Models of Democracy

For Peter

Models of Democracy

Third Edition

DAVID HELD

Stanford University Press
Stanford, California 2006

Contents

Figures and Tables

Figures

Tables

Preface to the Third Edition

Although it is easy to overgeneralize from one time period and from the culture of one's homeland, the development of the third edition of *Models of Democracy* is written in unsettling times. The events of 9/11 and the subsequent wars in Afghanistan (2002) and Iraq (2003) have created a ripple of change across the globe. Democracy, which seemed relatively untroubled in the 1990s, is experiencing intense pressures, from within and without. Security challenges, the 'war on terror', the attempt to impose 'regime change' on Iraq and to transform other Middle Eastern countries have been accompanied by a widespread sense of unease about whether democracies can deliver security to their citizens, whether they can sustain prosperity in tumultuous times and whether they embed ideals that can be defended adequately against, on the one hand, widespread despondency and apathy within and, on the other hand, fierce opponents, who do not hesitate to use indiscriminate violence, from without. The rise of fundamentalist elements in Islam, alongside the development of Christian and Jewish fundamentalist groupings elsewhere, raise questions about the legitimacy of contemporary political institutions, the separation of church and state, and the very possibility of democracy in the face of challenges to its underlying conception of human beings as free and equal, as active moral agents, with capacities for self-determination and political choice. There is a marked risk that in Western democracy a concern with security above all else will undo some of the important achievements of democracy and certain of the rights and liberties it presupposes. And there is a risk that cultures and religious forces that oppose the separation of politics and religion, state and civil society, will see 'democracy' as one of their enemies.

Elsewhere, most recently in *Global Covenant* (2004), I have analysed some of these trends and reactions. In *Models of Democracy* my aim is to clarify why democracy is so important in human affairs, why it is so contested and why, despite its vulnerabilities, it remains the best of all possible governing arrangements. Democracy is not a panacea for all human problems, but it offers the most compelling principle of legitimacy – 'the consent of the people' – as the basis of political order. It is important to understand this principle and the many debates it has given rise to, if an attractive and defensible conception of democracy is to be promulgated in the century ahead.

Given the difficulties of the present period it is easy to forget that, if there was ever an age of democracy, it is the present one. State socialism, which appeared so entrenched just a few decades ago, has crumbled in Central and Eastern Europe. In many of its essentials, democracy appears not only quite secure in the West but also widely adopted in principle beyond the West as a suitable model of government. Throughout the world's major regions there has been a consolidation of democratic processes and procedures. In the mid-1970s, over two-thirds of all states could reasonably be called authoritarian. This percentage has fallen dramatically; less than a third of all states are now authoritarian, and the number of democracies has grown. Democracy has become the leading standard of political legitimacy in the current era.

The tale of democracy from antiquity to the present seems, therefore, to be a relatively happy one. In more and more countries citizen-voters are, in principle, able to hold public decision-makers to account, while the decision-makers themselves represent the interests of their constituents – 'the people' in a delimited territory. However, the tale of democracy does not conclude with such developments. Although the victory of democratic movements across Central and Eastern Europe was of great moment, as was the transformation of political regimes in other places like South Africa, these events have left unresolved many important questions of democratic thought and practice. Democracy, as an idea and as a political reality, is fundamentally contested. Not only is the history of democracy marked by conflicting interpretations, but also ancient and modern notions intermingle to produce ambiguous and inconsistent accounts of the key terms of democracy, among them the proper meaning of 'political participation', the connotation of 'representation', the scope of citizens' capacities to choose freely among political alternatives, and the nature of membership in a democratic community.

These are significant and pressing matters, and the stock of a great deal of contemporary political debate. But even these important concerns by no means fully define the current agenda of democratic thought and practice. For any engagement with the contemporary meaning of democracy has to examine additional questions – questions not only about the 'internal' or 'domestic' character of democracy, but also about its 'external' qualities and consequences. This is so because one of the most conspicuous features of politics in the new millennium is the emergence of issues which transcend national democratic frontiers. Processes of economic globalization, the problem of the environment and the protection of the rights of minorities are increasingly matters for the international community as a whole. The nature and limits of national democracies have to be reconsidered in relation to processes of environmental, social and economic globalization; that is, in relation to shifts in the transcontinental or inter-regional scale of human social organization and of the exercise of social power.

Of course, there is nothing new about the emergence of global problems. Although their importance has grown considerably, many have existed for decades, some for centuries. But now that the old confrontation between East and West has ended, regional and global problems such as the spread of AIDS, the debt burden of the 'developing world', the flow of financial resources which escape national jurisdiction, the drugs trade, international crime and terrorism have an urgent place on the international political agenda. None the less, profound ambiguity still reigns as to where, how and according to what criteria decisions about these matters can be taken.

Democratic theory's exploration of emerging regional and global problems is still in its infancy. While democratic theory has examined and debated at length the challenges to democracy that emerge from within the boundaries of the nation-state, it has not seriously questioned whether the nation-state itself can remain at the centre of democratic thought. The questions posed by the rapid growth of complex interconnections and interrelations between states and societies, and by the evident intersection of national and international forces and processes, remain largely unexplored.

The challenges facing democratic thinking now are both numerous and substantial. *Models of Democracy*, as published initially in 1987, had two prime purposes: the first, to provide an introduction to central accounts of democracy and, above all, to those of the Western tradition from ancient Greece to the present day; the second, to offer a critical narrative about successive democratic ideas in order to address the question, raised directly towards the end of the book: what should democracy mean today? These remained the objectives of the second edition, published in 1996, but in order to ensure their thorough execution it became necessary to revise the original text in a number of ways. *Models* needed revision in order to take account of transformations in politics some of which were either unanalysed or unanticipated by the first edition. It needed revision, moreover, in order to examine the considerable research and scholarship undertaken in political thought in the last decade, some of which has changed our understanding of aspects of the classic democratic heritage as well as of contemporary political ideas and notions. And it needed revision because the author of *Models* had altered the balance of his views in some respects, alterations which could usefully be reflected in a new text.

A similar set of issues lies behind the third edition. It has been updated to take account of political changes that are now shaping our world, and in the light of new theoretical and historical work that alters how we should interpret aspects of earlier political traditions. It has been revised because debates in political and social theory have led to new innovations in democratic thinking. Thus, a new chapter has been added on deliberative democracy (chapter 9), which is concerned with the quality of democratic reasoning and the justification for political action. Deliberative theorists focus on the development of citizenship, on how to encourage 'refined' and 'reflective' political preferences and on political rationality as inseparable from the idea of justification to others. These are important notions worthy of careful analysis in a separate chapter.

The first two editions of *Models of Democracy* emerged, in part, as a set text for an Open University course, 'Democracy: From Classical Times to the Present'. Many of my colleagues at the Open University offered detailed commentaries on them. I would like to thank, in particular, Donna Dickenson, Bram Gieben, David Goldblatt, Paul Lewis, Tony McGrew and David Potter for their extensive advice. Moreover, in the preparation of the first and second editions I benefited enormously from the comments of friends and colleagues at other universities. I would like to thank David Beetham, Richard Bellamy, John Dunn, Anthony Giddens, John Keane, Joel Krieger, Quentin Skinner, Michelle Stanworth and John B. Thompson, among others.

Nearly twenty years after its inception, the Open University course has been phased out, but *Models of Democracy* continues to be used as an introduction to democratic thought throughout the world. Cillian McBride has been extraordinarily helpful in the development of the third edition. He has guided me through the deliberative democracy literature (now vast) and has been a sounding board when needed. I am deeply indebted to him. Ann Bone, Neil de Cort, Anne DeSayrah, Ellen McKinlay, Gill Motley, Breffni O'Connor, Sue Pope and Marianne Rutter provided indispensable aid in the process of the manuscript's publication. I am very grateful to them all.

I owe a special debt to my father, Peter Held, to whom the third edition is dedicated. He is a wise and reflective citizen, and a great supporter and interlocutor.

Finally, I want to acknowledge my children, as I did in previous editions, for constantly showing me that there is more to life than the *polis* and for being good enough citizens – just! Thank you Rosa, Joshua and Jacob.

DH

Introduction

The history of the idea of democracy is curious; the history of democracies is puzzling.

There are two striking historical facts. First, political leaders of extraordinarily diverse views profess to be democrats. Political regimes of all kinds describe themselves as democracies. Yet what these regimes say and do is often substantially different from one another throughout the world. Democracy appears to legitimate modern political life: rule-making and law enforcement seem justified and appropriate when they are 'democratic'. But it has not always been so. From ancient Greece to the present day the majority of political thinkers have been highly critical of the theory and practice of democracy. A general commitment to democracy is a very recent phenomenon.

Second, while many states today may be democratic, the history of their political institutions reveals the fragility and vulnerability of democratic arrangements. The history of twentieth-century Europe alone makes clear that democracy is a remarkably difficult form of government to create and sustain: fascism, Nazism and Stalinism came very close to eradicating it altogether. Democracy has evolved through intensive social struggles and is frequently sacrificed in such struggles. This book is about the idea of democracy, but in exploring the idea we cannot escape too far from aspects of its history in thought and practice.

While the word 'democracy' came into English in the sixteenth century from the French *démocratie*, its origins are Greek. 'Democracy' is derived from *demokratia*, the root meanings of which are *demos* (people) and *kratos* (rule). Democracy means a form of government in which, in contradistinction to monarchies and aristocracies, the people rule. Democracy entails a political community in which there is some form of *political equality* among the people. 'Rule by the people' may appear an unambiguous concept, but appearances are deceptive. The history of the idea of democracy is complex and is marked by conflicting conceptions. There is plenty of scope for disagreement.

Definitional problems emerge with each element of the phrase: 'rule'? – 'rule by'? – 'the people'? To begin with 'the people':

- Who are to be considered 'the people'?
- What kind of participation is envisaged for them?
- What conditions are assumed to be conducive to participation? Can the disincentives and incentives, or costs and benefits, of participation be equal?

The idea of 'rule' evokes a plethora of issues:

- How broadly or narrowly is the scope of rule to be construed? Or, what is the appropriate field of democratic activity?
- If 'rule' is to cover 'the political' what is meant by this? Does it cover: (a) law and order? (b) relations between states? (c) the economy? (d) the domestic or private sphere?

Does 'rule by' entail the obligation to obey?

- Must the rules of 'the people' be obeyed? What is the place of obligation and dissent?
- What roles are permitted for those who are avowedly and actively 'non-participants'?
- Under what circumstances, if any, are democracies entitled to resort to coercion against some of their own people or against those outside the sphere of legitimate rule?

The potential areas for disagreement do not stop here. For, from ancient Greece to the contemporary world, there have also been fundamentally different opinions expressed about the general conditions or prerequisites of *successful* 'rule by the people'. Do the people have, for instance, to be literate before becoming democrats? Is a certain level of social wealth necessary for the maintenance of a democracy? Can democracies be maintained during times of national emergency or war? These and a host of other issues have ensured that the meaning of democracy has remained, and probably always will remain, unsettled.

There is much significant history in the attempt to restrict the meaning of 'the people' to certain groups: among others, owners of property, white men, educated men, men, those with particular skills and occupations, white adults, adults. There is also a telling story in the various conceptions and debates about what is to count as 'rule' by 'the people'. The range of possible positions includes, as one commentator usefully summarized them:

1 That all should govern, in the sense that all should be involved in legislating, in deciding on general policy, in applying laws and in governmental administration.
2 That all should be personally involved in crucial decision-making, that is to say, in deciding general laws and matters of general policy.
3 That rulers should be accountable to the ruled; they should, in other words, be obliged to justify their actions to the ruled and be removable by the ruled.
4 That rulers should be accountable to the representatives of the ruled.
5 That rulers should be chosen by the ruled.
6 That rulers should be chosen by the representatives of the ruled.
7 That rulers should act in the interests of the ruled. (Lively, 1975, p. 30)

Positions taken derive in part from different ways of justifying democracy. Democracy has been defended on the grounds that it comes closest among the alternatives to achieving one or more of the following fundamental values or goods: rightful authority, political equality, liberty, moral self-development, the common interest, a fair moral compromise, binding decisions that take everyone's interest into account, social utility, the satisfaction of wants, efficient decisions. Within the history of the clash of positions lies the struggle to determine whether democracy will mean some kind of popular power (a form of life in which citizens are engaged in *self*-government and *self*-regulation) or an aid to decision-making (a means to legitimate the decisions of those voted into power – 'representatives' – from time to time). What should be the scope of democracy? To what domains of life should it be applied? Or, alternatively, should democracy be clearly delimited to maintain other important ends?

These are extremely difficult questions. Analysis of the variants of democracy, the chief task of this book, does not resolve them, although it may help to illuminate why certain positions are more attractive than others. In focusing on the chief variants, this volume will set out some of the political options we face today. But it is as well to say that these options do not present themselves in a simple, clear-cut manner. The history of democracy is often confusing, partly because this is still very much an *active* history, and partly because the issues are very complex (R. Williams, 1976, pp. 82–7). It is important to say also that my account of the myriad of issues is helped, as are all such accounts, by a particular position within this active history: a belief that democratic ideas and practices can in the long run be protected only if their hold on our political, social and economic life is *extended* and *deepened*. The precise nature of this view and the reasons I have for holding it will, I hope, be clarified later, but it does mean that I am inevitably more sympathetic to some democratic theorists than others.

The book is divided into three parts. Part One sets out four classic models of democracy: the classical idea of democracy in ancient Athens; the republican conception of a self-governing community (elaborated in two variants: protective and developmental republicanism);[1] liberal democracy (again, elaborated in two different variants: protective democracy and developmental democracy); and the Marxist conception of direct democracy. Part Two explores five more recent models that have spawned intensive political discussion and conflict: competitive elitist democracy, pluralism, legal democracy, participatory democracy and deliberative democracy. Part Three examines some of the central problems of democratic theory and practice, and addresses the question: what should democracy mean today? This question is pursued by means of an appraisal of the contemporary relevance of the democratic heritage within the context of the nation-state as well as against the background of the development of dense interconnections among states and societies.

Thus, the concerns of *Models of Democracy* span some of the earliest conceptions of democracy, the eclipse of these ideas for nearly two millennia, the slow re-emergence of democratic notions in the course of the Renaissance and, from the late sixteenth century, during the struggle of liberalism against tyranny and the absolutist state, the reformulation of the idea of democracy in the late eighteenth and nineteenth centuries in both the liberal and Marxist

---

[1] It is important to note that not all conceptions of republicanism were democratic. Chapters 2 and 3 explore the leading conceptions and their relation to democracy.

traditions, and the clash of contemporary perspectives. In focusing *Models of Democracy* in this way, prime attention is given to the development of democracy in the West. This is because the story of the development of different variants of democracy is in part the story of the formation of certain political ideas and practices which crystallized most clearly in the West. Debates about the nature of democracy have been particularly intensive within the European and North American intellectual traditions, although to state this is by no means to claim that everything of importance about the nature of democracy originated in, or was fully understood or expressed in, Europe and North America alone (see Bernal, 1987; Springborg, 1992). Although the emphasis here will be on the Western democratic tradition, the significance of other strands of thought and of other political regions will be introduced later.[2]

The models of democracy at the centre of the following chapters are set out in figure 1, as are the very general relations between them. All but one of the models could reasonably be divided into two broad types: direct or participatory democracy (a system of decision-making about public affairs in which citizens are directly involved) and liberal or representative democracy (a system of rule embracing elected 'officers' who undertake to 'represent' the interests and/or views of citizens within the framework of 'the rule of law').[3] These broad classificatory labels will occasionally be used for the purpose of grouping together a number of models. However, they will be deployed only on a highly restricted basis; for one of the central purposes of this volume is to explicate and assess a far wider range of arguments about democracy than are suggested by these two general notions alone. There is a great deal to be learned, for instance, about the differences between classical democracy, developmental republicanism, direct democracy and participatory democracy, even though they all might be labelled a type of 'direct democracy'. To focus on them merely as forms of the latter is to risk missing significant divergencies between them – divergencies which justify a more complex classificatory system. A similar point can be made about 'variants' of liberal democracy. Accordingly, the terms listed in figure 1 will be generally used. The context of their use should clarify any ambiguity about the type of democracy under discussion and the similarities and differences between them.[4]

---

[2] In addition, it should be noted that the origins of certain ideas in particular cultures and nations do not necessarily restrict their value or utility to those places. The language of self-determination and autonomy cannot simply be appraised in relation to its initial social context (see, in particular, chs 10 and 11 below).

[3] Deliberative democracy, as will be seen in chapter 9, seeks to break this mould directly.

[4] There are additional terminological difficulties which should be mentioned. Among the most central political traditions, at least for modern Western political thought, is, of course, liberalism. It is important to bear in mind that the 'modern' Western world was liberal first, and only later, after extensive conflicts, liberal democratic (see chs 2 and 3). It should be stressed that by no means all liberals, past and present, were democrats, and vice versa. However, the development of liberalism was integral to the development of liberal democracy. Therefore, while I shall treat liberalism and liberal democratic theory as distinguishable modes of political thought in certain contexts, I shall also, especially in later chapters, use the term 'liberalism' to connote both liberalism and liberal democracy. Again, the context in which these terms are used will, I hope, leave no ambiguity as to their meaning.

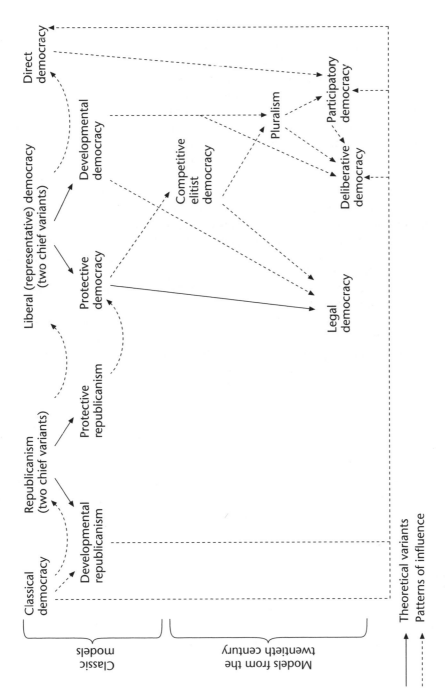

Figure 1 Variants of democracy

The development of democracy encompasses a long and much contested history. The field of democratic theory comprises a vast range of considerations and debates. Both this history and the debates need to be understood if the changing meaning of democratic discourse over time – its key concepts, theories and concerns – is to be grasped. In cutting a path through this terrain, *Models of Democracy* offers a map of the key positions and arguments, as well as a series of critical reflections upon them. However, although the book covers a substantial range of issues, it is as well to stress that it is selective. In including four classic models (and some of their variants), I have been guided by the supposition that a fairly extensive coverage of a number of the most central ideas and theories is preferable to a superficial glimpse of them all. Therefore, I have not included an analysis of certain political traditions which, in some people's lexicon, have made significant contributions to democratic theory, for example, that of the anarchists. There are other lacunae. I had originally planned to dwell at considerable length on the origin, source and context of each major theoretical trajectory in democratic theory. It was necessary to forgo this in order to keep the length of the volume to a manageable level, although I have tried to provide a brief historical and theoretical introduction to each model. In addition, I should perhaps emphasize that I have selected only those 'models of democracy' which I consider to be of central importance to classic and/or contemporary political debate.

There are three additional matters I should like to stress about the approach taken in this book and about the assumptions that underpin it. First, a word about the notion of 'models'.[5] As I use the term here it refers to a theoretical construction designed to reveal and explain the chief elements of a democratic form and its underlying structure of relations. An aspect of public life or set of institutions can be properly understood only in terms of its connections with other social phenomena. Models are, accordingly, complex 'networks' of concepts and generalizations about aspects of the political realm and its key conditions of entrenchment, including economic and social conditions.

Moreover, models of democracy involve necessarily, as will presently be seen, a shifting balance between descriptive-explanatory and normative statements; that is, between statements about how things are and why they are so, and statements about how things ought to or should be. While the classical Greek theorists often intended their work to be both descriptive and prescriptive, offering a unified teaching of ethics, politics and the conditions of human activity, many 'modern' theorists from Hobbes to Schumpeter claimed to be engaged in an essentially 'scientific' exercise which was non-normative, as they saw it. Hobbes fundamentally altered the tradition of political theory by sharply separating morals and politics; for him political analysis was to be a 'civil science' built upon clear principles and closely reasoned deductions. The rise of the social sciences (in particular, the disciplines of 'government' and sociology) in the late nineteenth and twentieth centuries added momentum to the view that the study

---

[5] In setting out the idea of 'models' of democracy, I am indebted to the work of C. B. Macpherson (1977). The terms 'protective' and 'developmental' democracy also derive from his work (1966, 1973, 1977). However, I shall develop these ideas in a substantially different way.

of democracy must be based on the pursuit of science. There has been a marked shift in the weight granted to 'scientific method' in the explication of the meaning of democracy. But 'science' has by no means triumphed everywhere over 'philosophy'; and a purely empirical approach to democratic theory has been extensively criticized. Furthermore, irrespective of the proclaimed method used in political analysis, one can find in all models of democracy an intermingling of the descriptive and the normative. As one observer put it:

> Some democratic theorists have seen clearly enough that their theories are such a mixture. Some have not, or have even denied it. Those who start from the tacit assumption that whatever is, is right, are apt to deny that they are making any value judgements. Those who start from the tacit assumption that whatever is, is wrong, give great weight to their ethical case (while trying to show that it is practicable). And between these two extremes there is room for a considerable range of emphasis. (Macpherson, 1977, p. 4)

In examining past, present and perhaps future models of democracy, it is important to inquire into their key features, their recommendations, their assumptions about the nature of the society in which democracy is or might be embedded, their fundamental conceptions of the political capabilities of human beings, and how they justify their views and preferences. And in assessing these models we must attend to the nature and coherence of theoretical claims, to the adequacy of empirical statements and to the practicality of prescriptions.

Second, in presenting a diversity of democratic models, I have tried to keep my own 'prejudices' under tight rein, so that an accurate representation of these models is given. But all 'representation' involves interpretation – interpretation which embodies a particular framework of concepts, beliefs and standards. Such a framework is not a barrier to understanding; on the contrary, it is integral to it (see Gadamer, 1975). For the framework we bring to the process of interpretation determines what we 'see', what we notice and register as important. Accordingly, particular interpretations cannot be regarded as *the* correct or final understanding of a phenomenon; the meaning of a phenomenon is always open to future interpretations from new perspectives. Interpretations are, therefore, always open to challenge. In the story that I tell some of my concerns, standards and beliefs – 'prejudices' – do inevitably appear. While I believe that the most defensible and attractive form of democracy is one in which citizens can, in principle, extend their participation in and deliberation about decision-making to a wide array of spheres (political, economic and social), I do not think any one existing model alone provides a satisfactory elucidation of the conditions, features or rationale of this democratic form. Part of my approach to assessing 'models of democracy' involves considering not only what democracy has been and is, but also what it might be.

Finally, in focusing above all on democratic 'ideas', I do not mean to imply that these ideas alone have been decisive in shaping political and social life. Rather, in general, I believe that it is only when ideas are connected to propitious historical circumstances and structural forces that they develop sufficient influence to alter the nature and workings of institutional forms. However, this statement itself needs careful qualification; for there are unquestionably circumstances in which the impact of particular political ideas has either lingered with potent effects or had the most dramatic consequences. The place of ideas in the historical process does not lend itself to easy generalization. But whatever the relation between 'ideas' and 'social conditions', an examination of models of democracy has its own justification, especially in a world like our own where there is pervasive scepticism and cynicism about many aspects of political life. In such a world it is more important than ever to examine the possible ways in which politics – democratic politics – might be transformed to enable citizens more effectively to shape and organize their own lives. It is hard to see how this task is possible without, among other things, an attempt to come to terms with the development and fate of democratic ideas, practices and institutions.

Accordingly, the chapters which follow have four overall objectives: first, to introduce leading models of democracy in terms of their central ideas and broad historical conditions; second, to set out the distinctiveness of each model in contrast with previous models; third, to explore the strengths and weaknesses of each model both in relation to what critics have said and in relation to the general argument developed in the book as a whole; and, fourth, by way of a conclusion, to present a novel understanding of democracy, albeit one that leaves further questions to be addressed. Throughout, I have tried to ensure that the reader has the clear opportunity to reflect upon arguments and positions independently, but obviously I hope to interest the reader in the critical views I develop. *Models of Democracy* is both an introduction and an interpretative work, a work which takes one from the politics of city-states to nation-states and, ultimately, to the terrain of international politics and global transformations. The story of democracy, thus told, is the story of fundamental alterations in the nature of political community and some of the key political possibilities that we face, now and in the future.

PART ONE

CLASSIC MODELS

1 Classical Democracy: Athens

In the fifth century BC, Athens emerged as the most innovative and sophisticated 'city-state' or *polis* among many rival Greek communities.[1] The reasons for its development and for the establishment of its extraordinary 'democratic' way of life are not of prime concern here, although a few comments are in order.

From 800 to 500 BC, urban patterns of civilization slowly crystallized in the Greek world; many small, often tightly knit communities hugged the coastline, while few could be found very far inland (see Finley, 1963, 1973a; P. Anderson, 1974a, pp. 29–44). Initially, these cities were typically controlled by local kingships but later, often after violent conflicts, they came to be dominated by 'clan' and 'tribal' hierarchies. One commentator describes these cities as essentially 'residential nodes of concentration for farmers and landowners: in the typical small town of this epoch, the cultivators lived within the walls of the city and went out to work in the fields every day, returning at night – although the territory of the cities always included an agrarian circumference with a wholly rural population settled in it' (P. Anderson, 1974a, pp. 29–30). The growth of land and overseas trade stimulated the development of particularly well-placed coastal cities, some of which came to enjoy periods of sustained growth.

The political continuity of the early city-states was broken by the rise of the 'tyrants' or autocrats (*c.*650–510 BC), who represented the interests of those who had recently become wealthy through either landownership or commerce and trade. The clan and tribal order gave way to more tyrannous regimes. But the stability of these regimes was vulnerable to shifting alliances and coalitions. The growth of wealth for some was not matched by improvements in the conditions of the poorer classes, particularly those who were landless or owned small farms and peasant holdings. An expansion in the population increased pressure on the privileged, and a period of intensive social struggle ensued. In the complex and intensive politics of the cities, concessions often had to be made to preserve a balance of power; and the concessions that were made, notably in Athens but also elsewhere, strengthened the economic autonomy of small and medium-sized farmers as well as of some categories of peasants, creating a community of smallholders (see Hornblower, 1992, pp. 3–4). The status of these groups was elevated further by important changes in military organization which made moderately prosperous farmers and peasants, among others, central to the

---

[1] For the Greek term *polis* I shall use the term 'city-state' and, occasionally, 'city-republic'. The issues which underpin some scholars' preference for 'city-republic' – issues concerning when the idea of 'the state' was first formulated – will be addressed in the following two chapters.

community's defence (see Mann, 1986, pp. 197–204). It was this change, perhaps more than any other, that affected the future political structure of city-states.

A growing number of independent citizens enjoyed a substantial increase in the scope of their activities with the expansion of slavery (a point returned to at greater length below). It was the formation of a slave economy – in mining, agriculture and certain craft industries – which, as has been remarked, 'permitted the sudden florescence of Greek urban civilization . . . the free citizen now stood out in full relief, against the background of slave labourers' (P. Anderson, 1974a, pp. 36–7; cf. Dickenson, 1997, ch. 2). Greek city communities acquired a growing sense of identity and solidarity. Clear lines of demarcation were drawn between 'insiders' (citizens) and 'outsiders' (slaves and other categories of people including all those, however respectable, who had come from other communities and resettled). This identity was reinforced by a growth in literacy which also aided the administration and control of people and resources (although the ancient world remained predominantly an oral culture).

Innovations in the 'constitutions' of city-states followed, transforming the written and unwritten legal codes which had been passed down through the generations (see Finley, 1975). It appears that during the mid-sixth century the first 'democratic' polity emerged in Chios, though others, all with their own particularities and idiosyncrasies, soon formed. While Athens stands out as the pinnacle of this development, the new political culture became fairly widespread throughout Greek civilization, enfranchising the whole of the free citizenry (cf. Hornblower, 1992, pp. 1–2). It is worth stressing that the emergence of these early democracies did not result from a single set of events; rather, their development was marked by a process of continuous change over many generations. But the question remains: why was it that the developments referred to above led to the creation of a type of democracy?

This is a difficult question, the answer to which is by no means fully clear. Of all the factors that could be stressed, it was the conjunction perhaps of the emergence of an economically and militarily independent citizenry in the context of relatively small and compact communities that nurtured a democratic way of life (cf. Finley, 1983; Mann, 1986, ch. 7; Dunn, 1992, chs 1–3). Political changes took place within geographically and socially demarcated communities of a few thousand people living closely together either within one urban centre or within the surrounding countryside.[2] In these communities, communication was relatively easy, news travelled quickly and the impact of particular social and economic arrangements was fairly immediate. Questions of political culpability and responsibility were almost unavoidable, and the kinds of obstacle to political participation posed by large, complex societies were not yet significant. These factors – size, complexity and degree of political heterogeneity – are of great importance in democratic theory, although, I shall argue, the eventual demise of classical Greek democracy does not mean the end of all historical opportunities for extensive participation in public affairs. But having said this, it is as well to bear in mind that even in Athens the

---

[2] In fifth-century Athens, for a significant period the largest of the city-states, there were estimated to have been between 30,000 and 45,000 citizens.

composition of the *demos* consisted entirely of free adult males of strictly Athenian descent.[3]

Political ideals and aims

The development of democracy in Athens has been a central source of inspiration for modern political thought (cf. Finley, 1983; Bernal, 1987). Its political ideals – equality among citizens, liberty, respect for the law and justice – have influenced political thinking in the West, although there are some central ideas, for instance, the modern liberal notion that human beings are 'individuals' with 'rights', that cannot be directly traced to Athens. The legacy of Athens was, however, by no means accepted uncritically by the great Greek thinkers who examined its ideas and culture, including Thucydides (*c.*460–399 BC), Plato (*c.*427–347 BC) and Aristotle (384–322 BC) (see Jones, 1957; Farrar, 1992). Their works contain some of the most challenging and durable assessments of the limitations of democratic theory and practice that have been written. It is a remarkable fact that there is no major ancient Greek democratic theorist whose writings and ideas we can turn to for the details and justification of the classical democratic *polis*. Our record of this flourishing culture must be pieced together from sources as diverse as fragments of writing, the work of the critical 'opposition' and the findings of historians and archaeologists.

The ideals and aims of Athenian democracy are strikingly recounted in the famous funeral speech attributed to Pericles, a prominent Athenian citizen, general and politician. The speech, written down and probably recomposed by Thucydides some thirty years after its delivery, extols the political strengths and importance of Athens (see Finley, 1972). There are two passages in particular that deserve to be highlighted:

> Let me say that our system of government does not copy the institutions of our neighbours. It is more the case of our being a model to others, than of our imitating anyone else. Our constitution is called a democracy because power is in the hands not of a minority but of the whole people. When it is a question of settling private disputes, everyone is equal before the law; when it is a question of putting one person before another in positions of public responsibility, what counts is not membership of a particular class, but the actual ability which the man possesses. No one, so long as he has it in him to be of service to the state, is kept in political obscurity because of poverty. And, just as our political life is free and open, so is our day-to-day life in our relations with each other. We do not get into a state with our next door neighbour if he enjoys himself in his own way, nor do we give him the kind of black looks which, though they do no real harm, still do hurt people's feelings. We are free and tolerant in our private lives; but in public affairs we keep to the law. This is because it commands our deep respect.
>
> We give our obedience to those whom we put in positions of authority, and we obey the laws themselves, especially those which are for the protection of the oppressed, and those unwritten laws which it is an acknowledged shame to break.

[3] Citizenship was on rare occasions granted to others but only with the approval of the Assembly, the key 'sovereign' body.

> ... Here each individual is interested not only in his own affairs but in the affairs of the state as well: even those who are mostly occupied with their own business are extremely well-informed on general politics – this is a peculiarity of ours: we do not say that a man who takes no interest in politics is a man who minds his own business; we say that he has no business here at all. We Athenians, in our own persons, take our decisions on policy or submit them to proper discussions: for we do not think that there is an incompatibility between words and deeds; the worst thing is to rush into action before the consequences have been properly debated. (Pericles' Funeral Oration, in Thucydides, *The Peloponnesian War*, pp. 145, 147)

There are several important points that can be drawn from these lines. Pericles describes a community in which all citizens could and indeed should participate in the creation and nurturing of a common life. Formally, citizens faced no obstacles to involvement in public affairs based on rank or wealth. The *demos* held sovereign power, that is, supreme authority, to engage in legislative and judicial functions. The Athenian concept of 'citizenship' entailed taking a share in these functions, participating *directly* in the affairs of the state. As Pericles says: 'We do not say that a man who takes no interest in politics is a man who minds his own business; we say that he has no business here at all.'

Athenian democracy was marked by a general commitment to the principle of *civic virtue*: dedication to the republican city-state and the subordination of private life to public affairs and the common good. 'The public' and 'the private' were intertwined, although, as Pericles points out, tolerance is essential in order that people can enjoy themselves 'in their own way'. None the less, Athenian democrats tended to the view that 'the virtue of the individual is the same as the virtue of the citizen' (see Lee, 1974, p. 32). Individuals could only properly fulfil themselves and live honourably as citizens in and through the *polis*; for ethics and politics were merged in the life of the political community. In this community the citizen had rights and obligations; but these rights were not attributes of private individuals and these obligations were not enforced by a state dedicated to the maintenance of a framework to protect the private ends of individuals (see Sabine, 1963, pp. 16–17). Rather, a citizen's rights and obligations were connected to *his* station; they followed from *his* existence *qua* citizen: they were 'public' rights and duties. In contrast to later liberal positions, politics in this conception demanded a great deal of people, yet this was not seen as a violation but as an affirmation of their capacity for autonomy. Political order was presented as a vehicle for expressing and realizing their nature (Farrar, 1992, p. 37). A fulfilled and good life was only possible in the *polis*.

The peculiarly modern distinctions which began to emerge with Niccolò Machiavelli (1469–1527) and Thomas Hobbes (1588–1679) between state and society, specialized officials and citizens, 'the people' and government, are not part of the political philosophy of the Athenian city-state. For this city-state celebrated the notion of an active, involved citizenry in a process of *self-government*; the governors were to be the governed. All citizens met to debate, decide and enact the law. The principle of government was the principle of a form of life: *direct participation*. And the process of government itself was based on what Pericles refers to as 'proper discussions', i.e. free and unrestricted discourse, guaranteed by *isegoria*, an equal right to speak in the sovereign assembly (Finley, 1973b, pp. 18–19). Accordingly, the ancient democratic *polis* can be thought of as an attempt to enable men of different backgrounds and attributes 'to express and transform their understanding of the good through political interaction' (Farrar, 1992, p. 38). Decisions and laws rested, it was claimed, on conviction – the force of the better argument – and not mere custom, habit or brute force. (The importance of public deliberation was not emphasized again in political theory for a long time: see chs 2, 3 and 9.) The law of the state was the citizens' law. Before the law everyone was equal and, hence, as Pericles puts it, 'we keep the law'. Law is juxtaposed with tyranny, and freedom, therefore, implies respect for the law. As one commentator aptly put it: 'The Athenian did not imagine himself to be wholly unconstrained, but he drew the sharpest distinction between the restraint which is merely subjection to another man's arbitrary will and that which recognizes in the law a rule which has a right to be respected and hence is in this sense self-imposed' (Sabine, 1963, p. 18). If the law is properly created within the framework of the common life, it legitimately commands obedience. In this sense, the notions of the rule of law, due process and constitutional procedure find their earliest expression in the politics of the Athenian city-state.

It seems that Athenians on the whole prided themselves on a 'free and open' political life in which citizens could develop and realize their capacities and skills. It was clearly recognized that not everybody had the ability, for instance, to command and lead the army or navy: differences in ability and merit were acknowledged. But when Pericles proudly proclaimed that 'our city is an education to Greece', he was speaking, above all, of a form of life in which 'each single one of our citizens, in all the manifold aspects of life, is able to show himself the rightful lord and owner of his own person, and do this, moreover, with exceptional grace and exceptional versatility' (Thucydides, *The Peloponnesian War*, pp. 147–8). Through independence, status, education, art, religion and, above all, participation in the common life of the city, the individual could fulfil his 'material powers' and the *telos* (goal or objective) of the common good. And the securing and realization of the citizen's proper role and place in the city-state was precisely what was meant by justice.

One of the most remarkable descriptions of ancient democracy can be found in Aristotle's *The Politics* (written between 335 and 323 BC), a book which, while examining 'lawful' and durable forms of rule, provided a detailed account of democracy, albeit as a model of rule which Aristotle himself could not approve of (indeed, he referred to it as a 'transgression' of good government). The account analyses 'the claims, ethical standards and aims' of democracy and clearly refers to the key features of a number of Greek democracies. The second paragraph contains probably the finest and most succinct statement of classical democratic institutions. The account is worth quoting at length:

> A basic principle of the democratic constitution is liberty. People constantly make this statement, implying that only in this constitution do men share in liberty; for every democracy, they say, has liberty for its aim. 'Ruling and being ruled in turn' is one element in liberty, and the democratic idea of justice is in

fact numerical equality, not equality based on merit;[4] and when this idea of what is just prevails, the multitude must be sovereign, and whatever the majority decides is final and constitutes justice. For, they say, there must be equality for each of the citizens. The result is that in democracies the poor have more sovereign power than the rich; for they are more numerous, and the decisions of the majority are sovereign. So this is one mark of liberty, one which all democrats make a definitive principle of their constitution. Another is to live as you like. For this, they say, is a function of being free, since its opposite, living not as you like, is the function of one enslaved. This is the second defining principle of democracy, and from it has come the idea of 'not being ruled', not by anyone at all if possible, or at least only in alternation. This ['to be ruled by alternation'] is a contribution towards that liberty which is based on equality.

From these fundamentals, and from rule thus conceived, are derived the following features of democracy: (a) Elections to office by all from among all. (b) Rule of all over each and of each by turns over all. (c) Offices filled by lot, either all or at any rate those not calling for experience or skill. (d) No tenure of office dependent on the possession of a property qualification, or only on the lowest possible. (e) The same man not to hold the same office twice, or only rarely, or only a few apart from those connected with warfare. (f) Short terms for all offices or for as many as possible. (g) All to sit on juries, chosen from all and adjudicating on all or most matters, i.e. the most important and supreme, such as those affecting the constitution, scrutinies, and contracts between individuals. (h) The assembly as the sovereign authority in everything, or at least the most important matters, officials having no sovereign power over any, or over as few as possible. . . . Next, (i) payments for services, in the assembly, in the law-courts, and in the offices, is regular for all (or at any rate the offices, the law-courts, council, and the sovereign meetings of the assembly, or in the offices where it is obligatory to have meals together). Again (j), as birth, wealth, and education are the defining marks of oligarchy, so their opposites, low birth, low incomes, and mechanical occupations, are regarded as typical of democracy. (k) No official has perpetual tenure, and if any such office remains in being after an early change, it is shorn of its power and its holders selected by lot from among picked candidates.

These are the common characteristics of democracies. (Aristotle, *The Politics*, pp. 362–4)

For the democrat, liberty and equality are, according to Aristotle, inextricably linked. There are two criteria of liberty: (1) 'ruling and being ruled in turn', and (2) 'living as one chooses'. In order to establish the first criterion as an effective principle of government, equality is essential: without 'numerical equality', 'the multitude' cannot be sovereign. 'Numerical equality', i.e. an equal share of the practice of ruling, is said by classical democrats to be possible because (1) participation is financially remunerated so that citizens are not worse off as a result of political involvement, (2) citizens have equal voting power, and (3)

---

[4] Pericles' conception of the democratic principle of equality indicates a place for an explicit recognition of merit. Aristotle's account, in contrast, stresses that the democratic idea of equality is equality of condition and outcome. Aristotle's discussion of these two kinds of equality in *The Politics* is among the earliest statements of this important distinction. (See Aristotle, *The Politics*, pp. 195–8.)

there are in principle equal chances to hold office. Thus understood, equality is the practical basis of liberty. It is also the moral basis of liberty; for the belief that people should have an equal share of ruling justifies the first criterion of liberty ('ruling and being ruled in turn'). While this strong commitment to equality might conflict (as many, including Aristotle, have argued) with liberty as measured by the second criterion ('living as one chooses'), democrats hold that there must be some limits to choice if one citizen's freedom is not to interfere unjustly with another's. So long as each citizen has the opportunity of 'ruling *and* being ruled in turn', the risks associated with equality can be minimized and, therefore, both criteria of liberty can be met. On Aristotle's account, then, classical democracy entails liberty and liberty entails strict political equality – a matter which caused him to express grave reservations about democracy, despite his general affirmation of the nation, which was to be highly influential in the development of Renaissance political thought, that human beings are political animals who can only find fulfilment within the *polis* (see ch. 2 below).

Institutional features

The institutions described in Aristotle's second paragraph further clarify the truly radical nature of ancient democracy. It is hardly surprising that Marx and Engels took it as a source of inspiration; their own model of a properly democratic order, the Paris Commune of 1871, is outlined by them in a way that suggests a remarkable number of common features with Athens. Figure 1.1 sets out the basic Athenian institutional structure.[5]

The citizenry as a whole formed the key sovereign body of Athens: the Assembly. The Assembly met over forty times a year and had a quorum of 6,000 citizens (the minimum number of people whose presence was required for the proper or valid transaction of business). All major issues such as the legal framework for the maintenance of public order, finance and direct taxation, ostracism and foreign affairs (including assessing the performance of the military and navy, forming alliances, the declaration of war, the concluding of peace) came before the assembled citizens for deliberation and decision. The Assembly decided the political commitments of the Athenian state. While unanimity (*homonoia*) was always sought in the belief that problems could only be resolved correctly in the common interest, the possibility of major differences of opinion and clashes of individual interest was clearly recognized. The Assembly allowed intractable issues to go to a formal vote with majority rule (Larsen, 1948). Voting was both a way of making explicit differences of judgement and a procedural mechanism to legitimate a solution to pressing matters. The Greeks probably invented the use of formal voting procedures to legitimate decisions in the face of conflicting positions. But the ideal remained consensus, and it is not clear that even a majority of issues was put to the vote (see Mansbridge, 1983, pp. 13–15).

[5] The basic structure of Athenian democracy developed in the context of, and existed side by side with, a number of regulatory institutions (for instance, the Areopagus, a Council of Elders) which predated it and continued to have some influence even after the end of democracy in Athens in the late 320s (see Hornblower, 1992).

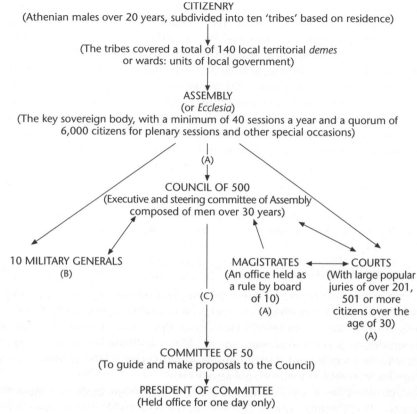

CITIZENRY
(Athenian males over 20 years, subdivided into ten 'tribes' based on residence)

(The tribes covered a total of 140 local territorial *demes*
or wards: units of local government)

ASSEMBLY
(or *Ecclesia*)
(The key sovereign body, with a minimum of 40 sessions a year and a quorum of
6,000 citizens for plenary sessions and other special occasions)

(A)

COUNCIL OF 500
(Executive and steering committee of Assembly
composed of men over 30 years)

10 MILITARY GENERALS
(B)

MAGISTRATES   COURTS
(An office held as   (With large popular
a rule by board   juries of over 201,
(C)   of 10)   501 or more
(A)   citizens over the
age of 30)
(A)

COMMITTEE OF 50
(To guide and make proposals to the Council)

PRESIDENT OF COMMITTEE
(Held office for one day only)

Methods of election or selection

(A) The ten tribes each sent fifty councillors to the Council, drawn from the *demes*. Demes
elected candidates in rough proportion to their size to 'represent' them in Council
and in other offices. The initial choice of candidates was determined by lot. Those
'elected' were put forward into a 'pool' of candidates. Finally, the candidates who
would actually serve were selected from the pool, again by lot. This method was said
to equalize everybody's chance of holding office. The terms of office were short
(one year) with typically no provision for immediate re-election. All elected officials
were paid for their services, as was attendance in the Assembly at certain times.

(B) These were chosen by the citizenry by direct election and eligible for repeated
re-election.

(C) The Committee was made up by rotation from the Council and served for one-tenth
of the yearly term of office.

Figure 1.1 Classical democracy: Athens. (Based on the constitution of Kleisthenes, reforms of
which were adopted in 507 BC and later amended in the 460s and 403 to include payment for
public office and payment for attendance in the Assembly.)
Sources: Finley (1963, 1983); Sabine (1963); P. Anderson (1974a); Hornblower (1992).

The Assembly was too large a body to prepare its own agenda, to draft
legislation and to be a focal point for the reception of new political initiatives
and proposals. A Council of 500 took responsibility for organizing and proposing
public decisions; it was aided, in turn, by a more streamlined Committee of 50

(which served for one month) with a president at its head (who could only hold office for one day). While courts were organized on a similar basis to the Assembly, the executive functions of the city were carried out by 'magistrates', although their own power was diffused by ensuring that even these posts were held by a board of ten. Nearly all such 'officials' were elected for a period of one year (with service typically restricted to two occasions in a lifetime). Further, in order to avoid the dangers of autocratic politics or clientage associated with direct elections, a variety of methods of election was deployed to preserve the accountability of political administrators and the state system more generally, including the rotation of tasks, sortition or lot and direct election.

The exclusivity of ancient democracy

The extraordinary innovations of Athenian democracy rested in large part on its exclusivity. The classical *polis* was marked by unity, solidarity, participation, public deliberation and a highly restricted citizenship. The state reached deeply into the lives of its citizens, but embraced only a small proportion of the population. Citizens were engaged together not only in activities such as administration, military service, lawmaking, jury service, religious ceremonies, games and festivals, but also in the surveillance and control of large numbers of people who could play no part at all in the state. In the first instance, Athenian political culture was an adult male culture. Only Athenian men over the age of 20 were eligible for active citizenship. Ancient democracy was a democracy of the patriarchs; women had no political rights and their civic rights were strictly limited (although married women fared rather better in this latter respect than single women). The achievements of classical democracy were directly linked to the politically unrecognized work and domestic service of women (and children).[6]

There were large numbers of residents in Athens who were also ineligible to participate in the formal proceedings. These included 'immigrants' whose families had settled in Athens several generations earlier. But perhaps by far the biggest category of politically marginalized people was the slave population. It is estimated that the proportion of slaves to free citizens in Periclean Athens was at least 3:2, a slave population of some 80,000–100,000 (Andrewes, 1967; P. Anderson, 1974a). Slaves were utilized in nearly all forms of agriculture, industry and mining, as well as in domestic settings. Athenian slavery and democracy seem to have been indivisible. The hiatus between the formal and actual basis of Athenian political life is striking. Classical conceptions of political equality were far removed from ideas about 'equal power' for all adults; political equality was a form of equality for those with equal status (male and Athenian born), and even then, as we shall shortly note, equal status did not really mean the opportunity for equal political influence. The legendary democracy was intimately connected to what one might call the 'tyranny of citizens'.

Thus, whether we can legitimately refer to Athens as a democracy at all is a question that at least has to be posed. Unquestionably, the politics of ancient

---

[6] Athenian native freewomen were regarded as 'citizens' only for genealogical purposes; they could not participate in politics. Their citizenship was instrumental for the purpose of producing citizen sons (see Dickenson, 1997, ch. 2).

Athens rested on a highly undemocratic base. But it is worth stressing, as Finley has done, that the choice between 'rule by the few' or 'rule by the many' was 'a meaningful choice', and that the 'rights' that various groups claimed for themselves, and bitterly fought for, were of the greatest significance, even though '"the many" were a minority of the population' (Finley, 1983, p. 9). Both the remarkable achievements and the strict limits of Athenian democracy need to be appreciated.

If one puts aside for a moment the issues concerning the restricted membership of the city-republic and the tensions and conflicts it would have inevitably generated, and focuses instead on some of the internal features of the new democratic order, then it is possible to glimpse significant difficulties created by the innovative form of Athenian politics: difficulties which, arguably, contributed to its incapacity to endure beyond the fifth and fourth centuries BC. Recorded history gives us very little access to the actual experiences and practices of ancient democracy. But one of the most intriguing accounts we have of its most compelling and negative qualities can be found in the writings of Xenophon (in Rodewald, 1974). In the following excerpt he illustrates many of the institutional features elaborated earlier by describing (or *re*-creating) a series of incidents and debates that took place in about 406 BC. The illustration highlights both the striking political accountability established in Athens – the direct involvement of citizens in the actual process of public decision-making – and some of the sources of its difficulties. The extract refers to a notable Athenian naval victory which, however, left many of the victor's sailors dead. Those in charge of the expedition were accused of unnecessarily leaving men in wrecked boats to drown. As with many of the other accounts we have, it should be remembered that this story was written by someone who was far from sympathetic to democratic ideas. None the less, it does seem a vivid illustration of political life as it was then and, hence, is worth reproducing:

> Back home, the People removed from office all the Generals except Konon. Two of the Generals who had taken part in the battle, Protomachos and Aristogenes, did not return to Athens. When the other six – Perikles [son of the famous Pericles], Diomedon, Lysias, Aristokrates, Thrasyllos and Erasinides – arrived, Archedemos, who was at that time a leading popular politician and controller of the War-Relief Fund, proposed the imposition of a fine on Erasinides and brought him before a Court of Justice ... The Court decided that Erasinides should be remanded in custody. After this the Generals made statements at a meeting of the Council about the battle and the violence of the storm. Timokrates then proposed that these Generals too should be taken into custody and brought before the Assembly, and the Council had them taken into custody.
>
> Afterwards there was a meeting of the Assembly, at which a number of people, and in particular Theramenes, attacked the Generals, saying that they should be called on to explain why they had not rescued the men who had been shipwrecked ... Each of the Generals then spoke in his own defence – briefly, for they were not offered the opportunity to deliver a speech as the law required. They explained what had happened: they themselves were to sail in pursuit of the enemy, and they had given the job of rescuing the shipwrecked to some of the ship-captains, who were capable men and had served as Generals in the past

... If anyone must be blamed, there was no-one whom they could blame for the failure of the rescue operations other than those to whom the job had been given. 'And we shall not', they added, 'make the false assertion that they are to blame, just because they are now making charges against us. We maintain that it was the violence of the storm that made the rescue impossible.' For this they offered as witnesses the helmsmen and many others who had sailed with them. With such arguments they were on the point of convincing the Assembly; many citizens were standing up and offering to go bail for them. However, it was decided that the matter should be adjourned to another meeting of the Assembly, for by then it was late and it would have been impossible to count votes, and that the Council should draft a motion as to what sort of trial the men should have.

After this came the Apaturia festival, at which fathers and their families meet together. Thus Theramenes and his supporters were able to arrange for men dressed in black and with their hair close-shaven, of whom there were large numbers at the festival, to attend the Assembly, as if they were kinsmen of those who had perished; and they induced Kallixenos to attack the Generals in the Council. Then came the meeting of the Assembly, at which the Council presented its motion, which was moved by Kallixenos. It was in the following terms: 'Resolved, that, since speeches in accusation of the Generals and speeches of the Generals in their own defence have been heard at the previous Assembly, all the Athenians do now is proceed to hold a ballot by constituencies; that for each constituency there be two urns; that in each constituency a herald proclaim that whoever thinks the Generals did wrong in failing to rescue those who won the victory in the naval battle shall cast his vote in the first urn and whoever does not think so shall cast his vote in the second urn; and that, if it be decided that they did wrong, they be punished with death and handed over to the Eleven[7] and their property be confiscated...'

Then a man came forward and said that he had been saved by clinging to a flour barrel and that those who were drowning told him, if he were saved, to report to the People that the Generals had failed to rescue those who had fought most gallantly for their fatherland.

Next a summons was served on Kallixenos for having made an illegal proposal; Euryptolemos son of Peisianax and a few others were the sponsors of it. Some of the People showed their approval of this, but the great mass shouted out that it was monstrous if the People were not allowed to do whatever they wished. Lykiskos took up this theme and proposed that, unless the summons be withdrawn, those who had served it should be judged by the same vote as the Generals; and as the mob broke out again in shouts of approval, they were forced to withdraw the summons.

Then some members of the Presiding Committee declared that they would not put the motion to the vote, since it was illegal. At this Kallixenos again mounted the platform and made the same complaint against them as had been made against Euryptolemos, and the crowd shouted that if they refused to put the motion to the vote they should be prosecuted. This terrified the members of the Committee, and all of them agreed to put the motion, except Socrates the son of Sophroniskos; Socrates said that he would do nothing at all that was contrary to law.

---

[7] The translator of this passage explains the Eleven as 'a board of officials, chosen annually by lot, who were, inter alia, in charge of the prison and of executions' (Rodewald, 1974, p. 128).

Euryptolemos then rose and spoke as follows in defence of the Generals:

'I have come to the platform, men of Athens, partly to accuse Perikles, although he is my kinsman and dear to me, and Diomedon, although he is a friend of mine, partly to speak in their defence, partly to recommend the measures that seem to be in the best interests of the community at large . . . The course of action that I recommend is one that will make it impossible for you to be misled, either by me or by anyone else, and will enable you to act with full knowledge, in punishing those who have acted wrongly, and to inflict on them, collectively and individually, whatever punishment you please. What I propose is that you should allow them at least one day, if not more, to speak in their own defence, so that you will be relying on your own judgement rather than that of others . . . Give these men a legal trial, men of Athens . . . a separate trial for each of them. If this procedure is followed, those who have done wrong will suffer the extreme penalty and those who are blameless will be set free, men of Athens, by your decision; men who have done no wrong will not be put to death. You will be observing the dictates of piety and the terms of your oath in giving them a legal trial . . . What are you afraid of, that makes you want to act in such excessive haste? . . .'

After making this speech, he put forward a motion that the men should be tried in accordance with the decree of Kannonos, each of them separately: the Council's motion was that judgement should be passed on all of them together by a single vote. When there was a show of hands to decide between the two motions, they decided at first in favour of Euryptolemos' proposal, but when Menekles put in an objection under oath (alleging illegality), there was a fresh vote, and this time the Council's proposal was approved. They then voted on the eight Generals who had taken part in the battle. The vote went against them, and the six who were in Athens were put to death.

Not long afterwards the Athenians repented and voted that preliminary plaints be lodged against those who had deceived the People, that they furnish sureties until they come up for trial, and that Kallixenos be included among them. Plaints were lodged against four others also and they were taken into custody by their sureties, but later, during a civil disturbance, they escaped, before being brought to trial. Kallixenos [later] returned . . . to the city, but everyone loathed him, and he died of starvation. (Xenophon, *History of Greece* 1.7, in Rodewald, 1974, pp. 2–6)

Xenophon's story highlights the accountability of officials and citizens to the Assembly, popular control of commanding officers, extensive open debate, and decisions by mass meetings, as well as a variety of other features of the Athenian city-state. It illustrates also how this rich texture of participation was shaped by the dependence of full participation on skills in oratory; clashes between rival groups of leaders; informal networks of communication and intrigue; the emergence of strongly opposed factions which were prepared to push for quick and decisive measures; the vulnerability of the Assembly to the excitement of the moment; the unstable basis of certain popular decisions; and the potential for political instability of a very general kind due to the absence of some system of checks on impulsive behaviour (see Rodewald's helpful remarks, 1974, pp. 1–2, 19). A number of constitutional checks were built into the structure of Athenian democracy at a later date to safeguard it precisely against hasty irreversible decisions. These changes tried to balance popular sovereignty with a constitutional framework capable of protecting enacted law and procedure, although it is doubtful whether these changes were sufficient for this purpose (if constitutional procedure alone can ever be, faced with highly determined opponents).

Athenian politics seems to have been extraordinarily intensive and competitive. Further, those who dominated the Assembly and Council tended to be of 'high' birth or rank, an elite from wealthy and well-established families, who had ample time to cultivate their contacts and pursue their interests. Since power was not structured by a firm constitutional and governmental system, political battles often took a highly personal form, often ending in the physical removal of opponents through ostracism or death (Finley, 1983, pp. 118–19). It is easy to exaggerate the frequency of these battles, to overstress the representativeness of Xenophon's narrative as an account of Athenian politics, and to forget that Athens enjoyed relatively long periods of political stability. None the less, Athens's political stability is probably to be explained less in terms of the internal workings of the political system, and more in terms of its history as a successful 'conquest-state'.[8] Successful military engagement accompanied the development of Athens; there were few years without war or military conflict. And military success brought material benefits to nearly all strata of the Athenian citizenry, which no doubt contributed to the formation of common ground among them, ground which is likely to have been quite solid – while victory lasted.

The critics

Citizens' equal rights to participate in the Assembly, to be heard before it and to hold public office, while they certainly did not come close to creating equal power for all citizens, were sufficient in themselves to be regarded with dismay by Athens's most famous critics, among them Plato. Plato's indictment of democracy in *The Republic* is worth dwelling on for a moment, for it contains criticisms that are still often levelled at democracy if it is taken to mean something more than a vote on periodic occasions, and even by some (legal democrats) if it is taken to mean merely the latter.

Plato's youth was overshadowed by the Peloponnesian war, which ended in defeat for Athens. Disillusioned with the city's demise, and with the deteriorating standards of leadership, morality and law, culminating in the trial and death of Socrates in 399 BC, Plato came ever more to the view that political control must be placed in the hands of a minority (Lee, 1974, pp. 11ff). He set out his views against a backdrop of four types of constitution: oligarchy (a system of rule modelled on Sparta's military aristocracy), timocracy (rule by the wealthy), democracy (rule by the people) and tyranny (rule by a single dictator). In discussing democracy, Plato was essentially drawing on his experience in Athens. While he was critical of aspects of all four constitutions, he was scathing about democracy, which he defined as a form of society which 'treats all men as equal, whether they are equal or not' and ensures that 'every individual is free to

---

[8] All these points are made superbly by Finley (1983).

do as he likes' (Plato, *The Republic*, pp. 375, 376).[9] This commitment to 'political equality' and 'liberty' is, according to Plato, the hallmark of democracy and the basis of its most regrettable characteristics.

Democracy has a series of interconnected failings (see Lee, 1974, pp. 27–30). These can be unfolded from, among other sources, the two famous metaphors in *The Republic* of the ship's captain (p. 282) and the keeper of a 'large and powerful animal' (p. 288). It is worth beginning with the tale of the ship's captain.

> Suppose the following to be the state of affairs on board a ship or ships. The captain [or ship-owner] is larger and stronger than any of the crew, but a bit deaf and short-sighted, and similarly limited in seamanship. The crew are all quarrelling with each other about how to navigate the ship, each thinking he ought to be at the helm; they have never learned the art [or the skill or technique] of navigation and cannot say that anyone ever taught it them, or that they spent any time studying it; indeed they say it can't be taught and are ready to murder anyone who says it can. They spend all their time milling round the captain and doing all they can to get him to give them the helm. If one faction is more successful than another, their rivals may kill them and throw them overboard, lay out the honest captain with drugs or drink or in some other way, take control of the ship, help themselves to what's on board, and turn the voyage into the sort of drunken pleasure-cruise you would expect. Finally, they reserve their admiration for the man who knows how to lend a hand in controlling the captain by force or fraud; they praise his seamanship and navigation and knowledge of the sea and condemn everyone else as useless. They have no idea that the true navigator must study the seasons of the year, the sky, the stars, the winds and all the other subjects appropriate to his profession if he is to be really fit to control a ship; and they think that it's quite impossible to acquire the professional skill needed for such control (whether or not they want it exercised) and that there's no such thing as an art of navigation. With all this going on aboard aren't the sailors on any such ship bound to regard the true navigator as a word-spinner and a star-gazer, of no use to them at all? (Plato, *The Republic*, p. 282)

The 'true navigator' denotes the minority who, equipped with the necessary skill and expertise, has the strongest claim to rule legitimately. For the people (the crew) conduct their affairs on impulse, sentiment and prejudice. They have neither the experience nor the knowledge for sound navigation, that is, political judgement. In addition, the only leaders they are capable of admiring are sycophants: 'politicians . . . are duly honoured . . . [if] they profess themselves the people's friends' (*The Republic*, p. 376). All who 'mix with the crowd and want to be popular with it' can be directly 'compared . . . to the sailors' (p. 283). There can be no proper leadership in a democracy; leaders depend on popular favour and they will, accordingly, act to sustain their own popularity and their own positions. Political leadership is enfeebled by acquiescence to popular demands and by the basing of political strategy on what can be 'sold'. Careful judgements,

---

[9] Note the equation of 'individuals' with 'all men' when Plato is, in fact, referring here to male citizens.

difficult decisions, uncomfortable options, unpleasant truths will of necessity be generally avoided. Democracy marginalizes the wise.

The claims of liberty and political equality are, furthermore, inconsistent with the maintenance of authority, order and stability. When individuals are free to do as they like and demand equal rights irrespective of their capacities and contributions, the result in the short run will be the creation of an attractively diverse society. However, in the long run the effect is an indulgence of desire and a permissiveness that erodes respect for political and moral authority. The young no longer fear and respect their teachers; they constantly challenge their elders and the latter 'ape the young' (*The Republic*, p. 383). In short, 'the minds of citizens become so sensitive that the least vestige of restraint is resented as intolerable, till finally . . . in their determination to have no master they disregard all laws' (p. 384). 'Insolence' is called 'good breeding, licence liberty, extravagance generosity, and shamelessness courage' (p. 380). A false 'equality of pleasures' leads 'democratic man' to live from day to day. Accordingly, social cohesion is threatened, political life becomes more and more fragmented and politics becomes riddled with factional disputes. Intensive conflict between sectional interests inevitably follows as each faction presses for its own advantage rather than that of the state as a whole. A comprehensive commitment to the good of the community and social justice becomes impossible.

This state of affairs invariably leads to endless intrigue, manoeuvring and political instability: a politics of unbridled desire and ambition. All involved claim to represent the interests of the community, but all in fact represent themselves and a selfish lust for power. Those with resources, whether from wealth or from a position of authority, will, Plato thought, inevitably find themselves under attack; and the conflict between rich and poor will become particularly acute. In these circumstances, the disintegration of democracy is, he contended, likely. 'Any extreme is likely to produce a violent reaction . . . so from an extreme of liberty one is likely to get an extreme of subjection' (*The Republic*, p. 385). In the struggle between factions, leaders are put forward to advance particular causes, and it is relatively easy for these popular leaders to demand 'a personal bodyguard' to preserve themselves against attack. With such assistance, the popular champion is a short step from grasping 'the reins of state'. As democracy plunges into dissension and conflict, popular champions can be seen to offer clarity of vision, firm direction and the promise to quell all opposition. It becomes a tempting option to support the tyrant of one's own choice. But, of course, once possessed of state power tyrants have a habit of attending solely to themselves.

For Plato tyranny in itself was not a stable resolution to the problems of democracy. Tyrants are rarely 'true navigators'. In the second well-known metaphor involving the 'large and powerful animal' (the mass of the people), Plato makes it clear that it is not enough for its keeper to know how to control the beast by a study of its moods, wants and habits. If the animal is to be properly cared for and trained it is important to know which of the creature's tastes and desires are 'admirable or shameful, good or bad, right or wrong' (*The Republic*, p. 288). Plato's position, in brief, is that the problems of the world cannot be resolved until philosophers (the class of 'guardians') rule; for only they, when fully educated and trained, have the deliberative faculty to harmonize all elements of life under 'the rule of wisdom'. Following Socrates, Plato believed that 'virtue is knowledge'; that is, that 'the good life', for both individuals and collectivities, is an objective phenomenon: it exists independently of the diverse states of being at any given moment and can be grasped through systematic study. It is the philosopher's rigorously acquired knowledge that justifies his suitability for power. It is his capacity to arrange things in the most advantageous way that recommends that the principle of government be the principle of enlightened despotism.

The details of Plato's position need not concern us here at any length; it will suffice to know that his position in *The Republic* is motivated by the desire to answer the question 'What is justice?' Starting from a conception of a natural division of labour in which classes of individuals can find their proper role (roughly as rulers, soldiers or labourers), the task set for the philosopher becomes one of investigating this division in order (1) to encourage the particular virtues proper to each kind of labour (wisdom, courage, temperance), and (2) to ensure that individuals perform their correct functions. Individuals and states are conceived as organic wholes in which, when the whole is healthy, it is possible for people to perform their functions, satisfy their needs, fulfil themselves and, thus, dwell in an efficient, secure and strong state (see Ryle, 1967). Under these circumstances justice can prevail and the good life can be realized (see Annas, 1981).

In Plato's view and, more generally, in ancient Greek thought, it is worth bearing in mind that the freedom the state secures is not so much for the individual *per se*, but for his ability to fulfil his role in the universe. Such a theory differs markedly, as one commentator aptly noted, 'from one which pictures social relations in terms of contract or agreement [between human beings as "individuals"] and which therefore conceives the state as primarily concerned with maintaining liberty of choice' (Sabine, 1963, p. 49). This notion, dominant in the liberal tradition from the seventeenth century, would have been anathema to Plato. His work defends the idea of a harmonious unity between 'the public' and 'the private'. The state secures the basis for the citizen to practise his calling.

The position Plato set out in *The Republic* was modified in subsequent works, notably in *The Statesman* and *The Laws*. These books acknowledge that, in an actual as opposed to an ideal state, rule cannot be sustained without some form of popular consent and participation. The importance of the rule of law as a mode of circumscribing the legitimate scope of those in positions of 'public' power – philosopher-kings – is also affirmed. Significantly, a theory of a 'mixed state', combining elements of monarchy and democracy, was introduced, anticipating positions later developed by Aristotle and Renaissance republicans.[10] Plato even devised a system of proportional voting which later

---

[10] The idea of a 'mixed state', deploying different principles of organization in order to counter one another and achieve a balance of political forces, is of course of great significance in the history of political theory and practice. Plato may have been the first to elaborate this idea, although this cannot be confirmed. The theory of a 'mixed state', or separation of powers, will be discussed later when the thought of Machiavelli, Locke and Montesquieu is examined.

was to find a parallel in the writings of figures like John Stuart Mill. But these ideas were not on the whole developed systematically, and Plato's attempt to introduce an element of democracy into his conception of a desirable system of rule did not amount to a novel democratic model.

The classical model of democracy (summarized in model I) and its critique have both had an enduring impact on modern Western political thought: the former as a source of inspiration for many democratic thinkers and the latter as a warning of the dangers of democratic politics. However, neither the model nor its critique had immediate theoretical and practical influence beyond the life of the ancient city-states. The model itself did not re-enter European political thought until the Italian Renaissance and the flourishing of the Italian city-republics, and it was not until Rousseau (1712–78) and, later still, Marx (1818–83) and Engels (1820–95) that many aspects of the idea of direct citizen participation were fully re-examined, rearticulated and readvocated (see chs 2 and 4 below). Plato's critique, along with the critical reflections of other Greek political thinkers, has had a particularly profound influence in relatively recent times. For his writings about the moral limitations of democracy 'have never', as one commentator aptly noted, 'been surpassed in force and urgency' (Dunn, 1979, p. 17). How seriously we must take the critique and its application to other democratic models is something that will have to be returned to later. Certainly, positions similar in spirit to that of Plato's have been of the utmost significance

In sum: model I

Classical Democracy

Principle(s) of justification
   Citizens should enjoy political equality in order to be free to rule and be ruled in turn

Key features
   Direct participation of citizens in legislative and judicial functions

   Assembly of citizens has sovereign power

   The scope of sovereign power to include all the common affairs of the city

   Multiple methods of selection of candidates for public office (direct election, lot, rotation)

   No distinctions of privilege to differentiate ordinary citizens and public officials

   With the exception of positions connected to warfare, the same office not to be held more than twice by the same individual

   Short terms of office for all

   Payment for public services

General conditions
   Small city-state with agricultural hinterland

   Slave economy creating 'free' time for citizens

   Domestic service, that is, the labour of women, freeing men for public duties

   Restriction of citizenship to relatively small numbers

historically. As one critic of democratic theory rightly stressed, 'the great preponderance of political thinkers ... have insisted upon the perversity of democratic constitutions, the disorderliness of democratic politics and the moral depravity of the democratic character' (Corcoran, 1983, p. 15). Until the early eighteenth century few who recorded their views at length thought democracy a desirable way of organizing political life.

The eclipse of Athenian democracy, in the context of the rise of empires, strong states and military powers, can be traced both to internal factors and to its changing fortunes overseas. The Athenian state rested upon a productive system that depended in large measure on slaves – to work, above all, the Laureion silver mines which funded vital corn imports (cf. P. Anderson, 1974a, chs 1 and 2; Hansen, 1991). This economic structure was vulnerable to unrest and conflict at home and abroad. The radically democratic nature of the state appears to have increased this vulnerability; for the absence of a bureaucratic centre, along with, at best, only loosely coordinated institutional divisions within 'government', exacerbated difficulties of managing the economy and an extended trade and territorial system. Moreover, given an increase in the costs of warfare as a result of changes in fighting techniques, weapons and the deployment of mercenaries, Athens could not easily manage the central coordination of larger and more varied military forces without undermining its own political and social structures (see Mann, 1986, pp. 223–8). More extensively organized and authoritarian states did not have this difficulty and, accordingly, Athens, along with other Greek cities, eventually lost its independent status and was incorporated into rival empires and powers.

The Athenian city-state shared features with republican Rome (see Finley, 1983, pp. 84ff). Both were predominantly face-to-face societies and oral cultures; both had elements of popular participation in governmental affairs; and both had little, if any, centralized bureaucratic control. Furthermore, both sought to foster a deep sense of public duty, a tradition of civic virtue or responsibility to 'the republic' – to the distinctive matters of the public realm. And in both polities, the claims of the state were given a unique priority over those of the individual citizen. But if Athens was a democratic republic, contemporary scholarship generally affirms that Rome was, by comparison, an essentially oligarchical system. Despite the inclusion of Hellenic conceptions of the state in the works of Roman thinkers (notably in Cicero, 106–43 BC), and the inclusion of the citizen-born peasants and emancipated slaves in the political community, elites firmly dominated all aspects of Rome's politics. Rome's military history – its extraordinary record of territorial expansion and conquest – helps to explain how and why Rome was able to sustain formal commitments to popular participation, on the one hand, and very limited actual popular control, on the other. Although, as will be seen in the following chapter, Rome was to have a fundamental influence on the dissemination of ideas associated with a self-governing order, from the ancient world it is the heritage of the classical Greek tradition, and of the model of Athenian democracy in particular, that it is especially important to come to terms with in the history of democratic thought and practice.

2 Republicanism: Liberty, Self-Government and the Active Citizen

In ancient Athens a citizen was someone who participated in 'giving judgement and holding office' (Aristotle, *The Politics*, p. 169). Citizenship for free adult men meant participation in public affairs. This classical definition is noteworthy in two respects. First, it suggests that the ancient Greeks would have found it hard to locate citizens in modern democracies, except perhaps as representatives and office holders. The limited scope in contemporary politics for active involvement would have been regarded as most undemocratic (see Finley, 1973b). Second, the classical Greek idea of citizenship would have found resonance in few communities during or after its initial elaboration (cf. Bernal, 1987). The ancient democracies are quite atypical regimes in recorded political history. The idea that human beings could be active citizens of a political order – citizens of their state – and not merely dutiful subjects of a ruler has had few advocates from the earliest human associations to the early Renaissance and the demise of absolutism. This chapter will focus on the revival of the ideal of active citizenship, beginning with the discourse and practice of the Renaissance republican tradition. But before exploring this remarkable political development, it is useful to dwell on some of the factors which help account for why the ideal of 'the active citizen in a republic' fell from view for so long in political theory and practice.

The eclipse and re-emergence of *homo politicus*

The eclipse in the West of the ideal of the active citizen, whose very being is affirmed in and through political action, is hard to explain fully. But it is clear enough that the antithesis of *homo politicus* is the *homo credens* of the Christian faith; the citizen whose active judgement is essential is displaced by the true believer (Pocock, 1975, p. 550). While it would be misleading to suggest that the rise of Christianity effectively banished secular considerations from the life of rulers and ruled, it unquestionably shifted the source of authority and wisdom from the citizen (or the 'philosopher-king') to other-worldly representatives. The Christian world-view transformed the rationale of political action from that of the *polis* to a theological framework. The Hellenic view of man as formed to live in a city was replaced by a preoccupation with how humans could live in communion with God (Pocock, 1975, p. 84). In sharp contrast to the Greek view that the *polis* was the embodiment of political good, the Christian worldview insisted that the good lay in submission to God's will. How the will of God was to be interpreted, and articulated with systems of secular power, preoccupied Christian Europe for centuries, until the very notion of a single religious truth was shattered by the Reformation.

Christianity certainly did not ignore questions about the rules and goals that humans ought to accept in order to live a productive life. Although Christianity was imposed on many communities, it could scarcely have become a world religion unless it bore values and aspirations which commended themselves to some extent by virtue of their role in human affairs (see MacIntyre, 1966, ch. 9, esp. pp. 114–20). Moreover, it would be wrong to regard Christianity as a complete retreat from a concern with the kinds of ideal which had been so central to parts of the ancient world. The ideal of political equality, for example, was to a degree preserved in Christianity, despite being embedded in a wholly different context. It has been suggested that the Christian affirmation of the 'equality of men before God', with its gesture to the possibility of a community in which nobody has superior moral or political rights, was the only basis on which values of political equality could be preserved for society as a whole in a world of minimal economic surpluses, where the mass of people lived at, near or below subsistence level (MacIntyre, 1966, pp. 114–15). Under such conditions, the religious vision of equality was, at least, a way of maintaining the vision of a better life. Clearly, Christianity was used to justify a diverse array of institutions, including slavery and serfdom. But it contained contradictory elements, some of which were later to become seeds of its own difficulties.

St Augustine's *The City of God*, written between AD 410 and 423, has frequently been regarded as the most authoritative statement of the superiority of ecclesiastical power over the secular. Augustine's insistence that the history of the Church was 'the march of God in the world' and that the true Christian ought not to focus on the problems of 'this temporal life' was immensely influential in medieval Europe. Written during the early stages of the fall of the Roman Empire, *The City of God* recommended firmly the harnessing of 'the desire for earthly things' to 'the desire for the heavenly city'. The illumination offered by God could guide the true believer to 'the everlasting blessings that are promised for the future'.

The Middle Ages did not give rise to extensive reflection on the nature of the democratic *polis* or to a comprehensive body of texts and writings which enriched the political philosophy of democracy. Moreover, while there were some important political innovations in Europe, these did not crystallize into a major new form of democratic system (see Poggi, 1978, ch. 2). Undoubtedly, the Eurocentric nature of much contemporary political theory has prevented an adequate grasp of important developments outside Europe during medieval times; and no doubt a great deal has been lost to the historical record. But until the work of St Thomas Aquinas in the thirteenth century, the influence of the Church Fathers, and of Augustine in particular, on political thought was profound, and an important factor in explaining its relative stagnation (cf. Coleman, 2000).

The distinction between the spheres of secular and spiritual jurisdiction was re-examined by Aquinas (1225–74), who attempted to integrate the rediscovered work of Aristotle (which had been lost to the West for many centuries, and had been translated from Arabic into Latin by the middle of the thirteenth century) with the central teachings of Christianity. Among the many unsettling aspects of Aquinas's writings was the contention that while monarchy was the best form of government it ought not to be ascribed unlimited authority. In his view, a monarch's rule was legitimate only to the extent that it upheld natural law – that part of the 'eternal law' disclosed to human reason. Since the state had no authority in the interpretation of religious doctrine, the Church could 'stand in judgement' over rulers. Furthermore, rebellion against a ruler was justified if natural law was repeatedly violated. Thus, the idea of limited government, central to the development of the liberal democratic tradition, was anticipated by Aquinas, despite his ultimate overriding concern for the development of the Christian community.

So much was the medieval view of society conceived as a whole – a divinely ordained hierarchy of rank and order in the 'Great Chain of Being' – that the idea of secular political power, in anything like its modern form, could not be found. There was no theoretical alternative – no alternative 'political theory' – to the theocratic positions of pope and Holy Roman Emperor.[1] The integration of Christian Europe came to depend above all on these authorities. This order has been usefully characterized as the order of 'international Christian society' (Bull, 1977, p. 27). International Christian society was conceived as being formed and constituted by Christianity first and foremost; it looked to God for the authority to resolve disputes and conflicts; its primary political reference point was religious doctrine; and it was overlaid with assumptions about the universal nature of human community. It was not until Western Christendom was under challenge, especially from the conflicts generated by the rise of national states and by the Reformation, that the idea of the modern state was born, and the ground was created for the general development of a new form of political regulation.

Within medieval Europe the economy was dominated by agriculture, and any surplus generated was subject to competing claims. A successful claim constituted a basis to create and sustain a degree of political power. Against the background of Christendom, a complex web of kingdoms, principalities and duchies developed alongside the emergence of new power centres in the towns and cities. Cities and urban federations depended on trade and manufacture and relatively high accumulations of capital. They formed distinctive social and political structures and frequently enjoyed independent systems of rule specified by charters. Among the best known were the Italian city-states of Florence, Venice and Siena, but across Europe hundreds of urban centres developed. While these centres alone did not determine the pattern of rule or political identity, they were the basis of a distinctive new trajectory in civic life and political ideas, especially in Italy.

---

[1] The Holy Roman Empire existed in some form from the eighth until the early nineteenth century. For while the Roman imperial title had lapsed in the fifth century, it was revived in 800 by Pope Leo III and conferred on Charlemagne, King of the Franks. Later, the title of Holy Roman Emperor was borne by successive dynasties of German kings, although its actual significance, like that of the Empire more generally, varied considerably over time. At its height, the Holy Roman Empire represented an attempt, under the patronage of the Catholic Church, to unite and centralize the fragmented power centres of Western Christendom into a politically unified Christian empire. The polities federated under the Empire spread from Germany to Spain, and from northern France to Italy. However, the actual secular power of the Empire was always limited by the complex power structures of feudal Europe on the one hand, and the Catholic Church on the other (see P. Anderson, 1974b; Mann, 1986; Held, 1992).

The reforging of republicanism

Republicanism began to enjoy something of a revival by the late eleventh century. At this time, a number of northern Italian communities established their own 'consuls' or 'administrators' to run their judicial affairs in defiance of papal as well as imperial claims to legal control (see Skinner, 1992, pp. 57–69). Towards the end of the twelfth century the consular system was replaced by a form of government comprising ruling councils headed by officials known as *podestà* with supreme power in executive as well as judicial matters. Such councils were in place in Florence, Padua, Pisa, Milan and Siena, among other cities, by the century's end, effectively making them independent city-states, or city-republics, as some commentators prefer.[2] Moreover, the *podestà* were elected positions, held for strictly limited periods of time, accountable to the councils and, ultimately, to citizens of the city – male householders with taxable property, born or resident continuously in their locales. The structure of institutional arrangements which could be commonly found is depicted in figure 2.1.

Measured against the extent and depth of political participation engendered by classical Athenian democracy, the Italian city-republics may not seem so extraordinary or innovative. But against the background of the structures of authority of feudal Europe – with its complex web of overlapping claims and powers – these developments were remarkable. They were so above all because, as the historian Quentin Skinner has written, 'they represented an explicit challenge to the prevailing assumption that government must be regarded as a God-given form of lordship' (1992, p. 57). Accordingly, it is not surprising that they inspired, and continued to inspire during many periods of modern European and American history, those who questioned tyrannical and absolutist rulers who maintained that they alone held the legitimate right of decision over state affairs. But reservations need to be registered about the degree to which the republics can be regarded as democracies (Skinner, 1992, pp. 58–60).

As in Athens, the citizenry was composed of a highly exclusive group of men, with the *podestà*, in many cases, initially the nominees of the nobility. This frequently resulted in civil instability, with groups of excluded citizens mobilizing to form their own separate councils and institutions; this, in turn, heightened political conflict, the consequences of which were sometimes violent and chaotic. (The most famous account of such a case can be found in Shakespeare's *Romeo and Juliet* with its depiction of the battle between the Montagues and the Capulets.) Ironically, many later political theorists were to reflect on these experiences only to draw the conclusion that, despite their initial classical inspiration, these republics were a prescription for disorder and weakness and, thus, an argument for the necessary return to strong monarchical government. Venice was the only city-republic to survive as a self-governing regime until the late eighteenth century, the rest being superseded much earlier by new systems of hereditary power.

---

[2] If the idea of the state is reserved for the notion of an impartial or legally circumscribed system of power, separate from both ruler and ruled, with supreme jurisdiction over a delimited territory, it is best thought of as a late sixteenth-century invention (see ch. 3).

CITIZENRY
(Male householders with taxable property,
born or continuously resident in their city)
↓
Divided into electoral districts or *contrada*
|
(A)
↓
GRAND RULING COUNCIL
(The key sovereign authority with up to 600 members)
|
(B)
↓
HEAD OF GRAND COUNCIL
(Officials, known as *podestà*,with supreme authority to act in executive and
judicial affairs, appointed by, and accountable to, the Council)

Methods of election or selection

(A) Citizens eligible to vote commonly drew lots to determine who should serve
as electors on the Council.

(B) Councils frequently drew lots to establish a selection committee (of up to
twenty) to consider suitable people to head the Council; names of three
possible candidates would be put to the Council, which would have the final
say. The elected officer, who would receive a salary from the city, was
appointed for a period of up to one year, and could not directly serve the
Council thereafter for a minimum of three years.

Figure 2.1 City-republics: innovations of government
Source: Adapted from Skinner (1992).

The second reservation relates directly to the use of the word 'democracy' in
connection with city-republics. For the first century of the republics'
development, the term was unknown to their supporters; it did not become part
of European political language until the reappearance of Aristotle's *The Politics*
(in the mid-thirteenth century). Thereafter, following Aristotle's usage, it took on
a pejorative connotation and became associated with the politics of the rabble;
government conducted for the benefit of the poor rather than the public
interest; and a form of power (to anticipate later nineteenth-century sceptics of
democratic government) in which the 'common people' can become tyrannical,
threatening to level all social distinctions and earned privileges (cf. Aquinas, *De
regimine principum*, pp. 2–82). In fact, some strains of Renaissance
republicanism are better thought of as a form of aristocratic or noble
republicanism than as a form of democratic politics at all. Certainly, few of their
defenders would have called themselves 'democrats', and they would have been
repelled by the idea that their governments were 'democratic'. In addition, it is
important to note that Italian city-republics bore little resemblance to modern
democratic polities with their emphasis on universal suffrage, the right of all
adults to oppose their government and stand for office, and so on (see ch. 3).

None the less, the contribution of city-republics to democratic theory and
practice has been considerable both from their institutional innovations, which, in

the context of the prevalence of Christian monarchism, offered an important example of the possibility of self-government, and from the extensive political treatises and texts which informed and reflected upon the new politics. The city-republics marked the first occasion in post-classical political thinking when arguments were developed for and on behalf of self-determination and popular sovereignty; and these were to have wide influence not only in Italy but, in the wake of the Reformation and the revival of political discourse in the seventeenth and eighteenth centuries, across Europe and America as well.

The core of the Renaissance republican case was that the freedom of a political community rested upon its accountability to no authority other than that of the community itself. Self-government is the basis of liberty, together with the right of citizens to participate – within a constitutional framework which creates distinct roles for leading social forces – in the government of their own common business. According to this position, the freedom of citizens consists in their unhindered pursuit of self-chosen ends; and the highest political ideal is the civic freedom of an independent, self-governing people. The community in its entirety 'must retain the ultimate sovereign authority', assigning its various rulers or chief magistrates 'a status no higher than that of elected officials' (Skinner, 1989, p. 105). Such 'rulers' must ensure the effective enforcement of the laws created by the community for the promotion of its own good; for they are not rulers in a traditional sense, but 'agents' or 'administrators' of justice.

The distinctive development of Italian city life during the Renaissance stimulated new ideas about political power, popular sovereignty and civic affairs. While many city republicans traced the origins of their new-found beliefs to ancient Greece and Rome, it was the Roman republic especially which inspired their thinking. Unlike the democracies of ancient Greece, which, in their view, were prone to instability, civil strife and internal weakness, Rome set out a model of governance which linked liberty not only with virtue but also with civic glory and military power. Rome offered a conception of politics which connected political participation, honour and conquest, and which, accordingly, could defeat the claims made in monarchical polities that only a king, enjoying personal authority over his subjects, could guarantee law, security and the effective projection of power. In this context, for many republicans, 'freedom meant freedom from the arbitrary power of tyrants, together with the right of citizens to run their common affairs by participating in government. "Virtue" meant patriotism and public spirit, a heroic willingness to set the common good above one's own or one's own family's interests' (Canovan, 1987, p. 434).

Republicans drew heavily in support of their arguments upon the classical writings of such figures as Cicero (106–43 BC), Sallust (86–c.35 BC) and Livy (59 BC–AD 17) and, in particular, on their histories and celebrations of the ancient Roman republic. The vision of how government may be structured so as to serve in principle the common business of citizens is set out by Cicero in *De re publica*:

> The commonwealth [*res publica*] is the people's affair [*populi res*]; and the people is not every group of men, associated in any manner, but is the coming together of a considerable number of men who are united by a common agreement about law and rights and by the desire to participate in mutual advantages. (*De re publica*, p. 124)

Sallust linked the rise of Rome with its achievement of liberty, and argued that it is when civic virtue prevails that citizens are the most able successfully to pursue glory for themselves. Indeed, he wrote in glowing terms that 'it almost passes belief what rapid progress was made by the whole state [Rome] when once it had gained its liberty; such was the desire for glory that had possessed men's hearts' (*The Conspiracy of Catiline*, p. 179). And Livy, in his *History of Rome*, held that the expansion of republican power could be linked directly to respect for authority, religious and secular, and to the 'modesty, fairness and nobility of mind' which belonged to the whole people. Such a frame of mind could be sustained when civic virtue presided over factionalism; that is, when the common business of citizens, conducted by them for the public good, prevailed over the tendency to corrupt political practices – the pursuit of private interests in public affairs. But while Rome's greatness was linked to the virtue of its citizens, it was also connected by some writers to its balance of institutions, especially, as will be noted later, to its mixed constitution, which sought to forestall factionalism by ascribing a role, albeit a limited role, to all the main social forces which operated within the public domain.

However, the Renaissance republican tradition, like nearly all traditions of political thought, was not a simple unity. In fact, two strands of republicanism can clearly be distinguished for analytical purposes, strands which have been referred to as 'civic humanist republicanism' and 'civic' or 'classical republicanism' (see Skinner, 1986), but which I shall refer to as 'developmental' and 'protective' republicanism. I shall use these terms because they are general enough usefully to encompass the different ways political freedom and participation are articulated in both republicanism and liberalism. The terms capture, as will be shown, important differences within and across these traditions. In the broadest sense, developmental theorists stress the *intrinsic* value of political participation for the development of citizens as human beings, while protective theorists stress its *instrumental* importance for the protection of citizens' aims and objectives, i.e. their personal liberty. Developmental republican theory builds on elements of the classical democratic heritage and on themes found among the philosophers of the Greek *polis*, notably their exploration of the inherent value of political participation and of the *polis* as a means to self-fulfilment. In this account, political participation is a necessary aspect of the good life. By contrast, protective republican theory, which can be traced to the influence of republican Rome and its historians, emphasizes the highly fragile nature of civic virtue and its vulnerability to corruption if dependent solely upon the political involvement of any one major grouping, whether it be the people, the aristocracy or the monarchy. Accordingly, protective republican theorists stress the overriding importance of civic involvement in collective decision-making for all citizens if their personal liberty is to be safeguarded.

Developmental republicanism received a profound and striking articulation in the work of Marsilius of Padua, although it was not until the writings of Rousseau in the eighteenth century that it probably acquired its most elaborate statement. At the same time, Wollstonecraft added important critical insights. Protective republicanism can be most closely associated with Machiavelli, although it was also elaborated later by such figures as Montesquieu and Madison. Figure 2.2 summarizes these two republican threads. Taking these developments chronologically, the focus below, in the first instance, is on Marsilius of Padua.

Republicanism, elective government and popular sovereignty

The formation of Renaissance republican thought can be traced through the work of diverse thinkers, such as Brunetto Latini (d. 1294), Ptolemy of Lucca (d. 1327) and Remigio de' Girolami (d. 1319) (see Rubinstein, 1982), but it is in the writings of Marsilius of Padua (1275/80–1342), particularly in his *Defensor pacis* (*The Defender of Peace*, issued 1324), that one can find one of the most remarkable early accounts of the significance of elective government and popular sovereignty. Seeking to refute the papalist claims to a 'plenitude of power' and to establish the authority of secular rulers over the Church, Marsilius argued that laws should be made by 'all the people or its weightier part' through the articulation of its will in a general assembly (see *Defensor pacis*, pp. 29–49).[3] The teaching of divine law and the administration of religious ceremony should mark out the limits of the powers of the priesthood. In championing a secular polity, under the control of an elective government, Marsilius placed himself in complete opposition to the traditional powers of the Church and to the prevailing conceptions of kingship. *Defensor pacis*, as one interpreter of his work aptly put it, 'was a book at which solid men of the age shuddered. When popes, cardinals, and writers simply concerned with preserving the social order wished to condemn heretics ... they charged them with having gotten their ideas from the "Accursed Marsilius". To be a Marsilian was regarded as subversive in a way similar to that which, centuries later, attached to being a Marxist' (Gewirth, 1980, p. xix). Marsilius was, in fact, branded as a heretic by Pope John XXII and forced to flee to Nuremberg.

There are three major themes in Marsilius's thought (see Gewirth, 1951, 1980). The first comprises an emphasis on civil communities as, in principle, products of reason and as the basis for humans to enjoy what they most naturally desire, a 'sufficient life'. According to this doctrine, each part of the community can be defined in terms of its contribution to the attainment of this end, while government is the just means to ensure that it is attained. Government properly consists of a regulative function which, if pursued adequately, can mean that all citizens can live well and realize the opportunities before them. The adequate pursuit of this function is revealed when government operates for the common benefit – and not for the private interests of a single faction or group, notably the 'common mass' (in Marsilius's terms, farmers, artisans and financiers). Marsilius distinguished 'temperate' and 'diseased' forms of rule by, among other things, whether or not they act on behalf of the common good (*Defensor pacis*, p. 32).

---

[3] The doctrine of the papal 'plenitude of power' was elaborated in the thirteenth and fourteenth centuries. It has been frequently taken to mean that the pope, as vicar of Christ, possessed an authority which was superior to all secular claims; and that the pope was the supreme ruler in temporal as well as spiritual affairs. While this interpretation can be contested, the debate over the doctrine's exact meaning is not of prime significance here. For at issue is Marsilius's concern to restrict the scope of papal authority in all aspects of governance.

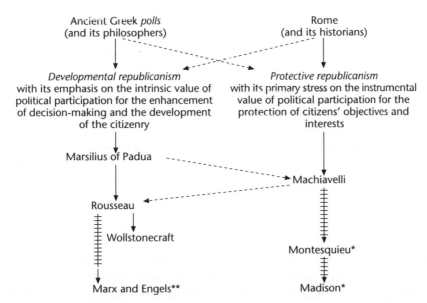

Ancient Greek *polis*
(and its philosophers)

Rome
(and its historians)

Developmental republicanism
with its emphasis on the intrinsic value of
political participation for the enhancement
of decision-making and the development
of the citizenry

Protective republicanism
with its primary stress on the instrumental
value of political participation for the
protection of citizens' objectives and
interests

Marsilius of Padua

Machiavelli

Rousseau

Wollstonecraft

Montesquieu*

Marx and Engels**

Madison*

Note: The figure is offered as an initial means of orientation to the two leading forms of republicanism, and the key figures associated with them here. There is, of course, a great deal of cross-fertilization between the strands as well as significant differences among the political theorists within each strand. And writers sometimes shifted between these analytical types.

⟶ Political thinkers within each republican strand discussed in this chapter.
--‣ Patterns of influence across the two forms of republicanism.
╫ Patterns of influence which combined with later currents of thought.
* Discussed in chapter 3.
** Discussed in chapter 4.

Figure 2.2 Forms of republicanism

The second major theme unfolds from Marsilius's judgement that the work of government is unending due to ever present strife in human affairs which can undermine political associations. Conflicts among people are inevitable and, therefore, the effective exercise of coercive authority is essential for the peace and prosperity of the community. Rival authorities (above all, those of Church and state) are a recipe for the erosion of law and order. A *unitary* coercive authority is a condition of the survival of civil associations. Effective rule depends on the effective deployment of coercive authority. Good government emerges less from a community dedicated to virtue than from rulers governing in the public interest, backed by coercive power.

These arguments may seem at some considerable distance from the concept of a republican community, but their meaning is not fully articulated without regard for the third theme which runs the course of Marsilius's *magnum opus*; that is, that the ultimate 'legislator' or source of legitimate political authority in the community is 'the people' (*Defensor pacis*, pp. 32, 45). The people's will is the key test of the proper interpretation of the ends to which the community is orientated and the only basis on which coercive power may be legitimately deployed. The authority to make the law belongs to 'the whole body of the citizens'; they alone have the authority to determine the law (p. 47). In a well-ordered civil community the source of both law and order is 'the people or the whole body of citizens, or the weightier part thereof, through its election or will expressed by words in the general assembly of the citizens, commanding or determining that something can be done or omitted with regard to human civil acts, under a temporary pain or punishment' (p. 45). Authority and force are legitimately deployed when they are deployed *rightfully*, that is, with the *consent* of citizens.

For Marsilius, the people's will is a more effective guarantee of government for the common benefit than rule by the one (kingship or lordship) or the few (aristocracy). Laws made by the many are both superior to and more likely to be upheld than those made by other forms of rulership. They are superior because when individuals publicly test their views and ends against those of others, they are forced to modify them and accommodate to others (*Defensor pacis*, pp. 46–7). As Marsilius explained: 'the common utility of a law is better noted by the entire multitude, because no one knowingly harms himself. Anyone can look to see whether a proposed law leans toward the benefit of one or a few persons more than of the others or of the community, and can protest against it' (p. 47). Thus:

> The authority to make laws . . . cannot belong to one man alone . . . for through ignorance or malice or both, this one man could make a bad law, looking more to his own private benefit than to that of the community, so that the law would be tyrannical. For the same reason, the authority to make laws cannot belong to a few; for they too could sin, as above, in making the law for the benefit of a certain few and not for the common benefit, as can be seen in oligarchies. The authority to make the laws belongs, therefore, to the whole body of citizens or to the weightier part thereof, for precisely the opposite reason. For since all the citizens must be measured by the law according to due proportion, and no one knowingly harms or wishes injustice to himself, it follows that all or most wish a law conducing to the common benefit of the citizens. (*Defensor pacis*, pp. 48–9)

Laws made by and for citizens establish a legal structure which can sustain a well-ordered, that is, just, community. In these circumstances, the community is also likely to be a peaceful one because laws made with the consent of citizens are laws which citizens feel an obligation to uphold. Law is 'better observed by every citizen' if each one is involved in 'imposing it upon himself' (p. 47).

By these arguments Marsilius did not mean to imply that all citizens must govern simultaneously. Rather, he advocated a conception of government not dissimilar to that depicted in figure 2.1, which entrenches popular sovereignty, creates self-governing councils, and establishes, through elections, 'rulers' or 'administrators' of city life – those whose duty it is to uphold the law for the benefit of all citizens (*Defensor pacis*, pp. 22–33). All citizens can, in principle, stand for office and enjoy, in turn, the opportunity to participate in public life. Marsilius concluded that 'elected kings' rule 'more voluntary subjects' and that the method of election alone can obtain 'the best ruler' and, as a result, a proper standard of justice (pp. 32–3). Finally, while 'rulers' are necessary to uphold this 'proper standard', they are in office as *delegates*, Marsilius insisted. Accordingly, those elected 'are not and cannot be the legislator in the absolute sense, but only in a relative sense and for a particular time in accordance with the authority of the primary legislator', that is, 'the whole body of citizens' (p. 45). Executive and judicial officers hold their office on the authority of the people and can be removed from power if they fail to pursue the common interest.

Marsilius, in accord with classical Athenian democracy and Aristotle's conception of politics, conceived of a citizen 'as one who participates in the civil community', either in the government or in 'the deliberative or judicial function' of the polity (*Defensor pacis*, p. 49; cf. Aristotle, *The Politics*, p. 169). Citizenship is the means to involvement in a shared enterprise orientated towards the realization of the common good; and political participation is the necessary vehicle for the attainment of the good. Following precedent as well, Marsilius noted, bluntly, that 'by this definition, children, slaves, aliens, and women are distinguished from citizens, although in different ways' (p. 46). One might expect at this point a detailed account of why these groups are excluded in 'different ways'; but the only qualifying remark Marsilius offered concerns the boys who are sons of citizens, lest anyone think they are to be permanently excluded. Marsilius asserted that 'the sons of citizens are citizens in *proximate potentiality*, lacking only in years' (p. 46, emphasis added). Citizenship extends to the ranks of men with taxable property, born or resident for a long period in their city, but excludes all others, a matter which apparently required little explanation.

Moreover, Marsilius's conception of citizenship, like nearly all others at the time, entailed a conception of political participation uniquely adapted to small-scale communities – self-government for city-republics. Few republicans reflected on the relevance of republican government to large, extended territories, a matter of considerable concern to later republican thinkers such as Montesquieu (see ch. 3 below). And none advocated institutions and procedures which bore any direct resemblance to democracy in its contemporary dominant form: liberal democracy, with its commitment to embrace all mature adults (Skinner, 1992, p. 63; and ch. 3 below). Renaissance republicans took for granted that popular government was a form of self-rule for those with entrenched (property-based) interests in their local community, who alone were thought to be capable of enjoying and developing the network of public relations and duties to which it gave rise.

The unqualified authority claimed by previous forms of rulership – Church and kingship – is also found in Marsilius's doctrine of popular sovereignty, for 'it entails an absolutism whereby any value, group, or institution can be brought under the authority of the people's will' (Gewirth, 1980, p. xli). The authority of 'the people' is, in principle, monistic, unchecked and ultimately unbalanced. In other words, there is no argument to be found here – urgently expressed by later liberal constitutionalists and advocates of a modern polity separate, in principle, from ruler and ruled – in support of the contention that for political power to be effective it must be impartial and circumscribed, so that the powers of the state can clearly be distinguished from the power of those who are entrusted with state duties and the power of those who are presided over. City-republicans and their protagonists placed their trust in the judgement of men of civil honour, and in the theory and practice of ancient self-government. For them, self-government was a form of direct democracy among trusted 'club members' –

not yet a view of the nature of popular rule for a more sceptical age, one which casts doubt on the beneficence and prudence of all, rulers and ruled alike.

From civic life to civic glory

By the time Marsilius published *Defensor pacis*, the institutions of elective government were in decline in Padua and being replaced by hereditary rule. The infighting and factional disputes that had characterized Paduan politics found parallels in many other cities. The attempt to defend republican ideals in the unstable circumstances of Italian public life required particularly compelling arguments. Given that the ancient republics had suffered decline and defeat, the question of how, and in what ways, the values of the classical *polis* could be adapted and upheld in radically changed circumstances was a pressing one. Few understood this question better than Niccolò Machiavelli (1469–1527), who linked the case for forms of elective government and participative politics to the prospects of civic welfare and civic glory, a connection more easily forged perhaps in his native Florence than elsewhere due to its particular pre-eminence during the Renaissance. Machiavelli, with a firm foot both in the political theory of the ancient world and in that of the new emerging European political order, was able to offer an account of the republican tradition – that is, of protective republicanism – which sought to locate in civic involvement the conditions of independence, self-rule and glorious endeavour. Florentine political culture articulated many of these notions and provided a rich context for his politics.

Often regarded as the first theorist of modern state politics, Machiavelli sought to explore how a proper balance might be found between the powers of the state and the powers of the citizen in two key texts, *The Prince* and *The Discourses*. For too long *The Prince* has been taken as Machiavelli's major contribution, and this has led to a quite distorted reading of his work. If one places greater stress on *The Discourses*, as contemporary scholars argue we should (see Gilbert, 1965; Pocock, 1975; Skinner, 1981), then a distinctive and, in many respects, compelling position emerges. The study of classical history reveals, Machiavelli argued, that the three major forms of government – monarchy, aristocracy and democracy – are inherently unstable and tend to create a cycle of degeneration and corruption. In passages which parallel strands in Plato and Aristotle, Machiavelli held that after an initial period of positive development monarchy tends to decay into tyranny, aristocracy into oligarchy and democracy into anarchy, which then tends to be overturned in favour of monarchy again (*The Discourses*, pp. 104–11). When the generation that created the ancient democracies died, a situation emerged:

> in which no respect was shown either for the individual or for the official, and which was such that, as everyone did what he liked, all sorts of outrages were constantly committed. The outcome was inevitable. Either at the suggestion of some good men or because this anarchy had to be got rid of somehow, principality was once again restored. And from this there was, stage by stage, a return to anarchy, by way of transitions . . . This, then, is the cycle through which all commonwealths pass, whether they govern themselves or are governed. (*The Discourses*, pp. 108–9)

Machiavelli pointed directly to Athens as an example of a democracy which degenerated because of its inability to protect itself from 'the arrogance of the upper class' and 'the licentiousness of the general public' (*The Discourses*, p. 110). The political world, he contended, was always one of flux and potential chaos.

Unlike Marsilius before him, or Hobbes and Locke after him, Machiavelli did not believe that there was a given principle of organization (for instance, a fixed view of the state as subserving the good life or the natural rights of individuals) which it was the task of government to articulate and sustain. There was no natural or God-given framework to order political life. Rather, it was the task of *politics* to create order in the world. Machiavelli conceived politics as the struggle to win, utilize and contain power. Politics is thus ascribed a pre-eminent position in social life as the chief constitutive element of society. Like many other political thinkers from Plato onwards, Machiavelli conceived of 'the generality of men' as self-seeking, lazy, suspicious and incapable of doing anything good unless constrained by necessity (see *The Discourses*, pp. 200–1, 256–7). The question was: under what circumstances might people support political order and commit themselves to the state? Or, to put the question in more Machiavellian terms, how might *virtú* – 'a willingness to do whatever may be necessary for the pursuit of civic glory' – be instilled in people?[4]

Machiavelli stressed two key institutional devices as critical to the inculcation of civic virtue: the enforcement of law and upholding religious worship. The former, in particular, provides the basis to compel people to place the interests of the community above their own interests: the law can 'make citizens good'. But how can good and bad laws be distinguished? The answer is disclosed by historical investigation into the ways the law has been used to foster civic culture and greatness. The instability of all singular constitutional forms suggests that only a governmental system combining elements of monarchy, aristocracy and democracy can promote the kind of culture on which *virtú* depends. The best example of such a government was, in Machiavelli's opinion, Rome: Rome's 'mixed government' (with its system of consuls, Senate and tribunes of the people) was directly linked to its sustained achievement of glory.

It is not only the historical route to this conclusion that is important; Machiavelli's reasoning is theoretically innovative as well. A 'mixed government', structured to compensate for the defects of individual constitutional forms, is most likely to be able to balance the interests of rival social groupings, particularly those of the rich and the poor. Machiavelli's argument should not be confused with later arguments for the separation of powers within the state and for representative government based on party competition. None the less, his argument is a precursor of them, anticipating important aspects of their rationale. If the rich and the poor can be drawn into the process of government, and their interests found a legitimate avenue of expression through a division of offices between them, then they will be forced into some form of mutual accommodation. Ever watchful of their own positions,

---

[4] In putting the question in this way, and in exploring a response, I am following Skinner's admirable analysis of Machiavelli's writings on this theme (1981, pp. 51–77).

they will expend great efforts to ensure that no laws are passed that are detrimental to their interests. The outcome of such efforts is likely to be a body of law that all parties can agree on in the end. Against the dominant traditions of his time, Machiavelli contended that the existence of opposed social forces and dissension, far from eroding all possibility of good and effective laws, might be the condition of them (Skinner, 1981, pp. 63–6). A quite unconventional conclusion was reached: the basis of liberty may not just be a self-governing regime and a willingness to participate in politics, but may also be conflict and disagreement through which citizens can promote and defend their interests.

Writing against the background of competition and war between sixteenth-century Italian city-states, Machiavelli's views were of particular significance; for his argument was that communities have never increased in 'dominion or wealth' except when they have been able to enjoy liberty (*The Discourses*, p. 275). Under tyranny, whether imposed by an external power or by a 'local' tyrant, cities or states degenerate in the long run. By contrast, if a community can enjoy liberty, as Machiavelli hoped his native city would continue to do and a united Italy would do in the future, it is likely that it will flourish. Machiavelli sought to reinforce this point by referring (not wholly consistently) to classical Athens (with its factional disputes) and Rome (with its conflicts between Senate and Commons) as examples of cities which enjoyed liberty and 'grew enormously' in relatively short periods of time (*The Discourses*, p. 275).

The preservation of liberty, however, depended on something more than just a mixed constitution: 'eternal vigilance'. There are always threats to liberty posed by, on the one hand, the particular interests of factions and, on the other hand, competing states. While a mixed constitution is essential to containing the former, the best way of meeting the challenge of competing states is to contain them before one is contained. A policy of expansion is, therefore, a necessary prerequisite to the preservation of a collectivity's liberty: the application of force is integral to the maintenance of freedom. In so arguing, Machiavelli was firmly placing the ends of the state or community above those of the individual, both at home and abroad; 'reasons of state' held priority over the rights of individuals. A person's duties were first and foremost those required by citizenship. However, Machiavelli linked this classical emphasis on the primacy of civic life directly to the requirements of 'power politics'. Accordingly, 'Machiavellianism' in its more 'popular' contemporary sense emerged: the politics of statecraft and the relentless pursuit of power had priority over individual interests and private morality. Machiavelli thus anticipated certain of the dilemmas of liberalism (see ch. 3, pp. 59–60), but resolved them ultimately in a profoundly anti-liberal way, by granting priority to the preservation of society by whatever means necessary.

Political life is ambiguous. In order to create liberty and political stability, it may not always be possible to resort to law and the minimum use of force. Machiavelli unquestionably preferred liberty to tyranny, but he thought the latter might often be necessary to sustain the former. His judgement moved uneasily between admiration of a free, self-governing people and admiration of a powerful leader able to create and defend the law. He tentatively sought to reconcile these preferences by distinguishing between, on the one hand, the kind of politics necessary for the inauguration of a state or for the liberation of a state from corruption and, on the other hand, the kind of politics necessary for the maintenance of a state once it had been properly established. An element of democracy was essential to the latter, but quite inappropriate to the former.

In general, however, Machiavelli believed that 'free government' was difficult if not impossible to sustain in the actual political circumstances of Europe. Thus, there was a clear necessity for the resourceful despot to impose his vision of state and society and to create the possibility of order and harmony. The free state would depend on the strong, expansionary state to secure the conditions of its existence. The good state was first and foremost the secure and stable state. Therefore, while we find in Machiavelli the germs of a theory of democracy – elements of democracy are necessary to protect the governed from the governors, and to protect the governed from each other – they have a somewhat precarious existence in the context of other aspects of his thought.

Further, when Machiavelli is said to defend elements of democratic government, it is very important to be clear what is meant (see Plamenatz, 1963, pp. 36–40). By the standards of his day he was, it should be stressed, a democrat; that is, he conceived of political participation in broader terms than simply the involvement of the wealthy and/or noble in public affairs. Along with the ancient Greek democrats, and many republican thinkers like Marsilius of Padua, he wanted the process of government to include artisans and small traders. 'The people' or citizenry were to be those with 'independent' means who might be expected to have a substantial interest in public affairs. Foreigners, labourers, servants and 'dependants', a category which included all women and children, were not, however, regarded as having such an interest (see Pitkin, 1984). Citizens were men with a 'stake in the country' of unambiguously local descent. Public affairs were their affairs. Moreover, his conception of a self-governing community is by no means yet a conception of democracy embodying many of the elements (such as individual democratic rights entrenched irrespective of class, race and sex, and majority rule) that became central to modern liberalism and democratic thinking. None the less, his distinctive understanding of politics, linking closely the case for self-determination with that of self-protection, was a fundamental moment in political thought. It is summarized in model IIa, which provides a useful contrast with what is taken here as the leading account of developmental republicanism, the work of Jean-Jacques Rousseau (1712–78).

The republic and the general will

Protective republicans hold, it has been shown, that political participation is a necessary condition of liberty; a self-governing republic requires involvement in the political process. Moreover, freedom is marked by the ability to participate in the public sphere, by the subordination of egoistic concerns to the public good, and by the subsequent opportunity this creates for the expansion of welfare, individual and collective. This emphasis on the significance of participating as a full member in a *polis* was given another remarkable restatement by Rousseau, who, like many of his Renaissance republican predecessors, stood between ancient and modern thought about democracy, but who, writing in the very different context of the eighteenth century, sought to rearticulate this position in

In sum: model IIa

Protective Republicanism

Principle(s) of justification
   Political participation is an essential condition of personal liberty; if citizens do not rule themselves, they will be dominated by others

Key features
   Balance of power between 'the people', aristocracy and the monarchy linked to a mixed constitution or mixed government, with provision for all leading political forces to play an active role in public life

   Citizen participation achieved via different possible mechanisms, including election of consuls, or representatives to serve on ruling councils

   Competing social groups promoting and defending their interests

   Liberties of speech, expression and association

   Rule of law

General conditions
   Small city community

   Maintenance of religious worship

   Society of independent artisans and traders

   Exclusion of women, labourers and 'dependants' in politics (expanding opportunities for male citizens to participate in the public realm)

   Intensive conflict among rival political associations

the face of both the absolutist claims of kings and the liberal onslaught against them. Born in a small city-republic, the city of Geneva, Rousseau hoped to defend the idea of 'assembly politics' where the people can readily meet together and where each citizen can 'with ease' know the rest. Rousseau was aware that this was democracy for small states and that many of his ideal stipulations could not be met by the world developing before him, with its spread of commercial networks, industrial developments, large states and complex problems posed by size. None the less, his account of the core republican ideas is among the most radical, if not *the* most radical, ever developed, and it is linked to a new view of the rights and duties of citizens. It is important to examine Rousseau's position, not only because of the significance of his thought, but because he had a considerable (though ambiguous) influence on the ideas in currency during the French Revolution as well as, according to some writers at least, on the development of the key counterpoint to liberal democracy: the Marxist tradition, discussed in chapter 4 (see, for example, Colletti, 1972).

   Rousseau has been described as 'the Machiavelli of the eighteenth century' (Pocock, 1975, p. 504). He referred to his own preferred political system as 'republican', stressing the centrality of obligations and duties to the public realm. And, indeed, Rousseau's account of the proper form of 'the republic' is clearly indebted to his republican forebear. Like Machiavelli, Rousseau was critical of the notion of 'democracy', which he associated with classical Athens. In his view,

Athens alone could not be upheld as a political ideal because it failed to incorporate a clear division between legislative and executive functions and, accordingly, became prone to instability, internecine strife and indecision in crises (*The Social Contract*, pp. 112–14, 136ff). Moreover, like his forebear, he tended to emphasize continuity between his conception of a defensible form of government and the legacy of republican Rome (although, in fact, it is not hard to see elements of continuity with the Athenian heritage). But while Rousseau appears to have admired Machiavelli, referring to him as 'a gentleman and a good citizen', he also regarded his work as something of a compromise with the power structures of the actual republics of his age (*The Social Contract*, p. 118). In his theoretical writing about the ideal government at least, Rousseau was not prepared to make any such compromise, developing an interpretation of the proper form of 'the republic' which was, and came to be seen as, unique in many respects.

In his classic *The Social Contract*, published in 1762, Rousseau explored how human beings were contented in their original 'state of nature', a period before the development of civil governments. During this time humans were fundamentally equal, living somewhat isolated but free lives in a diversity of natural circumstances. However, people were driven from their original state to develop new institutions by a variety of obstacles to their preservation: individual weaknesses and egoistic desires, common miseries and natural disasters. Human beings would have 'perished' if they had not 'changed their mode of existence' (*The Social Contract*, p. 59). They came to realize that their survival, the development of their nature, the realization of their capacity for reason and their fullest experience of liberty could be achieved only by the establishment of a system of cooperation upheld by a law making and enforcing body. Thus, people joined together to create through a 'social contract' – a new basis of understanding and agreement, 'perhaps never formally stated ... everywhere tacitly admitted and recognized' – the possibility of living together under laws which treat all individuals equally and give all the opportunity to develop their capacities securely (p. 60). The public association thus formed was 'once called the *city*, and is now known as the *republic* or the *body politic*' (p. 61). For Rousseau the fundamental question was: 'How to find a form of association which will defend the person and goods of each member with the collective force of all, and under which each individual, while uniting himself with the others ... remains as free as before' (p. 60).

Rousseau saw individuals as ideally involved in the direct creation of the laws by which their lives are regulated, and he affirmed the notion of an active, involved citizenry: all citizens should meet together to decide what is best for the community and enact the appropriate laws. The ruled should be the rulers. In Rousseau's account, the idea of self-rule is posited as an end in itself; a political order offering opportunities for participation in the arrangement of public affairs should not just be a state, but rather the formation of *a type of society*: a society in which the affairs of the state are integrated into the affairs of ordinary citizens (see *The Social Contract*, pp. 82, 114, and for a general account book 3, chs 1–5). Rousseau set himself firmly against the post-Machiavellian distinctions between state and civil society, government and 'the people' (although he accepted, and this will be returned to below, the importance of dividing and limiting both access to 'governmental power' and governmental power itself). For him, sovereignty originates in the people, and it ought to stay there (Cranston, 1968, p. 30). In a justly famous passage he wrote:

> Sovereignty cannot be represented, for the same reason that it cannot be alienated . . . the people's deputies are not, and could not be, its representatives; they are merely its agents; and they cannot decide anything finally. Any law which the people has not ratified in person is void; it is not law at all. The English people believes itself to be free; it is gravely mistaken; it is free only during the election of Members of Parliament; as soon as the Members are elected, the people is enslaved; it is nothing. (*The Social Contract*, p. 141)

The role of the citizen is the highest to which an individual can aspire. The considered exercise of power by citizens is the only legitimate way in which liberty can be sustained. The citizen must both create and be bound by 'the supreme direction of the general will', the publicly generated conception of the common good (*The Social Contract*, pp. 60–1). Rousseau recognized that opinions may differ about the 'common good' and he accepted a provision for majority rule: 'the votes of the greatest number always bind the rest' (p. 153). But the people are sovereign only to the extent that they participate actively in articulating the 'general will'.

In order to grasp Rousseau's position, it is important to distinguish the 'general will' from the 'will of all': it is the difference, according to him, between the judgement about the common good and the mere aggregate of personal fancies and individual desires (pp. 72–3, 75). Citizens are only obliged to obey a system of laws and regulations on the grounds of publicly reached agreement, for they can only be genuinely obliged to comply with a law they have prescribed for themselves with the general good in mind (p. 65; cf. p. 82). It is freely chosen obligation, accepted by the citizen body acting as a whole with the well-being of the community in mind, which constitutes the basis of 'political right' (cf. Manin, 1987, pp. 338–68; and see the discussion of impartialism on pp. 239–41 below for some interesting parallels with elements of contemporary deliberative democracy).

Rousseau drew a critical distinction between independence and liberty:

> Many have been the attempts to confound independence and liberty: two things so essentially different, that they reciprocally exclude each other. When every one does what he pleases, he will, of course, often do things displeasing to others; and this is not properly called a free state. Liberty consists less in acting according to one's own pleasure, than in not being subject to the will and pleasure of other people. It consists also in our not subjecting the wills of other people to our own. Whoever is the master over others is not himself free, and even to reign is to obey. (From letter 8, *Oeuvres complètes de J. J. Rousseau*, quoted in Keane, 1984a, p. 255)

Independence comprises the pursuit of self-interested projects without regard for the position and will of others. Liberty, by contrast, is attained by participating in the generation and enactment of the general will, which establishes equality among citizens in that they can all enjoy 'the same rights' (*The Social Contract*, p. 76; cf. p. 46).

By 'the same rights' Rousseau did not simply mean equal political rights and the equal application of all political rules to each citizen. However equal political rights may be in law, they cannot be safeguarded, he maintained, in the face of vast inequalities of wealth and power. Rousseau regarded the right to property as sacred, but he understood it as a limited right to only that amount of property commensurate with an individual's need for material security and independence of mind. Free of economic dependence, citizens need not be frightened of forming autonomous judgements; for citizens can, then, develop and express views without risk of threats to their livelihood. Rousseau desired a state of affairs in which 'no citizen shall be rich enough to buy another and none so poor as to be forced to sell himself' (*The Social Contract*, p. 96). Only a broad similarity in economic conditions can prevent major differences of interest developing into organized factional disputes which would undermine hopelessly the establishment of a general will. But Rousseau was not an advocate, as he is sometimes taken to be, of absolute equality; for equality, he made clear, 'must not be taken to imply that degrees of power and wealth should be absolutely the same for all, but rather that power shall stop short of violence and never be exercised except by virtue of authority and law' (p. 96).

Rousseau argued in favour of a political system in which the legislative and executive functions are clearly demarcated. The former belong to the people and the latter to a 'government' or 'prince'. The people form the legislative assembly and constitute the authority of the state; the 'government' or 'prince' (composed of one or more administrators or magistrates) executes the people's laws (*The Social Contract*, book 3, chs 1, 11–14, 18).[5] Such a 'government' is necessary on the grounds of expediency: the people require a government to coordinate public meetings, serve as a means of communication, draft laws and enforce and defend the legal system (p. 102). The government is a result of an agreement among the citizenry and is legitimate only to the extent to which it fulfils 'the instructions of the general will'. Should it fail so to behave it can be revoked and changed; for its personnel are chosen either directly through elections or by lot (pp. 136–9, 148).

Rousseau's conception of republican government, summarized in model IIb, represents in many respects the apotheosis of the attempt throughout the republican tradition to link freedom and participation directly. Moreover, the connection he forged between the principle of legitimate government and that of self-rule in the collective interest challenged not only the political principles of the regimes of his day – above all those of the *ancien régime* – but also those of later liberal democratic states. For his notion of self-government has been among the most radical, contesting at its core some of the critical assumptions of liberal democracy, especially the notion that democracy is the name for a particular kind of state which can only be held accountable to the citizenry once in a while.

But Rousseau's ideas do not represent a completely coherent system or recipe for straightforward action. He appreciated some of the problems created by large-scale, complex, densely populated societies, but did not pursue these as far

---

[5] There are additional institutional positions set out by Rousseau, for instance, that of 'the Lawgiver', which will not be elaborated here (see *The Social Contract*, pp. 83–8, 95–6). For a critical discussion, see Harrison (1993, pp. 59–60).

In sum: model IIb

Developmental Republicanism

Principle(s) of justification
Citizens must enjoy political and economic equality in order that nobody can be master of another and all can enjoy equal freedom and development in the process of self-determination for the common good

Key features
Division of legislative and executive functions

The direct participation of citizens in public meetings to constitute the legislature

Unanimity on public issues desirable, but voting provision with majority rule in the event of disagreement

Executive positions in the hands of 'magistrates' or 'administrators'

Executive appointed either by direct election or by lot

General conditions
Small, non-industrial community

Diffusion of ownership of property among the many; citizenship depends on property holding, i.e. a society of independent producers

Domestic service of women to free men for (non-domestic) work and politics

as one must (see, for example, *The Social Contract*, book 3, ch. 4; and Part Three of this volume). Furthermore, Rousseau himself by no means thought that history would culminate in the fulfilment of his model of democratic reason. He did not think history unfolded progressively towards a better life; on the contrary, he was sceptical of the Enlightenment's view of progress, since, having left the state of nature, humans had unleashed political and economic forces and forms of competitive and self-seeking behaviour which had generated 'civilization' only at a very high cost (cf. Masters, 1968; J. Miller, 1984). Corruption and social injustice typically followed from the inequalities wrought by 'progress'. Rousseau's view seems to have been that the ethical democratic political community would have to surmount these inequalities if it were to have any chance of becoming entrenched, and that this was a highly unlikely prospect.

Rousseau's insistence on the democratic nature of a community's government, however, sits uneasily with a number of restrictions he himself imposed upon this polity. In the first instance, he too excluded all women from 'the people', i.e. the citizenry, as well as, it seems, the poor. Women are excluded because, unlike men, their capacity for sound judgement is clouded by 'immoderate passions' and, hence, they 'require' male protection and guidance in the face of the challenge of politics (see Rousseau, *Émile*, esp. book V; Pateman, 1985, pp. 157–8). The poor appear to be outcasts because citizenship is conditional upon a small property qualification (land) and/or upon the absence of dependence on others (see Connolly, 1981, ch. 7).

There are other notable difficulties. Rousseau has been portrayed as advocating a model of democracy with, in the end, tyrannical implications (see, for example, Berlin, 1969, pp. 162–4). At the root of this charge is a concern that, because the majority is all-powerful in the face of individuals' aims and wishes, 'the sovereignty of the people' could easily destroy 'the sovereignty of individuals' (Berlin, 1969, p. 163). The problem is that Rousseau not only assumed that minorities ought to consent to the decisions of majorities but he also posited no limits to the reach of the decisions of a democratic majority. In fact, he thought that civic education ought to bridge the gap between the individual's will and the common good, while common beliefs ought to be enforced through a 'civil religion' (*The Social Contract*, book 4, ch. 8, esp. pp. 185–7). While questions posed by such positions do not engender fatal objections to all aspects of Rousseau's vision (see Pateman, 1985, pp. 159–62), it is hard to avoid the conclusion that he failed to reflect adequately upon the threats posed by 'public power' to all aspects of 'private life' (see Harrison, 1993, ch. 4). (This issue will be returned to in the next section of this chapter and in subsequent chapters.)

Rousseau's overriding concern was with what might be thought of as the future of democracy in a non-industrial community, that is, a community like his native 'republic of Geneva', which he greatly admired. His vision of democracy was evocative and challenging; but it was not systematically linked to an account of politics in a world faced by rapidly entrenching nation-states and by change of an altogether different kind, the industrial revolution, which was gathering pace at the end of the eighteenth century and beginning to undermine traditional community life. It was left to others to think through the nature of democracy in relation to these developments. In doing so, many came to see Rousseau's thought as utopian and/or irrelevant to 'modern conditions'. But this was – and is – by no means the judgement of all democratic theorists. For, as will be seen throughout the chapters which follow, there have been some political thinkers who have returned to the central 'moral' of the republican tradition, that is, that citizens must 'never put their trust in princes' and that '[i]f we wish to ensure that governments act in the interests of the people, we must somehow ensure that we the people act as our own government' (Skinner, 1992, p. 69). How enduring this moral has been can be disclosed by a critical assessment of the dominant model of democracy in modern politics: liberal democracy. However, before turning to it, the meaning of republican thought needs further explication in relation to one fundamental element of its conceptual framework which has as yet been insufficiently explored: its gendered conception of citizenship.

The public and the private

The history of republican thought is, as one critic aptly noted, 'ominously dismissive of femininity and women' (Phillips, 1991, p. 46). But one figure especially stands out against the 'male stream', Mary Wollstonecraft (1759–97), whose pioneering inquiry into the nature of the interconnections between the public and the private realms is discussed below. Wollstonecraft's work did not issue in a new model of a self-governing community or of democratic government, but it is properly understood as a central contribution to the analysis of the conditions for the possibility of democracy. As such, it sheds new light on the strengths and limitations of the traditions of thought discussed so far.

Reflecting on the significance of the French Revolution and the spread of radicalism across Europe at the close of the eighteenth century, Wollstonecraft found much in Rousseau's work to admire. Partly inspired by those events and the issues posed by Rousseau, Wollstonecraft wrote one of the most remarkable tracts of social and political theory, *Vindication of the Rights of Woman* (written in 1791 and published in 1792). While the text was received with considerable enthusiasm in the radical circles in which she moved (circles which included William Godwin and Thomas Paine), it was treated with the utmost scorn and derision in others (see Kramnick, 1982; Taylor, 1983; Tomalin, 1985). In fact, the latter reaction has largely characterized the reception of *Vindication of the Rights of Woman* since its inception. The reasons for this lie at the very heart of its argument, an argument barely considered in political theory again until the work of John Stuart Mill (1806–73), and, then, along with his work on the subjection of women, much neglected thereafter. Mary Wollstonecraft has rarely been considered one of the key theorists of democracy, but she ought to have been.

Wollstonecraft accepted the argument that liberty and equality were intertwined. Like Rousseau, she was of the view that all those who are 'obliged to weigh the consequences of every farthing they spend' cannot enjoy liberty of 'heart and mind' (*Vindication*, p. 255). Like Rousseau, she argued that from excessive respect for property and the propertied flow many 'evils and vices of this world'. The possibility of an active, knowledgeable citizenry depends on freedom from poverty as well as freedom from a system of hereditary wealth which instils in the governing classes a sense of authority independent of any test of reason or merit. Wollstonecraft was firmly of the view that while poverty brutalizes the mind, living off wealth created by others encourages arrogance and habitual idleness (pp. 252–3, 255). Human faculties can only be developed if they are used, and they will seldom be used 'unless necessity of some kind first set the wheels in motion' (p. 252). And Wollstonecraft maintained, like Rousseau, that more equality must be created in society if citizens are to gain an enlightened understanding of their world, and if the political order is to be governed by reason and sound judgement. In a typically bold passage, she declared:

> The preposterous distinctions of rank, which render civilization a curse, by dividing the world between voluptuous tyrants and cunning envious dependents, corrupt, almost equally, every class of people, because respectability is not attached to the discharge of the relative duties of life, but to the station, and when the duties are not fulfilled the affections cannot gain sufficient strength to fortify the virtue of which they are the natural reward. (*Vindication*, pp. 256–7)

However, unlike Rousseau and the republican tradition more broadly, Wollstonecraft could not accept the powerful strand in political thinking which subsumed the interests of women and children under those of 'the individual', that is, the male citizen. Wollstonecraft was critical of any assumption of an identity of interests among men, women and children, and deeply so of Rousseau's portrait of the proper relation between men and women, which denied women a role in public life (see *Vindication*, ch. 5). Although not the first to ask why it was that the doctrine of individual freedom and equality did not apply to women, she offered a more far-reaching analysis of this question than anyone before her and, indeed, after her for several generations to come (cf. Mary Astell, *Some Reflections upon Marriage*, first published 1700). For Wollstonecraft, the very failure to explore the issue of women's political emancipation had been detrimental not only to the equality of the lives of individual women and men, but also to the very nature of reason and morality itself. In her view, relations between men and women were founded on largely unjustified assumptions (about natural differences between men and women) and unjust institutions (from the marriage contract to the direct absence of female representation in the state). In Wollstonecraft's words, this state of affairs was 'subversive' of human endeavours to perfect nature and sustain happiness (*Vindication*, pp. 87, 91). If the modern world is to be free of tyranny, not only must 'the divine right of kings' be contested, but 'the divine right of husbands' as well (p. 127). Given this standpoint, it is scarcely surprising, then, that *Vindication of the Rights of Woman* was treated with such alarm by so many people.

Against the widely accepted portrait of women as weak, volatile, 'unable to stand alone' and passive, 'insignificant objects of desire', Wollstonecraft argued that to the extent that women were pitiful creatures this was because of the way they had been brought up (*Vindication*, pp. 81–3). What was at issue was not women's natural capacities, but marked inadequacies in their education and circumstances. Isolated in domestic routines and limited by restricted opportunities, women's abilities to become full citizens were constantly attacked and undermined. Women *learned* a 'feminine ideal' which they were pressured on all sides to uphold; they were taught to be delicate, well mannered and uninterested in worldly affairs. Women's rank in life *prevented* them from performing the duties of citizens and, as a result, profoundly degraded them (pp. 257–8). The position and education of 'ladies', for example, appeared to be designed to develop the necessary qualities for 'confinement in cages': 'like the feathered race, they have nothing to do but to please themselves, and stalk with mock majesty from perch to perch. It is true they are provided with food and raiment, for which they neither toil nor spin; but health, liberty and virtue are given in exchange' (p. 146). In short, what women are and can become is a product of human and historical arrangements, not a matter of natural differences.

It is necessary, therefore, Wollstonecraft contended, for political relations to be rethought in connection with 'a few simple principles', accepted by most thinkers who have sought to challenge arbitrary and despotic powers (*Vindication*, p. 90). The pre-eminence of human beings over 'brute creation' consists in their capacity to reason, to accumulate knowledge through experience and to live a life of virtue. Humans can – and have a right to – order their existence according to the dictates of reason and morality. Human beings are capable of understanding the world and seeking the perfection of their nature (p. 91). What distinguishes Wollstonecraft's invocation of these classic Enlightenment tenets, however, from that of nearly all her predecessors is that she turned them against the 'masculinist' assumptions of radical and liberal thinkers alike. Both men and women are born with a God-given capacity to reason, a capacity too often denied 'by the words or conduct of men' (p. 91). 'If the abstract rights of men will bear discussion and explanation,' Wollstonecraft avowed, 'those of women, by a parity of reasoning, will not shrink from the same test' (p. 87). And, she concluded, if women are to be effective both in public *and* private life (as citizens, wives and mothers), they must, first and foremost, discharge their duties to themselves as rational beings (p. 259).

In order for women to be in a position to discharge their duties as well as possible, it is not enough merely to reform their position by, for instance, altering the nature of their education, as some seventeenth- and eighteenth-century figures had held. For the rule of reason is stifled by arbitrary authority in many forms. It is, in particular, 'the pestiferous purple', she says in a memorable phrase, 'which renders the progress of civilization a curse, and warps the understanding' (*Vindication*, p. 99). Wollstonecraft directs most of her criticism at all those whose power and authority derive from inherited property and/or a system of titles. Three institutional groupings are singled out for especially harsh comment: the nobility, the Church and the army. Their privileges, idle lives and/or ill-thought-out projects – the corrupt relations which 'wealth, idleness, and folly produce' – oppress not only women but also 'a numerous class' of hard-working labourers (pp. 260, 317). Accordingly, it is the whole system of politics – 'if system it may courteously be called, consisting in multiplying dependents and contriving taxes which grind the poor to pamper the rich' – which must be altered if the rule of reason is to be created firmly (p. 256). Only when there is 'no coercion *established* in society', Wollstonecraft declared, will 'the sexes . . . fall into their proper place' (p. 88).

For women and men to enjoy liberty requires that they enjoy the conditions and opportunities to pursue self-chosen ends as well as social, political and religious obligations. What is especially important about Wollstonecraft's statement of this position is, it should be stressed, the deeply rooted connections it sets out between the spheres of 'the public' and 'the private': between the possibility of citizenship and participation in government, on the one hand, and obstacles to such a possibility anchored heavily in unequal gender relations, on the other. Her argument is that there can be little, if any, progressive political change without restructuring the sphere of private relations, and there can be no satisfactory restructuring of 'the private' without major transformations in the nature of governing institutions. Moreover, she endeavoured to show that private duties (to those closest to one, whether they be adults or children) 'are never properly fulfilled unless the understanding [reason] enlarges the heart', and that public virtue cannot properly be developed until 'the tyranny of man' is at an end; for 'public virtue is only an aggregate of private [virtue]' (*Vindication*, pp. 316, 318). The emancipation of women is, then, a critical condition of liberty in a rational and moral order.

Among the practical changes Wollstonecraft sought were a national system of education, new career opportunities for women ('women might ... be physicians as well as nurses') and, though 'I may excite laughter', a 'direct share' for women in 'the deliberations of government' (*Vindication*, pp. 252ff). With such changes a woman might come to enjoy the opportunity to make a major contribution to society: 'she must not, if she discharge her civil duties, want individually the protection of civil laws; she must not be dependent on her husband's bounty for her subsistence during his life, or support after his death; for how can a being be generous who has nothing of its own? or virtuous who is not free?' (p. 259). Given the financial wherewithal to sustain themselves and to contribute to the well-being of others, women would at last be in a position to become equal members of the polity. The social and political order would be transformed to the benefit of both women and men: order might then be based on no authority other than reason itself.

Wollstonecraft's work makes a significant contribution to the illumination of the interrelation between social and political processes and, thus, to a new appreciation of the conditions of democracy. Until the twentieth century, there were few, if any, writers who traced as perceptively as she did the relation between public and private spheres and the ways in which unequal gender relations cut across them to the detriment of the quality of life in both. The radical thrust of her argument posed new questions about the complex conditions under which a democracy, open to the participation of both women and men, can develop. After Wollstonecraft, it is hard to imagine how political theorists could neglect the study of the different conditions for the possibility of male and female involvement in democratic politics. Yet relatively few did pursue such a line of inquiry (see Pateman, 1988). The reasons for this no doubt lie, in part, in the dominance, as Mary Wollstonecraft would have understood it, of men in political and academic institutions; but a contributing factor lay in ambiguities in her thought itself.

To begin with, Wollstonecraft's work did not issue in a clear alternative model of democracy as, for instance, Rousseau's did before her or John Stuart Mill's after her. Wollstonecraft's arguments hovered uneasily between liberal principles familiar since Locke's *Second Treatise* (in *Two Treatises of Government*, discussed in the following chapter) and the more radical principles of a participatory democracy. In *Vindication of the Rights of Woman* she indicated that an additional volume was soon to be written which would pursue the political implications of her analysis (p. 90), but sadly it never appeared. Wollstonecraft's exact view of the proper role of government and the state is regrettably unclear. Although she often speaks of the need to extend the participation of women (and labouring men) in government, and argues clearly for the extension of the franchise, the implications of these views for the forms and limits of government are not spelt out in any detail. To the extent that implications are drawn, they point in different and sometimes competing directions: to a model of liberal democracy, on the one hand, and to quite revolutionary democratic ideas, on the other (see Taylor, 1983, pp. 1–7).

The difficulties in unfolding Wollstonecraft's position are highlighted by the rather surprising boundaries she herself drew around the relevant audience for her work; in 'addressing my sex ... I pay particular attention to those in the middle class, because they appear to be in the most natural state' (*Vindication*, p. 81). Leaving aside questions about what she meant by women living in 'the most natural state' (a phrase which is in some tension with her emphasis elsewhere on the historical nature of social relations), the issue is raised as to whether she was vindicating the rights of middle-class women only. Although such a position would itself have been quite a radical one to take at the time (most previous writers preoccupied with the position of women, as Wollstonecraft herself pointed out, had generally addressed themselves exclusively to upper-class 'ladies'), it is curious that she thought to limit the application of her doctrine to the middle classes. That she did so wish to limit it was made even clearer when she wrote that an emancipated woman would have a 'servant-maid to take off her hands the servile part of the household business' (*Vindication*, pp. 254–5). Despite many of her arguments being of great relevance to the conditions of all women, Wollstonecraft does not seem to have applied them to all women: in fact, the emancipated woman seems to require female servants. Further evidence of this view is found in Wollstonecraft's discussion of women (and men) in the 'ranks of the poor', who – destined for domestic employment or manual trades – would, even in a reformed society, still need philanthropic attention and specialized schooling if they were to attain a modicum of enlightenment (see Kramnick, 1982, pp. 40–4; *Vindication*, pp. 273ff).

None the less, Wollstonecraft set out central questions which any account of democracy which was not simply to assume that 'individuals' were men would have to address in the future. One of the few who actually addressed these questions was, as previously noted, John Stuart Mill, who attempted to integrate concerns about gender into a new version of liberal democratic arguments (see pp. 88–91 below). Mill's political thought is, of course, of the greatest importance. But even Mill, it should be borne in mind, did not pursue the implications for democracy of raising questions about gender as far as one must: it is only with the advent of contemporary feminism that the relevance and implications of many of Mary Wollstonecraft's ideas have begun to be appreciated fully (see chs 7 and 10).

Republicanism: concluding reflections

The revival of a concern with aspects of 'self-government' in Renaissance Italy had a significant influence on Britain, America and France in the seventeenth and eighteenth centuries. The problem of how civic life was to be constructed, and public life sustained, was one faced by diverse thinkers and political practitioners (see Pocock, 1975; Ball, 1988, ch. 3; Rahe, 1994). But different contexts yielded quite different results. In Britain, strands of republican thought continued to exert an impact, although they were most often enmeshed with powerful indigenous currents of thought dominated by monarchical and religious concepts. The relation between monarch and subjects was the main preoccupation (see Pocock, 1975, part III; Wootton, 1992). In America republican concepts remained contested, but their connotation shifted strikingly, and the meaning of the ideal of the active citizen was altered. In the debate surrounding the US constitution, some of America's 'founding fathers' repudiated ancient and Renaissance republicanism and sought to initiate a new republican order for a country with a large population, extended territory and complex commercial networks (cf. Ball, 1988, ch. 3; Rahe, 1994, pp. 3–18). In revolutionary France republican ideas remained uppermost and became part of the momentous challenge to the old monarchical order; however, even in France, republican ideas were transmuted many times, especially after the trajectory of the revolution – from popular revolt to terror – became more widely understood.

Across diverse backgrounds, thinking moved against reliance on virtuous citizens and civic restraint as the basis of political community and shifted towards a greater emphasis on the necessity to define and delimit the sphere of politics carefully, unleash individual energies in civil society, and provide a new balance between the citizen and government underwritten by law and institutions. Over time, the fundamental meaning of liberty as interpreted by the republican tradition changed; and liberty progressively came to evoke less a sense of public or political liberty, 'the right of the people to share in the government', and more a sense of personal or private liberty, 'the protection of rights against all governmental encroachments, particularly by the legislature' (Wood, 1969, pp. 608–9; and, for a discussion, Ball, 1988, pp. 54ff). Old words took on new meanings and were rearticulated with other threads of political language and tradition. The strengths and weaknesses of these political currents are explored in the chapter which follows.

3 The Development of Liberal Democracy: For and Against the State

The historical changes that contributed to the emergence of modern liberal and liberal democratic thought were immensely complicated. Struggles between monarchs and estates over the domain of rightful authority; peasant rebellions against the weight of excessive taxation and social obligation; the spread of trade, commerce and market relations; changes in technology, particularly military technology; the consolidation of national monarchies (notably in England, France and Spain); the growing influence of Renaissance culture; religious strife and the challenge to the universal claims of Catholicism; the struggle between church and state – all played a part. In the material that follows, a number of these developments will be dwelt on, but it is useful to clarify first the notion of the 'absolutist' state.

From the fifteenth to the eighteenth century two different forms of political regime were dominant in Europe: the 'absolute' monarchies of France, Prussia, Austria, Spain and Russia, among other places, and the 'constitutional' monarchies and republics of England and Holland (see Mann, 1986, ch. 14). There are significant conceptual and institutional differences between these regime types, although in terms of the history of state/society relations some of the differences have been more apparent than real. Constitutional states will be discussed shortly, but the focus in the first instance will be on absolutism.

Absolutism marked the emergence of a form of state based upon the absorption of smaller and weaker political units into larger and stronger political structures (at the beginning of the sixteenth century there were some 500 more or less independent political units in Europe); a strengthened ability to rule over a unified territorial area; an alteration and extension of fiscal management; a tightened system of law and order enforced throughout a territory (linked to a growing centralization of armed force); and the application of a more 'continuous, calculable, and effective' rule by a single, sovereign head (Poggi, 1978, pp. 60–1). Although the actual power of absolutist rulers has often been overstated, these changes signalled a substantial increase in 'public authority' from above (see P. Anderson, 1974b). Certainly, absolutist rulers proclaimed that they alone held the legitimate right of decision over state affairs. One of the most remarkable statements of this view has been attributed to Louis XV:

> In my person alone resides the sovereign power, and it is from me alone that the courts hold their existence and their authority. That ... authority can only be exercised in my name.... For it is to me exclusively that the legislative power belongs.... The whole public order emanates from me since I am its supreme guardian.... The rights and interests of the nation ... are necessarily united with my own and can only rest in my hands. (quoted in Schama, 1989, p. 104)

The absolutist monarch claimed to be the ultimate authority on all matters of human law, although it is important to note that this broad writ was understood to derive from the law of God. The king's legitimacy was based on 'divine right'.

The absolutist monarch was at the peak of a system of rule which was progressively centralized and anchored on a claim to supreme and indivisible power: *sovereign power* or *sovereignty*. This system was manifest in the routines and rituals of courtly life. However, linked to the court there developed a new administrative apparatus involving the beginnings of a permanent bureaucracy and army (Mann, 1986, p. 476). If the French monarchy of the seventeenth century represents the best example of an absolutist court, Prussia under the Hohenzollern dynasty provides the best example of the 'prototypes of ministries' (Poggi, 1990, p. 48). These 'prototypes' increased the state's involvement in the promotion and regulation of a hitherto unparalleled diversity of activities. Absolutism helped set in motion a process of state-making which began to reduce the social, economic, cultural and legal variation *within* states and expand the variation *among* them (Tilly, 1975, p. 19).

According to one interpretation of these changes, the expansion of state administrative power was made possible to a significant extent by the extension of the state's capacity for the collection and storage of information about members of society, and the related ability to supervise subject populations (Giddens, 1985, pp. 14–15, 198ff; cf. P. Anderson, 1974b, pp. 15–42). As the state's sovereign authority expanded and its administrative centres became more powerful, there was not simply, however, a concentration of power at the apex. For the increase in administrative power increased the state's dependence on cooperative forms of social relations; it was no longer possible for the state to manage its affairs and sustain its offices and activities by coercion alone. As a result, greater reciprocity was created between the governors and the governed, and the more reciprocity was involved, the more opportunities were generated for subordinate groups to influence their rulers. Absolutism, in short, created within itself a momentum towards the development of new forms of and limits on state power – constitutionalism and (eventually) participation by powerful groups in the process of government itself.

The proximate sources of the modern state were absolutism and the inter-state system it initiated. In condensing and concentrating political power in its own hands, and in seeking to create a central system of rule, absolutism paved the way for a national and secular system of power. But of all the developments that helped trigger new ways of thinking about the proper form of the state, it was perhaps the Protestant Reformation that was the most significant. For the Reformation did more than just challenge papal jurisdiction and authority across Europe; it raised questions about political obligation and obedience in a most stark manner. To whom allegiance was owed – the Catholic Church, a Protestant ruler, particular religious sects – was an issue that did not easily resolve itself. The bitter struggles between religious factions which spread across Europe during the last half of the sixteenth century, and reached their most intensive expression during the Thirty Years' War in Germany, made it clear that religion was becoming a highly divisive force (see Sigler, 1983). Very gradually it became apparent that the powers of the state would have to be separated from the duty of rulers to uphold any particular faith (Skinner, 1978, p. 352). This conclusion alone offered a way forward through the dilemmas of rule created by competing religions, all seeking to secure for themselves the kinds of privilege claimed by the medieval Church.

However, it was not just the strife created by the Reformation that had a lasting impact on political thought. For the teachings of Luther and Calvin contained at their very heart an unsettling conception of the person as 'an individual'. In the new doctrines, the individual was conceived as alone before God, the sovereign judge of all conduct, and directly responsible for the interpretation and enactment of God's will. This was a notion with profound and dynamic consequences. In the first instance, it loosened the individual from the direct 'institutional support' of the church and, in so doing, helped stimulate the notion of the individual agent as 'master of his destiny', the centrepiece of much later political reflection. It directly sanctioned, in addition, the autonomy of secular activity in all domains which did not directly conflict with moral and religious practice (see ch. 5 below, and Weber, *The Protestant Ethic and the Spirit of Capitalism*). This development, when joined with the momentum for political change initiated by the struggle among religions, and between religions and secular powers, constituted a major new impetus to re-examine the nature of state and society.

The impetus was given added force by a growing awareness in Europe of a variety of possible social and political arrangements, which followed in the wake of the discovery of the non-European world (see Sigler, 1983, pp. 53–62). The relationship between Europe and the 'New World', and the nature of the rights (if any) of non-Europeans, became a major focus of discussion. It sharpened the sense of a plurality of possible interpretations of the nature of politics (see S. Hall and Gieben, 1992, ch. 6). The direction these interpretations actually took was, of course, directly related to the context and traditions of particular European countries. The changing nature of politics was experienced differently throughout Europe. But it is hard to overestimate the significance of the processes and events which ushered in a new era of political reflection.

In modern Western political thought, the idea of the state is often linked to the notion of an impersonal and privileged legal or constitutional order with the capability of administering and controlling a given territory. While this notion found its earliest expression in the ancient world (especially in Rome), it did not become a major object of concern until the late sixteenth century. It was not an element of medieval political thinking. The idea of an impersonal and sovereign political order, i.e. a legally circumscribed structure of power separate from ruler and ruled with supreme jurisdiction over a territory, could not predominate while political rights, obligations and duties were closely tied to religious tradition, monarchical powers and the feudal system of property rights. Similarly, the idea that human beings were 'individuals' or 'a people', with a right to be citizens of their state, could not gain widespread currency until the constraining influence of such institutions was weakened.

Among the traditions of political thought that emerged during these times two were to become central: the republican tradition, discussed in the previous chapter, and the liberal tradition, of which Thomas Hobbes (1588–1679) and

John Locke (1632–1704) were among the first exponents. Hobbes marks an interesting point of transition between a commitment to absolutism and the struggle of liberalism against tyranny. Locke, by contrast, signals the clear beginnings of the liberal constitutionalist tradition, which became the dominant thread in the changing fabric of European and American politics from the eighteenth century.

It is important to be clear about the meaning of 'liberalism'. While it is a controversial concept, and its meaning has shifted historically, it is used here to signify the attempt to uphold the values of freedom of choice, reason and toleration in the face of tyranny, the absolutist system and religious intolerance (cf. Macpherson, 1966; Dunn, 1979; Pateman, 1985; Rahe, 1994, esp. the epilogue). Challenging clerical power and the Church, on the one side, and the powers of 'despotic monarchies', on the other, liberalism sought to restrict the powers of both and to define a uniquely private sphere independent of Church and state. At the centre of this project was the goal of freeing the polity from religious control and freeing civil society (personal, family and business life) from political interference. Gradually, liberalism became associated with the doctrine that individuals should be free to pursue their own preferences in religious, economic and political affairs – in fact, in most matters that affected daily life. While different 'variants' of liberalism interpreted this objective in different ways, they were all united around the advocacy of a constitutional state, private property and the competitive market economy as the central mechanisms for coordinating individuals' interests. In the earliest (and most influential) liberal doctrines, it is important to stress, individuals were conceived as 'free and equal', with 'natural rights'; that is, with inalienable rights they were endowed with at birth. However, it should also be noted from the outset that these 'individuals' were regarded (once again) as men (see Pateman, 1988). It was generally the male property-owning individual who was the focus of so much attention; and the new freedoms were first and foremost for the men of the new middle classes or the bourgeoisie (who were benefiting so directly from the growth of the market economy). The dominance of men in public and private life was largely left unquestioned by prominent thinkers.

The central problem facing liberal political theory was how to reconcile the concept of the state as an impersonal, legally circumscribed structure of power with a new view of the rights, obligations and duties of subjects. The question was: how was the 'sovereign state' to be related to the 'sovereign people' who were recognized as the legitimate source of the state's powers? Most liberal and liberal democratic theory has been faced with the dilemma of finding a balance between might and right, power and law, duties and rights. For while the state must have a monopoly of coercive power to provide a secure basis upon which 'free trade', business and family life can prosper, its coercive and regulatory capability must be contained so that its agents do not interfere with the political and social freedoms of individual citizens, with their pursuit of their particular interests in competitive relations with one another.

In order to understand the nature of liberalism more fully, it is important to examine its development in some detail. It is only by understanding the emergence of the liberal tradition – and the questions it raised about the nature of sovereignty, state power, individual rights and mechanisms of representation – that it is possible to grasp the foundations of the new liberal democratic models which began to emerge in the eighteenth and nineteenth centuries. Two such models will be examined in this chapter: 'protective' and 'developmental' democracy, models IIIa and IIIb, respectively. These have clear parallels with aspects of the republican models introduced in the previous chapter. Protective democracy holds that, given the pursuit of self-interest and individually motivated choices in human affairs, the only way to prevent domination by others is through the creation of accountable institutions; developmental democracy avers that political participation is a desirable end in itself and is a (if not *the*) central mechanism for the development of an active, informed and involved citizenry. In both strands of thinking elements of republican influence can be detected, but neither strand can be understood properly if its special origins in early liberal thought are not grasped. Accordingly, it is to the latter that this chapter now turns and, in particular, to the early modern debate about the nature and scope of the powers of monarchs and clergy. In this debate Hobbes occupies a critical (if somewhat ambiguous) place.

Power and sovereignty

In his great *Leviathan* (1651), Hobbes portrayed human beings as profoundly self-interested, always seeking 'more intense delight' and a strong position, as Machiavelli had held, from which to secure their ends. Conflicts of interest and the struggle for power define the human condition. Hobbes emphasized 'a generall inclination of all mankind, a perpetuall and restlesse desire of Power after power that ceaseth onely in Death' (*Leviathan*, p. 161). From this perspective, the idea that human beings might come to respect and trust one another, honour contracts and cooperate politically, seems remote indeed. However, writing against the backdrop of the English Civil War, Hobbes desired to show that a consistent concern with self-interest does not have to lead, and should not lead, to endless conflict and warfare. In order to prove this and to establish, thereby, the proper form of the state, he introduced a 'thought experiment'. It is worth briefly examining this 'experiment', for it reveals in a most acute form some of the issues that arise when considering the relation between the individual and the state.

Hobbes imagined a situation in which individuals are in a state of nature – that is, a situation without a 'Common Power' or state to enforce rules and restrain behaviour – enjoying 'natural rights' to use all means to protect their lives and to do whatever they wish, against whomever they like, and to 'possess, use, and enjoy all that [t]he[y] would, or could get' (*Leviathan*, part I, chs 13–15). The result is a constant struggle for survival: Hobbes's famous 'Warre of every one against every one'. In this state of nature individuals discover that life is 'solitary, poore, nasty, brutish, and short' and, accordingly, that to avoid harm and the risk of an early death, let alone to ensure conditions of greater comfort, the observation of certain natural laws or rules is required (part I, ch. 13). Natural laws are things the individual ought to adhere to in dealings with others if there is sufficient ground for believing that others will do likewise (see Plamenatz,

1963, pp. 122–32). Hobbes says of these laws that 'they have been contracted into one easie sum, intelligible, even to the meanest capacity; and that is, *Do not that to another, which thou wouldest not have done to thy selfe*' (see *Leviathan*, chs 14, 15). There is much in what he says about laws of nature that is ambiguous (above all, their relation to the 'will of God'), but these difficulties need not directly concern us here. For the key problem, in Hobbes's view, is: under what conditions will individuals trust each other enough to 'lay down their right to all things' so that their long-term interest in security and peace can be upheld? How can individuals make a bargain with one another when it may be, in certain circumstances, in some people's interest to break it? An agreement between people to ensure the regulation of their lives is necessary, yet it seems an impossible goal.

Hobbes's argument, in short, is as follows: individuals ought willingly to surrender their rights of self-government to a powerful single authority – thereafter authorized to act on their behalf – because, if all individuals do this simultaneously, the condition would be created for effective political rule, and for security and peace in the long term. A unique relation of authority would be created – the relation of sovereign to subject – and a unique political power would be established: sovereign power or sovereignty – the authorized, hence rightful, use of state powers by the person or assembly established as sovereign. The sovereign's subjects would have an obligation and duty to obey the sovereign; for the office of 'sovereign' is the product of their agreement, and 'sovereignty' is a quality of this agreed position rather than of the person who occupies it (cf. Benn, 1955; Peters, 1956; Skinner, 1989, pp. 112ff).

It is important to stress that, in Hobbes's opinion, while the office of sovereign must be self-perpetuating, undivided and ultimately absolute, it is established by the authority conferred by the people (*Leviathan*, pp. 227–8). The state's right of command and the subjects' duty of obedience are the result of 'consent', the circumstances individuals would have agreed to if there had actually been a social contract. Although there is little about Hobbes's conception of the state which today we would call representative, he argues in fact that the people rule through the sovereign. The sovereign is their representative: 'A Multitude of men, are made *One* Person, when they are by one man, or one Person, Represented' (*Leviathan*, p. 220). Through the sovereign a plurality of voices and interests can become 'one will', and to speak of a sovereign state assumes, Hobbes held, such a unity. Hence, his position is at one with all those who argue for the importance of government by consent and reject the claims of the 'divine right of kings' and, more generally, the authority of tradition. Yet, his conclusions run wholly counter to the inferences of those who often take such an argument to imply the necessity of some kind of popular sovereignty or democratic representative government (for a fuller discussion of this theme, see Held, 1995, ch. 2).

Hobbes's position stands at the beginning of modern liberal preoccupations with the need to establish both the liberty of the individual and sufficient power for the state to guarantee social and political order. It is a decisive contribution to the formation of liberalism, but it is a contribution that combines, like the thought of Machiavelli, profoundly liberal and illiberal elements. It is liberal because Hobbes was concerned to uncover the best circumstances for human nature to find expression; to explain or derive the most suitable form of society and state by reference to a world of 'free and equal' individuals; and to emphasize, in a novel way, the importance of consent in the making of a contract or bargain, not only to regulate human affairs and secure a measure of independence and choice in society, but also to legitimate, i.e. justify, such regulation. Yet Hobbes's position is also quite illiberal: his political conclusions emphasize the necessity of a virtually all-powerful sovereign to create the laws and secure the conditions of social and political life. Hobbes was not actually asking his fellow countrymen to make a contract; he was asking them to acknowledge the reasonable nature of the obligations that follow if one were to presume that such a contract had been made (*Leviathan*, p. 728; see Macpherson, 1968, p. 45). His conception of these obligations drastically tipped the balance between the claims of the individual on the one hand, and the power of the state on the other, in favour of the latter. The sovereign power of the modern state was established, but the capacity of citizens for independent action – albeit, it must be stressed again, male citizens with 'high standing' and substantial property – was compromised radically. Hobbes sought to defend a sphere free from state interference in which trade, commerce and the patriarchal family could flourish: civil society. But his work failed, ultimately, to articulate either the concepts or the institutions necessary to delimit state action satisfactorily.

Citizenship and the constitutional state

John Locke's famous objection to the Hobbesian argument that individuals could only find a 'peaceful and commodious' life with one another if they were governed by the dictates of an indivisible authority anticipated the whole tradition of protective democracy. He said of this type of argument: 'This is to think that Men are so foolish that they take care to avoid what Mischiefs may be done them by *Pole-Cats*, or *Foxes*, but are content, nay think it Safety, to be devoured by *Lions*' (Locke, *Two Treatises of Government*, p. 372, para. 93). In other words, it is hardly credible that people who do not fully trust each other would place their trust in an all-powerful sovereign to look after their interests. Locke approved of the revolution and settlement of 1688 in England, which imposed certain constitutional limits on the authority of the Crown. He rejected the notion of a great power pre-eminent in all spheres. For him, the institution of 'government' can and should be conceived as an 'instrument' for the defence of the 'life, liberty and estate' of its citizens; that is, government's *raison d'être* is the protection of individuals' rights as laid down by God's will and as enshrined in law (see Dunn, 1969, part 3).

Locke thought, as Hobbes had done, that the establishment of the political world followed from the prior existence of individuals endowed with natural rights. Like Hobbes, he was concerned about what form legitimate government should take and about the conditions for security, peace and freedom. But the way he conceived of these things was fundamentally different. In the important second of his *Two Treatises of Government* (which was first published in 1690),

Locke starts with the proposition that individuals were originally in a state of nature: a '*State of perfect Freedom* to order their Actions, and dispose of their Possessions and Persons as they think fit, within the bounds of the Law of Nature, without asking leave, or depending upon the will of any other Man' (*Two Treatises*, p. 309, para. 4).[1] This state of nature, the basic form of human association, is a state of liberty but not 'a state of license'. Individuals are bound by duty to God and governed by the law of nature. The law of nature (the precise meaning of which is difficult to pin down in the *Two Treatises*) specifies basic principles of morality: individuals should not take their own lives, they should try to preserve each other and should not infringe upon one another's liberty. The law can be grasped by human reason but it is the creation of God, the 'infinitely wise Maker' (*Two Treatises*, p. 311, para. 6).

Within the state of nature, humans are free and equal because reason makes them capable of rationality, of following the law of nature. Moreover, they enjoy natural rights. The right to govern one's affairs and to enforce the law of nature against transgressors is presupposed, as is the obligation to respect the rights of others. Individuals have the right to dispose of their own labour and to possess property. The right to property is a right to 'life, liberty and estate' (*Two Treatises*, p. 395, para. 123), though Locke also uses 'property' in the narrower sense to mean the exclusive use of objects (cf. Macpherson, 1962; Plamenatz, 1963; Dunn, 1969).

Adherence to the law of nature, according to Locke, ensures that the state of nature is not a state of war. However, the natural rights of individuals are not always safeguarded in the state of nature, for certain 'inconveniences' exist: not all individuals fully respect the rights of others; when it is left to each individual to enforce the law of nature there are too many judges and hence conflicts of interpretation about the meaning of the law; and when people are loosely organized they are vulnerable to aggression from abroad (*Two Treatises*, pp. 316–17, para. 13). The central 'inconvenience' suffered can be summarized as the inadequate regulation of property in its broad sense: the right to 'life, liberty and estate' (p. 308, para. 3, and pp. 395–6, para. 124). Property is prior to both society and government; and the difficulty of its regulation is the critical reason which compels 'equally free men' to the establishment of both. Thus, the remedy for the inconveniences of the state of nature is an agreement or contract to create, first, an independent society and, second, a 'civil association' or government (*Two Treatises*, pp. 372–6, paras 94–7; see Laslett, 1963). The distinction between these two agreements is important, for it makes clear that authority is bestowed by individuals in society on government for the purpose of pursuing the ends of the governed; and should these ends fail to be represented adequately, the final judges are the people – the citizens – who can dispense both with their deputies and, if need be, with the existing form of government itself.

In Locke's opinion, it should be stressed, the formation of a governmental apparatus does not signal the transfer of all subjects' rights to the political realm (*Two Treatises*, pp. 402–3, para. 135, and pp. 412–13, para. 149). The rights

---

[1] In so arguing, of course, Locke was laying important trails which others later pursued.

of lawmaking and enforcement (legislative and executive rights) are transferred, but the whole process is conditional upon government adhering to its essential purpose: the preservation of 'life, liberty and estate'. Sovereign power, i.e. the capacity to determine the proper use of political power, remains ultimately with the people. The legislative body enacts rules as the people's agent in accordance with the law of nature, and the executive (to which Locke also tied the judiciary) enforces the legal system. This separation of powers was important because:

> It may be too great a temptation to humane frailty apt to grasp at Power, for the same Persons who have the Power of making Laws, to have also in their hands the power to execute them, whereby they may exempt themselves from Obedience to the Laws they make, and suit the Law, both in its making and execution, to their own private advantage, and thereby come to have a distinct interest from the rest of the community, contrary to the end of Society and Government. (*Two Treatises*, p. 410, para. 143)

Thus, the integrity and ultimate ends of society require a constitutional government in which 'public power' is legally circumscribed and divided. Locke believed in the desirability of a constitutional monarchy holding executive power and a parliamentary assembly holding the rights of legislation, although he did not think this was the only form government might take and his views are compatible with a number of other conceptions of political institutions.

The government rules, and its legitimacy is sustained, by the 'consent' of individuals. 'Consent' is a crucial and difficult notion in Locke's writings. It could be interpreted to suggest that only the continually active personal agreement of individuals would be sufficient to ensure a duty of obedience, i.e. to ensure a government's authority and legitimacy (Plamenatz, 1963, p. 228). However, Locke seems to have thought of the active consent of individuals as being crucial only to the initial inauguration of a legitimate civil government. Thereafter, consent ought to follow from majority decisions of 'the people's' representatives, so long as they, the trustees of the governed, maintain the original contract and its covenants to guarantee 'life, liberty and estate'. (See Lukes, 1973, pp. 80–1, and Dunn, 1980, pp. 36–7, for a full discussion of the issues involved.) If they do, there is a duty to obey the law. But if those who govern flout the terms of the contract with a series of tyrannical political acts, rebellion to form a new government, Locke contended, might be not only unavoidable but justified.

Political activity for Locke is instrumental; that is, it secures the framework or conditions for freedom so that the private ends of individuals may be met in civil society. The creation of a political community or government is the burden individuals have to bear to secure their ends. Thus, membership of a political community, i.e. citizenship, bestows upon the individual both responsibilities and rights, duties and powers, constraints and liberties (Laslett, 1963, pp. 134–5). In relation to Hobbes's ideas, this was a most significant and radical view. For it helped inaugurate one of the most central tenets of modern European liberalism; that is, that government exists to safeguard the rights and liberties of citizens who are ultimately the best judges of their own interests; and that accordingly government must be restricted in scope and constrained in practice in order to ensure the maximum possible freedom of every citizen. In most respects it was Locke's rather than Hobbes's views that helped lay the foundation for the development of liberalism and prepared the way for the tradition of popular representative government. Compared to Hobbes, Locke's influence on the world of practical politics has been considerable (see Rahe, 1994, pp. 291–311).

Locke's writings seem to point in a number of directions at once. They suggest the importance of securing the rights of individuals, popular sovereignty, majority rule, a division of powers within the state, constitutional monarchy and a representative system of parliamentary government: a direct anticipation of key aspects of democratic government as it developed in the nineteenth and early twentieth centuries, and of the central tenets of the modern representative state. But, at best, most of these ideas are only in rudimentary form, and it is certain that Locke did not foresee many of the vital components of democratic representative government; for instance, competitive parties, party rule and the maintenance of political liberties irrespective of class, sex, colour and creed (cf. Laslett, 1963, p. 123). It is not a condition of legitimate government or government by consent, in Locke's account, that there be regular elections of a legislative assembly, let alone universal suffrage. (Locke would almost certainly not have dissented from a franchise based strictly on the property holdings of male adults. Cf. Plamenatz, 1963, pp. 231, 251–2; Dunn, 1969, ch. 10.) Moreover, he did not develop a detailed account of what the limits might be to political interference in people's lives and under what conditions civil disobedience is justified. He thought that political power was held 'on trust' by and for the people, but failed to specify adequately who were to count as 'the people' and under what conditions 'trust' should be bestowed. While Locke was unquestionably one of the first great champions of liberalism – and although his works clearly stimulated the development of liberal and liberal democratic government – he cannot, like many of his predecessors, be considered a democrat without careful qualification (cf. Dunn, 1980, pp. 53–77).

Separation of powers

It is sometimes said that while Locke advanced consideration of the principles of representative government, it was the French philosopher and political theorist Charles Louis de Secondat, Baron de Montesquieu (1689–1755), who understood better the necessary institutional innovations for the achievement of a reformed representative government. There is some truth in this. Montesquieu never justified at any length his preference for limited government. In broad terms, he was a follower of Locke, and an advocate of what he took to be the distinctively 'English' notions of freedom, toleration and moderation which, he claimed, were admirably expressed (after 1688) by the English constitution itself: 'the mirror of liberty'. Against the background of marked dissatisfaction with absolutist government (the government of Louis XIV in particular), he became preoccupied with how to secure a representative regime dedicated to liberty and capable of minimizing corruption and unacceptable monopolies of privilege. Locke wrote little about the desirable characteristics of public power, or about the ways in which public power should be organized, while Montesquieu devoted considerable energy to this question. He analysed a variety of conditions of freedom, but the one which is most notable concerns how constitutions might set inviolable limits to state action (see Bellamy, 1996).

Montesquieu championed constitutional government as the central mechanism for guaranteeing the rights of the (adult, male, property-owning) individual. Although he believed in a given, unchangeable natural law, his writings indicate as much, if not more, concern with the development of a system of positive law: a formal, explicitly designed legal structure for the regulation of public and private life. He defended urgently the idea of a society in which 'individuals'' capacities and energies would be unleashed in the knowledge that privately initiated interests would be protected. Montesquieu took for granted that there 'are always persons distinguished by their birth, riches or honours' who have 'a right to check the licentiousness of the people' (*The Spirit of Laws*, p. 71 (first published 1748)); and he took for granted that there are many people (among others, labourers and those without substantial wealth) who 'are in so mean a situation as to be deemed to have no will of their own'. None the less, his writings advanced decisively the idea of a constitutional state maintaining law and order at home and providing protection against aggression from abroad. He did not directly use the term 'constitutional state', but the arguments he developed were aimed in part at 'depersonalizing' the state's power structure so that it might be less vulnerable to abuse by individuals and groups.

Montesquieu much admired the classical *polis* (see N. O. Keohane, 1972). He held in high esteem the ideal of active citizenship, dedication to the life of the political community and the deep sense of civic duty which animated the ancient world. But the general conditions which had led to the florescence of the city-state in antiquity and Renaissance Italy had, he contended, disappeared for ever.

> As in a country of liberty, every man who is supposed a free agent ought to be his own governor; the legislative power should reside in the whole body of the people. But since this is impossible in large states, and in small ones is subject to many inconveniences, it is fit the people should transact by their representatives what they cannot transact by themselves. (*The Spirit of Laws*, p. 71)

The emergence of states controlling substantial territories and the spread of free trade and the market economy had created an irreversible trend towards social and political heterogeneity. Compare ancient and contemporary Greece: 'The politic Greeks, who lived under a popular government, knew no other support than virtue. The modern inhabitants of that country are entirely taken up with manufacture, commerce, finances, opulence, and luxury' (*The Spirit of Laws*, p. 21). The contrast between the ancient and the modern is, according to Montesquieu, one between particular locales, tightly knit communities, a frugal economy, a concern for virtue and civic discipline promoting active citizenship, on the one hand, and large nation-states, centralized bureaucratic hierarchies, loosely connected commercial societies, inequality of fortunes and the free pursuit of private interests, on the other (*The Spirit of Laws*, pp. 15–21, 44ff; Krouse, 1983, pp. 59–60; cf. Pangle, 1973). Under the conditions of modern life, Montesquieu's preferred form of government was a state system modelled on the constitutional monarchy of England. In so thinking, he wanted to connect notions of monarchic government rooted in claims to stability, honour and glory with a broader system of checks and balances. Rearticulating both republican and liberal concerns about the problem of uniting private interest and the public good, he sought in institutional means a way to take account of the interests of different groups in public life while not sacrificing the liberty of the community overall.

Montesquieu's interpretation of the English constitution has been subjected to much criticism; it is often regarded as neither particularly accurate nor original. However, what he had to say about it was influential, especially on the founders of new political communities, notably in North America (see Ball, 1988, pp. 52–4; Manin, 1994).[2] While classical Greek philosophers, as well as figures like Machiavelli and Locke, had grasped the significance of a 'mixed state' or 'division of powers' for the maintenance of liberty, Montesquieu made it pivotal to his overall teachings. The state must organize the representation of the interests of different powerful 'groups'; that is, it must be a 'mixed regime' balancing the position of the monarchy, the aristocracy and 'the people'. Without such representation the law, he argued, will always be skewed to particular interests, governments will stagnate and political order will be vulnerable in the long run. In his view, the aristocracy was essential to the effective maintenance of a balance between the monarchy and 'the people', both of whom, when left to their own devices, inclined to despotism. But the liberty of the individual and moderate government depended, above all, on particular guarantees against oppression:

> constant experience shows us that every man invested with power is apt to abuse it, and to carry his authority as far as it will go . . . To prevent this abuse, it is necessary from the very nature of things that power should be a check to power. A government may be so constituted, as no man shall be compelled to do things to which the law does not oblige him, nor forced to abstain from things which the law permits. (*The Spirit of Laws*, p. 69)

Montesquieu distinguished, in a more precise way than Locke had done, between the executive, the legislature and the judiciary. And he was firmly of the view that there would be no liberty worth its name 'were the same man or the same body, whether of the nobles or of the people, to exercise those three powers, that of enacting laws, that of executing public resolutions, and of trying the causes of individuals' (*The Spirit of Laws*, p. 70). In a famous chapter of *The Spirit of Laws* (book XI, ch. 6, pp. 69–75), Montesquieu argued that under modern conditions liberty can only be based on the careful creation of an

---

[2] It seems that it is scarcely an exaggeration to suggest that 'American republicans regarded selected doctrines of Montesquieu's as being on a par with Holy Writ', the central points of which they could recite 'as if it had been a catechism' (McDonald, 1986, pp. 80–1; and see the discussion of Madison, pp. 70–5, below).

institutionalized separation and balance of powers within the state. Previously, the idea of mixed government had tended to mean limited 'participation' of different estates within the state. By making the case for a constitution based upon three distinct organs with separate legal powers, Montesquieu recast this idea and established an alternative account that was to be critical in attempts to curtail highly centralized authority, on the one hand, and to ensure that 'virtuous government' depended less on heroic individuals or civic discipline and more on a system of checks and balances, on the other.

Executive power ought to be in the hands of the monarch; this branch of government 'having need of dispatch', Montesquieu reasoned, 'is better administered by one than by many' (*The Spirit of Laws*, p. 72). Decisive leadership, the creation of policy, the efficient administration of law and the capacity to sustain a clear set of political priorities are marks of a 'glorious executive'. Accordingly, the executive ought to have the power to veto unacceptable legislation (legislation deemed to encroach upon its power), regulate the meetings of the legislative body (their timing and duration) and control the army, for 'from the very nature of the thing, its business consists more in action than in deliberation' (pp. 70–4). On the other hand, the monarch's powers must be restrained in law. To this end, it is vital that legislative power consist not only of the right to deliberate over policy and to amend and alter the law, but also of the right to hold the executive to account for unlawful acts, restrict the executive's scope by retaining control of the fiscal basis of the state and, if necessary, disband the army or control it by the provision of finance on an annual basis (p. 74). All this Montesquieu claimed to glean from the English constitution of his day. From the latter he also found grounds for approving the division of legislative power into two chambers: the one for hereditary nobles and the other for the representatives of 'the people', i.e. periodically elected individuals of distinction serving as trustees for the electorate's interests (responsive to the latter, but not directly accountable to them). Between the two chambers the views and interests of all 'dignified' opinion would be respected. The nobles would retain the right to reject legislation while 'the commons' would have the power of legal initiative. Separate from both these bodies must be the judiciary. Locke had thought of the judiciary as an arm of the executive, but Montesquieu thought its independence was crucial to the protection of the rights of individuals. Without an independent judiciary, people might have to face the awesome power of a combined executor, judge and jury – and then their rights could certainly not be guaranteed.

Montesquieu's analysis of the separation of powers was neither systematic nor fully coherent (see Pangle, 1973; Ball, 1988, pp. 52–3; Bellamy, 1996). For instance, the precise powers of the executive and legislature were left quite ambiguous. However, his explication of these issues was far more penetrating than that of any of his predecessors. Moreover, his insights allowed him to offer clear reasons why the risks associated with government in extended territories – risks, that is, of succumbing to despotism or powerful interests – might be overcome. Montesquieu was aware that in 'an extensive republic there are men of large fortunes, and consequently of less moderation' and that 'the public good' could be 'sacrificed to a thousand private views' (*The Spirit of Laws*, p. 120). But he thought that the division of powers could pose a fundamental obstacle to 'immoderate fortune'; and that, if entrenched in a 'confederate republic' – a republic built upon smaller governmental units – it might be possible for some of the freedoms associated with city-republican government to be enjoyed while preserving sufficient legal and political competence to resist both 'internal corruption' and 'external enemies' (pp. 126ff).

The great significance of Montesquieu's political writings lies in his thesis that in a world in which individuals are ambitious and place their own particular interests above all others, institutions must be created which can convert such ambition into good and effective government (see Krouse, 1983, pp. 61–2). By institutionalizing a separation of powers, and by providing a forum within the state for contending groups and factions to clash, Montesquieu thought he had uncovered a most practical and valuable political arrangement for the modern world: a world properly divided into the 'public sphere' of state politics run by men, on the one hand, and the 'private sphere' of economy, family life, women and children, on the other. For him, liberty, as has been aptly remarked, 'does not flourish because men have natural rights or because they revolt if their rulers press them too far; it flourishes because power is so distributed and organized that whoever is tempted to abuse it finds legal restraints in his way' (Plamenatz, 1963, pp. 292–3).

However, in exploring the relation between state and civil society, Montesquieu ultimately failed to establish adequate arguments and mechanisms for the protection of the sphere of private initiative. He spent enormous energy trying to explain variations in political structures by reference to geographical, climatic and historical conditions. These determined, in his account, the specific nature of the laws and the customs and practices of nations and states. Political possibilities were circumscribed by geo-climatic factors as well as by the organization of power. This contention is certainly plausible, but it generated a number of difficulties about reconciling, on the one hand, the view that there was considerable scope for constitutional change and, on the other hand, the view that political life was determined by natural and historical circumstances beyond particular agents' control. Second, a fundamental difficulty lay at the very heart of his conception of liberty. Liberty, he wrote, 'is the right of doing whatever the law permits'. People are free to pursue their activities within the framework of the law. But if freedom is defined in direct relation to the law, there is no possibility of arguing coherently that freedom might depend on altering the law or that the law itself might under certain circumstances articulate tyranny. Despite Montesquieu's defence of important institutional innovations, he formally resolved the dilemma of balancing the relation between state and society in favour of the former; that is, in favour of the lawmakers. In democratic terms, the position would have been more acceptable if the lawmakers had been held accountable to the people. But Montesquieu thought of few people as potential voters; he did not conceive of legislators or representatives as accountable to the electorate, and he ascribed the monarch vast power, including the capacity to dissolve the legislature. In addition, he ignored important issues that had been central to Locke: the right of citizens to dispense with their 'trustees' or alter their form of government if the need arose. In Montesquieu's thought, the governed remained in the end accountable to the governors.

The idea of protective democracy: a résumé and elaboration

Since Hobbes, a (if not *the*) central question of liberal political theory has been how, in a world marked by the legitimate and reasonable pursuit of self-interest, government can be sustained, and what form government should take. Hobbes was the theorist *par excellence* who departed systematically from the assumptions of the classical *polis*; only a strong protective state could reduce adequately the dangers citizens faced when left to their own devices. Locke's modification of this argument was decisive: there were no good reasons to suppose that the governors would on their own initiative provide an adequate framework for citizens to pursue their interests freely. In different but complementary ways, Locke and Montesquieu argued that there must be limits upon legally sanctioned political power. But neither of these thinkers developed their arguments to what seems today at least their logical conclusion. The protection of liberty requires a form of political equality among all mature individuals: a formally equal capacity to protect their interests from the arbitrary acts of either the state or fellow citizens. It was not until this insight was developed systematically that the protective theory of democracy was fully expressed, although it has been contended here that many of the theory's central elements find their origin and most succinct analysis in the political writings of the seventeenth and eighteenth centuries.

Two classic statements of the protective theory of democracy will be focused upon now: the political philosophy of one of the key architects of the American constitution, James Madison (1751–1836); and the views of two of the key spokesmen of nineteenth-century 'English liberalism', Jeremy Bentham (1748–1832) and James Mill (1773–1836). In their hands, the protective theory of liberal democracy received arguably its most important elaboration: the governors must be held accountable to the governed through political mechanisms (the secret ballot, regular voting and competition between potential representatives, among other things) which give citizens satisfactory means for choosing, authorizing and controlling political decisions. Through these mechanisms, it was argued, a balance could be attained between might and right, authority and liberty. But despite this decisive step, who exactly were to count as 'individuals', and what the exact nature of their envisaged political participation was, remained either unclear or unsettled in the Anglo-American world.

The problem of factions

In a series of extraordinary writings in the *Federalist* (published in 1788), Madison translated some of Hobbes's, Locke's and Montesquieu's most notable ideas into a coherent political theory and strategy. He accepted, in the tradition of Hobbes, that politics is founded on self-interest. Following Locke, he recognized the central importance of protecting individual freedom through the institution of a public power that is legally circumscribed and accountable ultimately to the governed. And following Montesquieu, he regarded the principle of a separation of powers as central to the formation of a legitimate state. But his own position can perhaps best be grasped in relation to his assessment of classical democracy. For in his thought, classical democracy is thoroughly criticized, if not fully repudiated, and what threads remain of the republican tradition overall – especially its concern with the corruption of public life by private interests, its anti-monarchical focus and its advocacy of mixed government – are rearticulated and combined with liberal emphases.

Unlike Montesquieu, who admired the ancient republics but thought their 'spirit' undermined by the forces of 'modernization', Madison was extremely critical of both the republics and their spirit. His judgement is similar to Plato's (see pp. 23–7 above), and sometimes seems even more severe, underpinned as it is by Hobbesian assumptions about human nature. In Madison's account, 'pure democracies' (by which he means societies 'consisting of a small number of citizens, who assemble and administer the government in person') have always been intolerant, unjust and unstable. In the politics of these states a common passion or interest, felt by the majority of citizens, generally shapes political judgements, policies and actions. Moreover, the direct nature of all 'communication and concert' means invariably that 'there is nothing to check the inducements to sacrifice the weaker party or an obnoxious individual' (Madison, *The Federalist Papers*, no. 10, p. 20). As a consequence, pure democracies 'have been spectacles of turbulence and contention' and have always been 'incompatible with personal security or the rights of property'. It can come as no surprise that 'they have in general been as short in their lives as they have been violent in their deaths'. Madison is scathing about 'theoretic politicians' who have 'patronized this species of government and have erroneously supposed that by reducing mankind to a perfect equality in their political rights, they would, at the same time, be perfectly equalized and assimilated in their possessions, their opinions, and their passions' (no. 10, p. 20). History testifies, from classical times to the Renaissance, that such suppositions are far from the truth.

Dissent, argument, clashes of judgement, conflicts of interest and the constant formation of rival and competing factions are inevitable. They are inevitable because their causes 'are sown in the nature of man' (*The Federalist Papers*, no. 10, p. 18). Diversity in capacities and faculties, fallibility in reasoning and judgement, zeal for a quick opinion, attachment to different leaders, as well as a desire for a vast range of different objects – all these constitute 'insuperable obstacles' to uniformity in the interpretation of priorities and interests. Reason and self-love are intimately connected, creating a reciprocal influence between rationality and passion. Where civic virtue has been proclaimed, it has been a mask generally for ceaseless, self-interested motion. The search for pre-eminence, power and profit are inescapable elements of the human condition which have constantly

> divided mankind . . . inflamed them with mutual animosity, and rendered them much more disposed to vex and oppress each other than to co-operate for their common good. So strong is this propensity of mankind to fall into mutual animosities, that when no substantial occasion presents itself, the most frivolous and fanciful distinctions have been sufficient to kindle their unfriendly passions and excite their most violent conflicts. (*The Federalist Papers*, no. 10, p. 18)

But the most common and durable source of antagonism and factionalism, Madison argued, has always been 'the various and unequal distribution of property'. Those who hold property and those who are without have consistently formed 'distinct interests in society'. This emphasis on the role of property was shared by many of the most prominent political theorists from Plato onwards. (It is intriguing, though, that it has been rejected most frequently by twentieth-century liberals and liberal democrats.) In Madison's hands, it led to an appreciation that all nations are divided by classes founded on property, 'actuated by different sentiments and views'. Unlike Marx, Engels and Lenin, who later sought to resolve the political problems posed by class conflict by recommending the removal of their cause (i.e. the abolition of private ownership of productive property), Madison contended that any such ambition was hopelessly unrealistic. Even if 'enlightened statesmen' could radically reduce the unequal possession and distribution of property – and it is very doubtful that they could, for human beings always recreate patterns of inequality – a homogeneity of interests would not follow. Thus, Madison concluded, 'the inference to which we are brought' is that relief from factional disputes 'is only to be sought in the means of controlling its *effects*' (no. 10, p. 19). The formation of factions is inescapable; and *the* problem of politics is the problem of containing factions.

By a faction, Madison understood 'a number of citizens, whether amounting to a majority or minority of the whole, who are united and actuated by some common impulse or passion, or interest, adverse to the rights of other citizens, or the permanent and aggregate interests of the community' (*The Federalist Papers*, no. 10, p. 17). The task he set himself was to find ways of regulating 'the various and interfering interests' in such a way that they become involved in the 'necessary and ordinary operations of government'. Madison argued for a powerful American state as a safeguard against tyranny and as a means to control 'the violence of faction', but it was to be a state organized on 'representative principles', with government facing the judgement of all citizens on a regular basis; that is, facing the electoral power of citizens to change their leaders. Madison's arguments sometimes suggest that he thought of citizenship as a universal category, applying to all adults irrespective of sex, colour and the possession of property. But while he thought of the franchise as legitimately extending to more people than Locke or Montesquieu would ever have found acceptable, it is very improbable indeed, given the time when he was writing, that he would have supported the extension of the vote to women, white non-propertied working people and black slaves. Certainly, a much more restrictive view of the scope of the voting population is outlined in some of his writings (see Madison, in Meyers, 1973; Main, 1973). None the less, he clearly thought that a form of 'popular government' with a federal structure and a division of powers would not only ameliorate the worst consequences of factions, but crucially involve citizens in the political process of protecting their own interests.

The political difficulties caused by minority interest groups can be overcome by the ballot box, 'which enables the majority to defeat their sinister views by regular vote' (*The Federalist Papers*, no. 10, p. 19). The major difficulties posed by factions, however, occur when one faction forms a majority. For then there is a danger that the very form of popular government itself will enable such a group to 'sacrifice to its ruling passions or interests both the public good and the rights of other citizens'. The 'tyranny of the majority', as it has often been called, can only be forestalled by particular constitutional arrangements. Of these, a system of political representation and a large electoral body are essential.

Political representation involves the permanent transfer of government to 'a small number of citizens elected by the rest' (*The Federalist Papers*, no. 10, p. 21). It involves representatives acting as the trustees of the electors, making up their own minds and exercising their own judgement about their constituents' interests and how these might most appropriately be met (see Ball, 1988, pp. 61–7).[3] Such a system, Madison argued, is important, since public views can be 'refined and enlarged' when 'passed through the medium of a chosen body of citizens'. Representative government overcomes the excesses of 'pure democracy' because elections themselves force a clarification of public issues; and the elected few, able to withstand the political process, are likely to be competent and capable of 'discerning the true interest of their country', i.e. the interests of all citizens. But representative rule alone is not a sufficient condition for the protection of citizens: it cannot in itself stop the elected from degenerating into a powerful exploitative faction. At this point, Madison offered a novel argument, contrary to the whole spirit of 'pure democracies', about the virtue of scale in public affairs. An 'extended republic', covering a large territory and embracing a substantial population, is an essential condition of non-oppressive government. Several reasons are given. In the first instance, the number of representatives must be raised to a certain level 'to guard against the cabals of the few' (while not being so numerous, Madison quickly added, as to risk 'the confusion of a multitude') (*The Federalist Papers*, no. 10, p. 21). More importantly, if the proportion of 'fit characters' is constant in both a small and a large republic, the latter will possess a far greater number from whom the electorate can choose. Further, in a large state representatives will be chosen by an extended electorate, who are more likely to spot 'unworthy candidates'. And in a large state with an economy based on the pursuit of private wants, there is inevitably great social diversity and, therefore, less chance of a tyrannous majority forming among either the electorate or the elected. Social diversity helps create political fragmentation, which prevents an excessive accumulation of power.[4] Although representatives might become progressively more remote and impersonal in a large state, a federal constitution – which binds overlapping communities together – can offset this: 'the great and aggregate interests being referred to the national, the local and particular to the State legislatures' (no. 10, p. 22). If, finally, the respective legal powers of the executive, legislature and judiciary are separated at both national and local levels, freedom can best be protected.

---

[3] This view of representation is sometimes referred to as the 'independence' theory, since it places emphasis on citizens being best served by their representatives when the latter act to a significant degree independently of them. It contrasts with the 'delegate' account of representation, commonly advocated by the Marxist tradition, in which the duty of representatives is to present faithfully the immediate views and interests of their constituents (see Pitkin, 1967, ch. 7).

[4] This argument had a profound influence on the 'pluralist' tradition after World War II (see ch. 6 below).

Madison's concern with faction-based politics and his solution to the problem of how to unite the private interest to the public good was inspired partly by a Machiavellian conception of republicanism, emphasizing the necessity to shape politically and institutionally a commitment to the public realm (see pp. 40–3 above; Bellamy, 1996). Within this framework, he interpreted the role of representatives and of a strong federal state not simply negatively as devices to be adopted in the light of the undesirability of direct democracy, but also positively as institutional vehicles to establish a form of politics with the best chance of creating serious deliberation and effective decision-making in public life. But his account of the extended republic should not be confused with earlier classic interpretations of civic life and the public realm. The theoretical focus is no longer on the rightful place of the active citizen in the life of the political community; it is, instead, on the legitimate pursuit by individuals of their interests and on government as, above all, a means for the enhancement of these interests. Although Madison sought clear ways of reconciling particular interests to 'the republic', his position signals the clear interlocking of protective republican with liberal preoccupations (cf. Wood, 1969; Pocock, 1975, pp. 522–45). Thus, he conceived of the federal representative state as the key mechanism to aggregate individuals' interests and to protect their rights. In such a state, he believed, security of person and property could be sustained, and politics could be made compatible with the demands of large, modern nation-states with their complex patterns of trade, commerce and international relations. To summarize his views, in the words of one commentator:

> only . . . a sovereign national government of truly continental scope, can assure non-oppressive popular rule. A republican leviathan is necessary to secure life, liberty, and property from the tyranny of local majorities. The extended republic is not simply a means of adapting popular rule to new political realities, but an inherently desirable corrective for deep intrinsic defects in the politics of the small popular regime. (Krouse, 1983, p. 66)

Madison's preoccupation with faction and his desire to protect individuals from powerful collectivities was an ambiguous project in certain respects. On the one hand, it raised important questions about the principles, procedures and institutions of popular government and about the necessity to defend them against impulsive, unreasonable action, whatever its source. Critics of democracy have frequently raised these matters: how 'popular' regimes remain stable, how representatives are held to account, how citizens understand the 'rules of the political game' and in what ways they follow them are all legitimate considerations. On the other hand, if these questions are pursued at the expense of all others, they can readily be associated with an unjustified conservative desire to find a way of protecting, above all, 'the haves' (a minority) from the 'have nots' (the rest). Madison insisted, as have all critics of democracy and nearly all theorists of protective democracy, on a natural right to private property. The basis of this right remains mysterious and it was precisely this mystery (as we shall see) that Marx and Engels sought to disentangle. Madison was in favour of popular government so long as there was no risk that the majority could turn the instruments of state policy against a minority's privilege. Despite the considerable novelty and significance of his overall arguments, Madison was unquestionably a reluctant democrat. He had this in common with Jeremy Bentham and James Mill, who, for my purposes here, can be discussed together.

Accountability and markets

Bentham and Mill were impressed by the progress and methods of the natural sciences and were decidedly secular in their orientations. They thought of concepts like natural right and social contract as misleading philosophical fictions which failed to explain the real basis of citizens' interests, commitment and duty to the state. This basis could be uncovered, they argued, by grasping the primitive and irreducible elements of actual human behaviour. The key to their understanding of human beings lies in the thesis that humans act to satisfy desire and avoid pain. Their argument, in brief, is as follows: the overriding motivation of human beings is to fulfil their desires, maximize their satisfaction or utility and minimize their suffering; society consists of individuals seeking as much utility as they can get from whatever it is they want; individuals' interests always conflict with one another for 'a grand governing law of human nature' is, as Hobbes thought, to subordinate 'the persons and properties of human beings to our pleasures' (see Bentham, *Fragment on Government*). Since those who govern will naturally act in the same way as the governed, government must, if its systematic abuse is to be avoided, be directly accountable to an electorate called upon frequently to decide whether their objectives have been met.

With these arguments, the protective theory of democracy received its clearest explication (see Macpherson, 1977, ch. 2; cf. Harrison, 1993, ch. 6). For Bentham and Mill, liberal democracy was associated with a political apparatus that would ensure the accountability of the governors to the governed. Only through democratic government would there be a satisfactory means for generating political decisions commensurate with the public interest, i.e. the interests of the mass of individuals. As Bentham wrote: 'A democracy ... has for its characteristic object and effect ... securing its members against oppression and depredation at the hands of those functionaries which it employs for its defence' (Bentham, *Constitutional Code*, book I, p. 47). Democratic government is required to protect citizens from despotic use of political power whether it be by a monarch, the aristocracy or other groups. For the temptation to abuse power in the public sphere – to act corruptly – is as universal as the force of gravity. Only through the vote, the secret ballot, competition between potential political representatives, a separation of powers, and freedom of the press, speech and public association could 'the interest of the community in general' be sustained (see Bentham, *Fragment on Government*, and J. Mill, *An Essay on Government*).

Bentham, Mill and the utilitarians generally (i.e. all those who defended the utility principle) provided one of the clearest justifications for the liberal democratic state, which ensures the conditions necessary for individuals to pursue their interests without risk of arbitrary political interference, to participate freely in economic transactions, to exchange labour and goods on the market and to appropriate resources privately. These ideas were at the core of nineteenth-century 'English liberalism': the state was to have the role of umpire or referee while individuals pursued in civil society, according to the rules of economic competition and free exchange, their own interests. Periodic elections, the abolition of the powers of the monarchy, the division of powers within the state, plus the free market, would lead to the maximum benefit for all citizens. The free vote and the free market, were *sine qua non*. For a key presupposition was that the collective good could be properly realized in many domains of life only if individuals interacted in competitive exchanges, pursuing their utility with minimal state interference.

Significantly, however, this argument had another side. Tied to the advocacy of a 'minimal' state, whose scope and power were to be strictly limited, there was a commitment in fact to certain types of state intervention, for instance the curtailment of the behaviour of the disobedient, whether individuals, groups or classes (see J. Mill, 'Prisons and prison discipline'). Those who challenged the security of property or the market society threatened the realization of the public good. In the name of the public good, the utilitarians advocated a new system of administrative power for 'person management' (cf. Foucault, 1977, part 3; Ignatieff, 1978, ch. 6). Prison systems were a mark of this new age. Moreover, whenever *laissez-faire* was inadequate to ensure the best possible outcomes, state intervention was justified to reorder social relations and institutions. The enactment and enforcement of law, and the creation of policies and institutions, were legitimate to the extent that they all upheld the principle of utility; that is, to the extent they contributed directly to the achievement, by means of careful calculation, of the greatest happiness for the greatest number – the only scientifically defensible criterion, Bentham and Mill contended, of the public good. Within this overall framework government ought to pursue four subsidiary goals: to help provide subsistence by protecting workers and by making them secure in the knowledge that they will receive the fruits of their labour; to help produce abundance by ensuring no political obstacles to 'natural incentives' to meet one's needs through work; to favour equality, because increased increments of material goods do not bring successively more happiness to those who possess them (the law of diminishing utility); and to maintain security of individual goods and wealth (see Bentham, *Principles of the Civil Code*). Of these four objectives the last is by far the most critical; for without security of goods and property there would be no incentive for individuals to work and generate wealth: labour would be insufficiently productive and commerce could not prosper. Accordingly, given the necessity to choose between 'equality' and 'security' in public policy and law, the former must yield to the latter (*Principles of the Civil Code*, part I, ch. 11). If the state pursues security (along with the other goals to the extent that they are compatible), it will, Bentham maintained, be in the citizen's self-interest to obey it.

Utilitarianism, and its synthesis with the economic doctrines of Adam Smith (1723–90), had a most radical edge. First, it represented a decisive challenge to excessively centralized political power and, in particular, to hitherto unquestioned regulations imposed on civil society. Liberalism's constant challenge to the power of the state has in this respect been of enduring significance. Second, utilitarianism helped generate a new conception of the nature and role of politics; it provided a defence of selective electorally controlled state *intervention* to help maximize the public good. Bentham, for instance, became a supporter of a plan for free education, a minimum wage and sickness benefits. The utilitarian legacy has had a strong influence on the shaping of the politics of the welfare state (see ch. 6). On the other hand, it has to be stressed, Bentham's and Mill's conception of the legitimate participants in, and scope of, democratic politics has much in common with the typically restrictive views of the liberal tradition generally: 'politics', the 'public sphere' and 'public affairs' remained synonymous with the realm of men, especially men of property. From Hobbes to Bentham and James Mill the patriarchal structure of public (and private) life, and its relation to the distribution of property, were persistently taken for granted. For instance, in considering the extent of the franchise, Bentham and Mill found grounds at one time for excluding, among others, the female population and large sections of the labouring classes, despite the fact that many of their arguments seemed to point squarely in the direction of universal suffrage. It should be noted, however, that Bentham became much more radical on the question of the suffrage than Mill and, in later life, abandoned his earlier reservations about universal manhood suffrage, though he retained some reservations about the proper extent of women's political involvement.

Bentham's and Mill's ideas have been appropriately referred to as a 'founding model of democracy for a modern industrial society' (Macpherson, 1977, pp. 42–3). Their account of democracy establishes it as a logical requirement for the governance of a society, freed from absolute power and tradition, in which individuals have unlimited desires, form a body of mass consumers and are dedicated to the maximization of private satisfaction. Democracy, accordingly, becomes a means for the enhancement of these ends, not an end in itself for, perhaps, the cultivation and development of all people. As such, Bentham's and Mill's views represent at best, along with the whole tradition of protective democracy, a very partial or one-sided form of democratic theory (see Pateman, 1970, ch. 1).

What is democratic politics? While the scope of politics in Athenian democracy and in the Renaissance republican tradition extended to all the common affairs of the city-republic, the liberal tradition of protective democracy (summarized in model IIIa) pioneered a narrower view: the political is equated with the world of government or governments and with the activities of individuals, factions or interest groups who press their claims upon it. Politics is regarded as a distinct and separate sphere in society, a sphere set apart from economy, culture and family life. In the liberal tradition, politics means, above all, governmental activity and institutions. A stark consequence of this is that issues concerning, for instance, the organization of the economy or violence against women in marriage are typically thought of as non-political, an outcome of 'free' private contracts in civil society, not a public issue or a matter for the state (see Pateman, 1983, 1988).[5] This is a very restrictive view, and one that will be subsequently rejected. But having noted it, it is also important to stress that the liberal idea of protective democracy has had profound effects.

---

[5] Despite the broader conception of politics in Greek thought, it is not at all clear that the Greeks would have addressed themselves to these particular questions (see Okin, 1991; Saxonhouse, 1991). On Renaissance republicanism, cf. Pitkin (1984); Phillips (1991).

In sum: model IIIa

Protective Democracy

Principle(s) of justification

Citizens require protection from the governors, as well as from each other, to ensure that those who govern pursue policies that are commensurate with citizens' interests as a whole

Key features

Sovereignty ultimately lies in the people, but is vested in representatives who can legitimately exercise state functions

Regular elections, the secret ballot, competition between factions, potential leaders or parties, and majority rule are the institutional bases for establishing the accountability of those who govern

State powers must be impersonal, i.e. legally circumscribed, and divided among the executive, the legislature and the judiciary

Centrality of constitutionalism to guarantee freedom from arbitrary treatment and equality before the law in the form of political and civil rights or liberties, above all those connected to freedom of speech, expression, association, voting and belief

Separation of state from civil society, i.e. the scope of state action is, in general, to be tightly restricted to the creation of a framework which allows citizens to pursue their private lives free from risks of violence, unacceptable social behaviour and unwanted political interference

Competing power centres and interest groups

General conditions

Development of a politically autonomous civil society

Private ownership of the means of production

Competitive market economy

Patriarchal family

Extended territorial reach of the nation-state

Note: The model presents, like many of the others in this volume, a general summary of a tradition; it is not an attempt to represent accurately, nor could it, the particular positions and the many important differences among the political theorists examined.

The idea of freedom *from* overarching political authority ('negative freedom', as it has been called) shaped the attack from the late sixteenth century on the old state regimes of Europe and was the perfect complement to the growing market society; for freedom of the market meant in practice leaving the circumstances of people's lives to be determined by private initiatives in production, distribution and exchange. But the liberal conception of negative freedom is linked to another notion, the idea of choosing among alternatives. A core element of freedom derives from the *actual capacity* to pursue different choices and courses of action ('positive freedom'). This notion was not developed systematically by the liberal tradition we have considered, although some pertinent issues were pursued by James Mill's son, John Stuart Mill (1806–73), whose work is examined next. None the less, the liberal idea of political equality as a necessary condition of freedom – the formally equal capacity of citizens to protect their own interests – contains an implicitly egalitarian ideal with unsettling consequences for the liberal order (see Mansbridge, 1983, pp. 17–18). If individuals' interests must have equal protection because only individuals can decide in the end what they want and because, hence, their interests have equal weight in principle, then two questions arise: should not all mature individuals (irrespective of sex, colour, creed and wealth) have an equally weighted way of protecting their interests, i.e. a vote and equal citizenship rights more generally? Should not one consider whether in fact individual interests can be protected equally by the political mechanisms of liberal democracy, i.e. whether the latter creates an equal distribution of political power?

The first of these considerations was at the centre of the struggle for the extension of the franchise in the late nineteenth and twentieth centuries. Many of the arguments of the liberal democrats could be turned against the status quo to reveal the extent to which democratic principles remained in practice unapplied. The second consideration became central to Marxist, feminist and other radical traditions. While each step towards formal political equality is an advance, 'real freedom' is undercut by massive inequalities which have their roots in the social relations of private production and reproduction. The issues posed by this standpoint require careful examination, but they are not confronted directly in model IIIa. This is hardly surprising, given the model's preoccupation, in the last instance, with the legitimation of the politics and economics of self-interest.

Liberty and the development of democracy

If Bentham and James Mill were reluctant democrats but prepared to develop arguments to justify democratic institutions, John Stuart Mill was a clear advocate of democracy, preoccupied with the extent of individual liberty in all spheres of human endeavour. Liberal democratic or representative government was important for him, not just because it established boundaries for the pursuit of individual satisfaction, but because it was an important aspect of the free development of individuality. Participation in political life – voting, involvement in local administration and jury service – was vital, he maintained, to create a direct interest in government and, consequently, a basis for an informed and developing citizenry, male or female, and for a dynamic 'developmental polity'. Like Rousseau and Wollstonecraft before him, Mill conceived of democratic politics as a prime mechanism of moral self-development (cf. Macpherson, 1977, ch. 3; Dunn, 1979, pp. 51–3). The 'highest and harmonious' expansion of individual capacities was a central concern.[6] However, this concern did not lead him to champion any form of direct democratic rule or non-representative democracy; he was extremely sceptical, as we shall see, of all such conceptions.

John Stuart Mill largely set the course of modern liberal democratic thought. Writing during a period of intense discussion about the reform of British

---

[6] Mill likened periodic voting to the passing of a 'verdict by a juryman': ideally the considered outcome of a process of active deliberation about the facts of public affairs, not a mere expression of personal interest.

government, Mill sought to defend a conception of political life marked by enhanced individual liberty, more accountable government and an efficient governmental administration unhindered by corrupt practices and excessively complex regulations. The threats to these aspirations came, in his view, from many places, including 'the establishment', which sought to resist change, the demands of newly formed social classes and groups who were in danger of forcing the pace of change in excess of their training and general preparedness, and the government apparatus itself which, in the context of the multiple pressures generated by a growing industrial nation, was in danger of expanding its managerial role beyond desirable limits. Unfolding Mill's view on these issues brings into clear relief many of the questions that have become central to contemporary democratic thought.

Mill's distinctive approach to the liberty of the individual is brought out most clearly in his famous and influential study *On Liberty* (1859). The aim of this text is to elaborate and defend a principle which will establish 'the nature and limits of the power which can be legitimately exercised by society over the individual', a matter rarely explored by those who advocate direct forms of democracy (*On Liberty*, p. 59; and pp. 48–9, 119–22, of this volume). Mill recognized that some regulation and interference in individuals' lives is necessary but sought an obstacle to arbitrary and self-interested intervention. He put the crucial point thus:

> The object ... is to assert one very simple principle, as entitled to govern absolutely the dealings of society with the individual in the way of compulsion and control, whether the means used be physical force in the form of legal penalties or the moral coercion of public opinion. That principle is that the sole end for which mankind are warranted, individually or collectively, in interfering with the liberty of action of any of their number is self-protection. That the only purpose for which power can be rightfully exercised over any member of a civilized community, against his will, is to prevent harm to others. (*On Liberty*, p. 68)

Social or political interference with individual liberty may be justified only when an act (or failure to act), whether it be intended or not, 'concerns others' and then only when it 'harms' others. The sole end of interference with liberty should be self-protection. In those activities which are merely 'self-regarding', i.e. only of concern to the individual, 'independence is, of right, absolute'; for 'over himself, over his own body and mind, the individual is sovereign' (*On Liberty*, p. 69).

Mill's principle is, in fact, anything but 'very simple': its meaning and implications remain far from clear. For instance, what exactly constitutes 'harm to others'? Does inadequate education cause harm? Does the existence of massive inequalities of wealth and income cause harm? Does the publication of pornography cause harm? But leaving aside questions such as these for the moment, it should be noted that in his hands the principle helped generate a defence of many of the key liberties associated with liberal democratic government. These are, first, liberty of thought, feeling, discussion and publication (unburdening 'the inward domain of consciousness'); second, liberty of tastes and pursuits ('framing the plan of our life to suit our own character'); and third, liberty of association or combination so long as, of course, it causes no harm to others (*On Liberty*, pp. 71–2). The 'only freedom which deserves the name is that of pursuing our own good in our own way, so long as we do not attempt to deprive others of theirs or impede their efforts to obtain it' (p. 72). For Mill the principle of liberty provided a point of demarcation between the people and the power of government; and through its specification in clusters of distinct liberties it could help delineate 'the appropriate region' of human freedom and, thus, the necessary domains of action citizens require in order to control their own lives. And it is by and through this freedom, he argued, that citizens can develop and determine the scope and direction of their own polity. He contended, moreover, that the current practice of both rulers and citizens was generally opposed to his doctrine and, unless a 'strong barrier of moral conviction' could be established against such bad habits, growing infringements on the liberty of citizens could be expected as the state expanded to cope with the pressures of the modern age (*On Liberty*, ch. 5).

The dangers of despotic power and an overgrown state

The uniqueness of Mill's position becomes very clear if we set it, as he did, against what he took to be, first, the unacceptable nature of 'despotic power', which in various guises was still championed by some influential figures during his lifetime, and, second, the risk of ever greater infringements on the liberty of citizens if the state developed too rapidly in an attempt to control complex national and international problems. There was plenty of evidence, Mill maintained, to suggest that an 'overgrown state' was a real possibility.[7]

In *Considerations on Representative Government* (1861), Mill criticized the absolutist state (which he referred to as 'absolute monarchy') and, more generally, the despotic use of political power, first, for reasons of inefficiency and impracticality in the long run and, second, on the grounds of undesirability *per se*. Against all those who advocated a form of absolute power, Mill argued that it could lead to a 'virtuous and intelligent' performance of the tasks of government only under the following extraordinary and unrealizable conditions: that the absolute monarch or despot be not only 'good', but 'all-seeing'; that detailed information be available at all times on the conduct and working of every branch of government in every district of the country; that an effective share of attention be given to all problems in this vast field; and that the capacity exist for a 'discerning choice' of all the personnel necessary for public administration (*Considerations*, pp. 202–3). The 'faculties and energies' presupposed for the maintenance of such an arrangement are, Mill says, beyond the reach of ordinary mortals and, hence, all forms of absolute power are unfeasible in the long run. But even if, for the sake of argument, we could find supermortals fit for absolute power, would we want what we should then have:

---

[7] It is interesting to note that Mill's arguments against absolutism parallel contemporary arguments against the possibility of centralized planning, while his arguments against a large, unwieldy state parallel many aspects of today's debates on the same topic.

'one man of superhuman mental activity managing the entire affairs of a mentally passive people?' (p. 203). Mill's answer is an unambiguous 'no'; for any political system which deprives individuals of a 'potential voice in their own destiny' undermines the basis of human dignity, threatens social justice and denies the best circumstances for humans to enjoy 'the greatest amount of beneficial consequences deriving from their activities'.[8]

Human dignity would be threatened by absolute power, for without an opportunity to participate in the regulation of affairs in which one has an interest, it is hard to discover one's own needs and wants, arrive at tried-and-tested judgements and develop mental excellence of an intellectual, practical and moral kind. Active involvement in determining the conditions of one's existence is the prime mechanism for the cultivation of human reason and moral development. Social justice would be violated because people are better defenders of their own rights and interests than any non-elected 'representative' can be and is ever likely to be. The best safeguard against the disregarding of an individual's rights consists in his or her being able to participate routinely in their articulation. Finally, when people are engaged in the resolution of problems affecting themselves or the whole collectivity, energies are unleashed which enhance the likelihood of the creation of imaginative solutions and successful strategies. In short, participation in social and public life undercuts passivity and enhances general prosperity 'in proportion to the amount and variety of the personal energies enlisted in promoting it' (*Considerations*, pp. 207–8, 277–9).

The conclusion Mill draws from these arguments is that a representative government, the scope and power of which is tightly restricted by the principle of liberty, and *laissez-faire*, the principle of which should govern economic relations in general, are the essential conditions of 'free communities' and 'brilliant prosperity' (*Considerations*, p. 210).[9] Before commenting further on Mill's account of the 'ideally best form of polity' and the 'ideally best form of economy', it is illuminating to focus on what he considered a major modern threat to them: 'the tyranny of the majority' and the burgeoning of governmental power.

From popular government to the threat of bureaucracy

The questions posed by the possibility of a tyrannous majority have already been raised in a number of different contexts: as issues of direct concern to the critics of classical democracy and republicanism, and as a problem addressed directly by defenders of protective democracy (Madison). However, it was the French

---

[8] Mill extensively criticized many of the assumptions of Bentham's utilitarian doctrines, introduced to him directly by his father and by Bentham himself (to whom he, for a time, served as secretary), but he affirmed the general principle of utility as the fundamental criterion for determining what are just ends, or what is right. However, his defence of this principle by no means led him to apply it unambiguously (cf. Ryan, 1974, ch. 4; Harrison, 1993, pp. 105–12).

[9] I shall not be concerned here with many of the apparent inconsistencies in Mill's argument. For example, he was quite prepared to justify despotic rule over 'dependent' territories. For an interesting recent commentary see Ryan (1983), and for a full study see Duncan (1971).

theorist and historian Alexis de Tocqueville (1805–1859) who most influenced Mill on this issue. In his major study, *Democracy in America*, de Tocqueville had argued that the progressive enfranchisement of the adult population, and the extension of democracy in general, created a levelling process in the broad social conditions of all individuals. On behalf of the *demos*, government was inevitably being turned against the privileges of the old ranks and orders; in fact, against all traditional forms of status and hierarchy. These developments, in de Tocqueville's view, fundamentally threatened the possibility of political liberty and personal independence. Among the many phenomena on which he dwelt was the ever-growing presence of government in daily life as an intrusive regulatory agency. In the midst of 'the democratic revolution', the state had become the centre of all conflict: the place where policy, on nearly all aspects of life, was fought over. On the assumption that it was an essentially 'benign' apparatus, the state had come to be regarded as the guarantor of public welfare and progressive change. De Tocqueville thought that this assumption was gravely mistaken and, if not countered in theory and practice, would become a recipe for capitulation to 'the dictate' of the public administrator.[10]

This latter concern was among several issues taken up by Mill. His views can be set out in summary form as follows:

1 The modern apparatus of government, with each addition of function (transportation, education, banking, economic management), expands.
2 As government expands, more and more 'active and ambitious' people tend to become attached to and/or dependent on government (or on a party seeking to win control of the governmental apparatus).
3 The greater the number of people (in absolute and relative terms) who are appointed and paid by government, and the more central control of functions and personnel there is, the greater the threat to freedom; for if these trends are unchecked 'not all the freedom of the press and popular constitution of the legislature would make this or any other country free otherwise than in name' (*On Liberty*, p. 182).
4 Moreover, the more efficient and scientific the administrative machinery becomes, the more freedom is threatened.

Mill summarizes the essence of these points eloquently:

> If every part of the business of society which required organized concert, or large and comprehensive views, were in the hands of the government and if government offices were universally filled by the ablest men, all the enlarged culture and practised intelligence in the country, except the purely speculative, would be concentrated in a numerous bureaucracy, to whom

[10] De Tocqueville recommended a series of countervailing forces, including the decentralization of aspects of government, strong independent associations and organizations in political, social and economic life to stand between the individual and the state, and the nurturing of a culture which respected the spirit of liberty, to help form barriers to the exercise of excessive centralized power (see Krouse, 1983; Dahl, 1985, ch. 1). De Tocqueville's broad 'pluralistic vision of society' was largely shared by Mill, despite his criticism of several aspects of de Tocqueville's position (see J. S. Mill, 'M. de Tocqueville on democracy in America').

alone the rest of the community would look for all things – the multitude for direction and dictation in all they had to do; the able and aspiring for personal advancement. To be admitted into the ranks of this bureaucracy and when admitted, to rise therein, would be the sole objects of ambition. (*On Liberty*, pp. 182–3)

But his argument is by no means complete with these points, for there are other significant considerations concerning the special impact of an overgrown governmental apparatus on 'the multitude':

5 If administrative power expands ceaselessly, citizens – for want of practical experience and information – would become increasingly ill-informed and unable to check and monitor this power.
6 No initiatives in policy matters, even if they stemmed from public pressure, would be taken seriously unless they were compatible with 'the interests of the bureaucracy'.
7 The 'bondage' of all to the state bureaucracy would be still more complete and would even extend to the members of the bureaucracy themselves, '[f]or the governors are as much the slaves of their organization and discipline as the governed are of the governors' (*On Liberty*, p. 184). The routine of organizational life substitutes for the 'power and activities' of individuals themselves; under these conditions, creative mental activity and the potential progressiveness of the governing body become stifled.

Mill put the last point this way:

> Banded together as they are – working a system which, like all systems, necessarily proceeds in a great measure by fixed rules – the official body are under the constant temptation of sinking into indolent routine, or, if they now and then desert that mill-horse round, of rushing into some half-examined crudity which has struck the fancy of some leading member of the corps, and the sole check to these closely allied, though seemingly opposite, tendencies, the only stimulus which can keep the ability of the body itself up to a high standard, is liability to the watchful criticism of equal ability outside the body. It is indispensable, therefore, that the means should exist, independently of the government, of forming such ability and furnishing it with the opportunities and experience necessary for a correct judgement of great practical affairs. (*On Liberty*, pp. 184–5)[11]

Representative government

What, then, did Mill consider the 'ideally best polity'? In general terms, Mill argued for a vigorous democracy to offset the dangers of an overgrown, excessively interventionist state. He seemed to draw a sharp contrast between democracy and bureaucracy: democracy could counter bureaucracy. But several questions arose

[11] Among the examples Mill cites of the domination of officials over society is, most notably, 'the melancholy condition of Russia'. The tsar himself is 'powerless against the bureaucratic body' of the state: he can 'send any one of them to Siberia but he cannot govern without them or against their will' (*On Liberty*, p. 183).

from this general formulation which posed dilemmas for Mill, as they do for all liberals and liberal democrats. First, how much democracy should there be? How much of social and economic life should be democratically organized? Second, how can the requirements of participation in public life, which create the basis for the democratic control of the governors, be reconciled with the requirements of skilled administration in a complex mass society? Is democracy compatible with skilled, professional government? Third, what are the legitimate limits of state action? What is the proper scope for individual as against collective action? It is worth looking briefly at Mill's response to each of these questions.

According to Mill, the ancient Greek idea of the *polis* could not be sustained in modern society. The notion of self-government or government by open meeting is, he held (in accord with the liberal tradition as a whole), pure folly for any community exceeding a single small town. Beyond small numbers, people cannot participate 'in any but some very minor portions of the public business' (*Considerations on Representative Government*, pp. 217–18). Apart from the vast problems posed by sheer numbers, there are obvious geographical and physical limits to when and where people can meet together: these limits are hard to overcome in a small community; they cannot be overcome in a large one. The problems posed by coordination and regulation in a densely populated country are insuperably complex for any system of classical or direct democracy (pp. 175–6, 179–80). Moreover, when government is government by all citizens there is the constant danger that the wisest and ablest will be overshadowed by the lack of knowledge, skill and experience of the majority. This danger can be slowly countered by experience in public affairs (voting, jury service, extensive involvement in local government), but only to a limited extent. Hence, the 'ideally best polity' in modern conditions comprises a representative democratic system in which people 'exercise through deputies periodically elected by themselves the ultimate controlling power' (p. 228).

A representative system, along with freedom of speech, the press and assembly, has distinct advantages: it provides the mechanism whereby central powers can be watched and controlled; it establishes a forum (parliament) to act as a watchdog of liberty and centre of reason and debate; and it harnesses, through electoral competition, leadership qualities with intellect for the maximum benefit of all (*Considerations*, pp. 195, 239–40). Mill argued that there was no desirable alternative to representative democracy, although he was aware of certain of its costs. Today, he wrote, representative democracy and the newspaper press are 'the real equivalent, though not in all respects an adequate one, of the Pnyx and the Forum' (pp. 176ff). Participation in political life is sadly but inescapably limited in a large-scale, complex, densely populated society (cf. ch 9, in which the notions of political participation and informed participation are explained more thoroughly).

Mill ultimately, however, trusted extraordinarily little in the judgement of the electorate and elected. While arguing that universal suffrage was essential, he was at pains to recommend a complex system of plural voting so that the masses, the working classes, 'the democracy', would not have the opportunity to subject the political order to what he labelled simply as 'ignorance' (*Considerations*, p. 324). Given that individuals are capable of different kinds of things and only a few have developed their full capacities, would it not be appropriate if some citizens have more sway over government than others? Regrettably for the cogency of some of Mill's arguments, he thought as much and endorsed a plural system of voting; all adults should have a vote but the wiser and more talented should have more votes than the ignorant and less able. As he put it:

> It is important that every one of the governed should have a voice in the government ... A person who is excluded from all participation in political business is not a citizen ... But ought every one to have an *equal* voice? This is a totally different proposition; and in my judgement ... palpably false ... There is no one who, in any matter which concerns himself, would not rather have his affairs managed by a person of greater knowledge and intelligence, than by one of less. There is no one who, if he was obliged to confide his interest jointly to both, would not desire to give a more potential voice to the more educated and more cultivated of the two. ('Thoughts on parliamentary reform', pp. 17–18, 20–2)

Mill took occupational status as a rough guide to the allocation of votes and adjusted his conception of democracy accordingly: those with the most knowledge and skill (who were in the better rewarded and most privileged jobs) should not be outvoted by those with less, i.e. the working classes.[12] But, escape from the rule of 'the operative classes' and, for that matter, from the self-interested rule of the propertied classes – from political ignorance in its most dangerous form and class legislation in its narrowest expression – lay not only in a voting system to prevent this state of affairs ever coming about; it lay also in a guarantee of expertise in government (*Considerations*, p. 324). How could this be ensured?

There is a 'radical distinction', Mill argued, 'between controlling the business of government and actually doing it' (*Considerations*, pp. 229–30). Control and efficiency increase if people do not attempt to do everything. The business of government requires skilled employment (p. 335). The more the electorate meddles in this business, and the more deputies and representative bodies interfere with day-to-day administration, the greater the risk of undermining efficiency, diffusing lines of responsibility for action and reducing the overall benefits for all. The benefits of popular control and of efficiency can only be had by recognizing that they have quite different bases:

> There are no means of combining these benefits except by separating the functions which guarantee the one from those which guarantee the other; by disjointing the office of control and criticism from the actual conduct of affairs and devolving the former on the representatives of the many, while securing for the latter, under strict responsibility to the nation, the acquired knowledge and practised intelligence of a specially trained and experienced Few. (*Considerations*, p. 241)

[12] There is evidence in *Considerations on Representative Government* that Mill saw plural voting as a transitional educative measure which would eventually (when the masses attained higher moral and intellectual standards) be replaced by a system of one-person-one-vote. The reasons why those with several votes would be willing to give them up at a subsequent stage are not, however, fully explained.

Table 3.1 Summary of advantages and disadvantages of government by bureaucracy according to Mill

Advantages	Disadvantages
Accumulates experience	Inflexibility
Acquires well-tested maxims	Rigid routines
Ensures skills in those who actually conduct affairs	Loses its 'vital principle'
Persistent pursuit of ends	Undermines individuality and individual development, thus limiting innovation

Parliament should appoint individuals to executive positions; it should provide the central forum for the articulation of wants and demands and for the pursuit of discussion and criticism; it should act as the final seal of national approval or assent. But it should not administer or draw up the details of legislation; for it has no competence in this domain.[13]

Representative democracy, thus understood, can combine accountability with professionalism and expertise. It can combine the advantages of bureaucratic government without the disadvantages (table 3.1). The latter are offset by the vitality injected into government by democracy (*Considerations*, pp. 246–7). Mill valued both democracy and skilled government and believed firmly that each was the condition of the other: neither was attainable alone. And to achieve a balance between them was, he thought, one of the most difficult, complicated and central questions 'in the art of government' (*On Liberty*, p. 168).

The question remains: in what domains of life might or should the democratic state intervene? What are the proper limits of state action? Mill sought to specify these clearly via the principle of individual liberty: self-protection – the prevention of 'harm' to any citizen – is the sole end which warrants interference with freedom of action. The state's activity should be restricted in scope and constrained in practice in order to ensure the maximum possible freedom of every citizen. The latter can be secured through representative democracy combined with a free-market political economy. In *On Liberty* Mill spoke of the doctrine of *laissez-faire* as resting on grounds as solid as those of the principle of liberty. He regarded all restraints on trade as evil – *qua* restraints – and ineffective because they did not produce the desired result, that is, the maximization of the economic good: the maximum economic benefit for all (pp. 164–5). Although there are significant ambiguities in Mill's argument (over state intervention to protect workers in dangerous occupations, for instance), the thrust of *On Liberty* is that the pursuit of economic exchange in the market and minimal interference by the state are the best strategies for the protection of individual rights and the maximization of beneficial consequences including, importantly, the possibility of self-development. In other works (notably

---

[13] In fact, Mill went so far as to recommend that parliament should have a right only of veto on legislation proposed and drawn up by a non-elected commission of experts.

Principles of Political Economy, first published in 1848 but revised in significant ways by its third edition, 1852), Mill's defence of *laissez-faire* is more hesitant; extensive arguments are offered for government intervention to resolve 'coordination problems' and to provide public goods such as education.

None the less, Mill arrives at a vision of reducing to the lowest possible extent the coercive power and regulatory capacity of the state. It is a vision which can be referred to as liberal democracy's conception of 'dynamic harmonious equilibrium': dynamic, because it provides for the free self-development of individuals; harmonious equilibrium, because competitive political and economic relations, based on equal exchange, apparently make control of society in many respects superfluous. Arbitrary and tyrannical forms of power are not only challenged as a matter of principle but rendered unnecessary by competition which creates, as one commentator put it, 'the only natural and just organization of society: organization according to merit . . . everyone stands in the place [s]he merits' (Vajda, 1978, p. 856). The 'hidden hand' of the market generates economic efficiency and economic equilibrium in the long run, while the representative principle provides the political basis for the protection of freedom.

The subordination of women

If Mill accepts the equation of politics with, above all, the sphere of government and governmental activity, and the necessity to draw a sharp division between state and society, he is remarkable in breaking with the dominant masculine assumptions of the liberal tradition by counting women as 'mature adults' with a right to be 'free and equal' individuals. It is important to dwell on his position on these issues for a moment; for it raises, along with Wollstonecraft's reflections, vital questions about the conditions for the participation of women and men in a democracy. The liberal tradition has generally taken for granted that 'the private world' free of state interference is a non-political world and that women naturally find their place in this domain. Accordingly, women are located in a wholly marginal position in relation to the political and the public. While maintaining a strict conception of what should be and what should not be a public matter, Mill did not map the 'generic' split (man–woman) onto the political–non-political dichotomy (cf. Siltanen and Stanworth, 1984, pp. 185–208).

In the (until recently) much neglected *The Subjection of Women* (1869), Mill criticized directly, as Wollstonecraft had done before him, conceptions of women's nature based exclusively on domestic roles, affective relations and commitments to home and family life. If women have been conventionally *defined* in terms of the latter by men and sometimes, indeed, by women themselves, it is because for the vast portion of human history they have been restricted in the scope of their lives and activities. The subordination of women to men – in the home, in work life and in politics – is 'a single relic of an old world of thought and practice' (*Subjection*, p. 19). Despite the declaration by many that equality of rights has been achieved, there lingers, Mill affirmed, a 'primitive state of slavery' which has not lost 'the taint of its brutal origin' (pp. 5–6). The relation between men and women was 'grounded on force' and, although some of its most 'atrocious features' have softened with time, 'the law of the strongest' has been enshrined in 'the law of the land' (see *Subjection*, pp. 1–28). Ever since Locke rejected the view that some men have an inherent and natural right to govern, liberals have given a prominent place to the establishment of the consent of the governed as the means to ensure a balance between might and right. Yet the notion that men are the 'natural' masters of women has been left generally unquestioned. The position of women, Mill concluded, is a wholly unwarranted exception to the principles of individual liberty, equal justice and equality of opportunity – a world in which authority and privilege ought to be linked directly to merit, not to institutionalized force.

The Subjection of Women was certainly an argument for the enfranchisement of women, but it was not only that. Nor was it merely an extension of the arguments Mill made in *On Liberty* and *Considerations on Representative Government*, although in many respects it was that as well (Mansfield, 1980, pp. ix–xix). Mill's position was novel among those of liberal democrats in its insistence on the impossibility of the realization of human happiness, freedom and democracy while the inequality of the sexes persisted. The subordination of women has created fundamental 'hindrances to human improvement' (*Subjection*, p. 1). In the first instance, it has led to the underestimation of the significance of women in history and the overestimation of the importance of men. The result has been a distorting effect on what men and women think about their own capabilities: men's abilities have almost constantly been overinflated, while women's capacities have been almost everywhere underrated. The sexual division of labour has led, moreover, to the partial and one-sided development of the characters of women and men. Women have suffered 'forced repression in some directions', becoming, for instance, excessively self-sacrificing, and 'unnatural stimulation in others', searching, for example, for incessant (male) approval (pp. 21ff). On the other hand, men have become above all self-seeking, aggressive, vain and worshippers of their own will. The ability of both sexes to respect merit and wisdom has been eroded. Too often men believe themselves to be beyond criticism and women acquiesce in their judgement to the detriment of government and society generally.

> Think what it is to a boy, to grow up to manhood in the belief that without any merit or any exertion of his own, though he may be the most frivolous and empty or the most ignorant and stolid of mankind, by the mere fact of being born a male he is by right the superior of all and every one of an entire half of the human race: including probably some whose real superiority to himself he has daily or hourly occasion to feel; but even if in his whole conduct he habitually follows a woman's guidance, still, if he is a fool, he thinks that of course she is not, and cannot be, equal in ability and judgement to himself; and if he is not a fool, he does worse – he sees that she is superior to him, and believes that, notwithstanding her superiority, he is entitled to command and she is bound to obey. What must be the effect . . . of this lesson? (*Subjection*, p. 80)

The inequality of the sexes has deprived society of a vast pool of talent. If women had 'the free use of their faculties' along with 'the same prizes and encouragements' as men, there would be a doubling of the 'mass of mental faculties available for the higher service of humanity' (p. 83).

The injustice perpetuated against women has depleted the human condition:

> every restraint on the freedom of conduct of any of their human fellow-creatures (otherwise than by making them responsible for any evil actually caused by it) dries up *pro tanto* the principal fountain of human happiness, and leaves the species less rich, to an inappreciable degree, in all that makes life valuable to the individual human being. (*Subjection*, p. 101)

For Mill, only 'complete equality' between men and women in all legal, political and social arrangements can create the proper conditions for human freedom and a democratic way of life. In turning many key liberal principles against the patriarchal structure of state and society, Mill was arguing that the emancipation of humanity is inconceivable without the emancipation of women.

While Wollstonecraft reached this conclusion before Mill, and no doubt countless other unrecorded women reached it earlier, it was a striking conclusion for someone in Mill's position to champion.[14] *The Subjection of Women*'s uncompromising attack on male domination is probably the key reason for its relative obscurity when considered in relation to his, for example, 'academically acceptable' *On Liberty* (Pateman, 1983, p. 208). But radical as the attack unquestionably was, it was not without ambiguities. Two should be stressed. First, the whole argument rests rather uneasily with Mill's narrow conception of the political. The principle of liberty could be taken to justify a massive range of state initiatives to restructure, for instance, economic and childcare arrangements so that women might be better protected against the 'harm' caused by inequality and might gain the chance to develop their own interests. However, Mill does not appear to interpret the principle in this way. The new policies he defended were, while of the greatest significance, limited; they included the enfranchisement of women, reform of the marriage laws to strengthen the independent position of women in the family, and suggestions to help create equal educational opportunities (see Mansfield, 1980, pp. xxii–xxiii). The limits Mill placed on legitimate state action are to be explained in part by his belief that women, once they attained the vote, would be in an advantageous position to specify further the conditions of their own freedom. The position would be advantageous because if the 'emancipation' of women were left to existing political agencies, it would be distorted by traditional patriarchal interests: women must enjoy equal rights to enable them to explore their own capacities and needs. On the other hand, Mill probably did not think through more interventionist strategies because they would infringe upon the liberty of individuals to decide what was in their own best interests. Individuals must be free of political and social impediments to choose how to arrange their lives – subject, of course, to their choices causing no 'harm' to others. But this proviso

---

[14] Some scholars have argued that Mill's position owes a great deal to Harriet Taylor, for many years a friend and from 1851 until her death in 1858 his wife (see Eisenstein, 1980), while others have claimed it owes a good deal to William Thompson's *Appeal of One Half of the Human Race*, published in 1825 (see Pateman, 1983, p. 211).

radically weakens the political implications of Mill's analysis; for it leaves the powerful (men) in a strong position to resist change in the name of liberty and freedom of action.

Second, Mill does not analyse in any detail the domestic division of labour. Without the sharing of domestic duties, the ability of women actively to pursue courses of action of their own choosing is considerably weakened. Mill reveals his ultimate view of the role of women by assuming that even if there were a 'just state of things' most women would rightly choose – as 'the first call upon [their] exertions' – to marry, raise children and manage households exclusively (see *Subjection*, pp. 47–8; Okin, 1979; Pateman, 1983). Without pursuing arguments about the obligations men must accept with respect to the care of children and households, and about the loss of unjustifiable privileges to which they must adapt (issues returned to later), the conditions of human freedom and democratic participation cannot be analysed adequately. But despite Mill's failing in this regard (a failing he shares to some extent with Wollstonecraft, whose own esteem for motherhood led her on occasion to adopt a fairly uncritical view of the duties of fathers), it is hard to overestimate the importance of his contribution in *The Subjection of Women* and its unsettling consequences for the liberal democratic tradition as a whole – and, indeed, for political thought more generally.

Competing conceptions of the 'ends of government'

Liberty and democracy create, according to Mill, the possibility of 'human excellence'. Liberty of thought, discussion and action is a necessary condition for the development of independence of mind and autonomous judgement; it is vital for the formation of human reason or rationality. In turn, the cultivation of reason stimulates and sustains liberty. Representative government is essential for the protection and enhancement of both liberty and reason. A system of representative democracy makes government accountable to the citizenry and creates wiser citizens capable of pursuing the public interest. It is thus both a means to develop self-identity, individuality and social difference – a pluralistic society – and an end in itself, an essential democratic order. If, in addition, all obstacles to women's participation in politics are removed, there will be few 'hindrances to the improvement of humankind'. Model IIIb summarizes Mill's position in broad terms.

Towards the close of *Considerations on Representative Government*, Mill summarized the 'ends of government' in the following way: 'Security of person and property and equal justice between individuals are the first needs of society and the primary ends of government: if these things can be left to any responsibility below the highest, there is nothing, except war and treaties, which requires a general government at all' (p. 355). One needs to ask at this point whether Mill was trying to 'reconcile irreconcilables' (Marx, *Capital*, vol. I, p. 16). For Mill's work entails the attempt to link together into a coherent whole security of person and property, equal justice, and a state strong enough to prevent or prosecute wars and sustain treaties. In fact, Mill's work lends itself to a variety of interpretations concerning not only matters of emphasis but the very

In sum: model IIIb

Developmental Democracy

Principle(s) of justification
Participation in political life is necessary not only for the protection of individual interests, but also for the creation of an informed, committed and developing citizenry. Political involvement is essential to the 'highest and harmonious' expansion of individual capacities

Key features
Popular sovereignty with a universal franchise (along with a 'proportional' system of vote allocation)

Representative government (elected leadership, regular elections, secret ballot, etc.)

Constitutional checks to secure limitations on, and divisions in, state power and to ensure the promotion of individual rights, above all those connected with freedom of thought, feeling, taste, discussion, publication, combination and the pursuit of individually chosen 'life plans'

Clear demarcation of parliamentary assembly from public bureaucracy, i.e. the separation of the functions of the elected from those of the specialist (expert) administrator

Citizen involvement in the different branches of government through the vote, extensive participation in local government, public debates and jury service

General conditions
Independent civil society with minimum state interference

Competitive market economy

Private possession and control of the means of production alongside experiments with 'community' or cooperative forms of ownership

Political emancipation of women, but preservation in general of traditional domestic division of labour

System of nation-states with developed relations among states

Note: It is important to recall that Mill is building on and developing many aspects of the liberal tradition and, hence, several of the features and conditions of developmental democracy are similar to those in model IIIa (see p. 78 above).

political thrust of liberalism and liberal democracy. There are, at least, three possible interpretations worth emphasizing.

First, Mill tried to weave arguments for democracy together with arguments to 'protect' the modern political world from 'the democracy'. While he was extremely critical of vast inequalities of income, wealth and power (he recognized, especially in his later writings, that they prevented the full development of most human beings and especially the working classes), he stopped far short of a commitment to political and social equality. In fact, Mill's views could be referred to as a form of 'educational elitism', since they clearly seek to justify a privileged position for those with knowledge, skill and wisdom: in short, for a modern version of philosopher-kings. The leading political role in society is allotted to a class of intellectuals, who, in Mill's system of vote allocation, hold substantial voting power. He arrives at this view through his emphasis on the importance of education as a key force in liberty and emancipation. It is a position fully committed to the moral development of all individuals but which simultaneously justifies substantial inequalities in order for the educators to be in a position to educate the ignorant. Thus, Mill presents some of the most important arguments on behalf of the liberal democratic state alongside arguments which would in practice cripple its realization.

Second, Mill's arguments concerning free-market political economy and minimal state interference anticipate later 'neo-liberal' arguments (see model VII: legal democracy, in ch. 7, p. 207 below). According to this position, the system of law should maximize the liberty of citizens – above all, secure their property and the workings of the economy – so that they may pursue their chosen ends unhindered. Vigorous protection of individual liberty allows 'the fittest' (the most able) to flourish and ensures a level of political and economic freedom which benefits all in the long run.

Third, while Mill remained throughout most of his life firmly of the opinion that the liberal state should be neutral between competing individuals' goals and styles of life (individuals should be left as free as possible), some of his ideas can be deployed to justify a 'reformist' or 'interventionist' view of politics (see ch. 6 below). For Mill's liberal democratic state is assigned an active role in securing people's rights through the promotion of laws designed to protect groups such as ethnic minorities and to enhance the position of women. Additionally, if we take Mill's principle of liberty seriously, that is, explore those instances in which it would be justified to intervene politically to prevent 'harm' to others, we have, at the very least, an argument for a fully fledged 'social democratic' conception of politics. Occupational health and safety, maintenance of general health and protection from poverty (in fact, all those areas of concern to the welfare state from the early twentieth century) might be included as part of the sphere for legitimate state action to prevent harm. In the *Principles of Political Economy* (third edition), Mill adopted such a line of reasoning and argued not only that there should be many exceptions to *laissez-faire* economic doctrines but also that all workers should experience the educational effects of ownership and control of the means of production. While he certainly believed that the principle of individual private property would and ought to be the dominant form of property for the foreseeable future, he advocated practical experiments with different types of ownership to help find the most advantageous form for 'the improvement of humanity' (see *Principles of Political Economy* and Mill's essays on socialism, originally published in 1879, in G. L. Williams, 1976, pp. 335–58). Taken together, these views can be read as one of the earliest statements of the idea of the democratic welfare interventionist state and the mixed economy (Green, 1981).[15]

Summary remarks

From classical antiquity to the seventeenth century, democracy was largely associated with the gathering of citizens in assemblies and public meeting

---

[15] Towards the end of his life, in fact, Mill came to regard himself more as a socialist than a liberal democrat (see his *Autobiography*).

places. By the late eighteenth century it was beginning to be thought of as the right of citizens to participate in the determination of the collective will through the medium of elected representatives (Bobbio, 1989, p. 144). The theory of representative liberal democracy fundamentally shifted the terms of reference of democratic thought: the practical limits that a sizeable citizenry imposes on democracy, which had been the focus of so much critical (anti-democratic) attention, were practically eliminated. Representative democracy could now be celebrated as both accountable and feasible government, potentially stable over great territories and time spans (see Dahl, 1989, pp. 28–30). As one of the great advocates of the 'representative system' put it, 'by ingrafting representation upon democracy' a system of government is created that is capable of embracing 'all the various interests and every extent of territory and population' (Paine, *The Rights of Man*, in Paine, 1987, p. 281). Representative democracy could even be heralded, as James Mill wrote, as 'the grand discovery of modern times' in which 'the solution of all difficulties, both speculative and practical, would be found' (quoted in Sabine, 1963, p. 695). Accordingly, the theory and practice of popular government broke away from its traditional association with small states and cities, opening itself to become the legitimating creed of the emerging world of nation-states. But who exactly was to count as a legitimate participant, or a 'citizen' or 'individual', and what his or her exact role was to be in this new order, remained either unclear or unsettled in the leading theories of both protective and developmental democracy considered in this chapter.

It was left by and large to the extensive and often violently suppressed struggles of working-class and feminist activists in the nineteenth and twentieth centuries to accomplish a genuinely universal suffrage in some countries. Their achievement was to remain fragile in places such as Germany, Italy and Spain, and was in practice denied to some groups: for instance, many African-Americans in the US before the civil rights movement in the 1950s and 1960s. However, through these struggles the idea that the rights of citizenship should apply equally to all adults slowly became established; many of the arguments of the liberal democrats could be turned against existing institutions to reveal the extent to which the principles and aspirations of equal political participation and equal representation remained unfulfilled. It was only with the actual achievement of citizenship for all adult men and women that liberal democracy took on its distinctively contemporary form: a cluster of rules and institutions permitting the broadest participation of the majority of citizens in the selection of representatives who alone can make political decisions (that is, decisions affecting the whole community).

This cluster includes elected government; free and fair elections in which every citizen's vote has an equal weight; a suffrage which embraces all citizens irrespective of distinctions of race, religion, class, sex and so on; freedom of conscience, information and expression on all public matters broadly defined; the right of all adults to oppose their government and stand for office; and associational autonomy – the right to form independent associations including social movements, interest groups and political parties (see Bobbio, 1987, p. 66; Dahl, 1989, pp. 221, 233). The consolidation of representative democracy, thus understood, has been a twentieth-century phenomenon; perhaps one should even say a late twentieth-century phenomenon (see ch. 8). For it was only in the closing decades of that century that liberal representative democracy was securely established in the West and widely adopted in principle as a suitable model of government beyond the West (see Held, 1993d, esp. part IV).

4 Direct Democracy and the End of Politics

Karl Marx (1818–83) and Friedrich Engels (1820–95) relentlessly attacked the idea of a 'neutral' liberal state and 'free'-market economy. In an industrial capitalist world the state could never be neutral or the economy free. John Stuart Mill's liberal democratic state might claim to be acting on behalf of all citizens; it might defend its claim to legitimacy with the promise to sustain 'security of person and property' while promoting simultaneously 'equal justice' among individuals. But this promise cannot be realized in practice, Marx and Engels argued. 'Security of person' is contradicted by the reality of class society where most aspects of an individual's life – the nature of opportunities, work, health, life span – are determined according to his or her location in the class structure. What faith can be placed in the promise to guarantee 'security of person' after a comparison is made between the position of the unemployed, or the worker in a factory doing routinely dull and unrewarding tasks in dangerous conditions, and the position of the small and wealthy group of owners and controllers of productive property living in conditions of more or less sumptuous luxury? What meaning can be given to the liberal state's promise of 'equal justice' between individuals when there are massive social, economic and political inequalities?

Marx and Engels – who were born in Germany, but lived most of their working lives in England – broke decisively with the terms of reference of liberal and liberal democratic thought. Although Marx's works will be focused upon here, in order to understand how both men conceived of politics, democracy and the state it is necessary to grasp their overall assessment of the place of the individual in society, the role of property relations and the nature of capitalism. Only by unpacking their analysis of the latter can one fully appreciate their account of the fate of liberal democracy and their unswerving promotion of a wholly different model.

Class and class conflict

Human beings as 'individuals'; individuals in competition with one another; freedom of choice; politics as the arena for the protection of individual interests, the defence of 'life, liberty and estate'; the democratic state as the institutional mechanism for the articulation of the legal framework for the pursuit of private initiatives in civil society and public concerns in the 'process of government': all these are preoccupations of the liberal democratic tradition. While Marx and Engels did not deny that people had unique capacities, desires and an interest in free choice, they attacked the idea that the starting point of the analysis of political life and its most desirable organizational form can be the individual, and his or her relation to the state. As Marx put it, 'man is not an abstract being squatting outside the world. Man is the human world, the state, society' (*The Critique of Hegel's Philosophy of Right*, p. 131, modified translation). Individuals only exist in interaction with and in relation to others; their nature can only be grasped as a social and historical product. It is not the single, isolated individual who is active in historical and political processes, but rather human beings who live in definite relations with others and whose nature is defined through these relations. An individual, or a social activity, or an institution (in fact, any aspect of human life) can only be properly explained in terms of its historically evolving interaction with other social phenomena, a dynamic and changing process of inextricably related elements.

The key to understanding the relations between people is, according to Marx and Engels, class structure (see Giddens and Held, 1982, pp. 12–39, for an overview). Class divisions are not, they maintained, found in all forms of society: classes are a creation of history, and in the future will disappear. The earliest types of 'tribal' society were classless. This is because, in such types of society, there was no surplus production and no private property: production was based upon communal resources and the fruits of productive activity were distributed throughout the community as a whole. Class divisions arise only when a surplus is generated, such that it becomes possible for a class of non-producers to live off the productive activity of others. Those who are able to gain control of the means of production form a dominant or ruling class both economically and politically. Class relations for Marx and Engels are thus necessarily exploitative and imply divisions of interest between ruling and subordinate classes. Class divisions are, furthermore, inherently conflictual and frequently give rise to active class struggle.

It is striking, and worth stressing from the outset, that Marx wrote virtually nothing about possible intersections between class exploitation and the exploitation of women. Engels did attempt such a task, however, in *The Origins of the Family, Private Property, and the State*. In this book he tried essentially to link the origins of sexual domination to the emergence of private property, especially private ownership of the means of production, which in turn was regarded as the condition of the development of the state. The earliest forms of society, according to Engels, were matriarchal: women were more powerful than men. But this relation between the sexes became reversed with the formation of private property. Although Engels's view of how this process occurred is not altogether clear, he associated it directly with the advent of private property and therefore class, since men assumed supremacy to protect inheritance. Accordingly, sexual exploitation in Engels's analysis is explained as an offshoot of class exploitation.

> The modern individual family is based on the open or disguised domestic enslavement of women . . . Today, in the great majority of cases, the man has to be the earner, the bread-winner of the family . . . and this gives him a dominating position which requires no special legal privileges. In the family, he is the bourgeois; the wife represents the proletariat. (Engels, *The Origins*, p. 510)

Engels was not reluctant to draw the implications of this standpoint: with the transcendence of capitalism, and thus of class divisions, sexual exploitation will also disappear. The development of capitalism, he believed, paves the way for the overcoming of sexual exploitation because the main form of deprivation to which women are subject in capitalist society – exclusion from equal participation in the labour force – is to an extent overcome by an increase in female involvement in wage-labour. In a future society, equality of participation in production will be the basis of achieving equality in other spheres.[1] Engels and Marx adopted a similar position with respect to racial inequalities. For them, class and class struggle form the chief mechanism or 'motor' of historical development.

History as evolution and the development of capitalism

In order to understand historical development adequately, it is essential to analyse how 'people make history' but not always 'in circumstances of their own choosing', because the latter are 'given and transmitted from the past' (Marx, *The Eighteenth Brumaire of Louis Bonaparte*, p. 15). To grasp 'the basis of all history', as Marx put it, is to grasp how the creative acts of humans are constrained and enabled by the resources which people can command, by the productive techniques at their disposal and by the form of society which exists as a result of the efforts of preceding generations. To ignore this set of processes is to neglect the very foundations of human existence. To explicate it, by contrast, is to establish the conditions of different forms of human association, and of the possibilities of politics in each era.

Two general concepts – 'social formation' and 'mode of production' – help unlock the historical process (although only the latter was explicitly used by Marx and Engels). Social formation connotes a web of relations and institutions which constitute a society. The web consists of a combination of economic, political and cultural phenomena including a particular type of economy, system of power, state apparatus and cultural life, all of which have definite interconnections with one another. These interconnections, Marx maintained, can be uncovered by analysing the 'mode of production'. A mode of production designates the essential structure of a society: the social relations of production. These relations specify the dominant way in which surplus production is extracted and appropriated. Modern Western societies or social formations are, according to Marx and Engels, capitalist because they are characterized by the extraction of surplus production in the form of 'surplus value', the value generated by workers in the productive process over and above their wages and appropriated by the owners of capital (see, especially, Marx, 'Value, price and profit'). The division between those with capital and those who only have their labouring capacity to sell demarcates the fundamental basis of exploitation and

---

[1] Although opinion is somewhat divided on the matter, most commentators are agreed that there is little in Engels's account that can be defended today. The sources which Engels drew upon for evidence of the existence of a matriarchal stage of society have been substantially discredited. Contemporary anthropology seems to have been unable to come up with a single authenticated instance of a society in which women are wholly dominant over men, although there are considerable variations in relations of power between the sexes in different societies. The connection Engels drew between private property and male domination also appears invalid; no direct relation of this kind seems to exist (see Hartmann, 1976; Coward, 1983; H. Moore, 1987).

conflict in the modern epoch, and establishes the key social and political, i.e. class, relations. 'Capitalists' own factories and technology, while wage-labourers, or 'wage-workers', are propertyless. As capitalism develops, the vast majority of the population become wage-workers, who have to sell their labour power on the market to secure a living.

Modes of production are, however, complex combinations of relations and forces of production. What Marx meant by this is set out in summary form in table 4.1. While the social relations of production are pivotal, around them typically crystallizes a variety of interconnected relations and organizations (1(b) and (c) in table 4.1). The exact form these take (for instance, the structure of trade unions) depends on historical circumstances and the balance of struggle between social classes. Forces of production comprise those things which are directly employed in the productive process itself.

In some of Marx's and Engels's best-known writings, they elaborated a conception of history based upon the idea of successive stages of development. These stages were distinguished by different modes of production and change was propelled by the economic 'base', particularly the interaction between the progressively expanding forces of production, on the one hand, and the struggle of classes over the distribution of social wealth, on the other. How exactly Marx and Engels conceived this interaction or dynamic is not of prime importance here. What is essential to note is that it suggested a conception of history as an evolutionary process marked by periods of revolutionary change (see, for instance, Marx, Preface to *A Contribution to the Critique of Political Economy*). This interpretation of historical development is a standard feature of orthodox Marxism (from Engels to Bukharin and Stalin, among others) and involves the idea of human society passing through five stages of development, from the primitive communal to the ancient, feudal, capitalist and (eventually) post-capitalist modes of production.

Marx believed the bourgeois or capitalist mode of production was the last major stage before a fundamentally new political and economic order, in which the ideals of liberty and equality would be gradually realized: communism. Before analysing the state and democratic life as he conceived them, it is useful to outline why he thought capitalism was the final stage of exploitation and 'unfreedom'. His account of capitalism sheds direct light on his reasons for holding that a new form of political organization was not only desirable but possible. The points can be made (although inevitably in simplified form) in a number of theses.

1 Contemporary society is dominated by the capitalist mode of production. It is a society based on the private possession of the means of production and on exchange, the unequal exchange between capital and labour. Products are manufactured primarily for their realization of surplus value and profit and not for their long-term capacity to satisfy human needs and desires.

2 Capitalism is not a harmonious social order. It is based on contradictions both in the realm of production and in the realm of ideology (the system of beliefs, values and practices that serve the interests of dominant groups and classes). The capitalist relations of production impede the full development of the forces of production and produce a series of conflicts and crises.

Table 4.1 Elements of a mode of production

1 *Relations of production*
   (a) Social relations of production, e.g. wage-labour/capital relation
   (b) Secondary (or indirect) productive relations, e.g. labour and capital organizations, patterns of family life
   (c) Politically derivative relations, e.g. state, educational institutions, i.e. a complex of relations and institutions serving (a) and (b)

2 *Forces of production*
   (a) Means of production, i.e. material means or instruments of production
   (b) Technical methods
   (c) Natural and human resources employed in production
   (d) Organization of work, largely determined by 1(a), (b) and (c)

3 The foundations of capitalism are progressively undermined 'from within', i.e. as a result of the development of capitalism itself. The economy is vulnerable to political business cycles which involve booms followed by sharp downturns in economic activity. Booms are created by a growth in demand which leads manufacturers to increase production. As production expands the number of those employed increases and unemployment falls. As unemployment falls, class struggle over the distribution of income intensifies as workers become more 'valuable' assets and can capitalize on tight labour market conditions. In order to remain competitive and keep production costs down (costs grow with increases in wage rates and expansion in demand for raw materials) employers substitute capital (in the form of new technology) for labour. Productive capacity grows rapidly. Since all productive units are operating competitively and in isolation from one another, the outcome is eventually excess production and excess capacity. A crisis sets in (a downturn in economic activity or recession or depression); production is cut back, workers are laid off, unemployment increases, wage rates fall until 'supply' and 'demand' are once more in line, and the cycle starts again.

4 In addition, in periods of downturn, small and/or weak firms tend to be pushed out of business by larger enterprises better able to 'weather' the poor economic conditions. In this way the 'free' market of competitive firms is progressively replaced by the oligopolistic and monopolistic mass production of goods: there is, in other words, an inevitable tendency towards the growing 'concentration' of ownership in economic life. Such concentration tends also to go along with what Marx called the increasing 'centralization' of the economy; this refers primarily to the expansion of the activities of banks and other financial organizations and involves their enhanced coordination of the economy as a whole. These processes of concentration and centralization progressively reveal the necessarily social nature of capitalist production, which undermines the mechanisms of individualistic entrepreneurial competition. Moreover, the ever greater interdependence between commercial and financial enterprises ensures, at best, a delicate economic equilibrium, for any major disturbance or disruption can potentially affect the whole system.

The bankruptcy of a giant firm or bank, for example, has implications for numerous apparently sound enterprises, for whole communities and hence for political stability. Figure 4.1 sets out Marx's theory of crisis in summary form.[2]

5 As part of these developments class struggle intensifies both sporadically as a feature of the cyclical tendencies of the economy and more generally in the longer term. The position of the isolated worker is incomparably weaker than that of his or her employer, who not only can sack the worker, but can fall back on massive resources in the event of any sustained conflict. Workers discover that the individual pursuit of interests is ineffective and even self-defeating. A strategy of collective action is, therefore, the only basis for the pursuit of certain basic needs and wants (e.g. increased material benefits, control over everyday life, satisfying work). It is only through *collective* action that *individuals* can establish the conditions for a fulfilling life. Ultimately, workers realize that it is only through the abolition of the capitalist relations of production that they can be free. The collective struggle for the realization of freedom and happiness is part of the daily life of workers. It must be carried forward and developed if their 'general interests' are to be enhanced; that is, if the *free* development of individuals, a *just* allocation of resources and *equality* in community are to be established.

6 The development of the labour movement is the means for achieving revolution. The lessons workers learn in the workplace and via their unions become the basis for the extension of their activities into the sphere of the state. The formal right to organize political parties, in the apparatus of 'representative democracy', permits the formation of socialist organizations that can challenge the dominant order. Through such challenges, the revolution can be made, a process which Marx apparently believed could be a peaceful transition in certain countries with strong democratic traditions (like Britain), but was likely to involve violent confrontation elsewhere.

7 Communism, as a political doctrine, has several related sources apart from the tradition of the writings of 'utopian socialists' such as Saint-Simon (1760–1825), Fourier (1772–1837) and Owen (1771–1858). It emerges, for instance, from the daily struggle of workers to win dignity in and control over their lives. It emerges from the contradiction between the promise of capitalism to produce stable economic growth and its actual unstable reality. It emerges from the failure of the liberal democratic order to create the conditions for liberty, equality and justice. And it emerges from the contradiction that, although founded upon 'private appropriation' – the appropriation by capitalists of profit – capitalism is the most 'socialized' form of order that human beings have ever created. For a capitalist economy involves the cooperation and mutual dependence of everyone on a scale unknown in previous forms of society. Communism is the logical extension of this principle to a new type of society.

---

[2] There are, in fact, several different interpretations of Marx's theory of crisis available in the secondary literature (cf. Sweezy, 1942; Mattick, 1969; Mandel, 1972; Fine and Harris, 1979).

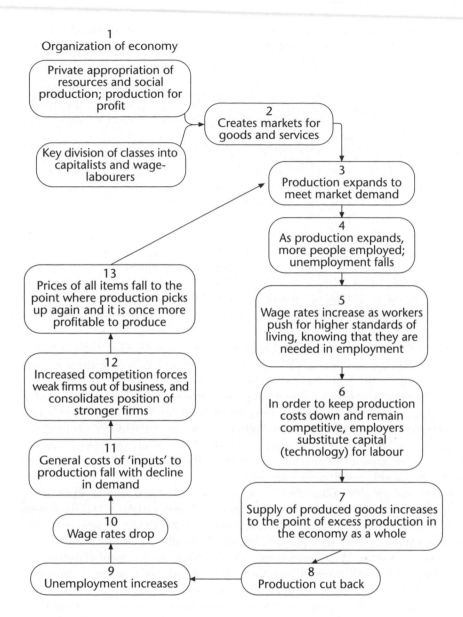

1
Organization of economy

Private appropriation of resources and social production; production for profit

Key division of classes into capitalists and wage-labourers

2
Creates markets for goods and services

3
Production expands to meet market demand

4
As production expands, more people employed; unemployment falls

5
Wage rates increase as workers push for higher standards of living, knowing that they are needed in employment

6
In order to keep production costs down and remain competitive, employers substitute capital (technology) for labour

7
Supply of produced goods increases to the point of excess production in the economy as a whole

8
Production cut back

9
Unemployment increases

10
Wage rates drop

11
General costs of 'inputs' to production fall with decline in demand

12
Increased competition forces weak firms out of business, and consolidates position of stronger firms

13
Prices of all items fall to the point where production picks up again and it is once more profitable to produce

Marx's theory sought to establish that: (a) crises are regular features of capitalist development; (b) crises are crises of overproduction; (c) there is a marked tendency to increased concentration and centralization of the economy which leads to a highly delicate economic 'equilibrium'; (d) the division of society into classes creates the predisposition to crises, and class struggle is the essential 'mechanism' of economic development as power shifts between employers and employees depending on labour market conditions.

Figure 4.1 Marx's theory of crisis

Two theories of the state

Marx believed that democratic government was essentially unviable in a capitalist society; the democratic regulation of life could not be realized under the constraints imposed by the capitalist relations of production. He thought it necessary to transform the very basis of society in order to create the possibility of a 'democratic politics'. To understand more precisely why Marx was of this view, it is important to examine how he conceived the position of the state – its role, function and limits – in the context of capitalism.

Central to the liberal and liberal democratic traditions is the idea that the state can claim to represent the community or public as a whole, in contrast to individuals' private aims and concerns. But, according to Marx and Engels, this claim is, to a large extent, illusory (see Maguire, 1978, ch. 1). The state defends the 'public' or the 'community' as if classes did not exist; as if the relationship between classes was not exploitative; as if classes did not have fundamental differences of interest; and as if these differences of interest did not largely define economic and political life. In formally treating everyone in the same way, according to principles which protect the freedom of individuals and defend their right to property, the state (by which Marx meant the whole apparatus of government from the executive and legislature to the police and military) may act 'neutrally' but it will generate effects that are partial; that is, it will inevitably sustain the privileges of those with property. By defending private ownership of the means of production, the state has already taken a side. It enters into the very fabric of economic life and property relations by reinforcing and codifying – through legislation, administration and supervision – its structure and practices. As such, the state plays a central part in the integration and control of class-divided societies; and in capitalist societies this means a central role in the reproduction of the exploitation of wage-labour by capital. The liberal notion of a 'minimal' state is, in fact, connected directly to a strong commitment to certain types of intervention to curtail the behaviour of those who challenge the inequalities produced by the so-called free market: the liberal or liberal democratic state is perforce in practice a coercive or strong state. The maintenance of private property in the means of production contradicts the ideals of a political and economic order comprising 'free and equal' citizens. The movement towards universal suffrage and political equality in general was, Marx recognized, a momentous step forward, but its emancipatory potential was severely undercut by inequalities of class and the consequential restrictions on the scope of many people's choices in political, economic and social life.

Moreover, the liberal claim that there is a clear distinction to be made between the private and the public, the world of civil society and that of the political, is, Marx maintained, dubious. The key source of contemporary power – private ownership of the means of production – is ostensibly *depoliticized*; that is, arbitrarily treated as if it were not a proper subject of politics. The economy is regarded as non-political, in that the massive division between those who own and control the means of production and those who must live by wage-labour is regarded as the outcome of free private contracts, not a matter for the state. But by defending private ownership of the means of production the state does not remain detached from the power relations of civil society as a set of institutions above all special concerns, i.e. a 'public power' acting for 'the public'. On the contrary, it is deeply embedded in socioeconomic relations and linked to particular interests. Furthermore, this link is sustained (for reasons which are explored further below) irrespective of the political views of the people's 'representatives' and the extent of the franchise.

There are at least two strands in Marx's account of the relation between classes and the state; while they are by no means explicitly distinguished by Marx himself, it is illuminating for analytical purposes to disentangle them. The first, henceforth referred to as position 1, stresses that the state generally, and bureaucratic institutions in particular, may take a variety of forms and constitute a source of power which need not be directly linked to, or be under the unambiguous control of, the dominant class in the short term. By this account, the state retains a degree of power independent of the dominant class; its institutional forms and operational dynamics cannot be inferred directly from the configuration of class forces: they are 'relatively autonomous'. The second strand, position 2, is without doubt the leading one in Marx's writings: the state and its bureaucracy are class instruments which emerged to coordinate a divided society in the interests of the ruling class. Position 1 is certainly a more complex and subtle conception. Both positions are elaborated below, beginning with position 1, for it is expressed most clearly in Marx's early writings and highlights the degree to which the second view involves a narrowing down of the terms of reference of his analysis of politics and the state.

Marx's engagement with the theoretical problems posed by state power developed from an early confrontation with Hegel (1770–1831), a central figure in German idealist philosophy and a crucial intellectual influence on his life. In the *Philosophy of Right*, Hegel argued that the state could potentially resolve intense conflicts between individuals by providing, on the one hand, a rational framework for their interaction in civil society and, on the other, an opportunity to participate (via a limited form of representation) in the formation of the 'general political will'. Over time, the modern state had become the centre of law, culture and national identity, the comprehensive basis of all development. By identifying with it, citizens could surmount the competitive anarchy of civil society and discover a true basis of unity. Only by virtue of the state could citizens achieve a 'rational existence'. (See Hegel, *Lectures on the Philosophy of World History*, first delivered in 1830, pp. 94–7, for a concise statement of this view.)

Hegel conceived of civil society as a sphere of 'self-regarding' actions where the pursuit of self-interest was entirely legitimate. While there had always been scope for self-interest, it is only with the progressive emancipation of individuals from religious, ethical and coercive political restraints that a fully distinct civil realm emerged. At the centre of this process lay the expansion of the free market, eroding tradition in its wake. But the meaning of the free market, and of civil society more generally, could not be properly grasped, Hegel insisted, simply by reference to a theory of human behaviour as self-seeking; it was fundamentally erroneous to abstract from the egoism of civil society, as many liberal thinkers had done, a general theory of human motivation and behaviour. Hegel accepted the pursuit of material wealth as a central basis for the realization of human needs but he argued, as one of his expositors has succinctly put it, 'that behind the self-seeking, accidentality and arbitrariness of civil society there looms inherent reason' (Avineri, 1972, p. 147). For civil society is an association of 'mutually interlocking' partial interests which has its foundation in both competing needs and the legal system (Hegel, *Philosophy of Right*, pp. 122ff). The latter guarantees security of person and property and, thereby, provides a mechanism for curbing the excesses of individuals (pp. 149–52). The existence of civil society is premised on the recognition that the 'general good' can only be realized through the enforcement of law and the conscious direction of the state (pp. 147ff). The history of the state makes apparent a strong desire for the rational (reasoned) pursuit of life. In Hegel's view, the state is the basis which enables citizens to realize their freedom in conjunction with others. Free of tyranny, it represents the potential unity of reason and liberty.

The actual institutional organization of the state is central to the degree to which individuals can enjoy freedom. Hegel admired (though with some qualifications) the Prussian state, which he portrayed as rightly divided into three substantive divisions – the legislature, the executive and the Crown – which together express 'universal insight and will'. For him, the most important institution of the state is the bureaucracy, an organization in which all particular interests are subordinated to a system of hierarchy, specialization, expertise and coordination on the one hand, and internal and external pressures for competence and impartiality on the other (*Philosophy of Right*, pp. 132, 179, 190–1, 193). According to Marx, however, Hegel failed to challenge the self-image of the state and, in particular, of the bureaucracy (*The Critique of Hegel's Philosophy of Right*, pp. 41–54).

The bureaucracy is the 'state's consciousness'. In marked contrast to Hegel, and figures like John Stuart Mill, Marx described the bureaucracy, the corps of state officials, as 'a particular closed society within the state', which extends its power or capacity through secrecy and mystery (*Critique*, p. 46). The individual bureaucrat is initiated into this closed society through 'a bureaucratic confession of faith' – the examination system – and the caprice of the politically dominant group. Subsequently, the bureaucrat's career becomes all-important, passive obedience to those in higher authority becomes a necessity and 'the state's interest becomes a particular private aim'. But the state's aims are not thereby achieved, nor is competence guaranteed (pp. 48, 51). For, as Marx wrote,

> The bureaucracy asserts itself to be the final end of the state . . . The aims of the state are transformed into aims of bureaus, or the aims of bureaus into the aims of the state. The bureaucracy is a circle from which no one can escape. Its hierarchy is a hierarchy of knowledge. The highest point entrusts the understanding of the particulars to the lower echelons, whereas these, on the other hand, credit the highest with an understanding in regard to the universal [the general interest]; and thus they deceive one another. (*Critique*, pp. 46–7)

Marx's critique of Hegel involves several points, but one in particular is crucial. In the sphere of what Hegel referred to as 'the absolutely universal interest of the state proper' there is, in Marx's view, nothing but 'bureaucratic officialdom' and 'unresolved conflict' (*Critique*, p. 54). Marx's emphasis on the structure and corporate nature of bureaucracies is significant because it throws into relief the 'relative autonomy' of these organizations and foreshadows the arguments elaborated in what may be his most interesting work on the state, *The Eighteenth Brumaire of Louis Bonaparte*.

The Eighteenth Brumaire is an eloquent analysis of the rise to power between 1848 and 1852 in France of Louis Napoleon Bonaparte and of the way power accumulated in the hands of the executive at the expense of, in the first instance, both civil society and the political representatives of the capitalist class, the bourgeoisie. The study highlights Marx's distance from any view of the state as an 'instrument of universal insight', 'ethical community' or 'judge' in the face of disorder. Marx emphasized that the state apparatus is simultaneously a 'parasitic body' on civil society and an autonomous source of political action. Thus, in describing Bonaparte's regime, he wrote: 'This executive power, with its enormous bureaucratic and military organization, with its ingenious state machinery, embracing wide strata, with a host of officials numbering half a million, beside an army of another half million, this appalling parasitic body . . . enmeshes the body of French society like a net and chokes all its pores' (*Eighteenth Brumaire*, p. 121). The state is portrayed as an immense set of institutions, with the capacity to shape civil society and even to curtail the bourgeoisie's capacity to control the state (see Maguire, 1978; Spencer, 1979). Marx granted the state a certain autonomy from society: political outcomes are the result of the interlock between complex coalitions and constitutional arrangements.

The analysis offered in *The Eighteenth Brumaire*, like that in *The Critique*, suggests that the agents of the state do not simply coordinate political life in the interests of the dominant class of civil society. The executive, under particular circumstances (for example, when there is a relative balance of social forces), has the capacity to take political initiatives as well as to coordinate change. But Marx's focus, even when discussing this idea, was essentially on the state as a conservative force. He emphasized the importance of its information network as a mechanism for surveillance, and the way in which the state's political autonomy is linked to its capacity to undermine social movements threatening the status quo. Moreover, the repressive dimension of the state is complemented by its ability to sustain belief in the inviolability of existing arrangements. Far then from being the basis for the articulation of the public interest, the state, Marx argued, transforms 'universal aims into another form of private interest' – the interest, that is, of its guardians and leaders.

There were ultimate constraints on the initiatives Bonaparte could take, however, without throwing society into a major crisis, as there are on any legislative or executive branch of the state. For the state in a capitalist society, Marx concluded (a conclusion which became central to his overall teachings), cannot escape its dependence upon that society and, above all, upon those who own and control the productive process. Its dependence is revealed whenever the economy is beset by crises; for economic organizations create the material resources on which the state apparatus survives. The state's overall policies have to be compatible in the long run with the objectives of manufacturers and traders, otherwise civil society and the stability of the state itself are jeopardized. Hence, though Bonaparte usurped the political power of the bourgeoisie's representatives, he protected the 'material power' of the bourgeoisie itself, a vital source of loans and revenue. Accordingly, Bonaparte could not help but sustain – and in this he was no different from any other politician in a capitalist society – the long-term economic interests of the bourgeoisie and lay the foundation for the regeneration of its direct political power in the future, whatever else he chose to do while in office (*Eighteenth Brumaire*, pp. 118ff).

Marx attacked the claim that the distribution of property lies outside the constitution of political power. This attack is, of course, a central aspect of Marx's legacy and of what I have called position 2. Throughout his political essays, and especially in his more polemical pamphlets such as *The Communist Manifesto*, Marx (and indeed Engels) insisted on the direct dependence of the state on the economic, social and political power of the dominant class. The state is a 'superstructure' which develops on the 'foundation' of economic and social relations (see Marx and Engels, *The Communist Manifesto* and Marx, Preface to *A Contribution to the Critique of Political Economy*). The state, in this formulation, serves directly the interest of the economically dominant class: the notion of the state as a site of autonomous political action is supplanted by an emphasis upon class power, an emphasis illustrated by the famous slogan of *The Communist Manifesto*: 'The executive of the modern state is but a committee for managing the common affairs of the whole bourgeoisie.' This formula does not imply that the state is dominated by the bourgeoisie as a whole: it may be independent of sections of the bourgeois class (see Miliband, 1965). The state, nevertheless, is characterized as essentially dependent upon society and upon those who dominate the economy: 'independence' is exercised only to the extent that conflicts must be settled between different sections of capital (industrialists and financiers, for example), and between 'domestic capitalism' and pressures generated by international capitalist markets. The state maintains the overall interests of the bourgeoisie in the name of the public or general interest.

There are, then, two (often interconnected) strands in Marx's account of the relation between classes and the state: the first conceives the state with a degree of power independent of class forces; the second upholds the view that the state is merely a 'superstructure' serving the interests of the dominant class. Position 1 has been emphasized because it is the more insightful of the two accounts (see Draper, 1977; Maguire, 1978; Perez-Diaz, 1978). Yet, it needs to be stressed, even this position was far from complete; it left several important questions insufficiently explored. What is the basis of state power? Is sovereignty just a chimera? What precise interests do political officials develop? How much scope is there for politicians to exercise initiative? Is politicians' capacity for autonomous action politically insignificant in the long run? Does the state – even within a framework of liberal democratic arrangements – have little general relevance other than its relation to class forces? Position 2 is even more problematic: it postulates a capitalist-specific organization of the state and takes for granted a simple causal relation between the facts of class domination and the vicissitudes of political life. Marx's work on the state and class politics left fundamental matters either unresolved or unaddressed.

But Marx's combined writings do indicate how central he regarded the state as being to the control of class-divided societies. Furthermore, his work suggests important limits to state action within capitalist societies. If state intervention undermines the process of capital accumulation, it simultaneously undermines the material basis of the state; hence, state policies must be consistent with the capitalist relations of production. Or, to put the point another way: constraints exist in liberal democracies – constraints imposed by the requirements of private capital accumulation – which systematically limit policy options. The system of private property and investment creates objective exigencies which must be met if economic development is to be sustained. If this system is threatened (for example, by a party elected into office with the firm intention of promoting greater equality), economic chaos can quickly ensue (as capital investment is placed overseas, for instance) and the acceptability of governments can be radically undermined.[3] Accordingly, a dominant economic class can *rule without directly governing*, that is, it can exert determinate political influence without even having representatives in government. This idea has retained a vital place in debates among Marxists, liberal democratic theorists and others (see chs 5 and 6). It is a key basis on which Marxists argue that freedom in a capitalist democracy is purely formal; inequality fundamentally undermines liberty and leaves most citizens free only in name. Capital rules.

The end of politics

Far from the state playing the role of emancipator, protective knight or umpire in the face of conflicting interests, the state is enmeshed in civil society. It is not the state, Marx wrote, that underlies the social order, but the social order that underlies the state. Marx did not deny the desirability of liberty – far from it. He recognized that the struggle of liberalism against absolutism and tyranny, and the struggle by liberal democrats for political equality, represented a major step forward in the battle for emancipation. But he thought liberty was impossible while human exploitation continued (a result of the very dynamics of the capitalist economy), supported and buttressed by the state. Freedom cannot be realized if freedom means first and foremost the freedom of capital. In practice, such freedom means leaving the circumstances of people's lives open to be determined by the pressures of private capitalist investment. It means succumbing to the consequences of the economic decisions of a wealthy minority, where those decisions are not taken with any reference to general costs or benefits. It means a reduction of freedom to unfettered capitalist competition, and the subordination of the mass of the population to forces entirely outside their control.

[3] It follows, as one commentator wrote, that liberal politics has a peculiarly 'negative character'. It becomes orientated towards the avoidance of risks and the eradication of dangers to the system: 'not, in other words, towards the *realization of practical goals* [that is, particular value choices] but towards the *solution* of *technical problems*' (Habermas, 1971, pp. 102–3).

Marx referred to this state of affairs (throughout his working life, I believe, although the matter is contentious) as one of 'alienation'; that is, a situation where the mass of people are estranged from the products of their labour, the process of their work, their fellow human beings and their fundamental capacities – what he called their 'species being' (see Marx, *Economic and Philosophical Manuscripts*, pp. 120–31, 202–3; Ollman, 1971). For the conditions are such that the products of work are appropriated privately and sold on the market by the employer; the worker has little, if any, control over the process of work and the conditions of his or her life; individuals are divided against each other by competition and possession; and men and women are in danger of losing their ability to be active, creative agents – people who can 'make their own history' with will and consciousness. Marx's theory of human nature departed radically from the rational, strategic, self-seeking person at the centre of much liberal thought, although there are some notable points of convergence with the views of J. S. Mill. For Marx, it is not the single human being who is active in the historical process; rather, it is the creative interplay of collectivities in the context of society: human nature is, above all, social. By 'species being' Marx referred to the distinctive characteristics of humans, as compared with other animals. Because humans are not merely driven by instincts, they do not adapt in a passive fashion to their environment, as most animals do. Human beings can and must actively, purposefully and creatively master their environment to survive; creativity and control of one's circumstances are thus an intrinsic part of what it is to be 'human'. A person doing routinely dull and unrewarding tasks in the context of minimal control of economic and political circumstances is reduced merely to adapting quiescently to his or her environment: in Marx's phrase, 'the animal becomes human and the human becomes animal'.

Liberal political doctrines effectively restrict freedom to a minority of the population by affirming a central place for the capitalist relations of production and the 'free' market; they legitimate an economic and political system that exploits the capacities, and threatens the 'species being', of humans. Only a conception of freedom that places equality at its centre (as Rousseau's vision of freedom sought to do), and is concerned above all with equal freedom for all (which Rousseau's vision ultimately failed to be), can restore to people the necessary power to 'make their own history' (*The Communist Manifesto*, p. 127). Freedom entails, in Marx's view, the complete democratization of society as well as the state; it can only be established with the destruction of social classes and ultimately the abolition of class power in all its forms.

How did Marx conceive the future after the revolution? How, in particular, did he see the future of democracy and the state? How should political power be organized when the capitalist relations of production are destroyed? No sooner are these questions posed, however, than a difficulty is encountered. Marx rarely wrote in any detail about what socialism or communism should be like. He was against the development of blueprints, which he likened to 'strait-jackets' upon the political imagination. The 'music of the future' could not and should not be composed in advance; rather, it must emerge in the struggle to abolish the contradictions of the existing order. Those involved in this struggle must play an equal part in defining the future. However, despite this general standpoint, Marx frequently gave indications of what a 'free and equal' society might be like.[4]

Marx set out his position in a framework which I shall refer to as the 'end of politics'. The end of politics (or the end of the era of the state) means the transformation of political life as it has been known in bourgeois societies; that is, the dismantling of politics as an institutionally distinct sphere in society used in the perpetuation of class rule. The emancipation of the working classes necessarily implies the creation of a new form of government. In *The Poverty of Philosophy*, Marx wrote: 'The working class, in the course of its development, will substitute for the old civil society an association which will exclude classes and their antagonism and there will be no more political power so-called, since political power is precisely the official expression of antagonism in civil society' (p. 182). And, discussing the way in which 'the proletariat will use its political supremacy', in *The Communist Manifesto*, he wrote:

> When, in the course of development, class distinctions have disappeared and all production has been concentrated in the hands of a vast association of the whole nation, the public power will lose its political character. Political power, properly so-called, is merely the organized power of one class for oppressing another. If the proletariat during its contest with the bourgeoisie is compelled, by the force of circumstances, to organize itself as a class; if, by means of a revolution, it makes itself the ruling class and, as such, sweeps away by force the old conditions of production, then it will, along with these conditions, have swept away the conditions for the existence of class antagonisms and of classes generally and will thereby have abolished its own supremacy as a class.
>
> In place of the old bourgeois society, with its classes and class antagonisms, we shall have an association, in which the free development of each is the condition for the free development of all. (p. 127)

With the destruction of the bourgeois class, the need for 'organized political power' will cease to exist.

The core of this position can be stated as follows:

1 since the state develops on the foundations of social and economic relations;
2 since the state secures and expresses the structure of productive relations and cannot determine the nature and form of these;
3 since, as an instrument or framework, it coordinates society in accordance with the long-term interests of the dominant class;
4 since class relations determine the key dimensions of power and axes of conflict in state and in society;
5 then, when classes are finally transcended, all political power will be deprived of its footing and the state – and politics as a distinct activity – will no longer have a role.

---

[4] These indications are found in scattered passages and in a few longer statements, notably in Marx, *The Critique of Hegel's Philosophy of Right* (1843); Marx and Engels, *The German Ideology* (1845–6); Marx, *The Poverty of Philosophy* (1847); Marx and Engels, *The Communist Manifesto* (1847); Marx, *The Civil War in France* (1871); and Marx, *Critique of the Gotha Programme* (1875).

Classes are 'inscribed' into the state. And precisely because so many of the apparatuses of the modern state are adjuncts of class domination (legal structures to protect property, forces to contain conflict, armies to support imperialist ambitions, institutions and reward systems for those who make a career in politics, and so on) the working classes cannot simply seize state power and turn it to their advantage in and after the revolution. 'The political instrument of their enslavement cannot serve as the political instrument of their emancipation' (see *The Civil War in France*, pp. 162–8). The 'master of society' will not become a 'servant' on request. The struggle to 'abolish' the state and to bring an 'end to politics' is thus the struggle for the 'reabsorption of the state by society' (*Civil War*, p. 168).

Marx linked the 'end of politics' not only to the political triumph of a socialist working class but also, importantly, to the eventual abolition of material scarcity. To a significant extent he believed that the potential for freedom was related directly to scarcity. Security from the ravages of nature, alleviation of the pressures of unmet physical need and time to pursue activities of one's own choice were among the essential conditions of real freedom. The 'mastery of nature' through the development of the forces of production was necessary for the advance of socialism and communism.

The triumph of capitalism can be explained with reference both to those who imposed it as a political and economic system and to its extraordinary productive achievements. Marx regarded the rapid expansion of the forces of production and the subsequent increase in economic growth under capitalism as in itself an immensely progressive phenomenon. The other side of this progress was, of course, the exploitative system of productive relations. The latter was, paradoxically, the condition of capitalism's success and of its inevitable downfall. The crisis-ridden nature of economic growth, the tendency to stagnation and, above all, the constant creation of conditions of suffering and degradation for the mass of citizens undermined the nature of capitalism's achievement in the long run. Thus, according to Marx, capitalism both contributed to the prospect of freedom – by helping generate its material prerequisites through modernizing the means of production – and simultaneously prevented its actualization.

The struggle against capital for 'the end of politics' allows the historical achievement of capitalism to be advanced radically. Once the capitalist relations of production have been destroyed, there will no longer be fundamental obstacles to human development. Marx conceived the struggle for 'the end of politics' in terms of 'two stages of communism'. In *State and Revolution* (1917), Lenin referred to these as, respectively, 'socialism' and 'communism'.[5] Since the latter terminology is compatible with Marx's stages, it will be adopted here for convenience (see S. Moore, 1980). For Marx 'socialism' and 'communism' were phases of political emancipation. Table 4.2 indicates their broad characteristics.[6] I shall focus below on how Marx conceived the

[5] Marx tended to use these terms more or less interchangeably.

[6] In setting out table 4.2 I have drawn upon a number of sources, most notably *The Communist Manifesto*, *The Civil War in France* and *Critique of the Gotha Programme*, as well as three excellent secondary discussions: Draper (1977), Ollman (1977) and S. Moore (1980).

Table 4.2 Broad characteristics of socialism and communism

	Socialism (or 'the dictatorship of the proletariat')	Communism
General goals	• Appropriation of all large-scale private capital • Central control of production in the hands of the state • Rapid increase of productive forces • Gradual dissolution of the bourgeois state • Defence of revolution against remnants of the old order	• End of the exploitation of labour in all forms; social ownership of property • Consensus on all public questions, therefore no laws, no discipline, no coercion • Satisfaction of all material needs • Collectively shared duties and work • Self-government (even democracy becomes redundant)
State	• Integration of executive and legislative functions • All government personnel to be subject to frequent elections, mandates from their constituencies and recall • Election and recall of magistrates and judges, as well as all administrative officials • Replacement of army and police force by a people's militia • Full local autonomy within framework of councils (pyramid structure)	• Abolition of legislative and executive functions (no longer necessary) • Distribution of administrative tasks by rotation and election • Dissolution of all armed and coercive forces
Economy	• Extension of state ownership of factories • State control of credit • State control of transportation and communication • Gradual abolition of private property in land, and cultivation of all land • Equal liability of all citizens to work; public direction of employment	• Elimination of markets, exchange and the role of money • End of division of labour, rotation of all tasks • People enjoy a variety of types of work and leisure • Work-time reduced to a minimum • With abolition of scarcity, all wants are satisfied and the idea of private property becomes meaningless
Society	• Heavy graduated taxation • No inheritance • Free education for all children • Reunion of town and country through more equitable distribution of population over country and integration of work and non-work environments	• Principle of cooperation extends to all public affairs • Social, cultural, regional and racial differences disappear as sources of conflict • People explore their capacities to the full with other people's freedom as the only constraint • Households are based on communal arrangements, monogamy persists, though not necessarily as a lifetime commitment
Overall objectives of both phases	• Planned expansion of production and abolition of material scarcity • 'Administration of persons' to be replaced by 'administration of things', i.e. 'withering away of the state' • Principle of justice to be gradually established: 'from each according to his ability, to each according to his need'	

future of state power and democracy, but it is interesting and necessary to locate this conception, as table 4.2 does, in the context of his overarching vision of social transformation.

One of the immediate objectives of the post-revolutionary era, according to Marx, is the establishment of the unrestricted authority of the state so that the constraints imposed on human development by the private ownership of the means of production can be overcome. The state in the hands of the working classes and their allies must transform economic and social relations while defending the revolution against remnants of the bourgeois order. But the extension of the authority of the state over the economy and society (over large-scale factories and investment funds, for instance) must go hand in hand with the establishment of the unrestricted accountability of the 'sovereign state' to the 'sovereign people'. Like the 'liberal' state, the socialist state must have the supreme right to declare and administer law over a given territory, but unlike the 'liberal state' it must be wholly accountable in all its operations to its citizens. Additionally, the socialist state must aim to become as fast as possible a 'minimal' state: an apparatus for the coordination and direction of social life without recourse to coercion.

Marx generally referred to the transitional stage in the struggle for communism as 'the revolutionary dictatorship of the proletariat' (see e.g. the *Critique of the Gotha Programme*). The 'dictatorship' is established during the revolution and will 'wither away' with the onset of communism. What did Marx mean by 'dictatorship'? He did *not* mean what this term is frequently taken to mean: the necessary domination of a small revolutionary group or party, reconstructing society according to its exclusive conception of the masses' interests. This fundamentally Leninist view (see pp. 116–19 below) should be distinguished from Marx's general position. By the 'dictatorship of the proletariat' Marx meant the democratic control of society and state by those – the overwhelming majority of adults – who neither own nor control the means of production. The question is, of course: how did Marx conceive the democratic control of state and society by the working classes and their allies?

When Marx referred to 'the abolition of the state' and the 'dictatorship of the proletariat' he had in mind after 1871, I think (although not all scholars would agree), the model of the Paris Commune.[7] The year 1871 witnessed a major uprising in Paris in which thousands of Parisian workers took to the streets to overthrow what they regarded as an old and corrupt governmental structure. Although the movement was eventually crushed by the French army, Marx thought of it as 'the glorious harbinger of a new society' (*Civil War*, p. 99). The rebellion lasted long enough for the planning of a remarkable series of institutional innovations and a new form of government: the Commune. Marx's description of the Commune is rich in detail and it is worth quoting at some length:

[7] Engels was certainly of this view: see, for instance, his Letter to A. Bebel, March 1875. But, for an alternative account, see Arendt (1963) and Anweiler (1974). Arendt argues that the Commune was only envisaged by Marx as a temporary measure 'in the political struggle to advance the revolution' (p. 259). In my view, the Commune provides a definite model for at least the 'first stage of communism'.

The Commune was formed of the municipal councillors, chosen by universal suffrage in the various wards of the town, responsible and revocable at short terms. The majority of its members were naturally working men, or acknowledged representatives of the working class. The Commune was to be a working, not a parliamentary, body, executive and legislative at the same time. Instead of continuing to be the agent of the Central Government, the police was at once stripped of its political attributes, and turned into the responsible and at all times revocable agent of the Commune. So were the officials of all other branches of the Administration. From the members of the Commune downwards the public service had to be done at workmen's wages. The vested interests and the representation allowances of the high dignitaries of State disappeared along with the high dignitaries themselves. Public functions ceased to be the private property of the tools of the Central Government. Not only municipal administration, but the whole initiative hitherto exercised by the State was laid into the hands of the Commune.

Having once got rid of the standing army and the police, the physical force elements of the old Government, the Commune was anxious to break the spiritual force of repression, the 'parson-power', by the disestablishment and disendowment of all churches as proprietary bodies. The priests were sent back to the recesses of private life, there to feed upon the alms of the faithful in imitation of their predecessors, the Apostles. The whole of the educational institutions were opened to the people gratuitously, and at the same time cleared of all interference of Church and State. Thus, not only was education made accessible to all, but science itself freed from the fetters which class prejudice and governmental force had imposed upon it.

The judicial functionaries were to be divested of that sham independence which had but served to mask their abject subserviency to all succeeding governments to which, in turn, they had taken, and broken, the oaths of allegiance. Like the rest of public servants, magistrates and judges were to be elective, responsible and revocable.

The Paris Commune was, of course, to serve as a model to all the great industrial centres of France. The communal *régime* once established in Paris and the secondary centres, the old centralized Government would in the provinces, too, have to give way to the self-government of the producers. In a rough sketch of national organization which the Commune had no time to develop, it states clearly that the Commune was to be the political form of even the smallest country hamlet, and that in the rural districts the standing army was to be replaced by a national militia, with an extremely short term of service. The rural communes of every district were to administer their common affairs by an assembly of delegates in the central town, and these district assemblies were again to send deputies to the National Delegation in Paris, each delegate to be at any time revocable and bound by the *mandat impératif* (formal instructions) of his constituents. The few but important functions which still would remain for a central government were not to be suppressed, as has been intentionally mis-stated, but were to be discharged by Communal, and therefore strictly responsible, agents. The unity of the nation was not to be broken, but, on the contrary, to be organized by the Communal Constitution, and to become a reality by the destruction of the State power which claimed to be the embodiment of that unity independent of, and superior to, the nation itself, from which it was but a parasitic excrescence. While the merely repressive organs of the old governmental power were to be amputated, its legitimate functions were to be wrested from an authority usurping pre-eminence over society itself, and restored to the responsible agents of society. Instead of deciding once in three to six years which member of the ruling class was to misrepresent the people in Parliament, universal suffrage was to serve the people, constituted in Communes, as individual suffrage serves every other employer in the search for the workmen and managers in his business. And it is well known that companies, like individuals, in matters of real business generally know how to put the right man in the right place, and, if they for once make a mistake, to redress it promptly. On the other hand, nothing could be more foreign to the spirit of the Commune than to supersede universal suffrage by hierarchic investiture. (*Civil War*, pp. 67–70)

The five points in table 4.2 that are listed as the broad characteristics of the state under socialism summarize the key issues in the quotation. The 'machinery' of the 'liberal' state would be replaced by the Commune structure. All aspects of 'government' would then, according to Marx, be fully accountable to the majority: 'the general will' of the people would prevail. The smallest communities would administer their own affairs and elect delegates to larger administrative units (districts, towns) which would, in turn, elect candidates to still larger areas of administration (the national delegation). This arrangement is known as the 'pyramid' structure of direct (or delegative) democracy. All delegates are revocable, bound by the instructions of their constituency and organized into a 'pyramid' of directly elected committees.

The post-capitalist state would not, therefore, bear any resemblance to a parliamentary regime. Parliaments create unacceptable barriers between the ruled and their representatives; a vote once in a while is a wholly insufficient basis, Marx thought, to ensure adequate representation of the people's views. A system of direct delegation overcomes this difficulty, as it does the fundamental lack of accountability introduced into state power by the principle of the separation of powers. The latter leaves branches of the state outside the direct control of the electorate. All state agencies must be brought within the sphere of a single set of directly accountable institutions (see Polan, 1984, pp. 13–20). Only when this happens will 'that self-reliance, that freedom, which disappeared from earth with the Greeks, and vanished into the blue haze of heaven with Christianity', gradually be restored (Marx, Letter two from the *Deutsch-Französische Jahrbücher*, 1843, modified translation). While Marx's model of direct democracy departs in many respects from the model of ancient Athens, and from Rousseau's related conception of a self-governing order, it is hard not to see in it, at least in part, an attempt to recover directly the radical heritage of these positions against the tide of the liberal tradition (see chs 1 and 2).[8]

---

[8] It could be argued that, if one considers the problems of holding delegates at national level strictly accountable, the Commune system might be better described as a highly *indirect* form of democracy. There is considerable force to this objection and I shall discuss some of the issues it raises later in the chapter. However, I find the term 'direct democracy' a useful one to help characterize a form of government which sought to combine local autonomy with a system of representatives who are in principle directly revocable delegates. Of course, whether 'direct democracy' is a more acceptable model of democracy than others considered in this volume is another question (see chs 10 and 11).

Marx always stressed that the transformation of society and state would be a slow process; those involved 'will have to pass through long struggles, through a series of historic processes, transforming circumstances and men' (*Civil War*, p. 73). But the struggle was both necessary and justified; for the goal was communism: a form of life in which society and state would be fully integrated, where people would govern their joint affairs collectively, where all needs would be satisfied and where the 'free development of each' would be compatible with the 'free development of all'. In this world of material abundance and self-regulation, the state would finally 'wither away' completely. Governments, legislatures and judiciaries would no longer be necessary. As institutions they are based on the assumption that there will be severe conflicts of interest in society and that these must be ordered and regulated. But in communism all remnants of classes will have disappeared and with them the basis of all conflicts. And since people's material needs will be satisfied and there will be no private property, the *raison d'être* for the forces of 'law and order' will have disappeared. Some coordination of tasks will be necessary in both community life and work generally, but this will be accomplished without creating a stratum of privileged officials. Bertell Ollman, who has reconstructed Marx's vision of communism in some detail, likens Marx's conception of the task of the communist administrator to 'traffic directing', 'helping people to get where they want to go' (Ollman, 1977, p. 33). The administrator or coordinator will be 'appointed' by a process of election which Marx describes as a 'business matter', i.e. a non-political affair. Furthermore, since everyone agrees on basic matters of public policy, elections are likely to be uncontested and to become mere mechanisms to ensure the rotation of administrative tasks. Thus, the 'end of politics' will, Marx thought, have been achieved.

Competing conceptions of Marxism

Twentieth-century Marxism evolved into at least three camps, which will be referred to here as the 'libertarians' (see e.g. Mattick, 1969), the 'pluralists' (see e.g. Poulantzas, 1980) and the 'orthodox' (e.g. Marxist-Leninists). Each of these groups (or schools of Marxism) has claimed, in part, the mantle of Marx.[9] I shall argue that they could all do this because Marx himself might have been trying, as he said of John Stuart Mill, to 'reconcile irreconcilables'. He conceived of the post-capitalist future in terms of an association of all workers, an association in which freedom and equality were combined through (1) the democratic regulation of society; (2) the 'end of politics'; (3) the planned use of resources; (4) efficient production; and (5) greater leisure. But is the democratic regulation of society compatible with planning? Is the model of the Commune, of direct democracy, compatible with a decision-making process that produces a

[9] While these three groups are important, they do not embrace fully the diversity of views found among writers and activists of different revolutionary movements, communist parties, social democratic parties (especially before World War I) and the many relatively small political groups and organizations which have claimed Marx's heritage. Such diversity testifies to the fact that the history of Marxism is much less monolithic and far more fragmented than is often thought.

sufficient number of decisions to coordinate a complex, large-scale society? Is efficient production compatible with the progressive abolition of the division of labour? Marx envisaged the full participation of all 'free and equal' workers in the institutions of direct democracy. But how exactly is such an association to function? How precisely is it to be secured? What happens if some people bitterly object to a decision of the central Commune? Assuming that the dissenters are a minority, do they have any rights, for instance, to safeguard their position? What happens if people simply disagree on the best course of action? What happens if differences of interest persist between groups of different ages, regions or religions? What happens if the new forms of association do not immediately work, or do not work at all adequately in the long run (see Vajda, 1978)? The rifts in Marxism are in part a consequence of Marx's insufficient reflection upon issues such as these (cf. the earlier discussion of Rousseau, pp. 43–9 above).

Marx, it should be emphasized, was not an anarchist; hence he saw a lengthy period of transition to communism which deployed the resources of the state, albeit a transformed state. But libertarian Marxists argue that his position can be interpreted adequately only if we read it as a consistent critique of all forms of division of labour, state bureaucracy and authoritarian leadership (whether created by the 'right' or the 'left'). They contend that Marx was trying to integrate the ideals of equality and liberty in his conception of the struggle for socialism (and the model of the Commune) and, hence, the aims of a non-coercive order must be embodied in the means used to establish that order. If the struggle is not organized democratically, utilizing a Commune or council structure, it will be vulnerable to modes of decision-making which can be exploited by new forms of despotic power. The end – a fully democratic life – necessitates a democratically organized movement in the struggle against capital and the state. Libertarian Marxists maintain, in short, that Marx was a champion of the democratic transformation of society and state and a consistent critic of hierarchy, centralized authority and all types of planning in detail. The struggle for socialism and communism must involve the creation of a mass movement, independent of the corrupting influence of the bourgeois state apparatus, to challenge all forms of established power. Libertarian Marxists make it clear that, in their view, there can be no associations or compromises with the state; for it is always everywhere the 'condensed power' and 'power instrument' of the dominant economic interests (see Held, 1989, ch. 5).

By contrast, pluralist Marxists emphasize that Marx saw the transition to socialism and communism taking place differently in different countries. Following his conception of state institutions as to a significant degree independent (or 'relatively autonomous') from the dominant class, pluralist Marxists stress the importance of the deployment of these institutions against the interests of capital. In countries where the liberal democratic tradition is well established, the 'transition to socialism' must utilize the resources of that tradition – the ballot box, the competitive party system – first, to win control of the state, and second, to use the state to restructure society. The principle of the 'ballot box' should not be overridden; for one cannot expect to create a new democratic order if one bypasses the achievements of past struggles for political emancipation. Unlike libertarian Marxists whose position is consistently anti-state and anti-party, pluralist Marxists argue that the implications of Marx's critique of the capitalist state are that the party of the working class and its allies can and must attain a legitimate and secure position in the state in order to restructure the political and social world.

In addition, pluralist Marxists contend (along with some libertarian Marxists) that Marx's concern to reduce non-coercive power to a minimum must not be interpreted (as Marx himself tended to do all too often) exclusively in terms of class-related issues (cf. McLennan, 1995). The power of men over women, of one race over another, of so-called 'neutral' administrators or bureaucrats over subject populations, must be confronted and its implications pursued, including, crucially, the implication that not all differences of interest can be interpreted in terms of class. Moreover, pluralist Marxists argue, the 'end of scarcity' is so far in the future – if it can be imagined at all – that there are bound to be major differences of position concerning the allocation of resources. It is inconceivable that people will have identical views about political priorities; for instance, about the objectives of public expenditure (investment in production v. current consumption, housing v. education programmes) or about the proper location of such expenditure (given the different needs of various regions and of particular strata in the population, the young, the old, the sick, etc.). Hence, the establishment of a socialist polity will, for all intents and purposes, be a long democratic road in which regular elections and the mobilization of competing interests through parties must – for all the reasons provided by liberal democrats – have a central role. In order to create the space for alternative ideas and programmes, and prevent power-holders from 'transforming themselves into a congealed, immovable bureaucracy', there must always be the possibility of being removed from office. (This position is often elaborated in terms of a 'participatory' model of democracy: see model VIII in ch. 7, p. 215 below.)

Orthodox Marxists, finally, emphasize (in common with libertarian Marxists) that the modern representative state is a 'special repressive force' for the regulation of society in the interests of the dominant economic class. The liberal democratic state might create the illusion that society is democratically organized, but it is no more than an illusion; for the exploitation of wage-labour by capital is secured within the framework of liberal democracy. Periodic elections do not alter this process at all (see Callinicos, 1991). Thus, the state cannot simply be taken over and contained by a democratic movement; its coercive structure has to be conquered and smashed. Preoccupied by the problems of seizing and controlling power, orthodox Marxists (from Lenin to Mao) argued consistently that the transition to socialism and communism necessitates the 'professional' leadership of a disciplined cadre of revolutionaries. Only such a leadership has the capacity to organize the defence of the revolution against counter-revolutionary forces, to plan the expansion of the forces of production and to supervise the reconstruction of society. Since all fundamental differences of interest are class interests, since the working-class interest (or standpoint) is the progressive interest in society and since during and after the revolution it has to be articulated clearly and decisively, a revolutionary party is essential. The party is the instrument which can create the framework for socialism and communism – a position still adhered to by some Marxists today, despite the revolutions of 1989–90 in Central and Eastern Europe (see ch. 8).

One may say, then, that while Marx offered one of the most profound challenges to the modern liberal and liberal democratic idea of the state and one of the most potent visions of a free, ultimately 'stateless' society (summarized in model IV), his views contain ambiguities which lend themselves to a variety of interpretations. Marx left an ambiguous heritage. But it needs to be considered, and this issue will be returned to later at greater length, whether the ambiguities have roots in more fundamental difficulties. Although the Marxist critique of liberalism is of great significance – showing as it does that the organization of the economy cannot be regarded as non-political, and that relations of production are central to the nature and distribution of power – its value is ultimately limited because of the direct connection drawn (even when the state is conceived as 'relatively autonomous') between political and economic life. By reducing political power to economic and class power – and by calling for 'the end of politics' – Marxism itself tended to marginalize or exclude certain types of issue from consideration in public discourse and from politics itself. This is true of all those issues (to be discussed further in later chapters) which cannot in the last analysis be reduced to class-related matters. Classic examples of this are the domination of women by men, of certain racial and ethnic groups by others, of some religions by other faiths, and of nature by industry and certain forms of consumption and energy usage (which raises ecological questions). Other central concerns include the power of public administrators or bureaucrats over their 'clients' and the role of 'authoritative resources' (the capacity to coordinate and control the activities of human beings) which build up in most social organizations.

However, it is not simply the marginalization of significant problems that is at stake; for the very meaning of politics and the grounds for legitimate political participation are at issue. The pluralist Marxist position makes a number of telling points, including that, if not all differences of interest can be reduced to class, and if differences of opinion about the allocation of resources are for all practical purposes inevitable, it is essential to create the institutional space for the generation of, and debate about, alternative political strategies and programmes. In order to prevent those who hold power – let us say at the pinnacle of the pyramid of Communes – from transforming themselves into an immovable political leadership, there must always be the possibility of removing this leadership, with its particular policies, from office. Politics involves discussion and negotiation about public policy – discussion and negotiation which cannot take place according to wholly 'objective criteria', for what might constitute such criteria and how they could be applied are matters of intense dispute. (Even the philosophy of science is well known for continuous controversy about what criteria are suitable for the resolution of disputes among competing theoretical positions.) Additionally, if differences of interest often underpin differences of political belief, a series of institutional procedures and mechanisms for debating and taking decisions about public

In sum: model IV

Direct Democracy and the End of Politics

Principle(s) of justification

The 'free development of all' can only be achieved with the 'free development of each'. Freedom requires the end of exploitation and ultimately complete political and economic equality; only equality can secure the conditions for the realization of the potentiality of all human beings so that 'each can give' according to his or her ability and 'receive what they need'

Key features

Socialism	Communism
Public affairs to be regulated by Commune(s) or council(s) organized in a pyramid structure	'Government' and 'politics' in all forms give way to self-regulation
Government personnel, law officers, administrators subject to frequent elections, mandates from their community and recall	All public affairs governed collectively
	Consensus as decision principle on all public questions
Public officers to be paid no more than workers' wages	Distribution of remaining administrative tasks by rotation or election
People's militia to sustain the new political order subject to community control	Replacement of all armed and coercive forces by self-monitoring

General conditions

Unity of working classes	All remnants of classes disappear
Defeat of bourgeoisie	Abolition of scarcity and private possession of the means of production
End of all class privileges	Elimination of markets, exchange and money
Substantial development of the forces of production so that all basic needs are met and people have sufficient time to pursue non-work activities	End of social division of labour
Progressive integration of state and society	

affairs is essential (see ch. 9). Marx defended, of course, the role of elections to choose among those who would represent local views and interests, delegates who were mandated to articulate particular positions and were subject to recall if they failed in this respect. He was aware of the practical importance of being able to remove delegates from office. But such a position is by no means sufficient.

The fundamental problem with Marx's view of the 'end of politics' is that it cannot accept a description of any serious political difference as 'genuine' or 'warranted'; that is, as an opinion which an individual or group has a right to

hold and negotiate about as an equal member of a polity (Polan, 1984, p. 77).[10]
Marx's conception of the end of politics in fact radically delegitimizes politics
within the body of the citizenry. After the revolution, there is a marked danger
that there can only be one genuine form of 'politics'; for there are no longer any
justified grounds for fundamental disagreement. The end of class means the end
of any legitimate basis for dispute: only classes have irreconcilable interests. It is
hard to resist the view that implicit in this position is a propensity to an
authoritarian form of politics. There is no longer a place for systematically
encouraging and tolerating disagreement and debate about public matters.
There is no longer a site for the institutional promotion, through the formation
of groups or parties, of opposing positions. There is no longer scope for the
mobilization of competing political views.

Without an institutional realm of public discourse, and procedures to protect
its autonomy and independence, the Commune structure would be granted
almost limitless power. In such circumstances there can be no guarantees that
those who are elected into the highest office will have their actions scrutinized
and their behaviour checked. One need not accept that individuals are simply
self-seeking to be reminded of telling points in Locke's critique of Hobbes's view
of the state, or J. S. Mill's defence of liberty against the threat of an overgrown
government. It appears, thus, that Marx underestimated the significance of the
liberal and liberal democratic preoccupation with how to secure freedom of
criticism and action, i.e. choice and diversity, in the face of centralized state
power, although this is by no means to say that the traditional liberal
formulations of the problem and its solution are fully satisfactory (cf. Arendt,
1963). It will be argued later that realms of social life where matters of general
interest can be discussed, where differences of opinion can be settled by
sustained argument and/or by clear-cut procedures for the resolution of
differences, are an essential institutional feature of public life (see Habermas,
1962), but that the classical democrats, republicans, liberals and Marxists all
failed to grasp fully their preconditions (see chs 9 and 10).

Marx did not produce an adequate political theory of socialism and
communism and, above all, an adequate theory of their institutional structures.
If political institutions are reduced to one undifferentiated type, to a complex of
organizations that are not clearly separated, power can congeal in a hierarchical
form. Marx tended to assume that the new political apparatus would be
accessible to all, fully transparent and open to change in the future. As one critic
aptly put it,

> It is ... a gigantic gamble; the gamble that it will be possible to set about
> constructing the state 'in the best of all possible worlds'. The odds against the
> gamble are astronomic. It does not simply demand the absence of the peculiarly
> unhelpful conditions of post 1917 Russia [economic underdevelopment,
> isolation of the Revolution from other socialist movements, pressures of
> encirclement by hostile powers, lack of resources as a result of war, civil war,
> etc.] – although those conditions themselves have for a long time conspired to

[10] Polan's excellent discussion of Lenin's account of the 'end of politics' has informed my
own assessment of Marx's original statement of this theme. (See Polan, 1984, esp. pp. 77–9,
125–30, 176.)

suggest the essential innocence of the model. It also demands a situation devoid of all political conflicts, of all economic problems, of all social contradictions, of all inadequate, selfish or simply human emotions and motivations, of all singularity, of all negativity. It demands, in short ... an absence of politics. (Polan, 1984, pp. 129–30)

The history of Marxism itself – marked by deep conflicts about how to define appropriate political goals and about how to develop political strategy in historical conditions often quite different from those envisaged by Marx – testifies against the desirability of this gamble (see ch. 8 for an extension of these arguments). But this by no means suggests that other gambles, partly inspired by Marx and appropriately defined, are not worthwhile – far from it.

PART TWO

VARIANTS FROM THE TWENTIETH CENTURY

5 Competitive Elitism and the Technocratic Vision

An optimistic and progressive view of human history informed the thought of John Stuart Mill, Karl Marx and many other nineteenth-century liberals and radicals. Guided by science, reason and philosophy, human beings could create a life marked by the 'highest and harmonious' expansion of their capacities and cooperative forms of self-regulation, although, of course, how the latter was interpreted was subject to the deepest dispute. By contrast, many of those who examined the prospects of democracy in the late nineteenth and early twentieth centuries had a much more sombre view of the future, a view shaped by sensitivity not only to some of the negative features of living in a technically developed civilization, but also to the unpredictable consequences of even the best intentioned political action.

Max Weber (1864–1920) and Joseph Schumpeter (1883–1950), upon whose work this chapter focuses, shared a conception of political life in which there was little scope for democratic participation and individual or collective development, and where whatever scope existed was subject to the threat of constant erosion by powerful social forces. Both thinkers believed that a high price was unavoidably attached to living in a modern, industrial society. Their work tended to affirm a very restrictive concept of democracy, envisaging democracy, at best, as a means of choosing decision-makers and curbing their excesses. Such a notion has much in common with aspects of the theory of protective democracy (see ch. 3), but it was elaborated in a quite distinct way.

It was in Max Weber's thought, above all, that a new model of democracy, which I shall generally refer to as 'competitive elitism', received its most profound expression. Weber wrote relatively little about this model directly, but much of his work, about the nature and structure of modern society, bears on the possibility of democracy. Weber has been called a 'liberal in despair' (Mommsen, 1974, pp. 95ff). He was preoccupied with the conditions of individual liberty in an age in which, as he saw it, many social, economic and political developments were undermining the essence of a liberal political culture: freedom of choice and freedom to pursue different courses of action. He came close to accepting that even the tenets of liberalism could no longer be upheld in the modern age. While he was firmly committed to the ideals of individuality and social difference, he feared for their survival in an epoch of ever larger organizations, whether they were companies, trade unions, mass parties or nation-states. He was particularly concerned about the fate of liberal values in his native Germany.

Unlike many liberal political theorists before him, who tended to argue from considerations of the most desirable form of political organization to characterizations of actual political organizations, Weber, like Marx, tended to argue along reverse lines: from descriptive–explanatory accounts of actual phenomena to assessments of the feasibility of various competing political options (see Weber's 'Politics as a vocation'). Unlike Marx, however, Weber believed that such 'feasibility' studies were value-free in the sense that they did not and could not specify what people should do. But it is quite apparent from his work that the 'is' and the 'ought' intermingle in more complex ways than he suggested. He did not think that science in any form, whether it be physics or the new discipline of sociology to which he was strongly committed, could answer the question: 'What shall we do and how shall we live?' (Weber, 'Science as a vocation', p. 143). Yet, he seems clearly to have made, like others before him, 'apparent historical necessities into positive theoretical virtues' (Krouse, 1983, pp. 76–7). In so doing, he effected a fundamental transformation in democratic theory. His characterization of the processes of modernity led him to a very particular conception of the proper form of politics and democracy.

Weber sought to rearticulate the liberal dilemma of finding a balance between might and right, power and law, expert government and popular sovereignty. He thought the problems posed by the pursuit of this goal were inescapable aspects of modern life, and could only be understood adequately in the light of dominant social tendencies, including those initiated by liberalism itself and its main alternative, Marxism (see Beetham, 1985). Weber's reflections on these problems suggest fundamental revisions to liberal doctrines: revisions that were to have a major influence on the development of political and social theory in the Anglo-American world, especially in the years following World War II. They also constitute one of the most coherent and compelling challenges to Marxism. What makes the challenge so significant, though by no means right in all respects, is its engagement with and assessment of the social and political circumstances in which liberal and Marxist values must survive. It is ultimately a distinctive meshing of sociology, politics and philosophy which gives Weber's work its force, a meshing which, formally at least, he would have strongly disapproved of.

Classes, power and conflict

What sense can be made of liberty, Weber asked, in a world increasingly dominated by the rivalry between capitalism and socialism, and where there is, almost irrespective of the type of political regime, a burgeoning of large-scale organizations which impose limited roles upon individuals? Weber accepted a great deal of what Marx had to say about the nature of capitalism, although he decisively rejected any attempt to argue that this entailed endorsing Marx's political ideas. If capitalism was in some respects a problematic socioeconomic system when judged by concerns about equality and liberty, socialism (in its social democratic or Bolshevik guise) had, according to Weber, even less to recommend it. In order to understand his overall position, it is useful to highlight some important differences between his views and those of Marx.

First, Weber accepted that intense class struggles have occurred in various phases of history and that the relationship between capital and wage-labour is of considerable importance in explaining many of the features of industrial capitalism. He agreed that class is first and foremost an 'objective' feature of economic relations, founded upon property relations, and that the emergence of modern capitalism involved the formation of a mass of propertyless wage-workers, who have to sell their labour to owners of capital in order to sustain a livelihood. He did not, however, accept the theory of surplus value, drawing instead mainly upon 'marginalist' economics, thus conceptualizing class in non-exploitative terms. According to Weber, classes consist of aggregates of individuals who share similar sets of 'life chances' in labour and commodity markets. Classes are not groups, although group action may be taken on the basis of common class interests; that is, on the basis of economic interests formed by a shared market position.

Weber did not believe in the likelihood, or the desirability, of proletarian revolution, and presented a more diversified view of conflicts in capitalist societies. He strongly disputed the notion that the analysis of conflict could be reduced to the analysis of classes. For him, classes constitute only one aspect of the distribution of and struggle for power. What he called 'status groups',[1] political parties and nation-states are at least as significant, if not more so. The fervour created by sentiments of group solidarity, ethnic community and nationalism is an absolutely vital part of the creation and mobilization of power and conflict in the modern age (see Weber's 'Class, status and party' and 'Status groups and classes', in Giddens and Held, 1982, pp. 60ff). While class and class conflict are important, they are not the main 'motor' of historical development.

Second, Weber saw industrial capitalism as a distinctively Western phenomenon in its origins, incorporating distinctive values and modes of activity that are divergent from those generated by other civilizations (Weber, *The Protestant Ethic and the Spirit of Capitalism*, and pp. 57–8 of this volume). The most important feature of this 'Western-ness' is what he referred to as the 'rationalized' character of capitalist production, something which stretches well beyond economic enterprise itself. Rationalization is a phenomenon which permeates each of the major institutions of capitalist society. 'Rationalization' is not an unambiguously formulated concept in Weber's writings. But its core meaning refers to the extension of calculative attitudes of a technical character to more and more spheres of activity, epitomized by scientific procedures and given substantive expression in the increasing role that expertise, science and technology play in modern life (Giddens, 1972, pp. 44ff).

The rationalization of the modern world has profound consequences, including the erosion of the credibility of belief systems which seek to provide a clear-cut interpretation of the 'meaning of life'. In all areas of the world where rationalization is advanced, religious beliefs give way, as do political and philosophical doctrines which emphasize a fixed arrangement of natural or human affairs, to a more fluid view of things. The idea of the earth as an

---

[1] Status groups are founded upon relations of consumption and take the form of 'styles of life' that separate one group from another. Weber maintained that status groups (in the shape of feudal estates, or castes in India) have been prominent elements in all pre-capitalist societies. While tending to be overshadowed by class relations in modern capitalism, status group affiliations by no means lose their significance.

'enchanted garden' – as a place where 'mysterious incalculable forces come into play' – is irreversibly undermined by an instrumental ethos, a firm view that one can 'master life by calculation' (Weber, 'Science', p. 139). Weber's attitude to this process was ambivalent. On the one hand, the world is progressively 'intellectualized', freeing people from the burden of theological and metaphysical illusions. On the other hand, rationalization also signals a loss which Weber termed 'disenchantment' ('Science', pp. 138ff). There are no longer any 'worldviews' that can legitimately command collective agreement; the traditional bases for resolving the 'struggle' between the huge array of possible attitudes to life have been fundamentally weakened. Today, Weber argued, there is no ultimate justification beyond individual choice as to 'which of the warring gods we should serve' ('Science', pp. 152–3). It is the responsibility of each individual to judge and decide which are the most appropriate values to uphold. This is, he memorably wrote, 'the fate of an epoch which has eaten of the tree of knowledge'.

While from one point of view Weber's position represented 'the apotheosis of individualism', from another it suggested a radical departure from the classic liberal tradition which, as we have seen, initially conceived the basis of individualism in natural law and natural rights (see ch. 3 and Beetham, 1985, pp. 4ff). For in an age of competing values, where none can be regarded as objectively valid, the idea that political life is founded upon a given or agreed morality cannot be maintained. In these circumstances, the liberal polity can only be defended, Weber held, on *procedural* grounds – grounds which emphasize its importance as a mechanism for promoting the 'competition of values' and 'freedom of choice' in a rationalized world (see Roth and Schluchter, 1979). Democracy is a vital component of the institutional arrangements necessary for the achievement of this end, i.e. for the maintenance of a liberal political culture.

Third, Weber thought rationalization was inevitably accompanied by the spread of bureaucracy. When Marx and Engels wrote about 'bureaucracy', they had in mind the civil service, the bureaucratic apparatus of the state. But Weber applied the concept much more broadly, as characterizing all forms of large-scale organization: the state, to be sure, but also industrial enterprises, unions, political parties, universities and hospitals. He agreed with Marx that bureaucracy is essentially undemocratic because bureaucrats are not accountable to the mass of the population affected by their decisions. However, he insisted that (1) the problem of bureaucratic domination is much more pervasive than Marx imagined, and (2) there is no way of transcending bureaucratic domination save by limiting the spread of bureaucracy itself. In particular, there can be no question of 'transcending the state'. The achievement of a socialist society, in Weber's view, would always have quite the contrary consequence to that predicted by socialist thinkers, for it would involve the extension of bureaucratic domination. By domination Weber meant 'a structure of superordination and subordination sustained by a variety of motives and means of enforcement', which can take many forms, the most potent of which is bureaucratic administration (Weber, *Economy and Society*, vol. I, p. xc; vol. II, pp. 941ff). Although he did not consider oppressive dominance by bureaucracy inescapable, modern politics must, he thought, find strategies for containing and limiting its development. He was absolutely convinced of one thing: if socialism or communism mean the direct and equal regulation of economic, social and political affairs by all citizens, then they are excessively naive and dangerously misleading doctrines.

Bureaucracy, parliaments and nation-states

The notion that the state, and its bureaucratic organization in particular, constitute 'parasitic' entities upon society is a position Marx and many other Marxists (especially Lenin) have espoused. But centralized administration may be inescapable. Weber came to this view partly through an appraisal of the impractical nature of direct democracy

> where the group grows beyond a certain size or where the administrative function becomes too difficult to be satisfactorily taken care of by anyone whom rotation, the lot, or election may happen to designate. The conditions of administration of mass structures are radically different from those obtaining in small associations resting upon neighborly or personal relationships... The growing complexity of the administrative task and the sheer expansion of their scope increasingly result in the technical superiority of those who have had training and experience, and will thus inevitably favor the continuity of at least some of the functionaries. Hence, there always exists the probability of the rise of a special, perennial structure for administrative purposes, which of necessity means for the exercise of rule. (*Economy and Society*, vol. II, pp. 951–2)

Weber did not think direct democracy[2] was impossible in all circumstances; rather, he believed it could only function in organizations which fulfil the following conditions:

> 1) the organization must be local or otherwise limited in the number of members; 2) the social positions of the members must not greatly differ from each other; 3) the administrative functions must be relatively simple and stable; 4) ... there must be a certain minimum development of training in objectively determining ways and means. (*Economy and Society*, vol. II, p. 949)

Direct democracy requires relative equality of all participants, a key condition of which is minimal economic and social differentiation. Accordingly, examples of such forms of 'government' can be found among the aristocracies in late medieval Italian city-republics, among certain townships in the United States and among highly selected occupational groupings, for instance, university teachers. However, the size, complexity and sheer diversity of modern societies make direct democracy simply inappropriate as a general model of political regulation and control.

Weber appreciated that the aim of direct democracy was the reduction of domination to its lowest possible extent, but in a heterogeneous society direct

---

[2] By 'direct democracy' Weber meant a system of decision-making about 'public affairs' in which citizens are directly involved. (In the terms of this volume, direct democracy, thus understood, would embrace models I, IIa, IIb, IV and elements of VIII.)

democracy would lead to ineffective administration, unwanted inefficiency, political instability and, ultimately, a radical increase in the probability (as Plato and other critics had remarked about classical democracy) of oppressive minority rule. The latter was likely precisely because of the coordination vacuum created by the absence of a technically effective administration. In addition, direct democracy has another notable characteristic that makes it singularly unsuitable to modern politics: its mode of political representation hinders the possibility of political deliberation, negotiation and compromise. This is particularly apparent where direct democracy is structured by a hierarchy of mandated or 'instructed' delegates (see model IV in ch. 4, p. 120 above). Direct mandates undermine the scope that representatives must have if they are to resolve conflict, balance clashing interests and develop policies which are flexible enough to meet shifting circumstances (see *Economy and Society*, vol. I, pp. 289–90, 292–3; vol. II, pp. 948–52, 983–7). Direct democracy has no suitable mechanism for mediating the struggles of factions.

It is misleading to conflate problems concerning the nature of administration with problems concerning the control of the state apparatus (see Albrow, 1970, pp. 37–49). In Weber's opinion, Marx, Engels and Lenin confused these matters by running together the question of the class nature of the state with that of whether a centralized bureaucratic administration is a necessary feature of political and social organization. Lenin's commitment to 'smashing' the state is perhaps the clearest example of the failure to see these as two distinct issues. Furthermore, Weber resisted all suggestions that modern state organization could be explained directly in terms of the activities of classes. In order to understand his position, it is useful to grasp his conception of the state.

Weber developed one of the most significant definitions of the modern state, placing emphasis upon two distinctive elements of its history: territoriality and violence. The modern state, unlike its predecessors, which were troubled by constantly warring factions, has the capability to monopolize the legitimate use of violence within a given territory; it is a nation-state in embattled relations with other nation-states rather than with armed segments of its own population. 'Of course,' Weber emphasized, 'force is certainly not the normal or only means of the state – nobody says that – but force is a means specific to the state . . . the state is a relation of men dominating men [and generally, one should add, of men dominating women], a relation supported by means of legitimate (i.e. considered to be legitimate) violence' ('Politics', p. 78). The state maintains compliance or order within a given territory; in individual capitalist societies this involves, crucially, the defence of the order of property and the enhancement of domestic economic interests overseas, although by no means all the problems of order can be reduced to these. The state's web of agencies and institutions finds its ultimate sanction in the claim to the monopoly of coercion, and a political order is only, in the last instance, vulnerable to crises when this monopoly erodes.

However, there is a third key term in Weber's definition of the state: legitimacy. The state is based on a monopoly of physical coercion which is legitimized (that is, sustained) by a belief in the justifiability and/or legality of this monopoly. Today, Weber argued, people no longer comply with the authority claimed by the powers that be merely on the grounds, as was once common, of habit and tradition or the charisma and personal appeal of individual leaders. Rather, there is general obedience by 'virtue of "legality", by virtue of the belief in the validity of legal statute and functional "competence" based on rationally created *rules*' ('Politics', p. 79). The legitimacy of the modern state is founded predominantly on 'legal authority', i.e. commitment to a 'code of legal regulations'. Thus, the activities of the modern state are bounded by the rule of law, a complex process of constraint. On the one hand, the rule of law implies that the state's agents must conduct their affairs in accordance with the principles of proper legislative procedure while, on the other hand, it implies that the people as 'citizens' should respect the state's authority by virtue of the maintenance of these principles. Officials of the modern state can claim obedience, not because of any particular appeal they might possess, although this might sometimes be very significant indeed, but because of the authority they hold temporarily as a result of their *office*, which people endorse or at least generally accept.

Foremost among the state's institutions are the administrative apparatuses: a vast network of organizations run by appointed officials. Although such organizations have been essential to states at many times and places in history, 'only the Occident', on Weber's account, 'knows the state in its modern scale, with a professional administration, specialized officialdom, and law based on the concept of citizenship'. These institutions had beginnings in antiquity and the Orient, but there they were never able to develop systematically (*General Economic History*, p. 232).

The modern state is not, Weber argued, an effect of capitalism; it preceded and helped promote capitalist development (*Economy and Society*, vol. II, pp. 1381ff). Capitalism, however, provided an enormous impetus in public as well as private life to the expansion of rational administration, that is, the type of bureaucracy founded on legal authority. In the contemporary world, Weber believed, public and private administration were becoming more and more bureaucratized (*Economy and Society*, vol. II, p. 1465). That is to say, there is a growth of the following organizational structures: office hierarchy ordered in a pyramid of authority; the existence of impersonal, written rules of procedure; strict limits on the means of compulsion at the disposal of each official; the appointment of officials on the basis of their specialist training and qualifications (*not* on the basis of patronage); clearly demarcated specialized tasks demanding full-time employees; and, significantly, the separation of officials from 'ownership of the means of administration' (*Economy and Society*, vol. I, pp. 220–1).

The last point needs some expansion. Weber generalized the Marxist idea of 'the expropriation of the worker from control of the means of production' beyond the sphere of production itself, relating it to the general expansion of bureaucracy in the modern world. The 'expropriation of the worker', he argued, is characteristic of all bureaucratic organizations and is a process that is irreversible. The 'alienation' of the workers should be understood as an ineluctable element of the centralization of administration. Individuals at the lower level of bureaucratic organizations inevitably lose control of the work they do, which is determined by those in higher echelons. Bureaucracies, in addition, tend to become impersonal forces; their rules and procedures take on a life of their own as they contain and restrict the activities of all who are subject to them, officials and clients alike. Moreover, bureaucratic decision-making is 'rigid' and 'inflexible', frequently (and necessarily) neglecting the particular circumstances of individuals. In sum, bureaucracy, according to Weber, forms a 'steel-hard cage' in which the vast majority of the population are destined to live out a large part of their lives. This is the price, referred to earlier, that has to be paid for the benefits of living in an economically and technically developed world.

There is no plausible way for the modern citizen to create 'non-bureaucratic' administration. For under virtually every imaginable circumstance, bureaucracy is 'completely indispensable' (*Economy and Society*, vol. I, p. 223). The choice is only 'between bureaucracy and dilettantism in the field of administration'. Weber explained the spread of bureaucracy in the following terms:

> The decisive reason for the advance of bureaucratic organization has always been its purely *technical* superiority over any other form of organization. The fully developed bureaucratic apparatus compares with the non-mechanical modes of production. Precision, speed, unambiguity, knowledge of the files, continuity, discretion, unity, strict subordination, reduction of friction and of material and personal costs – these are raised to the optimum point in the strictly bureaucratic administration. (*Economy and Society*, vol. II, p. 973)

As economic and political life become more complex and differentiated, bureaucratic administration becomes more critical.

Weber linked the indispensability of bureaucracy to the problems of coordination created by modern economic systems and by mass citizenship. A predictable political and legal environment is essential to the development of economic enterprises; without it, they cannot successfully manage their affairs and their relations with consumers. Organizational effectiveness and stability, which only bureaucracy can guarantee in the long term, was (and is) necessary to the expansion of commerce and industry (see *Economy and Society*, vol. II, pp. 969–80; Beetham, 1985, ch. 3). Mass citizenship itself led to increased demands upon the state of both a quantitative and qualitative kind. Not only were the newly enfranchised asking more of the state in areas such as education and health, but they were also asking for uniformity of treatment between persons with similar categories of need: the 'discharge of business according to *calculable rules*' without 'regard for particular persons' (*Economy and Society*, vol. II, p. 975).[3] Standardization and routinization of administrative tasks were crucial to the achievement of this end. Additionally, the increasing demands made upon the state were of an international as well as national type; and the more demands there are, the more an expert administration is necessary for their careful interpretation and management:

---

[3] Bureaucracy develops 'the more perfectly', Weber wrote, 'the more it is "dehumanized", the more completely it succeeds in eliminating from official business love, hatred, and all purely personal, irrational, and emotional elements which escape calculation' (*Economy and Society*, vol. II, p. 975).

> It is obvious that technically the large modern state is absolutely dependent upon a bureaucratic basis. The larger the state, and the more it is a great power, the more unconditionally is this the case . . . the greater the zones of friction with the outside and the more urgent the needs for administrative unity at home become, the more this character is inevitably and gradually giving way formally to the bureaucratic structure. (*Economy and Society*, vol. II, p. 971)

While rule by officials is not inevitable, considerable power accrues to bureaucrats through their expertise, information and access to secrets. This power can become, Weber thought, overwhelming. Politicians and political actors of all kinds can find themselves dependent on the bureaucracy. A central question for (if not preoccupation of) Weber was how bureaucratic power could be checked. He was convinced that, in the absence of checks, public organization would fall prey to overzealous officials or powerful private interests (among others, organized capitalists and major landholders) who would not have the national interest as their prime concern. Moreover, in times of national emergency, there would be ineffective leadership: bureaucrats, unlike politicians more generally, cannot take a decisive stand. They do not have the training – and bureaucracies are not structurally designed – for the consideration of political, alongside technical or economic, criteria. However, Weber's solution to the problem of unlimited bureaucratization was not one that depended merely on the capacity of individual politicians for innovation. Writing about Germany, he advocated a strong parliament which would create a competitive training ground for strong leadership and serve as a balance to public and private bureaucracy (see Mommsen, 1974, ch. 5).

Weber's political position can be clarified further by examining his critique of socialism. He believed that the abolition of private capitalism 'would simply mean that . . . the *top management* of the nationalized or socialized enterprises would become bureaucratic' (*Economy and Society*, vol. II, p. 1402). Reliance upon those who control resources would be enhanced, for the abolition of the market would be the abolition of a key countervailing power to the state. The market generates change and social mobility: it is the very source of capitalist dynamism.

> State bureaucracy would rule alone if private capitalism were eliminated. The private and public bureaucracies, which now work next to, and potentially against, each other and hence check one another to a degree, would be merged into a single hierarchy. This would be similar to the situation in ancient Egypt, but it would occur in a much more rational – and hence unbreakable – form. (*Economy and Society*, vol. I, p. 143)

While Weber argued that 'progress' towards the bureaucratic state is given an enormous impetus by capitalist development, he believed that this very development itself, coupled with parliamentary government and the party system, provided the best obstacle to the usurpation of state power by officials. Far from ending domination, socialism would inevitably recast it in a tight bureaucratic form, ultimately suppressing all expression of legitimately conflicting interests in the name of a fictitious solidarity – the bureaucratic state alone would rule. Elements of Weber's critique were unquestionably prophetic (see below, and chs 7 and 8).

Competitive elitist democracy

In advocating a capitalist economy, along with parliamentary government and a competitive party system, Weber was on ground familiar to many nineteenth- and twentieth-century liberals. But his defence of this institutional nexus rested on novel arguments. Before examining some of the limitations of his ideas, it is important to say something more about his model of democracy, a model he thought both 'unavoidable' and desirable.

Weber gave several reasons why parliamentary government is vital. First, parliament maintains a degree of openness in government. As a forum for debating public policy, it secures an opportunity for the expression of competing ideas and interests. Second, the structure of parliamentary discussion, the nature of debate, and the requirement that to be 'persuasive' a high standard of oratory must be reached make parliament an important testing ground for aspiring leaders; leaders must be capable of mobilizing opinion and of offering a plausible political programme. Third, parliament provides the space for negotiation about entrenched positions. Political representatives make decisions by criteria which are distinct from the logic of bureaucratic processes and market operations. They can make policy alternatives visible to individuals or groups with conflicting interests, thereby creating a possible opportunity for compromise. They are able consciously to formulate objectives which respond to shifting pressures and which are in accordance with strategies for electoral as well as national success. As such, parliament is an essential mechanism for the preservation of the competition of values.

But the role of parliament should not be romanticized. According to Weber, the idea of parliament as a centre of argument, deliberation and debate – the place where authoritative political programmes are formulated – is to a large extent a misrepresentation of the nature of modern parliamentary affairs ('Politics', p. 102). If parliaments were at one time 'centres of reason', this could no longer be confidently asserted. In contrast with the views of people like J. S. Mill, Weber argued that the extension of the franchise and the development of party politics undermined the classic liberal conception of parliament as a place where national policy is settled by rational reflection, guided only by the public or general interest. While formally parliament is the only legitimate body where law and national policy can be established, in practice, party politics is uppermost (see Mommsen, 1974, pp. 89–90). The mass franchise fundamentally alters the dynamics of political life, placing the *party* at the centre of political business.

It is only by grasping the nature of modern political parties that one can fully understand the meaning of the extension of the franchise in the nineteenth and twentieth centuries. Far from ensuring 'the sovereignty of the people' – an idea which Weber regarded as quite simplistic – the extension of the franchise has been mainly associated with the emergence of a new type of career politician. Why has this been the case? With the spread of the suffrage it became necessary 'to call into being a tremendous apparatus of political associations'. These associations or parties were dedicated to the organization of representation. In all communities larger than small rural districts, political organization is, Weber contended, 'necessarily managed by men interested in the management of politics . . . It is unimaginable how in large associations elections could function at all without this managerial pattern. In practice this means the division of the citizens with a right to vote into politically active and politically passive elements' ('Politics', p. 99).

The extension of the franchise ineluctably means the spread of political associations to organize the electorate, whose interests in most circumstances (the exceptions being national emergencies and wars) are fragmented and divided. A plurality of social forces vie for influence over public affairs. In order to attain influence, such forces need to mobilize resources, collect the financial wherewithal, recruit followers and attempt to win people to their cause(s). But in organizing they become dependent on those who continually work in the new political apparatuses. And these apparatuses become, in seeking to be effective, bureaucratic. Parties may aim to realize a programme of 'ideal' political principles, but unless their activities are based on systematic strategies for achieving electoral success they will be doomed to insignificance. Accordingly, parties become transformed, above all else, into means for fighting and winning elections. The development of competing parties irreversibly changes the nature of parliamentary politics. Party machines sweep aside traditional affiliations and establish themselves as centres of loyalty, displacing others as the key basis of national politics. Pressure builds up even on elected representatives to uphold the party line; representatives become 'normally nothing better than well disciplined "Yes" men' ('Politics', p. 106). The key steps in Weber's argument are summarized in figure 5.1.

Although Weber firmly believed that the advance of bureaucratization more or less meant a progressive decline in the autonomy of those in the lower echelons of political organizations, he was critical of the writings of Michels, whose own formulation of this tendency, 'the iron law of oligarchy', owed much to him (Michels, *Political Parties*; see Roth, 1978, pp. lxxi, xcii). Michels stated the 'iron law' in the following terms: 'It is organization which gives birth to the dominion of the elected over the electors, of the mandatories over the mandators, of the delegates over the delegators. Who says organization, says oligarchy' (*Political Parties*, p. 365). For Weber this statement represented a major oversimplification; not only was bureaucratization a highly complex process, but it was also compatible with both a degree of political democratization and the emergence of capable leaders.

Modern political parties, in fact, reinforce the importance of leadership. Leadership has to be understood as a necessary concomitant both of large-scale organizations which require firm political direction and of the essential passivity of the mass of the electorate. This passivity is partly the product of the modern bureaucratic world. But although Weber's analysis on the face of it offered a sound explanation of why the mass of people were passive (they have few meaningful opportunities to participate in institutional life, i.e. they do not have enough power to make such participation worth while), Weber himself tended to include in his explanation a low estimation of the bulk of the electorate. In his famous essay, 'Politics as a vocation', he referred to the 'emotionality' of the masses, which was not a proper basis for understanding or judging public

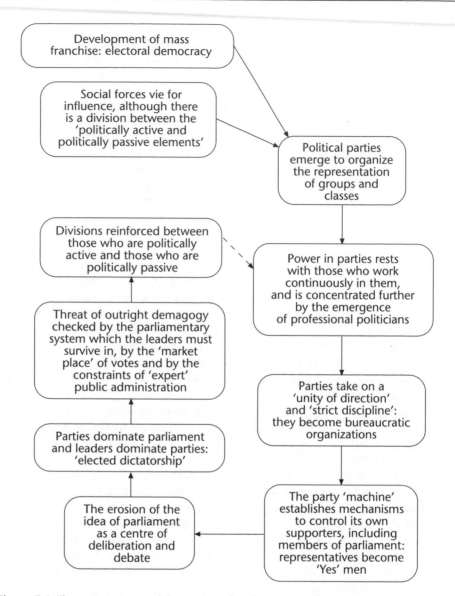

Figure 5.1 The party system and the erosion of parliamentary influence

affairs. He appears to have thought of the electorate as unable generally to discriminate among policies and as capable only of making some kind of choice among possible leaders. Hence, he portrays democracy as a testing ground for potential leaders. Democracy is like the 'market place', an institutional mechanism to weed out the weakest and establish those who are most competent in the competitive struggle for votes and power. Under current circumstances, there is only the choice, he wrote, 'between leadership democracy with a [party] "machine" and leaderless democracy, namely, the rule of professional politicians without a calling' ('Politics', p. 113).

Weber referred to modern representative democracy as 'plebiscitary leadership democracy': 'plebiscitary' because routine elections in Western countries (Britain, Germany, the United States) were progressively becoming indistinguishable from occasional direct votes of confidence (or lack of confidence) in government; 'leadership' because what was at stake in such elections was the popularity and credibility of particular groups of leaders, i.e. political elites. Weber went so far as to describe contemporary democracy as 'Caesarist'. Far from democracy being the basis for the potential development of all citizens, democracy is best understood as a key mechanism to ensure effective political and national leadership. In serving a selection function, and in legitimating the selected (via elections), democracy is indispensable. As one commentator aptly put it, 'Weber was an advocate of democracy on the grounds that, under the social and political conditions of a modern bureaucratic society, it offered a maximum of dynamism and leadership' (Mommsen, 1974, p. 87). And as another noted, 'Weber's enthusiasm for the representative system owed more to his conviction that national greatness depended on finding able leaders than on any concern for democratic values' (Albrow, 1970, p. 48). Weber took the establishment of competent leadership, able and willing to maintain power and prestige, as his prime concern.

The tension between might and right, power and law, was to a large extent resolved by Weber in favour of might and power. Although he was firmly committed to the 'rule of law', what was important about the democratic process was that it established a form of 'elected dictatorship'. Weber clearly affirmed this trend. He affirmed it by arguing that the social conditions which generated it were irreversible, and by setting out the benefits of such a system. He was well aware of the loss of a 'heroic' age of liberal individualism, an age which promised to unleash individual drives and capacities. But under contemporary circumstances, he believed, the costs simply had to be borne. It was no longer possible for freedom of action and initiative to be preserved for all individuals equally. Rather, the central issue facing liberals was how to preserve scope for initiative at the 'pinnacles of power'.

Weber was concerned to understand, and to find ways of ensuring, an effective balance between political authority, skilled leadership, efficient administration and a degree of political accountability. He by no means dismissed, it should be emphasized, the importance of the electorate being able to dispense with incompetent leaders. But this was virtually the only role he envisaged for the electors. A balance had to be found between political authority and accountability *without* surrendering too much power to the *demos*. In so arguing, Weber stood squarely in the classic liberal democratic tradition which has consistently sought to defend *and* limit the political rights of citizens. However, there is an important sense in which he altered it. For he articulated a new, highly restrictive model of democracy. It is restrictive because he envisaged democracy as little more than providing a way of establishing qualified political leaders. It is restrictive because the role of the electorate and possible avenues of extending political participation are treated highly sceptically. It is restrictive because, although Weber thought that the electoral system provided some semblance of protection for the electorate, he maintained that this protection was simply to be measured by the opportunity to dismiss the ineffective from office. In this sense Weber's work stands, as has been rightly stressed, 'more at the starting point than at the conclusion of a series of developments in the theory and practice of liberal democracy in the era of mass politics and bureaucratic organisations; it is much more as a precursor than as an "epigone" that he should be understood' (Beetham, 1985, p. 7).

Weber's writings represent a challenge both to traditional liberal ideas as well as to those who foresee the possibility of creating self-governing societies free of bureaucracy. Although some political theorists, particularly those of a traditional Marxist persuasion, are apt to dismiss rather cursorily his pessimistic appraisals of the modern world, these surely pose problems of major importance. Writing before the era of Stalinism and the emergence of the state socialist societies of Eastern Europe, Weber's work was, as previously noted, quite prophetic. His attempt to reappraise the nature of liberal democracy, in a world of highly complex sets of national and international institutions, echoes closely the views of many who do not believe that a radical reorganization of society is possible.

Liberal democracy at the crossroads

Weber feared that political life in both West and East would be ensnared ever more by a rationalized, bureaucratic system of administration. Against this, he championed the countervailing power of private capital, the competitive party system and strong political leadership, all of which could prevent the domination of politics by state officials. In putting his case in this way, the limitations of his political thought become apparent: some of the key insights and principles of both Marxist and liberal political theory seem to have been set aside. The significance of massive inequalities of political and class power is played down because of the priority of power – i.e. interleadership and interstate – politics. This priority leaves the balance between might and right in the end to the judgement of 'charismatic' political leaders locked into the competition between state and economic bureaucracies, a situation which comes perilously close to accepting that even the central tenets of classic liberalism can no longer be sustained in the contemporary age. It appears that there is only scope for those who 'rise to the top' to flourish as 'free and equal' individuals. This could be judged a 'realistic' assessment of empirical trends, or it might be regarded as making certain social and political developments into inadequately justified theoretical virtues. It is the latter position that I believe to be correct.

Weber's assumption that the development of bureaucracy leads to increased power for those at the highest levels of administration leads him to neglect the ways in which those in subordinate positions may increase their power. In modern bureaucratic systems there appear to be considerable 'openings' for those in 'formally subordinate positions to acquire or regain control over their organizational tasks' (for example, by hindering or blocking the collection of vital information for centralized decision-making) (Giddens, 1979, pp. 147–8). Bureaucracies may enhance the potential for disruption from 'below' and increase the spaces for circumventing hierarchical control. Weber did not adequately characterize internal organizational processes and their significance for developments in other political spheres.[4]

Further, his underestimation of the power of 'subordinates' is linked to another difficulty: an uncritical acceptance of the 'passivity' of the mass of citizens – their apparent lack of knowledge, commitment and involvement in politics. Weber's explanation of this is twofold: there are relatively few people who are both able and interested in politics; and only a competent leadership, coupled with a bureaucratic administration and parliamentary system, can manage the complexity, problems and decisions of modern politics. There are several difficulties with this view which will be explored below and again in later chapters.

First, Weber's position depends in part on a dubious claim about the electorate's capacity to discriminate between alternative groups of leaders and its incapacity to decide on policies on the grounds of merit. On what basis could such a claim be satisfactorily defended? If one takes the view that the electorate is unable to think through issues of political importance, why should one believe in the judgement of the electorate when it comes to choosing political leaders with rival claims to competence and imagination? It seems inconsistent and, indeed, dogmatic to consider the electorate capable of the latter while dismissing the implications of this for a more general (and higher) estimation of its overall talents.

Second, Weber's account of people's separation or estrangement from 'ownership of the means of administration' could be interpreted as entailing a vicious circle of limited or non-participation in politics. The dotted line in figure 5.1 above reveals the extent to which divisions between the politically 'active' and 'passive' may themselves be the result of a lack of significant opportunities to participate in politics, rather than natural (?) 'passivity' or 'emotionality'. The subordination of women has typically been linked to the latter in such a way as to mask and legitimate the social, economic and political conditions which prevent women's active political involvement (see chs 2, 3 and 10). There is plenty of evidence to suggest that for many people politics denotes an activity about which they feel a combination of cynicism, scepticism and mistrust (see Held, 1989, ch. 4). The affairs of government and national politics are not things many claim to understand, nor are they a source of sustained interest. Significantly, those closest to centres of power and privilege (above all, males in the dominant classes) are the ones who indicate the most interest in and are most favourable to political life. However, it may well be that those who express lack of interest in politics do so precisely because they experience 'politics' as remote, because they feel it does not directly touch their lives and/or that they are powerless to affect its course.

---

[4] One can, in addition, search his writings in vain for a satisfactory explanation of the precise character of the relation between the growing bureaucratic centralization of the state and modern capitalism (see Krieger, 1983). In his historical account of patterns of bureaucratization in diverse societies, he did not isolate the degree to which certain bureaucratic processes may be specific to, or influenced by, capitalist development *per se*. He failed to disentangle the impact of cultural, economic and technological forces on the growth of bureaucracy, and to say to what extent these were independent of capitalist development. In the end, the particular connection between the state, bureaucratization and capitalism is left obscure.

It is highly significant that participation in decision-making (of whatever type) is much more extensive the more it is related to issues that directly affect people's lives, and the more those affected can be confident that their input into decision-making will actually count; that is, that it will be weighted equitably with others, and will not simply be side-stepped or ignored by those who wield greater power (see Pateman, 1970; Mansbridge, 1983; Dahl, 1985, 1989; Saward, 2003; Beetham, 2005; cf. ch. 9 below). This finding has particular pertinence to those who have examined critically some of the conditions of political participation: advocates of classical democracy (who highlight, for instance, the necessity to have not only the time for politics, but the resources to be able to afford involvement); protagonists of (protective and developmental) republicanism (who stress that the public interest can easily be corrupted if citizens are excluded, for want of access or opportunity, from the business of government); Marxists (who point to the massive obstacles to equal involvement in political life posed by concentrations of economic power); and critics of systems of male dominance (who show how the sexual division of labour in 'private' and 'public' life obstructs the full participation of the vast majority of women in local and national politics) (see pp. 49–54, 88–91 of this volume; Siltanen and Stanworth, 1984; Pateman, 1985, 1988). It is of the utmost importance, then, to consider whether it is possible to break the vicious circle shown in figure 5.1, and all those other institutional circumstances that create vicious circles of limited or non-participation. In dismissing this possibility, Weber was too quick to reject alternative models of democracy and too ready to accept competition between rival groups of leaders as the only way history could be kept open to human will and the struggle of values.

The complexity and sheer scale of modern life might well make, as Weber claimed, centralized political control and decision-making inevitable. Weber's arguments on these themes are powerful. But it should by no means be taken for granted that the *form* and *limits* of centralized political organization need be as Weber described them. Weber tended to assume an unceasing pattern of bureaucratic development. While it would be unwise to deny all aspects of this view, organizational forms have proved far more varied than Weber's 'logic of bureaucracy' would suggest (see Crozier, 1964; Albrow, 1970; Giddens, 1979). Additionally, there are many different forms of representative democracy based on different types of electoral system which need careful specification and assessment. Weber did not provide an adequate account of the types and forms of possible political organizations, whether at a central or a local level (see ch. 10 below).

None the less, his attempt to analyse the internal workings of public (and private) organizations and his observations about trends in bureaucratization constitute a major contribution to understanding government and democracy. His work provides a counterbalance to the Marxist and, particularly, Leninist emphasis on the intimate connection between state activities, forms of organization and class relations (see Wright, 1978, ch. 4). The argument that private and public administrations are similarly structured – as opposed to causally determined by class power – is important, as is his argument, developing ideas in the liberal tradition, that skilled, predictable administration is a necessary condition for other important objectives: the end of arbitrariness, haphazardness and excessive political patronage in the regulation of public affairs; the availability of publicly known procedures for dealing with routine difficulties and for summoning bodies such as councils or parliaments to manage or resolve severe problems; and the establishment of relatively clear-cut public rules which allow people to investigate the legitimacy or otherwise of decisions and decision-making. Without skilled, predictable administration, public affairs can quickly become, as Weber rightly argued, a quagmire of infighting among factions and wholly ineffective in settling pressing collective issues – rather like aspects of classical democracy, on Plato's account at least. Of course, the form of such administration admits of further discussion.

Weber's writings have had an enormous influence on sociology and political science in the Anglo-American world. They have stimulated a rich variety of developments, two of which deserve attention: the theory of democracy developed by Schumpeter (which directly pursued aspects of Weber's concept of plebiscitarian leadership democracy) and empirical democratic theory or 'pluralism' (which took as a starting point Weberian ideas about the multi-dimensionality of power). Together, these developments represent well the tensions of Weber's political thought, although they elaborate quite different strands of his thinking. Schumpeter's work is discussed immediately below, and pluralism in chapter 6.

The last vestige of democracy?

Schumpeter, Austrian born, but a US citizen later in life, sought to develop an empirically based 'realistic' model of democracy. In opposition to the main streams of political theory from classical times, he sought to free thinking about the nature of public life from what he took to be excessive speculation and arbitrary normative preferences. His primary task was explanatory: to account for how actual democracies work. He wanted to produce a theory that was, in his words, 'much truer to life' than existing models. Although this objective did not mark as radical a departure from tradition as he claimed – Bentham, Marx and Weber, for example, all shared it to a large degree – his work did a great deal to revise accepted notions of democracy. His classic book, *Capitalism, Socialism and Democracy* (first published in 1942), had an extraordinary impact on the development of democratic theory in the aftermath of World War II, especially in the budding disciplines of political science and sociology (although in his own primary discipline – economics – it did not receive a great deal of attention). Subsequently, many social scientists sought to explore and amplify Schumpeter's main hypotheses concerning how political leaders and voters behave and affect one another (see, e.g., Berelson et al., 1954; Dahl, 1956, 1961; Almond and Verba, 1963; Sartori, 1987).

Schumpeter's concern with the empirical should not be accepted uncritically. As with Max Weber, his work has clear normative dimensions. Part of a large project examining the gradual supersession of capitalism by socialism in the

West,[5] Schumpeter's theory of democracy both focused on a highly delimited range of questions and championed a very particular set of tenets about the proper form of 'popular' government. The apparent correspondence between these tenets and the actual structure of the two most prominent postwar liberal democracies (Britain and the United States) might help to explain why Schumpeter and his followers could affirm them as the most 'realistic' view of democratic systems. Additionally, Schumpeter's highly critical account of more participatory schemes of democracy, found in the writings of figures such as Rousseau and Marx, echoed closely the opinions of many Western commentators and politicians at the time who felt 'excessive' participation might produce the mobilization of the *demos* with highly dangerous consequences: among the experiences uppermost in their minds were no doubt the Bolshevik revolution and the mass rallies which signalled the advent of Nazi Germany. Yet, it should be pointed out, Schumpeter's concept of democracy was far from original. Some scholars have claimed that there is a point-by-point correspondence between many of Schumpeter's ideas about democracy, party organization and bureaucracy and those of Weber in *Economy and Society* (Roth, 1978, p. xcii). While this overstates the position, Schumpeter's debt to Max Weber is, as will be seen, considerable. Unquestionably, Schumpeter popularized some of Weber's ideas, but he also developed them in a number of interesting ways.

By democracy, Schumpeter meant a political *method*, that is, an institutional arrangement for arriving at political – legislative and administrative – decisions by vesting in certain individuals the power to decide on all matters as a consequence of their successful pursuit of the people's vote (*Capitalism*, p. 269). Democratic life was the struggle between rival political leaders, arrayed in parties, for the mandate to rule. Far from democracy being a form of life marked by the promise of equality and the best conditions for human development in a rich context of participation, the democratic citizens' lot was, quite straightforwardly, the right periodically to choose and authorize governments to act on their behalf. Democracy could serve a variety of ends, e.g. the pursuit of social justice. But it was important, Schumpeter argued, not to confuse these ends with democracy itself. What political decisions were taken was a question independent from the proper form of their taking: the conditions of the *de facto* legitimacy of decisions and decision-makers as a result of the periodic election of competing political elites.

The essence of democracy was, as the protective theorists of liberal democracy rightly emphasized, the ability of citizens to replace one government by another and, hence, to protect themselves from the risk of political decision-makers transforming themselves into an immovable force. As long as governments can be changed, and as long as the electorate has a choice between (at least two) broadly different party platforms, the threat of tyranny can be

[5] Socialism was defined by Schumpeter as an 'institutional pattern in which control over means of production and over production itself is vested with a central authority – or ... in which, as a matter of principle, the economic affairs of society belong to the public and not to the private sphere' (*Capitalism*, p. 167).

checked. Democracy is a mechanism which allows the registration of the broad desires of ordinary people, while leaving actual public policy to the few who are sufficiently experienced and qualified to make it. Given the diversity of individual desires and the inevitably broad (fragmented) set of demands upon government, amply analysed in Weber's work, a mechanism is required to select those able to produce 'a set of decisions most agreeable to, or least disagreeable to, the whole lot of diverse individual demands' (Macpherson, 1977, pp. 78–80). Democracy is the only device which can remotely achieve this objective.

If democracy is an institutional arrangement to generate and legitimate leadership, then it has at best a most tenuous relation to the classical meaning of democracy: 'rule by the people'. Schumpeter himself was quick to point this out:

> democracy does not mean and cannot mean that the people actually rule in any obvious sense of the terms 'people' and 'rule'. Democracy means only that the people have the opportunity of accepting or refusing the men [*sic*] who are to rule them. . . . Now one aspect of this may be expressed by saying that *democracy is the rule of the politician*. (*Capitalism*, pp. 284–5, emphasis added)

It is a question of facing facts:

> If we wish to face facts squarely, we must recognize that, in modern democracies . . . politics will unavoidably be a career. This in turn spells recognition of a distinct professional interest in the individual politician and of a distinct group interest in the political profession as such. It is essential to insert this factor into our theory . . . Among other things we immediately cease to wonder why it is that politicians so often fail to serve the interest of their class or of the groups with which they are personally connected. Politically speaking, the man [*sic*] is still in the nursery who has not absorbed, so as never to forget, the saying attributed to one of the most successful politicians that ever lived: 'What businessmen do not understand is that exactly as they are dealing in oil so I am dealing in votes.' (*Capitalism*, p. 285)

This is not, Schumpeter stressed, a 'frivolous or cynical' view of politics. On the contrary, what is 'frivolous or cynical' is to pretend that democracy can become a self-regulated community guided only by the 'common good', while knowing all the time that one set of interests will be served above all others: the interests of those actually in charge. Democracy, understood as a mechanism of selection, provides not only a safeguard against such pretences but also the minimum conditions necessary to keep those in charge in check.

Like Weber, Schumpeter found the notion of 'popular sovereignty' unhelpful and full of dangerous ambiguities. The complex modern world could only be governed successfully if the 'sovereign state' were clearly demarcated from the 'sovereign people' and the role of the latter were tightly circumscribed. It is sometimes hard to understand (a point I shall return to later) why Schumpeter retained any faith in, what one might call, the last vestige of the idea of democracy – an occasional vote for all mature adults. He had a low estimation of the political and intellectual capacities of the average citizen. His portrayal of the latter is reminiscent in places of the typical inhabitant of Hobbes's state of nature, but Hobbes, more consistently than Schumpeter, was no democrat (see

Capitalism, pp. 256–64). In general terms, Schumpeter characterized the electorate, under the influence of crowd psychologists like Gustave Le Bon, as generally weak, prone to strong emotional impulses, intellectually unable to do anything decisive on their own and susceptible to outside forces. What particularly concerned him was the large range of ordinary circumstances, from a committee meeting to listening to the radio, in which there was a minimum sense of involvement, a low level of energy and thought, and great sensitiveness to non-logical influences, circumstances in which any 'attempt at rational argument only spurs the animal spirits' (p. 257). For people in these everyday situations politics is like a 'fictitious world': 'the great political questions take their place in the psychic economy of the typical citizen with those leisure-hour activities that have not attained the rank of hobbies, and with the subjects of irresponsible conversation' (p. 261).

Ignorance and lack of sound judgement mark the speculations of the uneducated, as well as many of the educated, when it comes to public affairs. Education, Schumpeter contended, rarely makes a significant difference: 'people cannot be carried up the ladder' (*Capitalism*, p. 262). Why? Most issues in domestic and foreign affairs are so remote from most people's lives that they hardly have 'a sense of reality'. In contrast to the business world, where people have routinely to weigh up the risks and dangers of various courses of action, the distance of the electorate from the political world makes an equivalent task of judgement extremely difficult: 'dangers may not materialize at all and if they should they may not prove so very serious' (p. 261). Without the sense of responsibility that comes from immediate involvement, ignorance persists. Thus, the typical citizen argues and analyses about politics in 'an infantile way': he or she becomes 'a primitive again' (p. 262). Two ominous consequences follow: first, irrational prejudice and impulse govern a great deal of what passes for the average citizen's contribution to politics; second, the 'public mind' becomes highly vulnerable to groups with 'an axe to grind': self-seeking politicians, business interests or 'idealists of one kind or another'.

Whether one takes as a benchmark the political philosophy of ancient Athens, republicanism (in its protective or developmental variant) or liberal democracy (again, in its protective or developmental variant), it appears that 'democratic theory' has come almost full circle: from the defence of a range of fairly tough grounds which might justify a commitment to a form of democratic life, to an argument which seems to cede almost everything to opponents of democracy. Schumpeter's case for democracy can support, at best, only minimum political involvement: that involvement which could be considered sufficient to legitimate the right of competing political elites to rule.

Democracy, capitalism and socialism

Schumpeter's conception of modern industrial society was indebted to both Marx and Weber (see Bottomore, 1985, ch. 3). Like Marx, he emphasized the ceaseless motion and dynamic nature of industrial capitalism. Like Marx, he affirmed a trend towards the domination of ever larger corporations in the production and distribution of goods. And, like Marx, he believed that the development of industrial capitalism would eventually destroy the foundations of capitalist society: the latter was based on contradictions which it could not solve (see Schumpeter, *Capitalism*, part II). Western capitalism would in all likelihood give way to a new economic order which, irrespective of what it was actually called, would be a form of socialism.

However, Schumpeter was a reluctant socialist. Socialism had to be understood as the result of a series of social trends; it was essentially a prediction, not an ethical ideal. In addition, socialism did not necessarily mean social or state ownership of property. Rather, it connoted above all a solution to the technical problem of maximizing national output in an efficient way in the context of an economy dominated by large companies. Schumpeter rejected the central role Marx ascribed to class and class conflict. He thought the whole area of class analysis was 'a hotbed of prejudice' and that the 'rhetoric of revolution' was quite misguided (*Capitalism*, p. 14, and see pp. 57–8, 346 there). The definitive element of socialism was the planning of resources: an institutional pattern which allowed a central authority control over the production system (p. 167). Interpreted in this manner, socialism was not necessarily incompatible, as Weber had asserted, with democracy. In an argument which had particular influence over later theorists of the mixed economy and the welfare state (see ch. 6 below), Schumpeter maintained that so long as democracy is defined in terms of 'general elections, parties, parliaments, cabinets and prime ministers' – that is, in terms of a system for the establishment of legitimate leadership – it may well prove to be the most appropriate and most convenient instrument for dealing with the political agenda of a capitalist or socialist order (*Capitalism*, p. 301).

Like Weber, Schumpeter regarded the application of a rational, calculating attitude to ever more sectors of life as having major consequences for the nature of modern society. Like Weber, he affirmed that capitalism had given an enormous impetus to 'the process of rationalization' (*Capitalism*, pp. 121–2; see Bottomore, 1985, pp. 39–40). Further, he agreed with Weber that rationalization is a necessary part of a complex world which demands impartial, functional ordering; that only 'governments of experts' can direct the state administrative apparatuses in their task of regulation and control; and that only a highly restrictive model of democracy can be sustained in contemporary circumstances. But he differed profoundly from Weber in thinking that, far from capitalism plus democracy providing a significant limit to the expansion of the process of rationalization, capitalism itself would be progressively eroded by the steady advance of 'technical' processes.

The growth of large-scale enterprises is accompanied by the expansion of a rationalized, bureaucratic form of management in the private and public sectors. Central control is increased over an array of phenomena hitherto subject to direct market regulation: innovation, output, prices and investment. Market-orientated industrial capitalism is, accordingly, slowly supplanted by organized or planned economic advance. Bureaucratic management makes an unambiguously positive contribution to this development; it is essential both to the growing scale of modern industrialism and to any future socialist organization. Schumpeter wrote:

I for one cannot visualize, in the conditions of modern society, a socialist organization in any form other than that of a huge and all-embracing bureaucratic apparatus. Every other possibility I can conceive would spell failure and breakdown ... this should not horrify anyone who realizes how far the bureaucratization of economic life – of life in general even – has gone already. (*Capitalism*, p. 206)

Neither socialism nor democracy is threatened by bureaucracy; on the contrary, the latter is an inevitable complement to both (*Capitalism*, p. 206, and see pp. 293–4 there). Socialism will be a successful form of economic organization only to the extent that it employs the 'services of a well-trained bureaucracy of good standing and tradition'. Bureaucratization is the basis of modern management and democratic government, irrespective of whether the economy is capitalist or socialist. Unlike Weber, Schumpeter held bureaucracy to be fully compatible with democracy and democracy to be, in principle, quite consistent with socialist organization.

The details of Schumpeter's own theory of capitalism and socialism are not of prime concern here, although his conception of their development is summarized in figure 5.2. The key points to stress in order to grasp the context of modern democracy, as he understood it, are, first, the erosion of market forces by the progressive increase in scale and concentration of the means of production; second, an increasing tendency towards the rationalization and bureaucratization of management; third, the growing indispensability of the planning of resources in economic and political life; and fourth, the importance of both bureaucracy and democracy for the regulation of the conditions of a 'centralist' economy.

'Classical' v. modern democracy

Schumpeter's advocacy of 'leadership democracy' or 'competitive elitism' rested on an explicit rejection of 'the classical doctrine of democracy'. By this he meant 'that institutional arrangement for arriving at political decisions which realizes the common good by making the people itself decide issues through the election of individuals who are to assemble in order to carry out its will' (*Capitalism*, p. 250). Thus put, the doctrine represents a curious amalgam of theories combining elements of a variety of quite different models; Rousseauian and utilitarian ideas are alluded to, as well as, I think, certain Marxist notions about the integration of state and society. The notion that there is *a* 'classical doctrine', as he called it, makes little sense and should be discarded; there are, as I have sought to show, a range of 'classic' models. Schumpeter has been rightly criticized for erecting a 'straw man' (Pateman, 1970, p. 17). None the less, his critique sets out in bold form a number of fundamental reasons for preferring 'competitive elitism' to other models. As such, it is well worth considering (see D. Miller, 1983, pp. 137–41).

Schumpeter began his critique by attacking the idea of a 'common good' which 'all people could agree on or be made to agree on by the force of rational argument' (*Capitalism*, p. 251). This notion is, he contended, both misleading and dangerous. It is misleading because people not only have different wants,

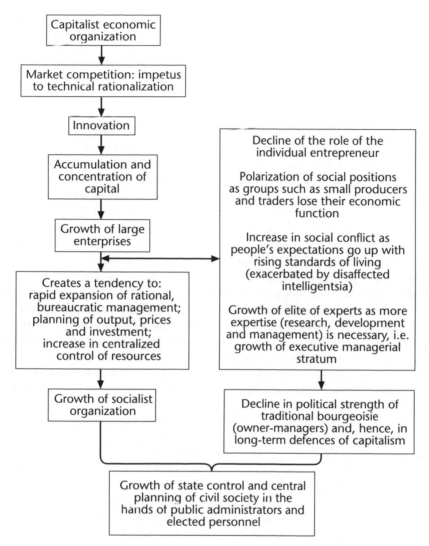

Figure 5.2   From capitalism to socialism: central elements of Schumpeter's theory

they also have different values. Individuals and groups rarely share the same ends and, even when they do, there can be profound disagreements about the most suitable means for the realization of a given objective. In modern, economically differentiated and culturally diverse societies, there are bound to be different interpretations of the common good. Rifts exist on questions of principle and policy, which simply cannot be resolved by an appeal to 'an all-embracing general will'. Moreover, these rifts cannot be bridged by rational argument. For 'ultimate values', Schumpeter argued in a similar vein to Weber, 'are beyond the range of mere logic'. There are irreducible differences between competing conceptions of what life and what society should be like (pp. 251–2). To play down such differences is, furthermore, politically dangerous. If one assumes the existence of a common good and asserts that it is a product of rationality, then it is a short step to dismissing all dissension as sectarian and irrational. Opponents who are merely 'sectarian and irrational' can be legitimately marginalized or ignored; they might even be restrained 'for their own good' if they are persistent in their protest. The notion of the common good is an unacceptable element of democratic theory (pp. 252ff). (The role of values in politics and the possibility of different levels of informed political engagement are revisited in chapter 9's discussion of deliberative democracy.)

It is not a necessary part of either Rousseau's or Marx's conception of democracy that law or policy must be based on the 'will of all' (cf. models IIb and IV). But even if we take the 'will of all' to be 'the will of the majority', it is by no means guaranteed that 'classical democracy' will achieve 'what people really want' (*Capitalism*, p. 254). Schumpeter's second argument against the 'classical doctrine' is that decisions of non-democratic agencies may sometimes prove more acceptable to people generally than 'democratic decisions', for such agencies can use their unique position to produce policies which the various affected parties, in the first instance, either would have failed to agree upon, or would have rejected on the grounds that they entailed unacceptable levels of sacrifice. He cited a religious settlement imposed by Napoleon Bonaparte in France at the very beginning of the nineteenth century as a classic example of a satisfactory policy being established by dictatorial means; and, Schumpeter claimed, the policy had unquestionably beneficial results for all parties in the long term. In his view, this example is far from isolated and therefore: 'if results that prove in the long run satisfactory to the people at large are made the test of government *for* the people, then government *by* the people, as conceived by the classical doctrine of democracy, would often fail to meet it' (p. 256).

Schumpeter's final argument against the 'classical heritage' is the most intriguing and the best known: it attacks directly the very nature of a 'popular will'. Drawing on the theories of crowd psychologists, mentioned earlier, and on observations about the success of advertising in shaping consumer preferences, he maintained forcefully that the 'popular will' (or the 'will of the people' or the 'voters' will') is a social construct which has little, if any, independent or rational basis (see *Capitalism*, pp. 256–68). The case of advertising is instructive. The clear ability of advertisers to create 'needs' for new products and to rekindle interest in old ones testifies to the susceptibility and manipulability of 'individual' desires and choices. The origin of the latter is clearly social and, from the standpoint of the individual, 'extra-rational' (p. 256). This is not to say that advertisers could sell anything; products must have some kind of 'use value' in the long run if they are to sustain an appeal. However, it is to say that consumers are amenable to the influence of advertisers who, by using the force of repetition or by playing on the subconscious (in attempts to evoke pleasant associations of an entirely extra-rational, frequently sexual, nature), can have the most profound effects (p. 258).

The world of consumption offers, at least, a routine way of testing promise against reality (does the product fulfil expectations?). In politics, unfortunately, this is not the case. The remoteness of the world of national and international affairs from the lives of most people leaves them in a very weak position to make sound judgements about competing ideologies and policies.

Moreover, the general susceptibility of individuals, and their vulnerability to the pressures of interest groups, undercuts any independent basis for political thought. In addition, the ever growing use by politicians of the techniques of advertisers themselves erodes further whatever faith one might have had in liberal or radical notions that the 'sovereign people' are, or could be, the source of and a check on the 'sovereign state's' powers (cf. J. B. Thompson, 1995). According to Schumpeter, what one confronts in politics is largely a 'manufactured' not a 'genuine' popular will. The *volonté générale* of 'classical democracy' is, in reality today, 'the product and not the motive power of the political process' (*Capitalism*, p. 263).

There are many worrying consequences of such a state of affairs: political issues, options and 'remedies' can be created by selective pressure, sales tricks and gimmicks; fashions and fads can rule the public mind; and political instability can readily become the norm. The dangers of falling victim to self-seeking 'salesmen', minimized to some extent in the realm of commerce by the daily process of actual consumption, are very high in public life. While Schumpeter does not wish to dismiss wholly Lincoln's dictum about the impossibility of 'fooling all the people all the time', he insisted that:

> history ... consists of a succession of short-run situations that may alter the course of events for good. If all the people can in the short run be 'fooled' step by step into something they do not really want, and if this is not an exceptional case which we could afford to neglect, then no amount of retrospective common sense will alter the fact that in reality they neither raise nor decide issues but that the issues that shape their fate are normally raised and decided for them. (*Capitalism*, p. 264)

The conclusion Schumpeter draws from these arguments is that, in order to avoid some of the worst dangers and risks of contemporary politics, 'lovers of democracy' must clear their creed of the 'make-believe' assumptions and theses of the 'classical doctrine' of democracy. Above all, they must banish the ideas that 'the people' hold definite and rational opinions about all political questions; that the electorate can only give effect to such opinions by either directly acting upon or choosing 'representatives' who will carry out their will; and that the power of decision is the prime element of democracy. If 'the people' cannot be thought of as 'deciders' or 'governors', then what, if any, role can be ascribed to them? In Schumpeter's view, 'the people' are, and can be, nothing more than 'producers of governments', a mechanism to select 'the men who are able to do the deciding' (*Capitalism*, p. 269). Hence, democracy should be understood as a political method in which the people as electors periodically choose between possible teams of leaders. 'Competitive elitism' is, thus, the most suitable, workable and appropriate model of democracy.

Schumpeter conceived the behaviour of politicians as analogous to the activities of entrepreneurs competing for customers. The reins of government properly belong to those who command 'the market' (*Capitalism*, p. 282). Just as voters do not define the central political questions of the day, so their 'choice' of candidates is highly restricted. Who they select is dependent upon rules governing eligibility for office, the initiatives of candidates who actually stand and the powerful forces behind such stands. Political parties form a further restriction on the available choice. Although it is tempting to think of parties as shaped 'by the principles upon which all their members agree', this is, Schumpeter maintained (in parallel to Weber), a dangerous rationalization: a capitulation to the self-image of parties. All parties have commitments to particular principles and platforms, but they cannot be understood in these terms. The explanation for why parties have, in fact, similar records in office and similar sets of policies in practice lies in their function as 'machines' invented for the purpose of winning the competitive struggle for power. And they had to be invented because of the inability of ordinary citizens to coordinate their own political activities:

> Party and machine politicians are simply the response to the fact that the electoral mass is incapable of action other than a stampede, and they constitute an attempt to regulate political competition exactly similar to the corresponding practices of a trade association. The psycho-technics of party management and party advertising, slogans and marching tunes, are not accessories. They are of the essence of politics. So is the political boss. (*Capitalism*, p. 283)

The role of the voter is confined to accepting or refusing one 'boss' or another. The 'boss' provides order and an ability to manage complexity in politics; the electorate's vote provides the legitimacy for subsequent political action.

A clear division of labour between representatives and voters is highly desirable: 'The voters outside of parliament must respect the division of labor between themselves and the politicians they elect. They must not withdraw confidence too easily between elections and they must understand that, once they have elected an individual, political action is his business' (*Capitalism*, p. 295). Not only should electors refrain from trying to instruct their representatives about what they should do but they should also refrain from any attempt to influence their judgement: 'the practice of bombarding them with letters and telegrams for instance . . . ought to come under the same ban' (p. 295)! The only means of political participation open to citizens in Schumpeter's theory are discussion and the occasional vote. In his opinion, democracy is most likely to be effective when leaders are able to set the terms of public policy unimpeded by 'back-seat driving'.

Democracy in any form carries the risk of becoming a breeding ground for administrative inefficiency. Even as an institutional arrangement for the establishment of leadership, democracy can hinder good management as a result of, among other things, the incessant struggle for political advantage and the adaptation of public policy to the long-run interests of politicians (for instance, managing the economy to enhance re-election chances). These risks are real, as are the host of other possible difficulties (see *Capitalism*, pp. 284–9). However, the problems can be minimized if the conditions for the satisfactory working of democracy are understood. The conditions, in Schumpeter's view, are these:

1 The calibre of politicians must be high.
2 Competition between rival leaders (and parties) must take place within a relatively restricted range of political questions, bounded by consensus on the overall direction of national policy, on what constitutes a reasonable parliamentary programme and on general constitutional matters.

3 A well-trained independent bureaucracy of 'good-standing and tradition' must exist to aid politicians on all aspects of policy formulation and administration.
4 There must be 'democratic self-control', i.e. broad agreement about the undesirability of, for instance, voters and politicians confusing their respective roles, excessive criticism of governments on all issues, and unpredictable and violent behaviour.
5 There must be a culture capable of tolerating differences of opinion.

The democratic method can function well when these five conditions are present but it is, Schumpeter stressed, 'at a disadvantage in troubled times' (p. 296). Democracy is likely to break down when interests and ideologies are held so steadfastly that people are not prepared to compromise. Such a situation usually signals the end of democratic politics.

Schumpeter argued that his account of democracy had a number of distinct advantages over other theories. It provided an efficient criterion for distinguishing democratic governments from others; it fully acknowledged the centrality of leadership; it affirmed the importance of competition in politics – even if it is imperfect – and it showed how governments could be created and evicted. In addition, the theory highlighted the nature of popular wishes while not exaggerating their significance. Schumpeter also felt that his theory clarified the relation between democracy and freedom. If by the latter is meant 'the existence of a sphere of individual self-government', then the democratic method requires that everyone is, in principle, free to compete for political leadership. For this requirement to be met there must be 'a considerable amount of freedom of discussion *for all*', and this entails both freedom of speech and freedom of the press (*Capitalism*, pp. 270–1).

It was an important part of Schumpeter's theory to show, furthermore, that democracy and freedom are compatible with either a capitalist or a socialist organization of the economy *so long as* the notion of politics is not stretched excessively. In a capitalist economy the latter is not likely to be the case because the economy is regarded as outside the direct sphere of the political, the world of governmental activity and institutions. This liberal and, fundamentally, 'bourgeois scheme of things' is, of course, rejected by socialists, for whom the power relations of the economy are a central part of what constitutes 'the political'. However, while the socialist concept has explanatory advantages, it also poses, Schumpeter pointed out, severe difficulties: it lacks a decisive restriction on the scope and limits of politics and thus opens all realms of activity to direct political intervention and control. 'Democracy', he stressed, is no answer to this difficulty. Further, the idea of 'democratizing' state and society, placing full political authority in citizens' hands, rests on all the illusions of the 'classical doctrine of democracy'; it is a dangerously misleading idea in the modern world. Therefore, democracy and socialism can only be compatible if democracy is understood as 'competitive elitism' and if the five conditions for its successful functioning are met. A socialist democracy will require, among other things, an extensive bureaucracy as well as an unambiguous separation of politics from all technical-administrative matters. Although Schumpeter's conception of politics is far from clear, it appears that, in his view, politics should be equated with party competition and the lawmaking and policy-making processes which establish the 'infrastructure' of state and civil society. Whether a socialist democracy could work adequately in the long run, Schumpeter contended, could not be determined in advance. But of one thing he was absolutely sure: the ideas enshrined in the 'classical doctrine of democracy' can never be met; a socialist future, whatever its exact outcome, will bear no relation to them.

A technocratic vision

Schumpeter's theory of democracy highlights many recognizable features of modern Western liberal democracies: the competitive struggle between parties for political power; the important role of public bureaucracies; the significance of political leadership; the way in which modern politics deploys many of the techniques of advertising; the way voters are subject to a constant barrage of information, written materials and messages; and the way, despite this barrage, many voters remain poorly informed about contemporary political issues and express marked uncertainty about them. Many of these ideas became central to the political and social sciences of the 1950s and early 1960s and were subjected to further investigation (see Duncan and Lukes, 1963, for a critical survey). The results of such studies are not of great significance here, although it is worth pointing out that many claimed to confirm the basic thrust of Schumpeter's portrait of democracy. What is important here, however, is to address directly a number of Schumpeter's key theoretical and empirical positions.

Throughout Schumpeter's account of democracy run two highly questionable claims: that there is 'a classical theory of democracy' which is fundamentally unfounded because it is 'unrealistic'; and that this theory can only be replaced by a 'competitive elitist' model. These claims are dubious for a number of reasons. First, as I have already pointed out, there is no such thing as 'a classical theory of democracy'; there are many 'classic' models. Schumpeter's concept of the classical heritage is a myth (Pateman, 1970, p. 17). Second, Schumpeter's claim to be replacing an 'unrealistic' model by a well-founded, empirically based alternative presupposes that the latter can account for all the key elements of contemporary democracy. All claims to comprehensiveness should invite scepticism, and the criticisms made below show that 'the alternative' cannot account for a range of vital aspects of modern democratic life. Third, the competitive leadership model by no means exhausts all defensible options within democratic theory. Like Weber, Schumpeter did not investigate a variety of different forms of democracy and political organization. He did not consider, for instance, the way aspects of the competitive model might be combined with more participatory schemes involving opportunities for face-to-face meetings to stimulate and create policy and/or decisions by majority vote and/or the election of representatives who are mandated to follow specified positions (see D. Miller, 1983).

But matters cannot simply be left here; for Schumpeter's whole attack on 'classical democracy' rests on 'a category mistake'. He wrongly supposed, as a number of critics have noted, that empirical evidence about the nature of contemporary democracies could straightforwardly be taken as the basis for refuting the normative ideals enshrined in classic models: for instance, the ideals of political equality and equal participation (cf. chs 1 and 2 above). As one commentator put it, 'the failure of contemporary societies to achieve such goals cannot in itself demonstrate that they are inherently incapable of achievement. . . . If "classical democracy" . . . does not exist it is not thereby proved that it is impossible' (Parry, 1969, p. 149; see Duncan and Lukes, 1963). Rousseau and Marx, two of the most radical of democrats, were well aware that their ideal conceptions of democracy were fundamentally at odds with the world of their lifetime; the point of much of their work, it scarcely needs restating, was to criticize that world. Moreover, they were also aware of the major obstacles preventing the transformation of reality in a more 'democratic' direction. Now, it might be possible to show that certain political ideals could never be realized by demonstrating that they were humanly impossible to achieve, or that the struggle to achieve them would involve such massive upheavals that they would never in practice be realized, or that they embodied contradictory goals (cf. Parry, 1969). But Schumpeter's attack is of a very different order. He did not make these kinds of argument. What he did was to define democracy and the range of 'real' political possibilities in terms of a set of procedures, practices and goals that were prevalent in the West at the time of writing. In so doing, he failed to provide an adequate assessment of theories which are critiques of reality – visions of human nature and of social arrangements which explicitly reject the status quo and seek to defend a range of alternative possibilities (Duncan and Lukes, 1963).

Schumpeter's broadside against 'the classical heritage', moreover, came very close to offering an explicit attack on the very idea of the individual human agent, an idea which has been at the heart of liberal thought from the late sixteenth century. Central to the whole liberal tradition has been the notion of human beings as 'individuals' who can be active citizens of their political order and not merely subjects of another's power. Schumpeter acknowledged that individuals can be 'active' in the realms of consumption and private life, but he came very close to denying that such a capacity existed in the sphere of politics. His emphasis both on the degree to which the 'popular will' is 'manufactured' and on the vulnerability of individuals to 'extra-rational' forces strikes at the very idea of individual human agency – the idea that humans can exert power by reasoning and making choices.

It is surely fundamental to any satisfactory conception of human agency that agents 'could have acted otherwise'. The concept of agency presupposes the 'knowledgeability of agents'. To be human is to be a purposive agent, who both has reasons for his or her activities and is able, if asked, to elaborate discursively upon those reasons (see Giddens, 1984; Held and Thompson, 1989). To emphasize the way in which human agents are capable of knowledgeable action is by no means to imply, of course, that such knowledgeability is unbounded. It is clearly bounded by, among other things, conditions of action which may be only poorly understood or unacknowledged altogether. While it is of vital importance to recognize the way in which individuality is structured by social forces, it is also important not to undercut completely the idea of agency. If one drops the notion that human beings are knowledgeable agents capable of making political choices, then it is but a short step to thinking that all that 'the people' need as 'governors' are engineers capable of making the right technical decisions about the ordering of human affairs. Schumpeter's 'competitive elites' are only one small step removed from this technocratic vision – a vision which is both anti-liberal and anti-democratic.

Schumpeter's problematic account of the nature of agency and his very low estimation of people's capacities created a number of other difficulties that parallel those found in Weber's thought. If the electorate is regarded as unable to form reasonable judgements about pressing political questions, why should it be regarded as capable of discriminating between alternative sets of leaders? On what basis could an electoral verdict be thought adequate? If the electorate is capable of assessing competing leaderships, it surely is able to understand key issues and discriminate between rival platforms. Furthermore, Schumpeter presupposed the existence of a group of political leaders who are competent to make political decisions. But very little by way of justification is offered for this view other than the unsupported assertions that there are some talented and tough people engaged in politics, that they possess a high degree of rationality, and that they are sufficiently affected by the 'real' problems of public life to be able to make sound political judgements. Schumpeter argued, it will be recalled, that the bulk of the population is uninvolved, uninterested and, therefore, unable to think about the stuff of politics because of, among other things, the remoteness of the latter from most people's lives. However, if one tries to define the 'stuff of politics', strangely left unspecified by Schumpeter, then it would surely include (on most people's account) matters such as health and education, employment and unemployment, inequality and social conflict, environmental degradation and regeneration, war and peace (see Held and Leftwich, 1984). It is hard to describe these things as 'remote' from everyday life: they are more accurately described as among those deep-rooted problems that face most people daily as citizens. Moreover, they are problems about which people are likely to have strong opinions. To fail to explore the relevance of these opinions is to strengthen the justification of politics as 'method', and it is to halt prematurely the inquiry into the most adequate form of democracy.

The above problems are linked to another difficulty: Schumpeter's propensity to exaggerate the degree to which the 'popular will' is manufactured. Although there is a large variety of evidence in the social sciences that suggests that the impact of the media, political institutions and other official 'socialization' agencies is great indeed, there is also evidence to suggest that their power should not be exaggerated. For it is clear that people's values, beliefs and the very frameworks within which they think do not simply reflect the stamp of powerful institutions. This area of inquiry is highly complex. But, at the very least, it is certain that major qualifications have to be entered about Schumpeter's argument. There is little evidence to support the view that people's political attitudes are overwhelmingly shaped by the messages that they receive 'from above'. In general, the evidence highlights both the general moral approval of dominant institutions by the politically powerful and mobilized, and the prevalence of value dissensus and of marked divisions of opinion among many working people; a fragmented set of attitudes is a more common finding than a coherent 'manufactured' standpoint. The views 'aired' in politics and the media intersect in complex ways with daily experience, local tradition and social structure (see J. B. Thompson, 1984, 1995).

Democracy is important for Schumpeter because it legitimates the position of those in authority. But in what precise ways may this be claimed? Can we take acquiescence to a competitive democratic system as indicating legitimacy? Does an occasional vote legitimate a political system? There are a number of important points that need to be made. Schumpeter assumed that voting entails a belief that the polity or political institutions are accepted, i.e. legitimated. But the difficulty with this conception of legitimacy is that it fails to distinguish between different grounds for accepting or complying, consenting or agreeing to something (cf. Mann, 1970; Habermas, 1976). We may accept or comply because:

1 There is no choice in the matter (*following orders* or *coercion*).
2 Little or no thought has ever been given to existing political circumstances and we do as we have always done (*tradition*).
3 We cannot be bothered one way or another (*apathy*).
4 Although we do not like a situation (it is not satisfactory and far from ideal), we cannot imagine things being really different and so we accept what seems like fate (*pragmatic acquiescence*).
5 We are dissatisfied with things as they are but nevertheless go along with them in order to secure another end; we acquiesce because it is in the long run to our advantage (*instrumental acceptance* or *conditional agreement*).
6 In the circumstances before us, and with the information available to us at that moment, we conclude it is 'right', 'correct', 'proper' for each of us as an individual or member of a collectivity: it is what we genuinely *ought to* or *should* do (*normative agreement*).
7 It is what in ideal circumstances – with, for instance, all the knowledge we would like, all the opportunity to deliberate over the circumstances and requirements of others – we would have agreed to do (*ideal normative agreement*).

These distinctions are analytical: in real life many different types of agreement are often fused together; and what I am calling an 'ideal normative agreement' is not a position anyone is likely to attain. But the idea of an 'ideal normative agreement' is interesting because it provides a benchmark which helps us to assess whether those whose acceptance of rules, laws and political systems is, for instance, pragmatic *would* have done as they did *if* they had had better knowledge, information, etc., at the moment of their action (cf. Held, 1995, chs 7–9; and see Part Three below).

Not only did Schumpeter's analysis fail to distinguish among the different possible meanings of acceptance entailed by an act like voting, but it actually provided good prima facie reasons for doubting whether political participation by voting should be equated with 'legitimacy'. In Schumpeter's own account, a competitive democratic system routinely enables those in powerful political positions to manipulate and distort the political will of citizens. Does not such a political system create the conditions of its own legitimacy? Schumpeter's work did not examine critically the circumstances under which it might be said that citizens confer legitimacy; that is, the circumstances under which citizens do things because *they* think them right, correct, justified – worthy.[6] Power and legitimacy intermingle in more complex ways than Schumpeter's analysis allowed.

Schumpeter believed his theory of democracy shed light on the relationship between democracy and freedom. Democracy entails, in his view, a state in which everyone is, in principle, free to compete for political leadership. The conditions of such participation are freedom of discussion and speech (*Capitalism*, pp. 270–1). Put thus, however, this is a quite inadequate view. In the first instance, many people cannot stand for political office, not because they do not enjoy freedom of discussion but because they do not, in fact, have the necessary resources (whether these be time, organizational skills, money or capital). It is patently clear that there is a large variety of groups that simply do not have the means to compete in the national arena with those, say, who own and control the bulk of economic resources, or who direct powerful political apparatuses. Some do not have access to the minimum facilities for political mobilization of any kind. The conditions of what was earlier called 'limited' or 'non-participation' need to be analysed, and they are not by Schumpeter. Like Weber, Schumpeter did not examine the vicious circles of non-participation, although even he acknowledged that without scope for political initiative people are likely to become apathetic even in the face of all the information needed for active involvement (*Capitalism*, p. 262). Effective participation depends both upon political will *and* upon having the actual capacity (the resources, skills and knowledge) to pursue different courses of action.

Finally, it is worth commenting on Schumpeter's claim that his model of democracy represents a fundamentally 'competitive' system. As one critic aptly noted, the model is far more appropriately referred to as 'oligopolistic'. That is to say,

> there are only a few sellers, a few suppliers of political goods... Where there are so few sellers, they need not and do not respond to the buyers' demands as they must do in a fully competitive system. They can set prices and set the range of goods that will be offered. More than that, they can, to a considerable extent, create ... [their own] demand. (Macpherson, 1977, p. 89)

In Schumpeter's democratic system, the only full participants are the members of political elites in parties and in public offices. The role of ordinary citizens is not only highly delimited, but it is frequently portrayed as an unwanted infringement on the smooth functioning of 'public' decision-making. All this places considerable strain on the claim of 'competitive elitism' to be democratic. Little remains of the case for democracy except the sheer 'protection against tyranny' argument (Macpherson, 1977, pp. 90–1). As the last four chapters have

---

[6] This issue will be returned to in chapters 6, 7 and 9, and in the final part of the volume, pp. 288–9 below.

In sum: model V

Competitive Elitist Democracy

Principle(s) of justification

Method for the selection of a skilled and imaginative political elite capable of making necessary legislative and administrative decisions

An obstacle to the excesses of political leadership

Key features

Parliamentary government with strong executive

Competition between rival political elites and parties

Domination of parliament by party politics

Centrality of political leadership

Bureaucracy: an independent and well-trained administration

Constitutional and practical limits on the 'effective range of political decision'

General conditions

Industrial society

Fragmented pattern of social and political conflict

Poorly informed and/or emotional electorate

A political culture which tolerates differences of opinion

Emergence of skilled strata of technically trained experts and managers

Competition between states for power and advantage in the international system

Note: This model encapsulates central elements of both Weber's and Schumpeter's views.

tried to show, this is a far from unimportant consideration; if it were merely a choice between tyranny and competitive elitism (monopoly or oligopoly in politics), the latter would of course be desirable. But the rich tradition of democratic thought indicates that these are far from the only avenues open. Along with Max Weber, Schumpeter too hastily closed off the exploration of other possible models in democratic theory and practice, beyond those posed by the control of public affairs by all citizens or by competitive elites. Along with Max Weber, he registered significant trends in modern politics – the development of the competitive party system, the ability of those with power to set agendas, the domination of elites in national politics – and uncritically cast them into rigid patterns: a basis for the claim that, ultimately, only one particular model of democracy is appropriate to the contemporary age. Taken together, their views, summarized in model V, are among the most intriguing and most problematic contributions to the analysis of modern politics.

6 Pluralism, Corporate Capitalism and the State

In Schumpeter's theory there is little that stands between the individual citizen and the elected leadership. The citizen is portrayed as isolated and vulnerable in a world marked by the competitive clash of elites. In this account, scarcely any attention is paid to 'intermediary' groups such as community associations, religious bodies, trade unions and business organizations which cut across people's lives and connect them in complex ways to a variety of types of institution. If judged in relation to this matter alone, Schumpeter's theory is partial and incomplete.

A school of political analysts, widely referred to as empirical democratic theorists or 'pluralists', attempted to remedy this deficiency by examining directly the dynamics of 'group politics'. Exploring the interconnections between electoral competition and the activities of organized interest groups, pluralists argued that modern democratic politics is actually far more competitive, and policy outcomes are far more satisfactory to all parties, than Schumpeter's model suggested. The fluid and open structure of liberal democracies helps explain, they contended, the high degree of compliance to dominant political institutions in the West. Pluralists gained a commanding position in American political studies in the 1950s and 1960s. While their influence is by no means as extensive now as it was then, their work has had a lasting effect on contemporary political thought. Many, particularly Marxists, have dismissed pluralism as a naive and/or narrowly ideological celebration of Western democracies, but the tradition has contributed important insights.

The intellectual ancestry of pluralism has not been thoroughly traced, although a number of strands of influence can readily be detected. Schumpeter's critique of the 'unreality' of both classic democratic ideals and the conception of representative government found in the writings of nineteenth-century liberals like John Stuart Mill had a decisive impact. Pluralists accepted Schumpeter's broad view that what distinguishes democracies from non-democracies are the ways (methods) by which political leaders are selected. Moreover, they affirmed as empirically accurate the claims that the electorate is more apathetic and less well informed than democratic theorists had generally admitted, that individual citizens have little, if any, direct influence on the political process and that representatives are often 'opinion makers'. But they did not think a concentration of power in the hands of competing political elites was inevitable. Following Weber, they took as a starting point the existence of many determinants of the distribution of power and, hence, many power centres. They deployed Weberian ideas to help challenge doctrines that suggested the overwhelming centrality of fixed groups of elites (or classes) in political life.

While the works of Schumpeter and Weber were the proximate sources of pluralism, its intellectual terms of reference were set by two streams of thought above others: the Madisonian heritage in American democratic theory, and utilitarian conceptions of the inescapability of the competitive pursuit of interest satisfaction. Madison provided, according to Robert Dahl (one of the earliest and most prominent exponents of pluralism),[1] 'a basic rationale for the American political system' (Dahl, 1956, p. 5). Unlike many liberals who emphasized the importance in democratic politics of an individual citizen's relation to the state, pluralists, following certain strands in Madison, have been preoccupied with the 'problem of factions' (see pp. 70–5). Pluralists put particular weight on the processes creating, and resulting from, individuals combining their efforts in groups in the competition for power. Like Madison, they stressed that factions – or, in their modern guise, 'interest groups' or 'pressure groups' – are 'the natural counterpart of free association' in a world where most desired goods are scarce and where a complex industrial system fragments social interests and creates a multiplicity of demands. Like Madison, they accepted that a fundamental purpose of government is to protect the freedom of factions to further their political interests while preventing any individual faction from undermining the freedom of others. Unlike Madison, however, pluralists argued (despite certain disagreements among themselves) that far from posing a major threat to democratic associations, factions are a structural source of stability and the central expression of democracy. For pluralists, the existence of diverse competitive interests is the basis of democratic equilibrium and of the favourable development of public policy (see Held and Krieger, 1984). They tended to take for granted the view that just as economics is concerned with individuals maximizing their personal interests, politics is concerned with sets of individuals maximizing their common interests. Accordingly, a very particular utilitarian conception of individuals as satisfaction maximizers, acting in competitive exchanges with others in the market and in politics, is also presupposed (see Elster, 1976).

In the modern competitive world, marked by complexity and divisions of interest, political life can never approach, pluralists admitted, the ideals of Athenian democracy, Renaissance republics or the kind of democracy anticipated by Rousseau or Marx. The world is unquestionably 'imperfect' if judged by such standards. But it ought not to be so judged. Rather, it should be analysed by a 'descriptive method' which considers the distinguishing characteristics and actual functioning of all those nation-states and social organizations that are commonly called democratic by social scientists (Dahl, 1956, p. 63). Pluralists aimed to describe the *real workings* of democracy and to assess its contribution to the development of contemporary society. Hence, they referred to their own brand of democratic theory as 'empirical democratic theory', a descriptive–explanatory account of the actuality of democratic politics. Like Weber and Schumpeter, their goal was to be 'realistic' and 'objective' in the face of all those thinkers who asserted particular ideals without

---

[1] Dahl has become, in some respects at least, a more radical thinker over time (see 1985, 1989; and see below).

due attention to the circumstances in which they found themselves. Since the pluralists' critique of such thinkers is similar in many respects to the critical treatment offered by Montesquieu, Madison, Mill, Weber and Schumpeter, the focus below will be on the pluralists' positive understanding of democracy. (A succinct account of Dahl's critique of 'populistic democracy', as he calls it, can be found in Dahl, 1956, ch. 2.)

Group politics, governments and power

Several pluralist theories have been expounded, but I shall examine initially what may be regarded as the 'classic version' found in the writings of, among others, Truman and Dahl (see, e.g., Truman, 1951; Dahl, 1956, 1961, 1971). This version has had a pervasive influence, although very few political and social scientists would accept it in unmodified form today (though many politicians, journalists and others in the mass media still appear to do so). Pluralism has been developed by some of its original exponents and a new variant, frequently referred to as 'neo-pluralism' or 'critical pluralism', has been established; this latter model will be discussed in subsequent pages.

The essence of the classic pluralist position stems from investigation into the distribution of power in Western democracies. By power, pluralists have generally meant a capacity to achieve one's aims in the face of opposition. As Dahl put it, 'by "power" we mean to describe a . . . realistic relationship, such as A's capacity for acting in such a manner as to control B's responses' (Dahl, 1956, p. 13).[2] A's capacity to act depends on the means at A's disposal and, in particular, on the relative balance of resources between A and B. Pluralists emphasized that resources can be of a vast variety of types; financial means are only one kind of resource, and can be easily outweighed by, for instance, an opposition with a substantial popular base. Clearly, there are many inequalities in society (of schooling, health, income, wealth, etc.) and not all groups have equal access to all types of resource, let alone equal resources. However, nearly every group has some advantage that can be utilized in the democratic process to make an impact. Since different groups have access to different kinds of resource, the influence of any particular group will generally vary from issue to issue.

In the pluralist account, power is non-hierarchically and competitively arranged. It is an inextricable part of an 'endless process of bargaining' between numerous groups representing different interests, including, for example, business organizations, trade unions, political parties, ethnic groups, students, prison officers, women's collectives, and religious groups. These interest groups may be structured around particular economic or cultural 'cleavages', such as

---

[2] There are other formulations of power in the pluralist literature. Dahl himself has also referred to power as involving 'a successful attempt by A' to get B to do something 'he would not otherwise do' (Dahl, 1957; cf. Nagel, 1975, pp. 9–15). Whether one emphasizes actual behavioural outcomes of the exercise of power, as Dahl's latter definition suggests, or capacities, as his original definition specified, the pluralist definition of power tends to hinge on the exercise of control over immediate events: the issue is the overcoming of B's immediate resistance to A's will or purpose (see Lukes, 1974, ch. 2).

social class, religion or ethnicity. But, in the long term, social forces tend to change their composition, alter their concerns and shift their positions. Hence, the determination of political decisions at either national or local level does not (and cannot) reflect a 'majestic march' of 'the public' united upon matters of basic policy, as imagined, albeit in quite different ways, by Locke, Bentham and Rousseau. Even when there is a numerical majority at an election, it is rarely useful, Dahl stressed, 'to construe that majority as more than an arithmetic expression ... the numerical majority is incapable of undertaking any coordinated action: it is the various components of the numerical majority that have the means for action' (Dahl, 1956, p. 146). Political outcomes are the result of government and, ultimately, the executive trying to mediate and adjudicate between the competing demands of groups. In this process, the political system or state becomes almost indistinguishable from the ebb and flow of bargaining, the competitive pressure of interests. Indeed, individual government departments are sometimes best conceived as just another kind of interest group, as they themselves compete for scarce resources. Thus, the making of democratic governmental decisions involves the steady trade-off between, and appeasement of, the demands of relatively small groups, although by no means all interests are likely to be satisfied fully.

There is no single, powerful decision-making centre in the classic pluralist model. Since power is essentially dispersed throughout society, and since there is a plurality of pressure points, a variety of competing policy-formulating and decision-making centres arises. How, then, can any equilibrium or stability be achieved in a democratic society like the United States? According to David Truman, another early analyst of group politics:

> Only the highly routinized governmental activities show any stability ... and these may as easily be subordinated to elements in the legislature as to the chief executive ... organized interest groups ... may play one segment of the structure against another as circumstances and strategic considerations permit. The total pattern of government over a period of time thus presents a protean complex of criss-crossing relationships that change in strength and direction with alterations in the power and standing of interests, organized and unorganized. (Truman, 1951, p. 508)

The clue to why democracy can achieve relative stability lies, Truman argued, in the very existence of a 'protean complex' of relationships. Starting from Madison's assumption that the very diversity of interests in society is likely to protect a democratic polity from 'the tyranny of a factious majority' (by fragmenting it into factions), Truman suggested that 'overlapping membership' between factions is an important additional explanatory variable. Since, in Truman's words, all 'tolerably normal' people enjoy multiple memberships among groups with diverse – and even incompatible – interests, each interest group is likely to remain too weak and internally divided to secure a share of power incommensurate with its size and objectives. The overall direction of public policy emerges as a result of a series of relatively uncoordinated impacts upon government, directed from all sides by competing forces, without any one force wielding excessive influence. Accordingly, out of the fray of interests, policy emerges – to a degree independently of the efforts of particular politicians – within 'the democratic mold' (Truman, 1951, pp. 503–16).

None of this is to say that elections and the competitive party system are of trivial significance in determining policy. They remain crucial for ensuring that political representatives will be 'somewhat responsive to the preferences of ordinary citizens' (Dahl, 1956, p. 131). But elections and parties alone do not secure the equilibrium of democratic states. The existence of active groups of various types and sizes is crucial if the democratic process is to be sustained and if citizens are to advance their goals.

Of course, some citizens are neither active in nor very concerned about politics. A series of large-scale voting studies initiated in North America, within the pluralist framework, found that voters were often hostile to politics, apathetic and uninformed about public issues (see, e.g., Berelson et al., 1954; Campbell et al., 1960). The evidence showed that less than one-third of the electorate was 'strongly interested' in politics. However, none of this was taken as evidence against the pluralist characterization of liberal democracies and, above all, of the US. For the classic pluralists maintained that it was only from the standpoint of the abstract ideals of 'classical democracy' that these findings could be judged regrettable. In the contemporary world, people were free to organize, they had the opportunity to press interest group demands and they enjoyed the right to vote out of office governments they found unsatisfactory. People's decisions to participate in political processes and institutions were theirs alone. Moreover, a degree of inaction or apathy might even be functional for the stable continuity of the political system. Extensive participation can readily lead to increased social conflict, undue disruption and fanaticism, as had been clearly seen in Nazi Germany, fascist Italy and Stalin's Soviet Union (see Berelson, 1952; Berelson et al., 1954; Parsons, 1960). Lack of political involvement can, in addition, be interpreted quite positively: it can be based upon trust in those who govern (see Almond and Verba, 1963). As one author put it, 'political apathy may reflect the health of a democracy' (Lipset, 1963, p. 32, n. 20). In so arguing, the merging of the normative and empirical (frequently found but often denied in writings on democracy) was clearly manifest. Empirical democratic theorists held that pluralist democracy was a major achievement, irrespective of the actual extent of citizen participation. Indeed, 'democracy' does not seem to require a high level of active involvement from all citizens; it can work quite well without it.

It was Dahl, perhaps more than anyone else, who sought to specify the exact nature of the 'pluralist democracies'. Unlike Truman, and many others writing in the pluralist tradition, Dahl insisted on the importance of separating two claims. He argued (1) that if competitive electoral systems are characterized by a multiplicity of groups or minorities who feel intensely enough about diverse issues, then democratic rights will be protected and severe political inequalities avoided with a certainty beyond that guaranteed by mere legal or constitutional arrangements; and (2) that there is empirical evidence to suggest that at least certain polities, for example, the US and Britain, satisfy these conditions. Concerned to discover who exactly has power over what resources (hence the title of his famous study of city politics in America, *Who Governs?*), Dahl found that power is effectively disaggregated and non-cumulative; it is shared and bartered by numerous groups in society representing diverse interests (Dahl, 1961). *Who Governs?* revealed multiple coalitions seeking to influence public policy. There were, to be sure, severe conflicts over policy outcomes, as different interests pressed their sectoral claims, but the process of interest bartering through governmental offices created a tendency towards 'competitive equilibrium' and a set of policies which was positive for the citizenry at large in the long run.

At the minimum, according to Dahl, 'democratic theory is concerned with processes by which ordinary citizens exert a relatively high degree of control over leaders' (Dahl, 1956, p. 3). In his view, empirical study shows that such control can be sustained if politicians' scope for action is constrained by two key mechanisms: regular elections and political competition among parties, groups and individuals. He emphasized that while elections and political competition do *not* make for government by majorities in any very significant way, 'they vastly increase the size, number, and variety of minorities whose preferences must be taken into account by leaders in making policy choices' (Dahl, 1956, p. 132). Moreover, he contended, if the full implications of this are grasped, then the essential differences between tyranny and democracy, the preoccupation of much political theory, can finally be unravelled.

Once liberalism achieved victory over the old 'absolute powers' of the state, many liberal thinkers, it will be recalled, began to express fear about the rising power of the *demos*. Madison, de Tocqueville and J. S. Mill, among others, were all concerned about the new dangers to liberty posed by majority rule: the promise of democracy could be undercut by 'the people' themselves acting in concert against minorities. For Dahl, this concern has been to a large degree misplaced. A tyrannous majority is improbable because elections express the preferences of various competitive groups, rather than the wishes of a firm majority. Supporters of democracy need not fear an 'excessively strong faction'. Rather, what Dahl calls 'polyarchy' – a situation of open contest for electoral support among a large proportion of the adult population – ensures competition among group interests: the safeguard of democracy. Thus, he wrote,

> The real world issue has not turned out to be whether a majority, much less 'the' majority, will act in a tyrannical way through democratic procedures to impose its will on a (or the) minority. Instead, the more relevant question is the extent to which various minorities in a society will frustrate the ambitions of one another with the passive acquiescence or indifference of a majority of adults or voters.
>
> ...if there is anything to be said for the processes that actually distinguish democracy (or polyarchy) from dictatorship ... the distinction comes [very close] ... to being one between government by a minority and government by minorities. As compared with the political processes of a dictatorship, the characteristics of polyarchy greatly extend the number, size, and diversity of the minorities whose preferences will influence the outcome of governmental decisions. (Dahl, 1956, p. 133)

The democratic character of a regime is secured by the existence of multiple groups or multiple minorities. Indeed, Dahl argued that democracy can be defined as 'minorities government'. For the value of the democratic process lies in rule by 'multiple minority oppositions', rather than in the establishment of the 'sovereignty of the majority'. Weber's and Schumpeter's scepticism about the concept of popular sovereignty was justified, albeit for reasons different from those they themselves gave.

Dahl reinforced the view that competition among organized interest groups structures policy outcomes and establishes the democratic nature of a regime. Whatever their differences, nearly all empirical democratic theorists defend an interpretation of democracy as a set of institutional arrangements that create a rich texture of interest group politics and allow, through competition to influence and select political leaders, the rule of multiple minorities. In Dahl's assessment, this is both a desirable state of affairs and one to which most liberal democracies actually approximate.

While majorities rarely, if ever, rule, there is an important sense in which they none the less 'govern'; that is, determine the framework within which policies are formulated and administered. For democratic politics operates, to the extent that it persists over time, within the bounds of a consensus set by the values of the politically active members of society, of whom the voters are the key body (Dahl, 1956, p. 132). If politicians stray beyond this consensus or actively pursue their own objectives without regard for the expectations of the electorate, they will almost certainly fail in any new bid for office:

> what we ordinarily describe as democratic 'politics' is merely the chaff. It is the surface manifestation, representing superficial conflicts. Prior to politics, beneath it, enveloping it, restricting it, conditioning it, is the underlying consensus on policy that usually exists in the society... Without such a consensus no democratic system would long survive the endless irritations and frustrations of elections and party competition. With such a consensus the disputes over policy alternatives are nearly always disputes over a set of alternatives that have already been winnowed down to those within a broad area of basic agreement. (Dahl, 1956, pp. 132–3)

Contrary to Schumpeter's view that democratic politics is steered ultimately by competing elites, Dahl (in common with many other pluralists) insisted that it is anchored to a value consensus that lays down the parameters of political life. True, there have always been politicians or political elites who have had a profound impact on the direction of a nation; however, their impact can only be properly understood in relation to the nation's political culture with which they were 'in tune'.

The social prerequisites of a functioning polyarchy – consensus on the rules of procedure; consensus on the range of policy options; consensus on the legitimate scope of political activity – are the most profound obstacles to all forms of oppressive rule. The greater the extent of consensus, the securer the democracy. In so far as a society enjoys protection against tyranny, it is to be found in non-constitutional factors above all (Dahl, 1956, pp. 134–5). Dahl did not deny the significance of, for example, a separation of powers, a system of checks and balances between the legislature, executive, judiciary and administrative bureaucracy – far from it. Constitutional rules are crucial in determining the weight of advantages and disadvantages groups face in a political system; hence, they are often bitterly fought over. But the significance of constitutional rules to the successful development of democracy is, Dahl argued, 'trivial' when compared to non-constitutional rules and practices (Dahl, 1956, p. 135). And, he concluded, as long as the social prerequisites of democracy are intact, democracy will always be 'a relatively efficient system for reinforcing agreement, encouraging moderation, and maintaining social peace' (p. 151).

Dahl's position does not require that control over political decisions is equally distributed; nor does it require that all individuals and groups have equal political 'weight' (Dahl, 1956, pp. 145–6). In addition, he clearly recognized that organizations and institutions can take on 'a life of their own', which may lead them to depart, as Weber predicted, from the wishes and interests of their members. There are 'oligarchical tendencies': bureaucratic structures can ossify and leaders can become unresponsive elites in the public or private sectors. Accordingly, public policy can be skewed towards certain interest groups which have the best organization and most resources; it can be skewed towards certain politically powerful state agencies; and it can be skewed by intense rivalries between different sectors of government itself. Policy-making as a process will always be affected and constrained by a number of factors, including intense political competition; electoral strategies; scarce resources; and limited knowledge and competence. Democratic decision-making is inevitably incremental and frequently disjointed. But the classic pluralist position does not explore these potentially highly significant issues very fully; their implications are not pursued. For the central premises of this position – the existence of multiple power centres, diverse and fragmented interests, the marked propensity of one group to offset the power of another, a 'transcendent' consensus which binds state and society, the state as judge and arbitrator between factions – cannot in the end shed light on, or explain, a world in which there may be systematic imbalances in the distribution of power, influence and resources. The full consideration of such issues is incompatible with the assumptions and terms of reference of classic pluralism.

Politics, consensus and the distribution of power

The account of interest group politics offered by classic pluralists was a significant corrective to the one-sided emphasis on 'elite politics', and the overemphasis on the capacity of politicians to shape contemporary life, found in the writings of the competitive elitists. Pluralists stressed, rightly, the many ways in which particular patterns of interaction, competition and conflict are 'inscribed' into, that is, embedded in, the organization, administration and policies of the modern state. Electoral constraints and interest group politics mean that the ability of political leaders to act independently of societal demands and pressures will almost always be compromised, with the exception perhaps of times of war and other types of national emergency. Democracy as a set of institutions cannot be adequately understood without detailed reference to this complex context.

However, the pluralist emphasis on the 'empirical' nature of democracy compounds a difficulty in democratic thought, a difficulty created, in part, by

Weber and Schumpeter. By defining democracy in terms of what is conventionally called 'democracy' in the West – the practices and institutions of liberal democracy – and by focusing exclusively on those mechanisms through which it is said citizens can control political leaders (periodic elections and pressure group politics), pluralists neither systematically examined nor compared the justification, features and general conditions of competing democratic models. The writings of the key pluralist authors tended to slide from a descriptive–explanatory account of democracy to a new normative theory (see Duncan and Lukes, 1963, pp. 40–7). Their 'realism' entailed conceiving of democracy in terms of the actual features of Western polities. In thinking of democracy in this way, they recast its meaning and, in so doing, surrendered the rich history of the idea of democracy to the existent. Questions about the nature and appropriate extent of citizen participation, the proper scope of political rule and the most suitable spheres of democratic regulation – questions that have been part of democratic theory from Athens to nineteenth-century England – are put aside, or, rather, answered merely by reference to current practice. The ideals and methods of democracy become, by default, the ideals and methods of the existing democratic systems. Since the critical criterion for adjudicating between theories of democracy is their degree of 'realism', models which depart from, or are in tension with, current democratic practice can be dismissed as empirically inaccurate, 'unreal' and undesirable.

Suggestions about ways in which democratic public life might be enriched cannot be explored adequately within the terms of reference of classic pluralism. This is illustrated most clearly by the use of the findings on the degree to which citizens are uninformed and/or apathetic about politics. For the most part, the classic pluralists regard such findings simply as evidence of how little political participation is necessary for the successful functioning of democracy. Limited or non-participation among large segments of the citizenry – for instance, non-whites – is not a troubling problem for them, because their theoretical framework does not invite discussion of the extent to which such phenomena might be taken to negate the definition of Western politics as democratic. Empirical findings, once again, become inadequately justified theoretical virtues.

The question remains, of course: how satisfactory is pluralism as an account of 'reality'? An intriguing place to begin an assessment of this matter is by examining further the underlying value consensus which, Dahl claimed, ultimately integrates state and society. While Schumpeter believed acquiescence to a competitive electoral system entails a belief in the legitimacy of the system, Dahl contended that it was from the depths of political culture that support for a political system derives. One of the most famous studies within the pluralist tradition, Almond and Verba's *The Civic Culture* (1963), set out to explore directly, through a comparative nationwide sample survey of political attitudes, whether modern Western political culture was a source of such support. It is worth reflecting upon the findings of this study for a moment.

According to Almond and Verba, if a political regime is to survive in the long run 'it must be accepted by citizens as the proper form of government per se' (Almond and Verba, 1963, p. 230). Democracy, in their view, is indeed accepted in this sense 'by elites and non-elites' (p. 180). They arrived at this conclusion by taking as a suitable index for the measurement of acceptance or legitimacy whether individuals reported pride in their country and its political institutions (pp. 102–3, 246). But a number of things need to be noted. First, only a minority, 46 per cent, of the British respondents (the second highest percentage after the US figure) expressed pride in their governmental system, and this despite the fact that Britain was regarded as a bastion of democracy (p. 102). Second, Almond and Verba's measure of legitimacy was, like the general pluralist treatment of this concept, very crude. For it failed to distinguish between the different possible meanings of pride and their highly ambiguous relation to legitimacy. For instance, one can express pride or pleasure in parliamentary democracy without in any way implying that it operates now as well as it might, or that it is the proper, or best or most acceptable, form of government. One can express pride in something while wishing it substantially altered. Almond and Verba did not investigate possibilities like this, and yet their study is probably the key pluralist study of political attitudes. Third, Almond and Verba appear to have misinterpreted their own data. It can be shown that a careful reading of the evidence presented in *The Civic Culture* reveals not only that the degree of common value commitment in a democracy like Britain is quite limited, but also that according to the only (and indirect) measure of social class used – the type of formal education of the respondent – working-class people frequently express views which Almond and Verba think reflect 'the most extreme feeling of distrust and alienation' (Almond and Verba, 1963, p. 268; see Mann, 1970; Pateman, 1980). Almond and Verba failed to explain the systematic differences in political orientation of social classes and, cutting across these, of men and women, which their own data revealed.

That value consensus did not exist to a significant extent in Britain and the United States, during the period in which classic pluralism was formulated, was confirmed by a survey of a large variety of empirical materials based on research conducted in the late 1950s and early 1960s (Mann, 1970). The survey disclosed that middle-class people (white-collar and professional workers), on the whole, tended to exhibit greater consistency of belief and agreement over values than did working-class people (manual workers). In so far as there were common values held by the working class, they tended to be hostile to the system rather than supportive of it. There was more 'dissensus' between classes than there was 'consensus'. Further, if one examines 'political efficacy', that is, people's estimation of their ability to influence government, noteworthy differences could also be recorded among classes: the middle class tended to assert far greater confidence than the working class. Considerable distance from, and distrust of, dominant political institutions were indicated among working-class people (cf. Pateman, 1971, 1980). Strong allegiance to the liberal democratic system and to 'democratic norms' appeared, in sum, to be correlated directly, as noted in chapter 5 above, to socioeconomic status.

It should be stressed that much of the research on value consensus is ambiguous and difficult to interpret. What matters here and what can be said with confidence is that any claim about widespread adherence to a common value system needs to be treated with the utmost scepticism. Further support for this view can be derived from the very history of the societies in which pluralism arose. Throughout the 1960s and early 1970s there was an escalation of tension and conflict within the United States and Western Europe which is hard to understand within the pluralist framework. In the context of an overarching trend to slowing rates of economic growth, growing unemployment, severe difficulties in public finances, mounting levels of industrial conflict, crisis in inner city areas and ethnic conflict, challenges grew to the 'rule of law' and public institutions.

The period of 1968–9 represents something of a watershed (S. Hall et al., 1978). The anti-Vietnam war movement, the student movement and a host of other political groups associated with the New Left altered the political pace: it was a time of marked political polarization. Demands for peace, the extension of democratic rights to workers in industry and to local communities, the emancipation of women and resistance to racism were just some of the issues which produced unparalleled scenes of protest in (postwar) London and Washington, and took France to the edge of revolution in May 1968. The new social movements seemed to define themselves against almost everything that the traditional political system defended. They defined the system as rigid, regimented, authoritarian and empty of moral, spiritual and personal content. While it is easy to exaggerate the coherence of these movements and the degree of support they enjoyed, it is not easy to exaggerate the extent to which they shattered the premises of classic pluralism. Within pluralist terms, the events and circumstances of the late 1960s were wholly unexpected. Moreover, the tangle of corruption and deceit revealed in the centres of American democracy during the Watergate scandal of the Nixon era brought the very idea of an 'open and trusted' government further into disrepute (McLennan, 1984, p. 84).

One of the most important reasons for the failure of classic pluralism to characterize Western politics adequately lies in fundamental difficulties with the way power and power relations were conceived. In an influential critique of the pluralist concept of power, Bachrach and Baratz drew attention to exercises of power which may have already determined the (observable) instances of control by A over B, which constitutes power in the pluralist view (Bachrach and Baratz, 1962, pp. 947–52). They rightly pointed out – adopting Schattschneider's concept of the 'mobilization of bias' – that persons or groups may exercise power by 'creating or reinforcing barriers to the airing of policy conflicts' (cf. Schattschneider, 1960). In other words, A may be able to control B's behaviour by participating in a *non-decision-making* process:

> Of course, power is exercised when A participates in the making of decisions that affect B. But power is also exercised when A devotes his energies to creating or reinforcing social and political values and institutional practices that limit the scope of the political process to public consideration of only those issues which are comparatively innocuous to A. To the extent that A succeeds in doing this, B is prevented, for all practical purposes, from bringing to the fore any issues that might in their resolution be seriously detrimental to A's set of preferences. (Bachrach and Baratz, 1962, p. 949)

Bachrach and Baratz's critique is of considerable significance, drawing attention as it does to the way in which power is deployed not only when things happen (decision-making) but also when they do not appear to do so (non-decision making). However, power cannot simply be conceived in terms of what individuals do or do not do, a position which Bachrach and Baratz themselves seemed to adopt. For, as Lukes observed in a telling analysis of the concept of power, 'the bias of a system is not sustained simply by a series of individually chosen acts, but also, most importantly, by the socially structured and culturally patterned behaviour of groups, and practices of institutions' (Lukes, 1974, p. 22). If power is defined in terms of the capacity of individuals to realize their wills against resistance, collective forces and social arrangements will be neglected. It is not surprising, then, that classic pluralists failed to begin to grasp those asymmetries of power – between classes, races, men and women, politicians and ordinary citizens – which were behind, in large part, the decay of what they called 'consensus politics'.

There is a range of other difficulties with the classic pluralist position, all of which stem from an inadequate grasp of the nature and distribution of power. The existence of many power centres hardly guarantees that government will (1) listen to them all equally; (2) do anything other than communicate with leaders of such centres; (3) be susceptible to influence by anybody other than those in powerful positions; (4) do anything about the issues under discussion, and so on (Lively, 1975, pp. 20–4, 54–6, 71–2, 141–5). While classic pluralists recognized some of these points, they did not pursue their implications for an analysis of the distribution of power and of political accountability. In addition, it is abundantly clear that, as already pointed out in the discussion of Schumpeter's analysis of the conditions of political participation, many groups do not have the resources to compete in the national political arena with the clout of, for instance, powerful lobby organizations or corporations. Many do not have the minimum resources for political mobilization. In retrospect, the pluralists' analysis of the conditions of political involvement was extraordinarily naive. It is hard to avoid the view that, in part, many pluralist thinkers must have been so anxious to affirm the achievements of Western democracy in the postwar era that they failed to appreciate a large range of potential objections.

Some of these objections would now be accepted by key 'pluralists', among them Dahl (1978, 1985, 1989). In fact, as a result of both conceptual and empirical problems with pluralist theory, classic pluralism has effectively been dissolved into a series of competing schools and tendencies, although the contours of a new 'neo-pluralist' position have crystallized (see McLennan, 1984, 1995). This is a noteworthy theoretical development, which is particularly apparent in Dahl's writings.

Democracy, corporate capitalism and the state

In *A Preface to Economic Democracy* (1985), Dahl argued that the main threats to liberty in the contemporary world have not turned out to be related, as de Tocqueville and others predicted, to demands for equality – the threat of a majority to level social difference and eradicate political diversity (Dahl, 1985, pp. 44ff, 50ff, 161–3). There may be tensions between equality and liberty, but equality is not in general inimical to liberty. In fact, the most fundamental challenge to liberty derives from *inequality*, or liberty of a certain kind: 'liberty to accumulate unlimited economic resources and to organize economic activity into hierarchically governed enterprises' (p. 50). The modern system of ownership and control of firms is deeply implicated in the creation of a variety of forms of inequality, all of which threaten the extent of political liberty. As Dahl put it:

> Ownership and control contribute to the creation of great differences among citizens in wealth, income, status, skills, information, control over information and propaganda, access to political leaders, and, on the average, predictable life chances, not only for mature adults but also for the unborn, infants, and children. After all due qualifications have been made, differences like these help in turn to generate significant inequalities among citizens in their capacities and opportunities for participating as political equals in *governing the state.* (1985, p. 55)

In stark contrast to *A Preface to Democratic Theory* (1956), Dahl averred, in a major concession to Marx's theories of the state (although he did not acknowledge this in so many words), that modern 'corporate capitalism' tends 'to produce inequalities in social and economic resources so great as to bring about severe violations of political equality and hence of the democratic process' (1985, p. 60).[3]

The nature of these violations, however, goes beyond the creation and immediate impact of economic inequalities. For the very capacity of governments to act in ways that interest groups may desire is constrained, as many Marxists have argued and as neo-pluralists like Charles Lindblom also now accept (Lindblom, 1977; cf. Dahl, 1985, p. 102). The constraints on Western governments and state institutions – constraints imposed by the requirements of private accumulation – systematically limit policy options. The system of private investment, private property, etc., creates objective exigencies that must be met if economic growth and stable development are to be sustained. If these arrangements are threatened, economic chaos quickly ensues and the legitimacy of governments can be undermined. In order to remain in power in a liberal democratic electoral system, governments must, in other words, take action to secure the profitability and prosperity of the private sector: they are dependent upon the process of capital accumulation which they have for their own sake to maintain. Lindblom has explained the point well:

> Because public functions in the market system rest in the hands of businessmen, it follows that jobs, prices, production, growth, the standard of living, and the economic security of everyone all rest in their hands. Consequently government officials cannot be indifferent to how well business performs its functions. Depression, inflation, or other economic disasters can bring down a government. A major function of government, therefore, is to see to it that businessmen perform their tasks. (Lindblom, 1977, pp. 122–3)

A government's policies must follow a political agenda that is at least favourable to, i.e. biased towards, the development of the system of private enterprise and corporate power.

---

[3] Dahl made the same point about 'bureaucratic socialism' without, however, developing it at any length (1985, p. 60).

Democratic theory is thus faced with a major challenge, a challenge far greater than de Tocqueville and J. S. Mill imagined, and far more complex than the classic pluralist theorists ever conceived. Political representatives would find it extremely difficult, if not impossible, to carry out the wishes of an electorate committed to reducing the adverse effects on democracy and political equality of corporate capitalism. Democracy is embedded in a socioeconomic system that systematically grants a 'privileged position' to business interests. According to Dahl, this ought to be a concern to all those interested in the relation between the liberties that exist in principle for all citizens in a democracy and those that exist in practice. A commitment to democracy can only be sustained in the contemporary era, he contended, if one recognizes that self-government cannot be fully achieved unless there is a major transformation in the power of the corporations. This, in turn, entails recognition of the superiority of the right to self-government over the right to productive property (Dahl, 1985, p. 162). The fulfilment of the promise of political liberty requires the establishment of a widespread system of cooperative forms of ownership and control in firms; that is, the extension of democratic principles to the workplace and to the economy in general (see Dahl, 1989, chs 22–3). Dahl's proposals for overcoming the economic obstacles to democracy will be returned to later (see ch. 10 below). The point to stress here is that in the view of neo-pluralists like Dahl and Lindblom, interest groups cannot be treated as necessarily equal, and the state cannot be regarded as a neutral arbiter among all interests: the business corporation wields disproportionate influence over the state and, therefore, over the nature of democratic outcomes.

The above considerations suggest the need to examine more closely the actual functioning of state institutions. It would not be surprising if sectors of the state – above all, the less accountable sectors like defence – were locked into the interest structure of a number of major manufacturers (see Duverger, 1974). But it would be quite wrong to suggest, neo-pluralists emphasized, that democratic institutions are controlled *directly* by the various economic interest groups with which they interact. In pursuing their own interests (e.g. the prestige and stability of their jobs, the influence of their departments), 'state managers' are more than likely to develop their own aims and objectives. Political representatives and state officials can constitute a powerful interest group, or a powerful set of competing interest groups, concerned to enhance (expand) the state itself and/or to secure particular electoral outcomes. Democratic politicians are engaged not only in satisfying the demands of leading groups in civil society, but also in pursuing political strategies which place on the agenda certain issues at the expense of others; mobilizing or undermining particular sectors of the community; appeasing or ignoring special demands; and stimulating or playing down electoral matters (see Nordlinger, 1981). In the context of these processes, neo-pluralists recognized the complex possible ramifications and dangers of the development of entrenched political interests and bureaucratic structures which always make it necessary to analyse 'who actually gets what, when and how' (see Pollitt, 1984). Despite the prominence granted to business interests, neo-pluralists have been careful not to portray a settled or fixed picture of the forces and relations underpinning contemporary democratic politics. They have retained some of the essential tenets of classic pluralism, including the account of the way liberal democracy generates a variety of pressure groups, an ever shifting set of demands and an ultimately indeterminate array of political possibilities. In addition, they have continued to affirm liberal democracy as a crucial obstacle to the development of a monolithic, unresponsive state: competitive political parties, an open electoral sphere and vigilant pressure groups can achieve, they hold, a degree of political accountability that no other model of state power can match. Model VI presents a summary of the classic pluralist and neo-pluralist positions.

What exactly democracies are and what exactly they ought to be are issues which have become perhaps more complicated with the passage of time. The trajectory of pluralism illustrates this well; theories of the character and desirable nature of democracy have been successively altered. Within pluralism, many of the central questions about the principles, key features and general conditions of democracy are now more open to debate than ever before. The same can be said, it is interesting to note, about developments in rival theoretical perspectives, especially neo-Marxism.

Accumulation, legitimation and the restricted sphere of the political

There are two significant theoretical strands in political studies which have extended the critique of pluralism: neo-Marxist developments in state theory and appraisals by social scientists of the significance of 'corporatist' tendencies in modern political institutions.[4] In setting out these developments below in broad outline, I shall not only examine their contributions to the discussion of pluralism and democratic theory, but also highlight the controversies among the leading authors. The main focus will be on the neo-Marxist discussion of the state, since, for my purposes here, it is of greater interest than the corporatist contribution. However, there is a discussion of the latter towards the end of the chapter, before a consideration of some of the outstanding issues posed by pluralism and its critics.

Throughout the 1960s and 1970s there was a notable revival of interest in the analysis of democracy and state power among Marxist writers (see Jessop, 1977; 1990, for a survey). As chapter 4 sought to show, Marx left an ambiguous heritage, never fully reconciling his understanding of the state as an instrument of class domination with his acknowledgement that the state might also have significant political independence. Lenin's emphasis on the oppressive nature of capitalist state institutions certainly did not resolve this ambiguity, and his writings seem even less compelling after Stalin's purges and the rise (and fall) of the Soviet state (see ch. 8 below). Since the deaths of Marx and Engels, many Marxist

---

[4] By 'corporatist' tendencies is meant here the progressive emergence of formal and/or informal, extraparliamentary arrangements between leaders of key labour, business and state organizations to resolve major political issues in exchange for the enhancement of their corporate interests (see Schmitter, 1974; Panitch, 1976; Offe, 1980, 1996a).

In sum: model VI

Pluralism

Principle(s) of justification

Secures government by minorities and, hence, political liberty

Crucial obstacle to the development of excessively powerful factions and an unresponsive state

Key features

Citizenship rights, including one-person-one-vote, freedom of expression, freedom of organization

A system of checks and balances between the legislature, executive, judiciary and administrative bureaucracy

Competitive electoral system with (at least) two parties

Classic pluralism	**Neo-pluralism**
Diverse range of (overlapping) interest groups seeking political influence	Multiple pressure groups, but political agenda biased towards corporate power
Governments mediate and adjudicate between demands	The state, and its departments, forge their own sectional interests
Constitutional rules embedded in a supportive political culture	Constitutional rules function in context of diverse political culture and system of radically unequal economic resources

General conditions

Power is shared and bartered by numerous groups in society	Power is contested by numerous groups
Different types of resource dispersed throughout population	Poor resource base of many groups prevents their full political participation
Value consensus on political procedures, range of policy alternatives and legitimate scope of politics	Uneven distribution of socioeconomic power provides opportunities for and limits to political options
Balance between active and passive citizenry sufficient for political stability	Unequal involvement in politics: insufficiently open government
International framework upholding the rules of pluralist and free-market societies	International order compromised by powerful multinational economic interests and dominant states

writers have made contributions of considerable importance to the analysis of politics (for instance, Lukács, Korsch and Gramsci explored the many complex and subtle ways classes sustain power), but it was not until the 1960s that the relation between state and society was fully re-examined in Marxist circles. The earliest of this work emerged as an attack on empirical democratic theory. It is useful, therefore, to start with this attack. The neo-Marxist 'alternative' to liberal democracy, to the extent to which one was explicitly developed, will be examined later, particularly in the following chapter.

Ralph Miliband provided a major stimulus to neo-Marxist thought with the publication of *The State in Capitalist Society* (1969). Noting the increasingly central position of the state in Western societies, he sought, on the one hand, to reassess the relationship Marx posited between class and state and, on the other, to evaluate the classic pluralist model of state–society relations which was then the reigning orthodoxy. Against those who held that the state is a neutral arbiter among social interests, he argued: (1) that in contemporary Western societies there is a dominant or ruling class which owns and controls the means of production; (2) that it has close links with powerful institutions, among them political parties, the military, universities and the media; and (3) that it has disproportionate representation at all levels of the state apparatus, especially in the 'command positions'. The social background of civil servants and public officers (overwhelmingly from the world of business and property, or from the professional middle classes), their special interests (a smooth career path), and their ideological dispositions (wholly accepting of the capitalist context in which they operate) mean that most, if not all, state institutions function as 'a crucially important and committed element in the maintenance and defence of the structure of power and privilege inherent in . . . capitalism' (Miliband, 1969, pp. 128–9). The capitalist class, Miliband insisted, is highly cohesive and constitutes a formidable constraint on Western governments and state institutions, ensuring that they remain 'instruments for the domination of society'. However, he maintained (defending what was earlier called Marx's position 1) that in order to be politically effective, the state must be able to separate itself routinely from ruling-class factions. Government policy may even be directed against the short-run interest of the capitalist class. He was also quick to point out that under exceptional circumstances the state can achieve a high order of independence from class interests: for example, in national crises.

In putting forward these arguments, Miliband was making a number of points – above all, about the political centrality of those who own and control the means of production – which were some years later to be considered plausible, as we have already seen, by neo-pluralists. But his unremitting emphasis on class as the central structural determinant of democratic politics and state action marks his position off from the later contributions of thinkers like Dahl: the emphasis on the capitalist class suggests an 'affinity' but not an 'identity' between perspectives, because neo-pluralists retain Weber's stress on the interrelated but to a significant degree independent dynamics of class relations and political processes (cf. McLennan, 1984, pp. 85–6). Nicos Poulantzas, Miliband's main neo-Marxist critic, developed a number of arguments which highlight even more sharply the gulf between these perspectives.

Poulantzas sought to clarify further Marx's position 1 (with its emphasis on scope for autonomous state action). He rejected what he considered Miliband's 'subjectivist' approach: his attempt to explore the relations between classes and the state through 'inter-personal relations'. As Poulantzas wrote: 'The *direct* participation of members of the capitalist class in the state apparatus and in government, even where it exists, is not the important side of the matter' (1972, p. 245). Much more important are the 'structural components' of the capitalist state which lead it to protect the long-term framework of capitalist production and to neglect wider issues of accountability.

In order to grasp these structural components, it is essential, Poulantzas argued, to understand that the state is the unifying element in capitalism. More specifically, the state must function to ensure (1) the 'political organization' of the dominant classes which, because of competitive pressures and differences of immediate interest, are continually broken up into 'class fractions'; (2) the 'political disorganization' of the working classes which, because of the concentration of production, among other things, can threaten the hegemony of the dominant classes; and (3) the political 'regrouping' of classes from non-dominant modes of production which, because they are economically and politically marginal, can act against the state (Poulantzas, 1973, pp. 287–8).

Since the dominant classes are vulnerable to fragmentation, their long-term interests require protection by a centralized political authority. The state can sustain this function only if it is 'relatively autonomous' from the particular interests of diverse fractions. But what exact autonomy a state has is a complicated matter. The state, Poulantzas stressed, is not a monolithic entity capable of straightforward direction; it is an arena of conflict and schism, the 'condensation of class forces' (Poulantzas, 1975). The degree of autonomy states acquire depends on the relations among classes and class fractions and on the intensity of social struggles. Insistent, at least in his early work, that power is 'the capacity to realize class interests', Poulantzas contended that state institutions are 'power centres', but classes 'hold power'. Relative autonomy 'devolves' on the state 'in the power relations of the class struggle' (Poulantzas, 1973, pp. 335–6).

Thus, the modern liberal democratic state is both a necessary result of the anarchic competition in civil society and a force in the reproduction of such competition and division. Its hierarchical bureaucratic apparatus, along with its electoral leadership, simultaneously seeks to construct and represent national unity – the 'people–nation' – and atomize and fragment the body politic (at least that part of 'the body' which potentially threatens the existing order) (Poulantzas, 1980). The state does not simply record socioeconomic reality, but enters into its very construction by codifying its form and reinforcing its forces.

There are, however, difficulties in Poulantzas's formulation of the relationship between classes, political power and the state. For he at one and the same time granted a certain autonomy to the state and argued that all power is class power.[5] Apart from such inconsistencies, he severely underestimated the state's

---

[5] In his last book Poulantzas took steps to resolve these problems: *State, Power, Socialism* (1980) was his most successful work. However, I do not think it fully surmounted the problems, although it contributed some important insights.

own capacity to influence and respond to social and economic developments. Viewing the state solely from a 'negative' perspective – that is, from the point of view of how far the state stabilizes capitalist economic enterprise, or prevents the development of potentially revolutionary influences – led to a peculiar de-emphasis of the capacity of the working classes, and of other groups and social movements, to influence the course and the organization of the state (see Frankel, 1979). To the extent that the state actually participates in the 'contradictions of class relations', it cannot merely be 'a defender of the status quo'. Further, Poulantzas's emphasis on the state as the 'condensation of class forces' meant that his account of the state was drawn without sufficient internal definition or institutional differentiation. How institutions operate and the manner in which the relationship among elites, government officials and parliamentarians evolves were neglected.

Invigorating the debate in neo-Marxist circles about democracy, class and state power, Claus Offe challenged – and attempted to recast – the terms of reference of both Miliband and Poulantzas (see Frankel, 1979; Keane, 1984b). For Offe, the state is neither simply a 'capitalist state' as Poulantzas contended (a state determined by class power) nor 'a state in capitalist society' as Miliband argued (a state that preserves a degree of political power free from immediate class interests). Starting from a conception of contemporary capitalism which stresses its internal differentiation into a number of sectors, Offe maintained that the most significant feature of the state is the way it is enmeshed in the contradictions of capitalism. In his account, there are four defining features of this situation.

First, privately owned capital is the chief foundation of economic enterprise; but economic ownership confers no direct political power. Second, the capital generated through private accumulation is the material basis upon which the finances of the state depend, these finances being derived from various modes of taxation upon wealth and income. Third, the state is dependent upon a source of income which it does not itself directly organize, save in nationalized industries. The state thus has a general 'interest' in facilitating processes of capital accumulation. This interest does not derive from any alliance of the state with capital as such but from the generic concern of the state with sustaining the conditions of its own perpetuation. Fourth, in liberal democratic states, political power has to be won by gaining mass electoral support. This political system helps mask the fact that state revenues are derived from privately accumulated wealth upon which the state, above all, relies.

The consequence of these characteristics of the capitalist state is that it is in a structurally contradictory position. On the one hand, the state must sustain the process of accumulation and the private appropriation of resources; on the other hand, it must preserve belief in itself as the impartial arbiter of class interests, thereby legitimating its power (Offe, 1984). The institutional separation of state and economy means that the state is dependent upon the flow of resources from the organization of profitable production. Since in the main the resources from the accumulation process are 'beyond its power to organize', there is an 'institutional *self-interest* of the state', and an interest of all those who wield state power, to safeguard the vitality of the capitalist economy.

With this argument, Offe differentiated his position from both Miliband and Poulantzas (and came close to the neo-pluralist view). As he put it, the institutional self-interest of the state 'does not result from alliance of a particular government with particular classes also interested in accumulation, nor does it result from any political power of the capitalist class which "puts pressure" on the incumbents of state power to pursue its class interest' (Offe and Ronge, 1975, p. 140). On its own behalf, the state is interested in sustaining accumulation.

The nature of political power is determined in a dual way: by formal rules of democratic and representative government which fix the institutional form of *access* to political power, and by the material content of the accumulation process which sets the *boundaries* of successful policies. Given that governments require electoral victory and the financial resources to implement policy, they are forced increasingly to intervene to manage economic problems. The growing pressure for intervention is contradicted, however, by capitalists' concern for freedom of investment and their obstinate resistance to state efforts to control productive processes (seen, for example, in efforts by business to avoid 'excessive regulation').

The modern state, therefore, faces contradictory imperatives: it must maintain the accumulation process without undermining either *private* accumulation or the belief in the market as a fair distributor of scarce resources. Intervention in the economy is unavoidable and yet the exercise of political control over the economy risks challenging the traditional basis of the legitimacy of the whole social order: the liberal belief that the collective good lies in private individuals pursuing their goals with minimal interference from an 'even-handed' state. The state, then, must intervene but disguise its preoccupation with the health of capital. Thus, Offe defined the liberal democratic capitalist state '(a) by its exclusion from accumulation, (b) by its necessary function for accumulation, (c) by its dependence upon accumulation, and (d) by its function to conceal and deny (a), (b) and (c)' (Offe, 1975, p. 144).

It is intriguing that while neo-pluralists have not been preoccupied with the kinds of issue raised by point (d) of Offe's definition, points (a)–(c) could be accepted readily by many neo-pluralist thinkers. The positions of Lindblom, Dahl and Offe converged on a number of fundamental issues: the dependence of Western democratic polities on privately generated resources; the degree to which liberal democratic states support (are necessarily biased towards) 'the corporate agenda'; and the extent to which the functioning of democracy is limited or constrained by private possession of the means of production. Although Offe ascribed a central role to the state as a mediator of class antagonisms and placed more emphasis on class than either Lindblom or Dahl would have accepted, they all also affirmed the view that 'state managers' can enjoy some independence from immediate economic and social pressures; that is, that the state cannot be understood exclusively in relation to, or reduced to, socioeconomic factors.

However, the prime emphasis of a great deal of Offe's work during the 1970s and early 1980s was on the state as a 'reactive mechanism'. He argued that if his definition of the modern state was valid, then 'it is hard to imagine that any state in capitalist society could succeed in performing the functions that are part of this definition simultaneously and successfully for any length of time' (Offe, 1975, p. 144). In order to examine this hypothesis, Offe investigated the nature of state administration and, in particular, its capacity for effective administrative action. The problems of administration are especially severe, Offe suggested, since many of the policies undertaken by contemporary governments do not simply complement market activities but actually replace them. Accordingly, Offe argued, in an interesting parallel to the corporatist view, that the state often selectively favours those whose acquiescence and support are crucial to the untroubled continuity of the existing order: leading corporate groups and organized labour. He contended, furthermore, that the representatives of these 'strategic forces' increasingly step in to resolve threats to political stability through a highly informal, extraparliamentary negotiation process (1979, p. 9). Thus, the liberal democratic state, in its bid to maintain the continuity of existing institutional arrangements, will tend to favour a compromise among powerful established interests: a compromise, however, that is all too often at the political and economic expense of vulnerable groups, for example the young, the elderly, the sick, the non-unionized and the non-white (see Offe, 1984, 1985, for a further discussion). The conditions of what I earlier called limited or non-participation of a large range of people are reproduced systematically, in Offe's view, as a result of the state's concern to sustain the overall institutional order in which capitalist mechanisms occupy a prime place.

There are many significant implications of Offe's analysis, including his view that key political problems are only 'solved' in modern capitalist democracies by either suppressing them or displacing them into other areas. Some of these implications will be examined in the following chapter, which focuses on theories of the 'crisis of democracy'. What need special emphasis here are the advantages of Offe's work over that of Miliband and Poulantzas as a contribution to the analysis of contemporary liberal democracies. Offe's emphasis on the way the state is enmeshed in class antagonisms surmounts some of the limitations of Miliband's and Poulantzas's 'negative' view of the state as functionally interlocked with the needs of capital or the capitalist class. Offe's work highlights the way that the state is pushed and pulled by a variety of forces into providing a range of policies and services which benefit not only capital but also some of the best organized sectors of the working class. The history of the labour movement is the history of a constant effort to offset some of the disadvantages of the power differential between employees and employers. In response, the state has introduced a variety of policies which increase the social wage, extend public goods, enhance democratic rights and alter the balance between public and private sectors. Offe's work clearly recognizes that social struggle is 'inscribed' into the very nature of the state and policy outcomes. While the state is dependent on the process of capital accumulation, the multiplicity of economic, social and electoral constraints on policy means, Offe rightly pointed out, that the state is by no means an unambiguous agent of capitalist reproduction. The democratic state's partiality and dependence can to a degree be both offset and masked by successive government attempts to manoeuvre within these conflicting pressures. In addition, Offe's emphasis on the frequent cost of this manoeuvring to the most vulnerable in society is, I believe, significant. To the extent that these issues can be placed at the heart of an 'empirical democratic theory', a basis is created for a more defensible account of the operations of existing democracies.

But Offe skewed his understanding of democracy and the state by underestimating the capacity of political representatives and administrators to be effective agents of *political strategy*. Although he formally recognized this capacity, he did not give it sufficient weight. His tendency to explain the development and limitations of state policy by reference to functional imperatives (the necessity to satisfy capital and labour, accumulation and legitimation) encouraged him to play down the 'strategic intelligence' which government and state agencies often display, and which is particularly apparent in a historical and comparative appreciation of the *diverse patterns* of state activity in liberal capitalist societies (see Bornstein et al., 1984; P. Hall, 1986). An additional shortcoming, related to this, involves his neglect of the different forms of institutional arrangement which constitute 'democracies' in different countries.[6] How these arrangements are reproduced over time, and how and why they differ from one country to another, with what consequences, are important considerations for any adequate assessment of democratic models (see Potter et al., 1997).

The changing form of representative institutions

One group of political analysts has attempted to overcome some of these gaps in democratic theory by studying the emergence of corporatism (see Schmitter, 1974; Panitch, 1976; Middlemas, 1979; cf. Jessop, 1990; Pierson, 1991). Although most 'corporatist' thinkers have overgeneralized the significance of their findings, it is useful to highlight the latter briefly, as they suggest a number of noteworthy trends. First, changes in the economy in the twentieth century have given rise to ever more concentrated economic power, which has often enabled private capital to gain the upper hand in struggles with labour. Faced with a recalcitrant labour force, capital can always move its centres of investment, making jobs more scarce and weakening the capacity of labour to press demands. Partly in response to the power of capital, and partly as a result of the sheer complexity of a modern economy, the labour movement has itself become more concentrated, more bureaucratized and more professionalized. Powerful organizations of both capital and labour have emerged to confront one another in the market place, each able and willing to disrupt the plans of the other. Before these developments there *was* a multiplicity of economic and social groups vying for political influence, as classic pluralism imagined, but there is no more. Any models in democratic theory which suggest that diverse interests are pursued, as a leading exponent of corporatist theory put it, by 'an unspecified number of multiple, voluntary, competitive, non-hierarchically ordered and self-determined . . . categories', are no longer valid (Schmitter, 1974, p. 93; see Held and Krieger, 1984, pp. 12–14).

---

[6] Many of these shortcomings have been addressed by Offe himself in his more recent writings (see, for example, 1996a, 1996b). These works examine the development of European democratic polities, West and East, shedding new light on the nature and prospects of democratic politics.

In the context of rising expectations and demands, especially in the first two decades following World War II, the ability of capital and labour to disrupt economic growth and political stability (by, respectively, withholding investment or taking strike action) posed ever more serious management problems for the state. But while class forces influenced state action, they never controlled the latter. Instead of the picture of classes dominating politics offered by Marxists, corporatist theorists focused on the centralized power of organized interest groups, and the attempts by the state to overcome the problems they generated by an *inventive* strategy of *political integration*. Thus, contemporary corporatism has been defined as:

> a system of interest representation in which the constituent units are organized into a limited number of singular, compulsory, hierarchically ordered and functionally differentiated categories, recognized or licensed (if not created) by the state and granted a deliberate representational monopoly within their respective categories in exchange for observing certain controls on their selection of leaders and articulation of demands and supports. (Schmitter, 1974, pp. 93–4)

Corporatist arrangements generally refer to 'tripartite' relations between organizations of employers, labour and the state, steered ultimately by the latter.

In the corporatist account, the directive capacities of the state have increased, allowing it to construct a framework for economic and political affairs. In return for direct channels of bargaining with state officials – a 'representational monopoly' – leaders of key organized interests (for example, the Trades Union Congress in Britain) were expected to deliver support for agreed policies and, if necessary, keep their own members firmly in line. The politics of negotiation became systematized along stricter, more formal lines, although most of the discussion between parties took place informally, behind closed doors and out of public view. A few key organizations participated in the resolution of pressing questions in exchange for relatively advantageous settlements for their members. Corporatist arrangements were, then, political strategies for securing the support of dominant trade unions, business associations and their respective constituencies.

There are several different accounts of the above developments to be found in the corporatist literature (e.g., Winkler, 1976; Schmitter, 1979; Panitch, 1980). In the context of this chapter, the differences between these accounts are, however, not as significant as the general political consequences that are said to follow from tripartite relations: the new political structures which crystallized with the 'post-liberal, corporate capitalist era'. Three central claims are pressed. First, it is argued that traditional representative political institutions have been progressively displaced by a decision-making process based on tripartism. The position of parliament as the supreme centre for policy articulation and agreement has been eroded; the passage of a bill through parliament is more than ever before a mere process of rubber stamping. Second, it is contended that parliamentary or territorial representation is no longer the chief way in which interests are expressed and protected. Although classic modes of representation remain (in the form of members of parliament, etc.), the most important work of

Figure 6.1 Corporatism and the erosion of parliament and party politics

political and economic management is carried out by functional represent-atives, i.e. by delegates from corporations, unions and branches of the state. Extraparliamentary political processes have steadily become the central domain of decision-making. Third, it is maintained that the scope for involvement in policy development by territorially based representatives, let alone by ordinary citizens, has declined steeply. Political participation becomes the preserve of organizational elites. In short, the sovereignty of parliament and the power of citizens are undermined by economic changes, political pressures and organizational developments. New 'flexible' avenues of negotiation replace the more complicated mechanisms of lawmaking and public authority. Those marginalized by these processes may object (e.g. the jobless and social activists of diverse kinds), sparking off 'unofficial' protest movements, but in general corporatist thinkers have tended to assume that the new institutional procedures forge a unity among the key societal factions. The major steps in the corporatist view are set out in figure 6.1.

The trends highlighted by corporatist thinkers are certainly noteworthy. The participation of organized interest groups in the governing process has major implications for democracy in the West (see Middlemas, 1979, p. 381). In focusing on the emergence of patterns of extraparliamentary negotiations about public issues, corporatists usefully shed light on one set of factors which help explain the limited effectiveness of formal representative structures, and the much discussed restricted scope of parliamentary bodies. If there has been a weakening of the sovereignty of the people, it would surely have to be explained in part by the terms of reference of corporatist thinkers. But several qualifications are in order.

To begin with, the idea that there was once a relatively unrestricted sphere of parliamentary discussion and initiative, now much denuded, should be treated with caution, as most political theorists from Marx to Weber, Lenin to Dahl, have done. It is clear that parliaments have always operated within a substantial range of constraints. The latter may indeed have changed over the years, but it would be very hard to justify the view that the effectiveness and authority of representative institutions have been particularly weakened in recent times. In addition, while corporatist theory has exposed some significant changes in the operations of post-war governments, few areas, if any, outside macroeconomic policy have been the subject of tripartite agreements; and even within macroeconomic policy very little besides incomes policies has fitted the 'corporatist' account. There are few sound reasons for supposing that functional representation has actually replaced the role of parties and parliaments. Moreover, to the extent that corporatist arrangements have developed, they have remained fragile because they require the presence of a relatively rare set of conditions which secure the integration of labour, including:

1 an attitude within the labour movement which favours 'cooperative management' over structural or redistributive measures in macroeconomic policy;
2 the presence of relevant state institutions for tripartite management initiatives;
3 the institutionalization of trade union power within a coordinated working-class movement;
4 sufficient centralization for decisions by labour confederations to be binding upon individual industrial unions;
5 adequate elite influence within unions to ensure rank-and-file compliance with agreed policies. (Adapted from Held and Krieger, 1984, p. 14)

Broad corporatist arrangements have taken hold in only a few countries, notably Austria, the Netherlands and Sweden; many of the conditions remain unmet elsewhere and in some countries like Britain only a few have been met for the shortest time (see Lehmbruch, 1979; cf. Williamson, 1989).

The prospects for the development of tripartite relations were brightest during the period of economic expansion from the 1950s to the early 1970s. The prosperity of these years certainly helped encourage the view that all key interests could be accommodated in the politics of the postwar era. Economic growth meant that management and labour, along with administrators of policy, might find scope for manoeuvre and a basis for satisfaction or future satisfaction. By contrast, the severe economic difficulties experienced in many countries from the mid-1970s to the late 1980s brought sharply into focus the limited common ground between labour and capital, and the poor prospects for the realization of institutions premissed upon the existence of a willingness to negotiate and compromise on core economic questions. In recognition of this, it is hardly surprising that the major concern of much later democratic theory shifted dramatically – to the 'crisis of democracy' (see ch. 7 below).

Attempts at constructing corporatist arrangements may themselves have contributed to some of the pressures that faced democracies from the mid-

1970s. The favouritism towards certain powerful or dominant groups expressed by corporatist strategies weakens the electoral/parliamentary support of the more vulnerable groups, which may be required for governments' stability. By placing certain issues high on the political agenda, tripartism leads inevitably to the marginalization or exclusion of others. More fundamentally, the attempt to enforce such strategies may erode respect for, and the acceptability of, institutions that have traditionally channelled conflict, e.g. party systems and conventions of collective bargaining. Thus, new arrangements may backfire, as some corporatist theorists have indeed suggested, encouraging the formation of opposition movements based on those excluded from key established political decision-making processes, e.g. ordinary workers, those concerned with environmental issues, anti-war campaigners, the women's movement activists and those in regional or nationalist movements (see Offe, 1980).

For corporatist arrangements to have fundamentally altered the character of democracy, they would probably have had to ensure not only a symmetry of power between the dominant organized interests – which would allow genuine bargaining – but also some way of involving in the process of decision-making all relevant interests and points of view. This they certainly have not done. To the extent that they represent a new form of representation, they mark an interesting but limited development in the theory and practice of democracy in capitalist society. However, the presence of corporatist institutions is certainly another factor to be considered, and certainly another force which further removes from ordinary citizens any substantial control over social, economic and political affairs.

Democratic theory is in a state of flux. There are almost as many differences among thinkers within each of the major strands of political analysis as there are among the traditions themselves. Many non-Marxists have come to appreciate the limitations placed on democratic life by, among other things, massive concentrations of ownership and control of productive property. The best of recent Marxist work has undertaken a reappraisal of liberal representative institutions and affirmed that state activity has to be partly understood in relation to the dynamics of electoral processes, changing patterns of interest constellations and the competitive pressure of groups, not all of which stem from class. In addition, there are interesting points of convergence in the normative aspirations of neo-pluralists and neo-Marxists. Although the former affirm the abiding importance of representative democracy, they concede that democratic life is unacceptably impaired by large concentrations of private economic power. Until recently, Marxists have not generally been prepared to rethink their commitment to the politics of Marx's classic vision (model IV, p. 120). But this has now changed. Partly in response to the state's growth in Western and Eastern Europe and the challenges to this, again, in West and East, there has been a reassessment by some Marxists of the liberal democratic emphasis on the importance of individual liberties and rights, as well as of groups and agencies organizing their activities independently of state or party control. The significance of certain liberal democratic innovations has, as chapters 7 and 8 will show in more detail, been more fully appreciated.

However, even the best contemporary models of democracy share a number of limitations which stem from their focus on, above all, state–economy relations. While Marxists have extended the concept of politics to embrace the power relations of production, none of the traditions has adequately examined those vicious circles of limited or non-participation in politics anchored in relations of sexual and racial domination, or pondered the implications of the work of figures like Wollstonecraft for democratic theory (see pp. 49–54). This partiality and one-sidedness mean unquestionably that the insights of contemporary models of democracy remain limited. Marxism, pluralism and the other non-Marxist approaches heretofore examined all appear to be premissed on a conception that the political coincides with the public sphere of state and/or economic relations, and that the latter is the proper domain of political activity and study. Accordingly, the world of 'private' relations, with its radically asymmetrical demands and opportunities for citizens, is excluded from view. How exactly one overcomes this deficiency, as one must, while reconciling some of the most important insights of the leading traditions of democratic theory remains an open question.

7 From Postwar Stability to Political Crisis: The Polarization of Political Ideals

The decade and a half following World War II has been characterized by many as a period of consent, faith in authority and legitimacy. The long war appeared to have generated a tide of promise and hope for a new era marked by progressive changes in the relationship between state and society on both sides of the Atlantic. In Britain, the coronation of Queen Elizabeth II in 1953 – at least two million people turned out in the streets, over twenty million watched on television, nearly twelve million listened on radio – reinforced the impression of a social consensus, a postwar social contract (Marwick, 1982, pp. 109–10). The monarchy signalled tradition and stability while parliament symbolized accountability and reform. In the US, the patriotic allegiance of all citizens seemed to be fully established. As one commentator put it, echoing much popular opinion,

> America has been and continues to be one of the world's most democratic nations. Here, far more than elsewhere, the public is allowed to participate widely in the making of social and political policy.... The people think they know what they want and are in no mood to be led to greener pastures. (Hacker, 1967, p. 68, quoted by Margolis, 1983, p. 117)

During the postwar years political commentators from right to left of the political spectrum remarked on the widespread support for the central institutions of society. A belief in a world of free enterprise, moderated and regulated by an interventionist state, was reinforced by the political excesses of the right (fascism and Nazism in central and southern Europe) and the left (communism in Eastern Europe). The Cold War exerted, in addition, an immense pressure confining all so-called 'respectable' politics to the democratic centre ground. Commenting on this period in British politics, A. H. Halsey wrote: 'Liberty, equality, and fraternity all made progress.' Full employment and growing educational and occupational opportunity marked it as a time 'of high net upward mobility and of slowly burgeoning mass affluence. The tide of political consensus flowed strongly for twenty years or more' (Halsey, 1981, pp. 156–7). The existence of this consensus was, as we have seen, strongly supported by academic studies like Almond and Verba's *The Civic Culture* which suggested that the leading Western democracies enjoyed a highly developed sense of loyalty to their system of government, a strong sense of deference to political authority, and attitudes of trust and confidence (see pp. 166–7 above).

The boundaries of the 'new politics' were set by a commitment to social and economic reform, by respect for the constitutional state and representative government, and by a desire to encourage individuals' pursuit of their interests while maintaining policies in the national or public interest. Underpinning these concerns was a conception of the state as the most suitable means for the promotion of 'the good' of both the individual and the collective. By protecting citizens from arbitrary interference and by aiding those who were vulnerable, governments could create a wider range of opportunities for all. Nearly all political parties throughout the 1950s and 1960s believed that in office they should intervene to reform the position of the unjustly privileged and aid the position of the underprivileged. Only the politics of a 'caring state', embodying concern and fair-mindedness, specialization and expertise, could create the conditions whereby the welfare and good of each citizen were compatible with the welfare and good of all.

This welfare or 'social democratic' or 'reformist' conception of politics had its origins in some of the ideas and principles of developmental democracy (see ch. 3, pp. 91–3, above). But it received its clearest expression in the actual politics and policies of the expanding, Keynesian, interventionist state in the years following World War II. The rapid economic growth of those years helped finance a programme of seemingly ever greater social welfare. But with the downturn in world economic activity in the mid-1970s the welfare state began to lose its attractiveness and came under attack from both the left (for having made few, if any, real inroads into the world of the privileged and powerful) and the right (for being too costly and a threat to individual liberty). The coalition of interests that had once supported it, including politicians from a wide variety of political parties, trade unionists committed to social reform and industrialists concerned to create a stable political environment for economic growth, began to break down. Whether the state should be rolled 'backward' or 'forward' became the subject of intense discussion. In the process, the synthesis of ideas that underpinned the welfare state began to look ever weaker. In arguing for individual rights, plus carefully guided state action to provide greater equity and justice for all, the advocates of a growing sphere of state management paved the way for a vastly expanded programme of state intervention in civil society. The trouble is that many of them said relatively little about the desirable forms and limits of state action and thus helped to engender, or so at least some would argue, paternalism, bureaucracy and hierarchy in and through state policies. The consequences of this for the nature and dynamics of democracy were considerable.

This chapter examines further the debate about the nature of liberal democracies by considering, initially, two sets of arguments. The first set is about the character of the postwar years of social 'consensus' (the 'end of ideology' and 'one-dimensional society' theses). The second set concerns the erosion of consensus and the growing 'crisis of democracy' from the late 1960s ('government overload' and 'legitimation crisis' theories). Each set of positions clarifies some of the key rifts in postwar political perspectives. In examining each set in turn the context is provided for an enhanced understanding of the actual condition of democratic politics as well as of two additional models of democracy: 'legal democracy', the model of the New Right; and 'participatory democracy', the model of the New Left. Figure 7.1 plots the broad relations between these positions and connects them to some pertinent models examined in earlier chapters. (It also provides a rough indication of where to locate 'deliberative democracy', which I shall discuss in chapter 9.)

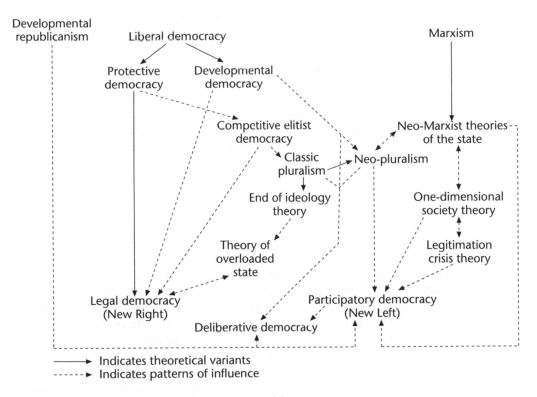

Figure 7.1 Theoretical trajectories of democratic models

A brief word of caution about terminology is in order. Many of the ideas of the New Right and New Left are not new; some were developed long before they became prominent as ideas of the New Right or New Left (and some will be quite recognizable from the theoretical positions considered in previous chapters). Nevertheless, the circumstances in which the New Right and New Left emerged have helped give 'old' ideas new force. They have, in addition, stimulated innovation within the sets of ideas themselves. It is noteworthy also that the New Right emerged partly in bitter opposition to the prominence of the New Left movements (broadly, a variety of left groupings, the women's movement, environmental campaigners and the peace movement) in the late 1960s and early 1970s. From the late 1960s something of a renaissance occurred in the political theory of democracy, albeit a renaissance marked by a fierce polarization of views.

A legitimate democratic order or a repressive regime?

Political analysts thinking about the extraordinary turmoil of the twentieth-century industrial capitalist world – two colossal wars, the Russian revolution, the depression of the 1930s, the rise of fascism and Nazism – were impressed by the relative political and social harmony which followed World War II, American, British and Continental political scientists and sociologists working in the late 1950s and early 1960s attempted to develop explanations of this state of affairs. One prominent group, arguing within the framework of classic pluralism, developed the 'end of ideology' thesis. It is a thesis that was markedly in tune with views expressed during the late 1950s and early 1960s in the media, in the main political parties, in official political circles and in many of the organizations of the labour movement. Another much smaller group expressed a radically dissenting view: it offered an interpretation of events which found little, if any, sympathy in the main institutions of state, economy and culture, although it had a major impact on students and the new radical protest movements of the 1960s. This second group, arguing within a modified Marxist framework, analysed the so-called 'end of ideology' as the realization of a highly repressive order: the 'one-dimensional society'.[1]

By the 'end of ideology' Lipset, one of the best-known exponents of this position, meant a decline in the support by intellectuals, labour unions and left-wing political parties for what he called 'red flag waving'; that is, the socialist project defined by Marxism-Leninism (Lipset, 1963). The general factors which explained this situation were the demise of Marxism-Leninism as an attractive ideology in the light of its record as a political system in Eastern Europe, and the resolution of the key problems facing Western industrial capitalist societies. More specifically, Lipset argued that, within Western democracies, 'the ideological issues dividing left and right have been reduced to a little more or a little less government ownership and economic planning', and that it 'really makes little difference which political party controls the domestic policies of individual nations'. All this reflects, he contended, the fact that the fundamental political problems of the industrial revolution have been solved: 'the workers have achieved political citizenship; the conservatives have accepted the welfare state; the democratic left has recognized that an increase in overall state power carries with it more dangers to freedom than solutions for economic problems' (Lipset, 1963, pp. 442–3). Arguing along parallel lines to Almond and Verba's, Lipset affirmed that a fundamental consensus on general political values – in favour of equality, achievement and the procedures of democracy – conferred legitimacy on present political and social arrangements. Accordingly, the Western democracies would come to enjoy a future defined by progressive stability, convergence in the political views of classes and parties, and the steady erosion of conflict. Such judgements were reinforced by other scholars studying particular political cultures, for instance Butler and Stokes in Britain (1974).

The 'end of ideology' theorists offered an interpretation of political life which Marcuse, who made famous the notion of the 'one-dimensional society', rejected (Marcuse, 1964). Yet curiously, as already noted, they all shared a common starting point: an attempt to explain the appearance of political harmony in Western capitalism in the immediate postwar years.

[1] Note that, unless indicated to the contrary, writers in both groups were writing about trends in advanced industrial societies generally.

Marcuse's analysis began by pointing to a multiplicity of forces which were combining to aid the management and control of the modern economy. First, he noted the spectacular development of the means of production, itself the result of the growing concentration of capital, radical changes in science and technology, the trend towards mechanization and automation, and the progressive transformation of management into ever larger private bureaucracies. Second, he emphasized the increasing regulation of free competition, a consequence of state intervention which both stimulates and supports the economy and leads to the expansion of public bureaucracy. Third, he described a reordering of national priorities by international events and the permanent threat of war, created by the Cold War and the ever present possibility of nuclear catastrophe. In short, the prevailing trends in society were leading, Marcuse contended, to the establishment of massive private and public organizations which threatened to engulf social life.

A crucial consequence of this state of affairs Marcuse labelled 'depoliticization': the eradication of political and moral questions from public life by an obsession with technique, productivity and efficiency. The single-minded pursuit of production for profit by large and small businesses, and the state's unquestioned support for this objective in the name of economic growth, set a highly limited political agenda. Moreover, these forces created a situation in which public affairs became concerned merely with debating different means – the end was given, i.e. more and more production. Depoliticization resulted from the spread of 'instrumental reason'; that is, the spread of the concern with the efficiency of different means with respect to pregiven ends.

This state of affairs was further reinforced, according to Marcuse, by the way the cultural traditions of subordinate classes and minorities were swamped by the mass media producing 'packaged culture'. The mass media were shaped to a significant extent by the concerns of the advertising industry with its relentless drive to increase consumption. The effect, he argued, was 'false consciousness'; that is, a state of awareness in which people no longer consider or know what is in their real interests. Marcuse did analyse counter-trends to this state of affairs but his general emphasis, at least in *One-Dimensional Man* (1964), was on the way the cult of affluence and consumerism (in modern industrial capitalist society) creates modes of behaviour that are adaptive, passive and acquiescent. Against the portrayal of the political order – from Schumpeter to Lipset – as one based on consent and legitimacy, Marcuse emphasized the way it is sustained by ideological and coercive forces. The idea of 'rule by the people' remains a dream.

The details of the above theories are not as important as their overall general claims. For despite their many differences – differences which centre on whether the legitimacy of the political order is genuine or contrived – the theorists of the end of ideology and one-dimensionality both emphasize (1) a high degree of compliance and integration among all groups and classes in society, and (2) that the stability of the political and social system is reinforced as a result. The argument of the two previous chapters suggests that doubt should be cast on both these claims. The research findings reviewed on political attitudes and opinions indicate that neither a system of 'shared values' nor one of 'ideological domination' simply conferred legitimacy on democratic politics after 1945. The situation was far more complicated. Moreover, the complications were acutely highlighted by the greatest difficulty to face the literature on consensus, be it voluntary or contrived; that is, the actual sequence of events which followed its publication. The simple picture of postwar political harmony and stable prosperity was heavily compromised by a whole variety of economic, political and cultural developments in the 1960s and 1970s. As the prosperity of the Western market economies came under question, so did the illusion that acquiescence by the mass of people meant political legitimacy.

Increasing economic difficulties, the oil crisis of 1973, the demise of the Bretton Woods international economic framework, retrenchment in many Western economies, mounting problems in meeting the costs of the welfare state, growing signs of disillusionment with the dominant political parties, electoral scepticism in the face of the claims of politicians: all of these were signs indicating that within and underlying the political system were deeply structured difficulties (see J. Cohen and Rogers, 1983; Held, 1984; Krieger, 1986). While the state had become immensely complex, it was in general much less monolithic and much less capable of imposing clear direction than Marcuse had suggested, and enjoyed less legitimacy than the proponents of the 'end of ideology' had thought. By the end of the 1960s few denied that dissensus was rife: the certitude and confidence of the middle ground (and largely of the middle and upper classes) were slipping away; and the conditional or instrumental consent of segments of the working classes seemed to be giving way to disillusionment and conflict.

Neither the theory of the 'end of ideology' nor that of 'one-dimensionality' can account adequately for the relation between state and society, the instability of the economy and government policy, and the persistence and escalation of tension and strife which emerged in the postwar years. While these phenomena did not culminate in a major revolutionary attack upon the state (except in France, where events, arguably, came close to this) and the clear-cut championing of a new model of democracy, they certainly constituted a severe test of the very foundation of the political order. As the 1960s went by, it seemed that a crisis of the liberal democratic state was developing. What exactly was the nature of the crisis? How were its dimensions to be analysed? What were its origins and causes?

Overloaded state or legitimation crisis?

What is a crisis? A distinction must be drawn between, on the one hand, a partial crisis (or phase of limited instability) and, on the other, a crisis that might lead to the transformation of a society. The former refers to such phenomena as the political–business cycle, involving booms and recessions in economic activity, which have been a chronic feature of modern economies. The latter refers to the undermining of the core or organizational principle of a society; that is, to the erosion or destruction of those societal relations which determine the scope of and limits to change for, among other things, political and economic activity. A crisis of this second type, which will be referred to here as a 'crisis with transformative potential', involves challenges to the very core of the political order.

In marked contrast to those political analysts of the 1950s and early 1960s who talked about 'integration', 'consensus' and 'political stability', those thinking about the late 1960s and 1970s were struck by almost the opposite. The work of political scientists and political sociologists during this period reflected preoccupations with 'a breakdown in consensus', 'a crisis of democracy' and 'political and economic decline'. This section will set out briefly the arguments of two contrasting theories of crisis – theories which tried to make sense of the events of the 1960s and early 1970s and the consequences they had for the whole modern state system, from representative institutions to administrative offices. The contrast is, again, between writers arguing from the premisses of a pluralist theory of politics and those arguing from the premisses of Marxist theory. Both groups of writers, it is worth stressing, were staunch 'revisionists'; they modified substantially the theories they took as their starting point.

The first group, arguing from pluralist premisses, can be referred to as theorists of 'overloaded government'; the second group, arguing from Marxist premisses, developed a theory of 'legitimation crisis'. The writers who discussed 'overloaded government' included Brittan (1975, 1977), Huntington (1975), Nordhaus (1975), King (1976) and Rose and Peters (1977). The theory of 'legitimation crisis' was developed by, among others, Habermas (1976) and Offe (1984), whose basic position has already been set out (see ch. 6 above).[2] For the purposes of this chapter it is unnecessary to follow all the details of these writers' analyses, or the differences in emphasis between them. It will be enough to present broad general summaries of the two positions.

It should be emphasized that both these contrasting accounts of the crises facing the modern democratic state focus on the possibility of 'crisis with transformative potential'. But while theorists of overload were clearly warning of this as a danger to the liberal democratic state (and suggested measures of containment and control), the theorists of 'legitimation crisis' saw this as presenting both difficult political dilemmas and potentiality for progressive, radical change. It is also noteworthy that overload theories were influential in party political circles and much discussed in general ways in the media; theories of legitimation crisis remained by and large the province of a few political analysts, although they gained influence in some academic circles.

To help comprehension of the arguments, the key steps of each are set out in figures 7.2 and 7.3. Each of these steps is briefly discussed below, and some of the major points are connected to political examples and illustrations.

The overloaded government

1a   A pluralist starting point: the theorists of the overloaded state frequently characterize power relations in terms of fragmentation: power is shared and bartered by numerous groups representing diverse and competing interests.

---

[2] Both overload and legitimation crisis theories were developed with reference to liberal democratic capitalist societies. Their advocates believed them to be applicable to many states within these societies, although it should be noted that legitimation crisis theory may shed more light on the collapse of communist regimes than on tensions in capitalist states (see ch. 8).

Hence, political outcomes are the result of numerous processes and pressures; governments try to mediate and adjudicate between demands.

1b   The postwar market society plus the early successes of Keynesian economic policy generated rising mass affluence and the general prosperity of the postwar years, e.g. booms in consumer goods, in new housing, and in the television and entertainment industries.

2   Accordingly, expectations increased, linked to higher standards of living, e.g. annual increments in income and welfare, availability of schooling and higher education.

3   Aspirations were reinforced by a 'decline in deference' or a decline in respect for authority and status. This was itself a result of growing affluence, 'free' welfare, health and education which undermined private initiative and responsibility, and egalitarian and meritocratic ideologies which promised much more than could ever realistically be achieved.

4   In this context, groups learnt to press politicians and governments hard to meet their particular interests and ambitions, e.g. higher wages (most employed groups), protection of jobs in declining industrial sectors (some trade unions), high interest rates (savers), low interest rates (borrowers, including domestic industry), low prices (consumer groups), higher prices (some business organizations).

5   In order to secure maximum votes politicians too often promised more than they could deliver, and sometimes promised to meet contradictory and therefore impossible sets of demands: competition between parties led to a spiral of ever greater promises.

6   Thus, aspirations were reinforced; political parties were seen as competing means to the same end, i.e. better standards of living.

7   In government, parties all too often pursued strategies of appeasement for fear of losing future votes. 'Firm action' to set the economy on the 'right path' or deal with 'young offenders', for example, was rarely if ever taken.

8   Appeasement strategies and the pursuit of self-interest by administrators generated ever more state agencies (in health, education, industrial relations, environmental protection, etc.) of increasingly unwieldy proportions. 'Faceless' bureaucracies developed which often failed to meet the ends for which they were originally designed.

9   The state was ever less able to provide firm effective management, faced as it was with, for instance, the spiralling costs of its programmes. Public spending became excessive and inflation just one symptom of the problem.

10   As the state expanded, it progressively destroyed the realm of individual initiative, the space for 'free, private enterprise'.

11   A vicious circle was set in motion (go back to section 4 on figure 7.2 and carry on round) which could be broken only by, among other things, 'firm', 'decisive' political leadership less responsive to democratic pressures and demands.

Legitimation crisis of the state

Overload theorists argued, in essence, that the form and operation of democratic institutions was essentially *dysfunctional* for the efficient regulation of economic and social affairs, a position broadly shared with the New Right.

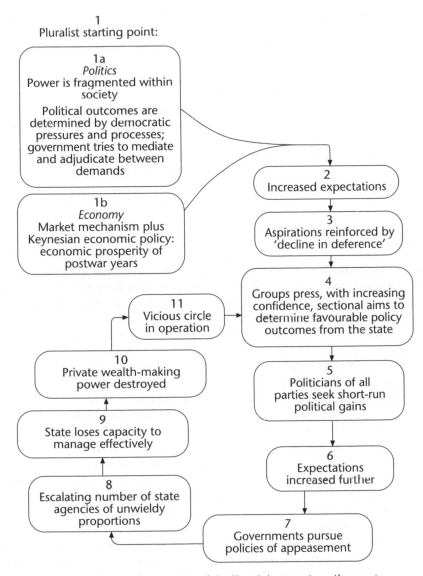

1
Pluralist starting point:

1a
Politics
Power is fragmented within society

Political outcomes are determined by democratic pressures and processes; government tries to mediate and adjudicate between demands

1b
Economy
Market mechanism plus Keynesian economic policy: economic prosperity of postwar years

2
Increased expectations

3
Aspirations reinforced by 'decline in deference'

4
Groups press, with increasing confidence, sectional aims to determine favourable policy outcomes from the state

11
Vicious circle in operation

10
Private wealth-making power destroyed

9
State loses capacity to manage effectively

8
Escalating number of state agencies of unwieldy proportions

5
Politicians of all parties seek short-run political gains

6
Expectations increased further

7
Governments pursue policies of appeasement

Figure 7.2 Overloaded government: crisis of the liberal democratic welfare regime

(Some of the theorists of the overloaded state became, in fact, advocates of New Right positions, although this was by no means true of all of them; cf. Huntington, 1975; King, 1976.) In contrast, legitimation crisis theorists held that it was only by focusing on class relations and the constraints on politics imposed by capital that an adequate basis could be established for understanding crisis tendencies. The main elements of their theory can be stated as follows:

1a A Marxist starting point: while political parties compete for office through the formal rules of democratic and representative processes, their power is severely constrained by the state's dependence on resources generated to a very large extent by private capital accumulation. The state must take decisions which are compatible in the long run with business (capitalist) interests while, at one and the same time, appearing neutral between all (class) interests so that mass electoral support can be sustained.

1b   The economy is organized through the private appropriation of resources which are socially produced (i.e. produced via a complex web of interdependence between people). Production is organized for profit maximization. The 'Keynesian state' in the immediate postwar period helped to sustain two decades of remarkable prosperity.

2   But the economy is inherently unstable: economic growth is constantly disrupted by crises. The increasingly extensive effects of changes within the system (high rates of unemployment and inflation at the troughs and peaks of the political–business cycle) and/or the impact of external factors (shortages of raw materials as a result of international political events, for instance) have to be carefully managed.

3   Accordingly, if the economic and political order of contemporary societies is to be maintained, extensive state intervention is constantly required. The principal concerns of the state become sustaining the capitalist economy and managing class antagonisms (through the agencies, for example, of welfare, social security and law and order). The state must act to ensure the acquiescence and support of powerful groups, especially the business community and leading trade unions.

4   In order to avoid economic and political crises, governments take on responsibility for more and more areas of the economy and civil society, e.g. the rescue of industries in trouble. Why? Because the bankruptcy of a large firm or bank has implications for numerous apparently sound enterprises, for whole communities and hence for political stability.

5   In order to fulfil their increasingly diversified roles, governments and the state more generally have to expand their administrative structures (e.g. enlargement of the civil service), thus increasing their own internal complexity. This growing complexity, in turn, entails an increased need for cooperation and, more importantly, requires an expanding state budget.

6   The state must finance itself through taxation and loans from capital markets, but it cannot do this in a way that will interfere with the accumulation process and jeopardize economic growth. These constraints help to create a situation of almost permanent inflation and crisis in public finances.

7   The state cannot develop adequate policy strategies within the systematic constraints it encounters; the result is a pattern of continuous change and breakdown in government policy and planning (e.g. a 'stop–start' approach to the economy, the fluctuating use of fiscal and monetary policy). Habermas and Offe refer to this as a 'rationality crisis' or a 'crisis of rational administration'. The state, controlled by a right-wing party, cannot drastically reduce its costs and spending for fear of the power of leading protest groups to cause large-scale disruption; the state, controlled by a left-wing party, cannot efficiently pursue strong socialist policies because business confidence would be undermined and the economy might be drastically weakened. Hence, governments of different persuasions come and go, and policy chops and changes.

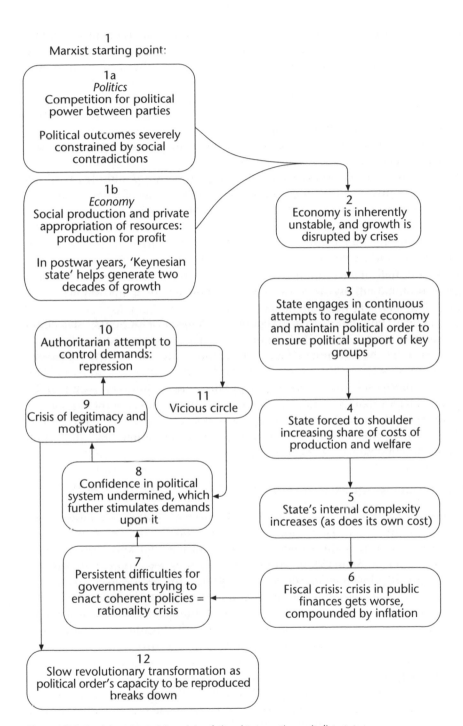

Figure 7.3 Legitimation crisis: crisis of the democratic capitalist state

8   The state's growing intervention in the economy and other spheres draws attention to issues of choice, planning and control. The 'hand of the state' is more visible and intelligible than 'the invisible hand' of the market. More and more areas of life are seen by the general population as politicized, i.e. as falling within the state's (via the government's) potential control. This development, in turn, stimulates ever greater demands on the state, for example for participation and consultation over decisions.

9   If these demands cannot be fulfilled within available alternatives, the state may face a 'legitimation and motivation crisis'. Struggles over, among other things, income, control over the workplace, and the nature and quality of the state's goods and services might spill beyond the boundaries of existing institutions of economic management and political control.

10   In this situation, a 'strong state' may emerge: a state which places 'order' above everything else, repressing dissent and forcefully defusing crises. Authoritarian states smashed most forms of opposition in the late 1930s and 1940s in Central and Southern Europe. One cannot rule out such attempts happening again or, much more likely, representative governments using progressively more 'strong arm' tactics.

11   If one of the two scenarios in section 10 occurs, a vicious circle may be set in motion. Move back to section 8 (figure 7.3) and carry on round.

12   However, the fundamental transformation of the system cannot be ruled out: it is unlikely to result from an event, an insurrectional overthrow of state power; it is more likely to be marked by a process, the continuous erosion of the existing order's capacity to be reproduced and the progressive emergence of alternative institutions, e.g. state agencies taking more industry under public control, state organization of ever more resources according to need not profit, the extension of democracy to the workplace and the local community.

Crisis theories: an assessment

How are we to assess these two contrasting theories of mounting political crisis in liberal democracies? There are many significant differences between the theorists of overloaded government and those of legitimation crisis, some of which will be discussed below. None the less, they also appear to share a common thread which can be set out in general terms. First, governmental, or more generally state, power is the capacity for effective political action. As such, power is the facility of agents to act within institutions and collectivities, and to apply the resources of these institutions and collectivities to chosen ends, even while institutional arrangements narrow the scope of their activities. Second, the power of the democratic state depends ultimately on the acceptance of its authority (overload theorists) or on its legitimacy (legitimation crisis theorists). Third, state power (measured by the ability of the state to resolve the claims and difficulties it faces) has been progressively eroded. The liberal democratic state has become increasingly hamstrung or ineffective (overload theorists, figure 7.2, sections 7–9) or short on rationality (legitimation crisis theorists, figure 7.3, section 7). Fourth, the capacity of the state to act decisively has been strained because its authority or legitimacy has declined. For overload theorists, the 'taut and strained' relationship between government and social groups can be explained by excessive demands related to, among other things, increased expectations and the decline in deference. Legitimation crisis theorists, in turn, focus on the way increased state intervention undermines traditionally unquestioned values and norms, and politicizes ever more issues, that is, opens them up to political debate and conflict.

Although the emphasis of Offe's and Habermas's work is more explicitly on legitimation, both overload and legitimation crisis theorists claim that state power has been eroded in the face of growing demands: in the one case these demands are regarded as 'excessive', in the other they are regarded as the virtually inevitable result of the contradictions within which the state is enmeshed. But, in both views, state power and political stability alter with changes to the pattern of values and norms. While both these theories offer a number of important insights, they also raise some fundamental questions: was the authority or legitimacy of the modern democratic state eroded during the late 1960s and 1970s to the point at which it was justified to talk about a mounting political crisis with transformative potential? Did the state become increasingly vulnerable to political and social turmoil?

There are three fundamental objections to the 'common thread' which runs through overload and legitimation crisis theory. First, there is no clear empirical evidence to support the claim of a progressively worsening crisis of the state's authority or legitimacy in the period in question. Second, it is not obvious that state power was eroding. Both overload and legitimation crisis theorists tend to treat the modern state as an 'empty' box through which things pass. This fundamentally underestimates the state's own capabilities and resources which derive from, for example, its bureaucratic, administrative and coercive apparatuses. Finally, while particular *governments* may be vulnerable when citizens fail to confer legitimacy, the *state* itself is not necessarily more vulnerable to collapse or disintegration. It is worth saying something briefly about each of these points in turn.

In order to address the question of whether the authority or legitimacy of the liberal democratic state was eroding from the late 1960s, it is useful to recall the different types of ground on which political institutions can be accepted, introduced in chapter 5 (pp. 155–6). The types are set out on the scale in figure 7.4. According to some political and social analysts (e.g.

Figure 7.4 Types of political acceptance

Schumpeter), the very fact that citizens comply with rules or laws means that the polity or political institutions are accepted, i.e. legitimated. But the problem with this conception of legitimacy, as pointed out in chapter 5, is that it does not take into account the different possible bases for obeying a command, complying with a rule, or agreeing or consenting to something. In the discussion below, the term legitimacy will be reserved for types 6 and 7 on the scale; that is, legitimacy will be taken to imply that people follow rules and laws because they actually think them right and worthy of respect. A legitimate political order is one that is normatively sanctioned by its population. (Although the distinction between categories 6 and 7 is important, it will not be dwelt on here; direct use of the idea of an ideal normative agreement will only be made in chapter 10.)

It is worth stressing that category 5 on the scale is ambiguous; it could be taken to imply a weak form of legitimacy, but because compliance or consent is instrumental or conditional it will not be taken to mean this. For when acceptance is instrumental it means that the existing state of affairs is only tolerated, or compliance granted, in order to secure some other desired end. If the end is not achieved the original situation will not be more agreeable; in all probability it will be much less so (cf. Beetham, 1991).

Many authors have been critical, to emphasize a point already made, about claims that a value consensus, or a common system of political attitudes and beliefs, is widespread (see Mann, 1973; Abercrombie et al., 1980; Kavanagh, 1980; Moss, 1982; F. Devine, 1993; cf. Crompton, 1993; Bradley, 1995; Saward, 2003; Beetham, 2005). Their studies generally disclose an affirmative attitude to existing political institutions among the middle and upper classes. However, they also show that this attitude 'does not extend very far down the stratification hierarchy'. Dissensus and frustration are common among some working-class groups and are associated with instrumental or conditional consent, rather than affirmation. The extent to which the state, parliament and politics are regarded as legitimate or 'worthy' is to a significant extent related to class.[3]

Is this phenomenon new? And does it constitute relevant evidence of a mounting crisis of the authority of the state (overload theorists) or of legitimacy and motivation (legitimation crisis theorists)? There does not seem much evidence to support these views. First, as argued in chapter 6, it is doubtful whether in the postwar years legitimacy was conferred as widely as is often thought. Second, while dissensus and conflict have been rife, it is not apparent that a massive protest potential has grown, leading to increased demands for participation in political decision-making and developing extensive criticism of the existing economic and political order. Third, the widespread scepticism and detachment of many men and women in their attitude to traditional forms of

---

[3] The focus of these works is on political attitudes in Britain with some comparative reference to other countries, notably the United States. This focus may seem somewhat narrow, but Britain is a particularly interesting case because it has so often been taken as an exemplar of the pluralist model (see, for example, Beer, 1969; cf. Beer, 1982). However, it ought to be borne in mind that the research on political attitudes to the state and parliamentary system has not been extensive and often leaves a lot to be desired (see Held, 1989, ch. 4; cf. Crompton, 1993).

politics have not given way to any clear demands for alternative kinds of institution: there has been a clear absence of images of alternatives, except among relatively marginal groups such as students and some civil society activists. Inequalities, privileges and disadvantages are often seen as the exclusive outcome of individual actions and bad luck rather than of structurally determined political and economic forces (Brown and Scase, 1991, pp. 21–2). A strong sense of fatalism linked to a culture of individualism serves to encourage the view that few, if any, alternatives to present arrangements exist. Moreover, to the extent that individual identities are shaped by changing consumption patterns and lifestyles, aspirations can come to be focused on particular goods and services with little regard for wider political questions (Featherstone, 1991; Bauman, 1991; S. Hall, 1992; cf. F. Devine, 1993). But what of the signs of conflict, the severe challenges (mentioned earlier) to the way resources and rights are distributed?

In a nutshell, it was *not* that the end of ideology was 'reversed', or a one-dimensional world collapsed, or that the authority of the state was suddenly in decline because demands became excessive, or that legitimacy was undermined; rather, it was that many people's cynicism, scepticism and detachment from conventional politics failed sometimes to be offset by prevailing political circumstances and/or economic conditions and/or the promise of future benefits by successive governments. The often expressed distrust was (and frequently is) translated into a range of political activities. During the late 1960s and early 1970s some of these activities were extremely intense, for instance the struggles launched by the New Left against the Vietnam war, while others were more diffuse, such as conflicts over public sector cutbacks. The possibilities of antagonistic stances against the state – prefigured or anticipated in people's dislike of politicians, respect for the local and for the common sense of ordinary people, and the rejection of 'experts' – were there, as indeed were germs of a variety of other kinds of political movement which sought to reassert the authority of 'the state'. That there should have been antagonism and conflict is not surprising: conditional consent or instrumental acceptance of the status quo is potentially unstable precisely because it is conditional or instrumental.

The above considerations, when linked to difficulties of national and international economic systems and to tensions over the future of, among other things, workplace relations, inner city areas and the environment, do suggest a number of fundamental questions. Is political and social conflict inevitable? In the absence of marked consensual values, how is the political order held together? It is clearly not simply legitimacy that provides the 'glue', that 'cements' or 'binds' the liberal democratic polity.

As long as governments and states are able to secure the acquiescence and support of those collectivities that are crucial for the continuity of the existing order (e.g. powerful financial interests, vital industrial organizations, unions with workers in key economic positions, dominant electoral groups), 'public order' can be sustained and is likely to break down only on certain 'marginal' sites. What can be called 'strategies of displacement' are crucial here; that is, strategies that disperse the worst effects of economic and political problems onto vulnerable groups while appeasing those able to mobilize claims most effectively (see Offe,

1984). This is *not* to argue that politicians or administrators necessarily desire or intend to displace the worst effects of economic problems onto some of the least powerful and most vulnerable of society. But if politics is the 'art of the possible', or if (to put it in the terms used hitherto) elected governments will generally try to ensure the smoothest possible continuity of the existing order (to secure support, expansion of economic opportunities and enhanced scope for their policies), then they will see little option but to appease those who are most powerful and able to mobilize their resources effectively. Successive governments have pursued strategies involving both appeasement and the uneven dispersal of the effects of economic crisis. The political capacity of governments and states to sustain these strategies – deriving from the concentration of resources at the disposal of the key executive branches of government and the central offices of state administration – should not be played down. For example, many of those who for one reason or another were most vulnerable suffered the worst effects of the crisis which faced the British political system between the mid-1970s and the 1990s. They include: the young (whose employment prospects radically deteriorated); non-whites (whose work opportunities, housing and general conditions of living became more difficult); single parent families (who found themselves often locked into cycles of poverty and dependency); the disabled and sick (who suffered a deterioration of services due to public sector cutbacks); the poor (who vastly increased in number); and those who lived in regions particularly hard hit (see Bradley, 1995; Hutton, 1995).

What, then, are the contributions of the theories of overload and legitimation crisis? How are they to be assessed? While the theorists of overload were right to point to the many different kinds of group pressing their demands on government, it follows from my argument that I find neither their starting point – classic pluralist premises – nor their diagnosis of problems of state power and conflict satisfactory. The model sketched by Habermas and Offe rightly suggests the necessity of a very different starting point, and the material presented in previous sections highlights the significance of stratified groups (demarcated by class among other categories) to the dynamics and instability of political life. In general terms, Habermas's and Offe's analysis of the way the state is enmeshed in conflict is insightful, as is their analysis of some of the pressures that can create a 'crisis of rational administration' (see figure 7.3 above, sections 1–7), but their subsequent focus on legitimation, and the likely spread of a legitimation crisis, is unconvincing. Both Habermas and Offe underestimate the contingent, fragmented and 'directionless' nature of much contemporary protest when taken as a whole. There are many highly specific single-issue campaigns, as well as a variety of powerful social movements, which have clear-cut political objectives. There is widespread scepticism about conventional democratic politics. But there is also considerable doubt about alternatives to existing institutions, doubt which cannot simply be regarded as the legacy of Cold War attitudes discrediting certain socialist ideas in the eyes of many (see ch. 4 above). There is uncertainty not only about what kinds of institution might be created but also about what general political directions should be taken. Thus, as possibilities for antagonistic stances against the state are realized, so too are the germs of a variety of other kinds of political movement, e.g. movements of the New Right. It is in this context that renewed concern about the direction of liberal democracy has given way to fresh consideration of the very essence of democracy.

Law, liberty and democracy

The New Right (or neo-liberalism or neo-conservatism, as it is sometimes called) has, in general, been committed to the view that political life, like economic life, is (or ought to be) a matter of individual freedom and initiative (see Hayek, 1960, 1976, 1982; Nozick, 1974). Accordingly, a *laissez-faire* or free-market society is the key objective, along with a 'minimal state'. The political programme of the New Right includes: the extension of the market to more and more areas of life; the creation of a state stripped of 'excessive' involvement both in the economy and in the provision of opportunities; the curtailment of the power of certain groups (for instance, trade unions) to press their aims and goals; and the construction of a strong government to enforce law and order.[4]

In the late 1970s and 1980s, the governments of Margaret Thatcher and Ronald Reagan advocated the 'rolling back of the state' on grounds similar to those of the New Right and of some of the theorists of 'overloaded government'. They insisted that individual freedom had been diminished because of the proliferation of bureaucratic state agencies attempting to meet the demands of those involved in group politics. In so arguing, they committed themselves to the classic liberal doctrine that the collective good (or the good of all individuals) can be realized properly in most cases only by private individuals acting in competitive isolation and pursuing their sectoral aims with minimal state interference. This commitment to the market as the key mechanism of economic and social regulation has, of course, a significant other side in the history of liberalism: a commitment to a 'strong state' to provide a secure basis upon which, it is thought, business, trade and family life will prosper (see ch. 3 above). In other words, this is a strategy for simultaneously increasing aspects of the state's power while restricting the scope of the state's actions.

At root, the New Right has been concerned to advance the cause of 'liberalism' against 'democracy' by limiting the democratic use of state power. The complex relationship between liberalism and democracy is brought out clearly in this confrontation, a confrontation which reminds one forcefully that the democratic component of liberal democracy was only realized after extensive conflict and remains a rather fragile achievement. In order to understand New Right thinking, it is worth examining briefly the work of two authors who have contributed to its formation: Robert Nozick and Friedrich Hayek. While it would be wrong to label Nozick simply as a spokesman of the New Right, since the political implications of his work are somewhat ambiguous, Hayek has probably been the New Right's most commanding figure (see Gamble, 1996). However, both men have been

[4] It might be noted that the last item of this programme is arguably inconsistent with the first two. In fact, a tension exists in conservatism generally, and in the New Right in particular, between those who assert individual freedom and the market as the ultimate concern, and those who believe in the primacy of tradition, order and authority because they fear the social consequences of rampant *laissez-faire* policies (see Gray, 1993). The account of the New Right here concentrates on the former group, who have been most influential in recent politics.

preoccupied with the refortification of liberalism in an age marked, as they understood it, by an ever more intrusive welfare state in the West and by a '1984'-type state in Eastern Europe (until it was dismantled in the 1990s: see ch. 8). For them, the contemporary state is a great Leviathan which threatens the foundations of liberty and, accordingly, must be radically 'rolled back'. The ideas which underpin this position are set out immediately below; in the last section of the chapter they will be juxtaposed with those of key New Left figures.[5]

In *Anarchy, State and Utopia* (1974), Nozick set out a range of arguments which form an intriguing restatement of liberal ideas from Locke to J. S. Mill. Beginning with the assumption that there is no social or political entity other than individuals – 'there are only individual people with their own individual lives' (Nozick, 1974, p. 33) – he argued that no general principles specifying particular priorities or patterns of distribution for society generally can be justified. The only legitimate organization (or mode of ordering) of human and material resources is that contingently negotiated by the unhindered activities of individuals in competitive exchanges with one another. Accordingly, the only political institutions that can be justified are those that uphold the framework for freedom, that is, those that contribute to the maintenance of individual autonomy or rights. By rights are meant 'various boundaries', demarcating legitimate spheres of action for an individual, that may not be crossed 'without another's consent' (Nozick, 1974, p. 325). Following Locke, Nozick contended that the only rights of which we can legitimately speak are the inalienable (natural) rights of the individual which are independent of society and which include, above all, the right to pursue one's own ends so long as they do not interfere with the rights of others. The right to pursue one's own ends is closely bound up, Nozick maintained, with the right to property and the accumulation of resources (even if this means a social order marked by considerable inequalities). Ownership of property and the appropriation of the fruits of one's own labour are fully justified if all that is acquired is justly acquired originally and/or the result of open and voluntary transactions between mature and knowledgeable individuals.

Nozick presented a number of arguments concerning what he called the 'minimal state' or the 'framework for utopia', the least intrusive form of political power commensurate with the defence of individual rights. He sought to establish that 'no more extensive state could be morally justified' because it would 'violate the rights of individuals' not to be forced to do certain things. In Nozick's view, individuals are extraordinarily diverse. There is no one community that will serve as an ideal for all people, because a wide range of conceptions of utopia exists. As he provocatively wrote:

> Wittgenstein, Elizabeth Taylor, Bertrand Russell, Thomas Merton, Yogi Berra, Allen Ginsberg, Harry Wolfson, Thoreau, Casey Stengel, The Lubavitcher Rebbe, Picasso, Moses, Einstein, Hugh Heffner, Socrates, Henry Ford, Lenny Bruce, Baba Ram Dass, Gandhi, Sir Edmund Hillary, Raymond Lubitz, Buddha, Frank

[5] Although Nozick's ideas were formulated more recently than Hayek's (most of the latter's work was written long before the New Right as such became prominent), I shall begin with Nozick's ideas because they provide a more accessible background to the central issues under consideration.

Sinatra, Columbus, Freud, Norman Mailer, Ayn Rand, Baron Rothschild, Ted Williams, Thomas Edison, H. L. Mencken, Thomas Jefferson, Ralph Ellison, Bobby Fischer, Emma Goldman, Peter Kropotkin, you, and your parents. Is there really *one* kind of life which is best for each of these people? (1974, p. 310)

The question is: how can radically different aspirations be accommodated? How can individuals and groups make progress towards their chosen ends? According to Nozick, we must get away from the idea that utopia represents *a single* conception of the best of all social and political arrangements. Rather, a society or nation in which utopian *experimentation* can be tried should itself be thought of as utopia. Utopia is a framework for utopias where people are 'at liberty to join together voluntarily to pursue and attempt to realize their own vision of the good life in the ideal community but where no one can *impose* his own utopian vision upon others' (Nozick, 1974, p. 312). To put the point another way, utopia is the framework for liberty and experimentation; it is the 'minimal state' (pp. 333–4).

Such a framework, Nozick argued, is 'libertarian and *laissez-faire*'. Only individuals can judge what they want and, therefore, the less the state interferes in their lives the better for them. The 'minimal state' is thus inconsistent with 'planning in detail' and with the active redistribution of resources, 'forcing some to aid others'. The state steps beyond its legitimate bounds when it becomes an instrument to promote equality, whether of opportunity or of result. What then is the proper role of the liberal democratic state in the future? It appears that it should only, in Nozick's opinion, be a 'protective agency' against force, theft, fraud and the violation of contracts. The state should sustain a monopoly of force so that it can protect individual rights in bounded territories. Within the framework of utopia this task amounts to enforcing the operation of the framework, adjudicating conflicts between communities, protecting the individual's right to leave a given community and doing all that might be required in the name of national defence and foreign relations.

The exact nature of the relationship between individual liberty, democracy and the state, as it is and as it should be, is left unclear in Nozick's writings, but it is confronted directly by Hayek. While Hayek upheld representative democracy in principle, he saw fundamental dangers in the dynamics of contemporary 'mass democracies'. These dangers are of two sorts: first, a propensity for arbitrary and oppressive majority rule, and second, the progressive displacement of the rule of the majority by the rule of its agents (Hayek, 1978, pp. 152–62). Both these points are familiar in political theory from Plato to Schumpeter, but Hayek pursued them with particular force and deployed them as part of an appeal for the restoration of a liberal order, what I call 'legal democracy' (see Hayek, 1960, 1976, 1982).

In Hayek's view, unless the *demos* is constrained in its actions by general rules, there is no guarantee that what it commands will be good or wise. To the 'doctrinaire democrat', what the majority wants 'is sufficient ground for regarding it as good ... the will of the majority determines not only what is law but what is good law' (1960, p. 103). This 'fetish' of democracy leads to the false suggestion that 'so long as power is conferred by democratic procedure, it cannot be arbitrary' (1976, p. 53). Democracy, Hayek argued, is by no means infallible or certain. And in parallel with Schumpeter he insisted we must not forget that 'there has often been much more cultural and spiritual freedom under an autocratic rule than under some democracies – and it is at least conceivable that under the government of a very homogeneous and doctrinaire majority democratic government might be as oppressive as the worst dictatorship' (1976, p. 52). It is the case that 'democratic control *may* prevent power from becoming arbitrary, but it does not do so by its mere existence' (1976, p. 53). It is only by distinguishing between 'limitations on power' and 'sources of power' that political arbitrariness can begin to be prevented.

The problems of arbitrary political power are compounded by all attempts to plan and regulate society, as is clearly demonstrated by the new 'welfare order' (Hayek, 1976, pp. 42ff). In the name of the 'common purpose' or the 'social good', the people's agents, whether representatives or bureaucrats, seek to reshape the social world through state economic management and the redistribution of resources. But Hayek maintained, echoing J. S. Mill's critique of despotic power (see ch. 3 above), that whatever the intentions behind such efforts, the result is coercive government. It is coercive because knowledge is inescapably limited; we know and can only know a very little about the needs and wants of those immediately around us, let alone of millions of people and how one might go about weighting their various aims and preferences (Hayek, 1976, p. 44). Any systematic attempt to regulate the lives and activities of individuals is perforce oppressive and an attack on their freedom: a denial of their right to be the ultimate judge of their own ends. This is not to say, Hayek pointed out, that there are no 'social ends', which he defined as 'the coincidence of individual ends'. But it is to limit the conception of the latter to areas of 'common agreement', and there are (and will always be) relatively few of these. In accord with Nozick, Hayek held that it is only in specifying 'the means capable of serving a great variety of purposes' that agreement among citizens is probable (1976, p. 45). Like Nozick, he took these means to be broadly synonymous with non-intrusive, non-directive organizations which provide a stable and predictable framework for the coordination of individuals' activities. While individuals alone can determine their wants and ends, organizations – above all, organizations like the state – can, in principle, facilitate the processes by which individuals successfully pursue their objectives. How can this be ensured?

Central to Hayek's argument is a particular distinction between liberalism and democracy. As he put it, 'liberalism is a doctrine about what the law ought to be, democracy a doctrine about the manner of determining what will be the law' (1960, p. 103). While liberalism regards it 'as desirable that only what the majority accepts should in fact be law', its aim is 'to persuade the majority to observe certain principles' (1960, pp. 103–4). So long as there are general rules which constrain the actions of majorities and governments, the individual need not fear coercive power. But without such constraints democracy will be in fundamental conflict with liberty. Like many other neo-liberals, Hayek made it clear that if democracy means 'the unrestricted will of the majority' he should not be counted as a democrat (1982, p. 39).

Coercive political power can be contained if, and only if, the 'Rule of Law' is respected. Hayek made a critical distinction for his argument between law (essentially fixed, general rules which determine the conditions of individuals' actions, including constitutional rules) and legislation (routine changes in the legal structure which are the work of most governments). Citizens can enjoy liberty only if the power of the state is circumscribed by law; that is, circumscribed by rules which specify limits on the scope of state action – limits based upon the rights of individuals to develop their own views and tastes, to pursue their own ends and to fulfil their own talents and gifts (1976, pp. 11, 63). Hayek's work placed at its centre Locke's dictum that 'Wherever Law ends Tyranny begins' and the notion that the law, properly constituted, binds governments to guarantee 'life, liberty and estate' (see ch. 3 above). The rule of law provides, in this account, the conditions under which individuals can decide how to use their energies and the resources at their disposal. It is, thus, the critical restraint on coercive power and the condition of individual freedom. 'Legal democracy' alone can satisfactorily place freedom at its centre.

In Hayek's view, democracy is not an end in itself; rather, it is a means – 'a utilitarian device' – to help safeguard the highest political end: liberty. As such, restrictions must, as the protective theorists of democracy rightly contended, be imposed upon the operations of democracy; democratic governments should accept limits on the legitimate range of their activities. The legislative scope of governments is, and must be, restrained by the rule of law. As Hayek explained:

> The Rule of Law . . . implies limits to the scope of legislation: it restricts it to the kind of general rules known as formal law, and excludes legislation either directly aimed at particular people, or at enabling anybody to use the coercive power of the state for the purpose of such discrimination. It means, not that everything is regulated by law, but, on the contrary, that the coercive power of the state can be used only in cases defined in advance by the law and in such a way that it can be foreseen how it will be used . . . Whether, as in some countries, the main applications of the Rule of Law are laid down in a Bill of Rights or a Constitutional Code, or whether the principle is merely a firmly established tradition, matters comparatively little. But it will readily be seen that whatever form it takes, any such recognized limitations of the powers of legislation imply the recognition of the inalienable right of the individual, inviolable rights of man. (1976, pp. 62–3)

Legislators should not meddle with the rule of law; for such meddling leads generally to a diminution of freedom.

Ultimately, Hayek's 'legal democracy' sets the contours for a free-market society and a 'minimal state'. He did not refer to this order as *laissez-faire* because every state intervenes to a degree in the structuring of civil society and private life (1960, p. 231; 1976, pp. 60–1). In fact, he regarded this term as 'a highly ambiguous and misleading description of the principles upon which a liberal order is based' (1976, p. 60). The question is why and how states intervene to condition economic and social affairs. In order to be consistent with the rule of law, intervention must be restricted to the provision of rules which can serve individuals as instruments in the pursuit of their various ends. A government can only legitimately intervene in civil society to enforce general rules, rules which broadly protect 'life, liberty and estate'. Hayek was unequivocal about this: a free, liberal, democratic order is incompatible with the enactment of rules which specify how people should use the means at their disposal (1960, pp. 231–2). Governments become coercive if they interfere with people's own capacity to determine their objectives. The prime example Hayek gave of such coercion is legislation which attempts to alter 'the material position of particular people or enforce distributive or "social" justice' (Hayek, 1960, p. 231). Distributive justice always imposes on some another's conception of merit or desert. It requires the allocation of resources by a central authority acting *as if* it knew what people should receive for their efforts and how they should behave. The value of individuals' services can, however, only justly be determined by their fellows in and through a decision-making system which does not interfere with *their* knowledge, choices and decisions. And there is only one sufficiently sensitive mechanism for determining 'collective' choice on an individual basis: the free market. When protected by a constitutional state, no system provides a mechanism of collective choice as dynamic, innovative and responsive as the operations of the free market.

The free market does not always operate perfectly; but, Hayek insisted, its benefits radically outweigh its disadvantages (1960, 1976; see Rutland, 1985). A free-market system is the basis for a genuinely *liberal* democracy. In particular, the market can ensure the coordination of the decisions of producers and consumers without the direction of a central authority; the pursuit by everybody of their own ends with the resources at their disposal; and the development of a complex economy without an elite which claims to know how it all works. Politics, as a governmental decision-making system, will always be a radically imperfect system of choice when compared to the market. Thus, 'politics' or 'state action' should be kept to a minimum, to the sphere of operation of an 'ultra-liberal' state (1976, p. 172). An 'oppressive bureaucratic government' is the almost inevitable result of deviation from this prescription – from the model of 'legal democracy', that is, summarized in model VII.

The causes of the expansion of modern 'bureaucratic government' are, however, as previous chapters have sought to demonstrate, far more complicated than Hayek's analysis allows. There are several major difficulties with this and other aspects of Hayek's thought. In the first instance, his model of the liberal free-market order (along with that of the New Right more generally) is ever more at odds with the modern corporate capitalist system (see Held, 1995, ch. 11). The idea that modern society approximates, or could progressively approximate, to a world where producers and consumers meet on an equal basis seems, to say the least, unrealistic when massive asymmetries of power and resource are (as both neo-pluralists and neo-Marxists recognize) not only systematically reproduced by the market economy but also buttressed by liberal democratic governments themselves. The resulting 'bias' in the political agenda appears to be recognized by nearly all schools of contemporary democratic theory other than the New Right. Liberalism generally, and the New Right in particular, project an image of markets as 'powerless' mechanisms of coordination and in so doing neglect the distorting nature of economic power

In sum: model VII

Legal Democracy

Principle(s) of justification

The majority principle is an effective and desirable way of protecting individuals from arbitrary government and of maintaining liberty. However, for political life, like economic life, to be a matter of individual freedom and initiative, majority rule must be circumscribed by the rule of law. Only under these conditions can the majority principle function wisely and justly

Key features

Constitutional state (modelled on features of the Anglo-American political tradition, including clear separation of powers)

Rule of law

Minimal state intervention in civil society and private life

Free-market society given fullest possible scope

General conditions

Effective political leadership guided by liberal principles

Minimization of excessive bureaucratic regulation

Restriction of role of interest groups, particularly trade unions

International free-trade order

Minimization (eradication, if possible) of threat of collectivism of all types

in relation to democracy (Vajda, 1978). The reality of the 'free market' is today marked by complex patterns of market formation, oligopolistic and monopolistic structures, the imperatives of the system of corporate power and multinational corporations, the short-term logic of many commercial banking houses and the rivalry of regional power blocs. This is not a world in which it is at all straightforward to sustain the claim that markets are simply free, responsive mechanisms of collective choice.

The New Right strategy of 'rolling back' the state has enjoyed, of course, a substantial measure of political support (up to the present), especially in the Anglo-American world. This is, in part, due to its success in mobilizing the considerable amount of cynicism, distrust and dissatisfaction with many of the institutions of the interventionist welfare state that have long existed. This is not to say that most of those who are disenchanted with aspects of the welfare state are neo-liberals (see, e.g., Whiteley, 1981; Taylor-Gooby, 1983, 1985, 1988; Jowell and Airey, 1984; Pierson, 1991). Rather, it is to highlight the evidence that points to marked dissatisfaction, including that among lower income groups and women, with their treatment by welfare state institutions, and to a tendency to regard the provision of benefits as excessively rigid, paternalistic and bureaucratic (see West et al., 1984; Hyde, 1985; Dominelli, 1991). The New Right successfully made political capital out of this disaffection, claiming it to be a natural outcome of 'mass democracies' in general and of interventionist socialist policies in particular. While social democratic parties were unquestionably outmanoeuvred by this attack in the late 1970s and 1980s, the New Right strategy is unlikely to work over a long period.

There are many reasons for this. Leaving the market to solve fundamental problems of resource generation and allocation misses entirely the deep roots of many economic and political difficulties: for instance, the vast inequalities within and between nation-states which are the source of considerable conflict; the erosion of trading opportunities in some countries while industries still enjoy protection and planned assistance in others; the emergence of huge global financial flows which can rapidly destabilize national economies and policies; and the development of serious transnational problems involving the global commons, including global warming, ozone depletion and the general spread of toxic pollutants (see ch. 11 below). Moreover, to the extent that pushing back the boundaries of the state means increasing the scope of market forces, national and transnational, and cutting back on services which have traditionally offered protection to the vulnerable, the difficulties faced by the poorest and the least powerful – North, South, East and West – are exacerbated. The rise of 'law and order' issues to the top of the political agenda reflects in part the need to contain the inevitable outcomes which such policies provoke (see Held, 2004).

The nature of the relationship between principle and practice in the New Right's programme can be illuminated further by considering its appeal to liberty. This appeal, as articulated by figures like Hayek and Nozick, is unquestionably potent, but it is based on a highly limited and contentious conception of freedom. By defining all 'distributional' questions as *ipso facto* against the rule of law, questions concerning economic, social and racial inequalities are treated as illegitimate matters for political analysis and examination, despite the fact that some of these inequalities are, as we have seen, central to a thorough account of the nature of liberty in a modern society. Further, while the distinction between 'law' and 'legislation' is important in many respects – for all the reasons given by thinkers from Locke to J. S. Mill – in Hayek's hands it is highly questionable. For it serves to remove certain critical issues from politics, to treat them as if they were not a proper subject of political action. This attempt to eradicate a range of questions from democratic consideration would, if successful, drastically restrict the sphere of democratic debate and control. Moreover, in a world where there is evidence of major and often increasing inequalities between classes, cultures, sexes and regions, it is hard to see how liberty – liberty to develop one's own tastes, views, talents and ends – could, in fact, be realized if we do not consider a far broader range of conditions than Hayek's analysis allows. It is here that neo-Marxists and, more recently, feminists have mounted their most powerful criticisms of liberal doctrines: to enjoy liberty means not only to enjoy equality before the law, important though this unquestionably is, but also to have the capacities (the material and cultural resources) to be able to pursue different courses of action (see Plant, 1985, 1992; Sen, 1999). While some versions of contemporary liberalism clearly recognize this (although they do not pursue these issues as far as one must), the neo-liberals certainly do not (see Sandel, 1984). The crucial issue of the relationship between types of liberty and democracy will be returned to below, as well as in the final part of the book.

Participation, liberty and democracy

Thinkers like Hayek and Nozick, along with the movement of the New Right more generally, have contributed significantly to a discussion about the appropriate form and limits of state action. They have helped to make the relationship between state, civil society and subject populations once again a leading political issue. Accordingly, conceptions about the proper character of this relationship have been unsettled, as have the very meanings of the concepts of liberty, equality and democracy. But the New Right is, of course, not the only tradition with a claim to inherit the vocabulary of freedom. From the late 1960s onwards, the New Left added serious claims of its own to this lexicon.

The New Left, like the New Right, consists of more than one strand of political thought: at the very least, it consists of ideas inspired by (developmental) republicans such as Rousseau, by anarchists and by what were earlier called 'libertarian' and 'pluralist' Marxist positions (see ch. 4). Many figures have contributed to the reformulation of left-wing conceptions of democracy and freedom (see Pierson, 1986, 1995), but the focus below will be on two people who have contributed, in particular, to the rethinking of the terms of reference of democracy: Carole Pateman (1970, 1985) and C. B. Macpherson (1977). While these two have by no means identical positions, they have a number of common starting points and commitments. Together, they represent a model of democracy which I shall simply refer to as 'participatory democracy'. This term is frequently used to cover a variety of democratic models from those of classical Athens to certain Marxist positions. This is not necessarily inaccurate in all respects, but the term will have a more restricted sense here in order to demarcate it from the other models considered so far. 'Participatory democracy' was, from the early 1970s to (at least) the early 1990s, the leading counter-model on the left to the 'legal democracy' of the right. (The anarchist or left libertarian position, while by no means insignificant, has attracted fewer supporters for reasons which will be considered briefly below.) It is worth stressing that the New Left model did not develop principally as a counter-attack on the New Right. While the presence of the New Right has in recent times sharpened New Left views, the latter emerged primarily as a result of the political upheavals of the 1960s, internal debates on the left and dissatisfaction with the heritage of political theory, liberal and Marxist.

The idea that individuals are 'free and equal' in contemporary liberal democracies is questioned by the New Left figures. As Carole Pateman put it, 'the "free and equal individual" is, in practice, a person found much more rarely than liberal theory suggests' (Pateman, 1985, p. 171). Liberal theory generally assumes what has, in fact, to be carefully examined: namely, whether the existing relationships between men and women, blacks and whites, working, middle and upper classes, and various ethnic groups allow formally recognized rights actually to be realized. The formal existence of certain rights is, while not unimportant, of very limited value if they cannot be genuinely enjoyed. An assessment of freedom must be made on the basis of liberties that are tangible, and capable of being deployed within the realms of both state and civil society. If freedom does not have a concrete content – as particular freedoms – it can scarcely be said to have profound consequences for everyday life.

From Hobbes to Hayek, liberals have all too often failed to examine these issues (see Pateman, 1985). While theorists of developmental democracy are among the exceptions to this generalization, even they failed to explore systematically the ways asymmetries of power and resources impinge upon the meaning of liberty and equality in daily relations (see Macpherson, 1977, pp. 69–76). If liberals were to take such an inquiry seriously, they would discover that massive numbers of individuals are restricted systematically – for want of a complex mix of resources and opportunities – from participating actively in political and civil life. What were referred to earlier as vicious circles of limited or non-participation directly illustrate this point. Inequalities of class, sex and race substantially hinder the extent to which it can legitimately be claimed that individuals are 'free and equal'.

Furthermore, the very liberal conception of a clear separation between 'civil society' and 'the state' is, Pateman argued, flawed, with fundamental consequences for key liberal tenets (Pateman, 1985, pp. 172ff). If the state is separate from the associations and practices of everyday life, then it is plausible to see it as a special kind of apparatus – a 'protective knight', 'umpire' or 'judge' – which the citizen ought to respect and obey. But if the state is enmeshed in these associations and practices, then the claim that the state is an 'independent authority' or 'circumscribed impartial power' is radically compromised. In Pateman's judgement (like that of many neo-Marxists and neo-pluralists), the state is inescapably locked into the maintenance and reproduction of the inequalities of everyday life and, accordingly, the whole basis of its claim to distinct allegiance is in doubt (Pateman, 1985, pp. 173ff). This is unsettling for the whole spectrum of questions concerning the nature of public power, the relation between the 'public' and the 'private', the proper scope of politics and the appropriate reach of democratic governments.

If the state is, as a matter of routine, neither 'separate' nor 'impartial' with respect to society, then it is clear that citizens will not be treated as 'free and equal'. If the 'public' and 'private' are interlocked in complex ways, then elections will always be insufficient as mechanisms to ensure the accountability of the forces actually involved in the 'governing' process. Moreover, since the 'meshing' of state and civil society leaves few, if any, realms of 'private life' untouched by 'politics', the question of the proper form of democratic regulation is posed acutely. What form democratic control should take, and what the scope of democratic decision-making should be, become an urgent matter. However, a straightforward traditional left-wing response to these issues needs to be treated with the utmost caution (see ch. 4 above). For New Left thinkers generally accept that there are fundamental difficulties with orthodox Marxist theory. Consequently, they have tried to develop a position that moves beyond a rigid juxtaposition of Marxism with liberalism. For instance, the development of Stalinism and a repressive state in the Soviet Union is not just understood as the result of the peculiarities of a 'backward' economy (as many

Marxists have argued) but also traced to problems in Marx's and Lenin's thought and practice. Marx's and Lenin's belief that the institutions of representative democracy can just be swept away by organizations of rank-and-file democracy is, New Left thinkers hold, erroneous. Lenin, in particular, mistook the nature of representative democracy when he labelled it simply as bourgeois. Underlying this typical Leninist view is a fundamentally mistaken distrust of the idea of competing power centres in society.

The whole relation between socialist thought and democratic institutions needs to be rethought in the light not only of the record of Eastern European socialism but also of the moral bankruptcy of the social democratic vision of reform. Major currents of social democratic politics have led to the adulation of 'social engineering', proliferating policies to make relatively minor adjustments in social and economic arrangements. The state has, accordingly, grown in size and power, undermining the vision that social democratic politics might once have had. But what then is the way forward? Institutions of direct democracy or self-management cannot simply replace the state; for, as Max Weber predicted, they leave a coordination vacuum readily filled by bureaucracy. Two sets of changes are often emphasized in New Left writings as vital for the transformation of politics in the West and East: the state must be democratized by making parliament, state bureaucracies and political parties more open and accountable, while new forms of struggle at the local level (through factory-based politics, the women's movement, ecological groups) must ensure that society, as well as the state, is subject to procedures which ensure accountability.

C. B. Macpherson's work is broadly in line with these general arguments, although he put special emphasis on the notion of participatory democracy as the key to a more democratic future. Macpherson derived some of his theoretical inspiration from a reassessment of aspects of the liberal democratic tradition. Of particular importance for him were some of the arguments put forward by J. S. Mill, but by maintaining that liberty and individual development can only be fully achieved with the direct and continuous involvement of citizens in the regulation of society and state, Macpherson gave Mill's ideas a more radical twist.

Macpherson has never been deterred from asking whether it is feasible in densely populated, complex societies to extend the realm of democracy from periodic involvement in elections to participation in decision-making in all spheres of life. The problems posed by the coordination of large-scale communities are, he admitted, considerable. It is hard – if not impossible – to imagine any political system, as J. S. Mill rightly pointed out, in which all citizens can be involved in face-to-face discussions every time a public issue arises. However, it does *not* follow from considerations such as this that society and the system of government cannot be transformed. Macpherson argued for transformation based upon a system combining competitive parties and organizations of direct democracy. There will, for as far as one can see, always be issues and major differences of interest around which parties might form, and only competition between political parties guarantees a minimum responsiveness of those in government to people at all levels below. The party system itself should, however, be reorganized on less hierarchical principles, making political administrators and managers more accountable to the personnel of the organizations they represent. A substantial basis would be created for participatory democracy if parties were democratized according to the principles and procedures of direct democracy, and if these 'genuinely participatory parties' operated within a parliamentary or congressional structure complemented and checked by fully self-managed organizations in the workplace and local community. Only such a political system, in Macpherson's view, would actually realize the profoundly important liberal democratic value of the equal right to liberty and self-development.

While Macpherson admitted that the obstacles to the realization of participatory democracy – from entrenched interests of all kinds – are formidable, the notion of 'participatory democracy' remained in his work a somewhat vague one. And yet it is critical that the grounds for and features of participatory democracy be specified thoroughly, if it is to be regarded as a compelling idea. In a more thorough statement of the case for the extension of the sphere of democratic participation, Pateman has argued, drawing upon central notions in Rousseau and J. S. Mill, that participatory democracy fosters human development, enhances a sense of political efficacy, reduces a sense of estrangement from power centres, nurtures a concern for collective problems and contributes to the formation of an active and knowledgeable citizenry capable of taking a more acute interest in government affairs (Pateman, 1970, chs 2, 6; cf. Dahl, 1985, pp. 95ff). Evidence from studies of innovations in democratic control of the workplace, while by no means unambiguous in all respects, highlights, according to Pateman, that 'a positive correlation between apathy and low feelings of political efficacy and low socio-economic status', typically found in most liberal democracies, can be broken by making democracy count in people's everyday life, i.e. by extending the sphere of democratic control to those key institutions in which most people live out their lives (Pateman, 1970, p. 104; Held and Pollitt, 1986; and cf. ch. 9 below).

If people know opportunities exist for effective participation in decision-making, they are likely to believe participation is worthwhile, likely to participate actively and likely, in addition, to hold that collective decisions should be binding. On the other hand, if people are systematically marginalized and/or poorly represented, they are likely to believe that only rarely will their views and preferences be taken seriously, weighted equally with those of others or assessed in a process that is fair or just. Thus, they are likely to find few good reasons for participating in, and regarding as authoritative, the decision-making processes which affect their lives.

As long as rights to self-determination only apply to the sphere of government, democracy will not only be restricted in meaning to the occasional periodic vote, as Schumpeter understood it, but will also count for little in the determination of the quality of many people's lives. For self-determination to be achieved, democratic rights need to be extended from the state to the economic enterprise and the other central organizations of society. The structure of the modern corporate world makes it essential that the political rights of citizens be complemented by a similar set of rights in the sphere of work and community relations.

Like Macpherson, Pateman rejected the view that the institutions of direct democracy could be extended to all political, social and economic domains while the institutions of representative democracy are swept aside, and that complete political and social equality could be created through the self-management of all spheres. Democracy in the workplace, if taken alone, will always have to contend with complex problems concerning the availability of different types of skill and labour, the coordination of resources and market instabilities – any one of which can impose restraints on democratic procedures and options. The types of problem faced by workplace democracy are likely to be radically compounded with the adoption of democratic mechanisms by all key social organizations (cf. P. Devine, 1988). There will always be within and between such organizations problems of resource allocation, difficulties coordinating decisions, pressures of time, differences of opinion, clashes of interest and problems reconciling the requirements of democracy with other significant ends: efficiency and leadership, for instance. In addition, Pateman conceded to Weberian and Schumpeterian views that 'it is doubtful if the average citizen will ever be as interested in all the decisions made at national level as [s]he would be in those made nearer home' (Pateman, 1970, p. 110). For the available evidence shows – apart from the fact that people learn to participate by participating – that people are most interested in, and likely to have a better grasp of, those problems and issues which immediately touch their lives. Whereas forms of direct participation are relevant in places like the workplace, we cannot avoid the conclusion, Pateman contended, that the role of the citizen will always be highly restricted in national politics, as theorists of competitive elitism have insisted.

> In an electorate of, say, thirty-five million the role of the individual must consist almost entirely of choosing representatives; even where [s]he could cast a vote in a referendum [her or] his influence over the outcome would be infinitesimally small. Unless the size of national political units were drastically reduced then that piece of reality is not open to change. (Pateman, 1970, p. 109)

Many of the central institutions of liberal democracy – competitive parties, political representatives, periodic elections – will be unavoidable elements of a participatory society. Direct participation and control over immediate locales, complemented by party and interest group competition in governmental affairs, can most realistically advance the principles of participatory democracy.

Concessions to the competitive elitists should not, Pateman stressed, be misunderstood. In the first instance, it is only if the individual has the opportunity to participate directly in decision-making at the local level that, under modern conditions, any real control over the course of everyday life can be achieved (Pateman, 1970, p. 100). Second and more importantly, the opportunity for extensive participation in areas like work would radically alter the *context* of national politics. Individuals would be presented with multiple possibilities to learn about key issues in resource creation and control and would, thus, be far better equipped to judge national questions, assess the performance of political representatives and participate in decisions of national scope when the opportunity arose. The connections between the 'public' and the 'private' would, as a result, be much better understood. Third, the exact structures of a participatory society, both at local and at national level, should be kept open and fluid so that people can experiment with and learn from new political forms. This is important because the evidence accumulated to date about the possibilities and effects of extensive participation is limited. There is not enough information to be able to recommend one institutional model above all others; relatively few experiments have been initiated and any fixed 'blueprint' could easily risk becoming an oppressive prescription for change. The participatory society must be an experimental society, a society able to experiment in the wake of the radical reform of the rigid structures hitherto imposed by private capital, class relations and other systematic asymmetries of power. 'It is this ideal, an ideal with a long history in political thought, that has become lost from view', Pateman contended, 'in the contemporary theory of democracy.' The classic ideal of freedom as self-government can be upheld, even if its institutional implications must be thoroughly revised (cf. ch. 2 above). We can still have, Pateman concluded, a modern, non-dogmatic democratic theory which 'retains the notion of participation at its heart' (1970, pp. 110–11; cf. Barber, 1984). A summary of the central features of participatory democracy can be found in model VIII.

It was suggested above that the 'legal democracy' of the New Right does not represent a plausible future, and that governments which champion it will run into severe difficulties. It was also suggested that the New Right model unjustifiably rules out of active consideration a range of 'distributional' questions which have to be addressed if individuals are to be 'free and equal' and if democracy is to be a phenomenon that provides people with equal opportunities to determine the framework of their lives. Many of these problems are taken up directly by New Left thinkers. It is, therefore, important to ask whether their model is compelling and defensible. If the views of the New Right are wanting, do those of the New Left represent a more plausible future? Certainly, the New Left model articulates fundamental concerns, concerns expressed by, among others, a variety of social movements which have pressed for a more participatory society. However, it also leaves a number of fundamental issues unaddressed, a particularly acute problem during a time of disenchantment in developed democracies with 'visionary politics'.

Macpherson and Pateman have both sought to combine and refashion insights from both the liberal and the Marxist traditions. While their efforts help move political debate away from the seemingly endless and fruitless juxtaposition of liberalism with Marxism, they say very little about fundamental factors such as how, for instance, the economy is actually to be organized and related to the political apparatus, how institutions of representative democracy are to be combined with those of direct democracy, how the scope and power of administrative organizations are to be checked, how households and childcare facilities are to be related to work, how those who wish to 'opt out' of the political system might do so, or how the problems posed by the ever changing international system could be dealt with. Moreover, their arguments pass over the question of how their 'model' could be realized, over the whole issue of

In sum: model VIII

Participatory Democracy

Principle(s) of justification
   An equal right to liberty and self-development can only be achieved in a 'participatory society', a society which fosters a sense of political efficacy, nurtures a concern for collective problems and contributes to the formation of a knowledgeable citizenry capable of taking a sustained interest in the governing process

Key features
   Direct participation of citizens in the regulation of the key institutions of society, including the workplace and local community

   Reorganization of the party system by making party officials directly accountable to membership

   Operation of 'participatory parties' in a parliamentary or congressional structure

   Maintenance of an open institutional system to ensure the possibility of experimentation with political forms

General conditions
   Direct amelioration of the poor resource base of many social groups through redistribution of material resources

   Minimization (eradication, if possible) of unaccountable bureaucratic power in public and private life

   An open information system to ensure informed decisions

   Re-examination of childcare provision so that women as well as men can take up the opportunity to participate in public life

Note: The model is drawn from the central elements of Macpherson and Pateman.

transitional stages and over how those who might be worse off in some respects as a result of its application (those whose current circumstances allow them to determine the opportunities of others) might react and should be treated. Furthermore, they tend to assume that people in general want to extend the sphere of democratic control over their lives. What if they do not want to do so? What if they do not really want to participate in the management of social and economic affairs? What if they do not wish to become creatures of democratic reason? Or, what if they wield democratic power 'undemocratically' – to limit or end democracy?

   These are complex and difficult questions, not all of which, of course, one could reasonably expect each theorist to address fully. None the less, they are important questions to ask of 'participatory democracy', precisely because it is a version of democratic theory which champions not only a set of procedures, but a form of life as well. As chapter 10 will indicate in more detail, the participatory theorists are right to pursue the implications of democratic principles for the organizational structure of society as well as of the state. However, this leaves them vulnerable to criticism. It leaves them, in particular, vulnerable to the charge that they have attempted to resolve prematurely the highly complex relations among individual liberty, distributional matters (questions of social justice) and democratic processes. By focusing squarely on the desirability of collective decision-making, and by allowing democracy to prevail over all other considerations, they tend to leave these relations to be specified in the ebb and flow of democratic negotiation. But it is precisely in criticizing such a standpoint that the New Right thinkers are at their most compelling. Should there be limits on the power of the *demos* to change and alter political circumstance? Should the nature and scope of the liberty of individuals and minorities be left to democratic decision? Should there be clear constitutional guidelines which both enable and limit democratic operations? By answering questions such as these in the affirmative, the New Right recognizes the possibility of severe tensions among individual liberty, collective decision-making and the institutions and processes of democracy. By not systematically addressing these issues, the New Left, in contrast, has too hastily put aside the problems.[6] In making democracy at all levels the primary social objective to be achieved, the New Left thinkers have relied upon 'democratic reason' – a wise and good democratic will – for the determination of just and positive political outcomes. Can an essentially democratic *demos* be relied upon? Can one assume that the 'democratic will' will be wise and good? Can one assume that 'democratic reason' will prevail? From Plato to Hayek, good grounds have been suggested for at least pausing on this matter (cf. Bellamy, 1996).

It was precisely around these issues that the New Right generated so much political capital by directly acknowledging the uncertain outcomes of democratic politics – the ambiguous results, for instance, of the 'well intentioned' democratic welfare state. By highlighting that democracy can lead to bureaucracy, red tape, surveillance and excessive infringement of individual options – and not just in communist societies – they have struck a chord with the actual experience of those in routine contact with certain branches of the modern state, experience which by no means necessarily makes people more optimistic about collective decision-making (see Pierson, 1991, ch. 5; Giddens, 1998). The New Right has, then, contributed to a discussion about the desirable limits of collective regulation with which others must engage if the model of a more participatory society is to be adequately defended. Such an engagement might well have to concede more to the liberal tradition than has hitherto been allowed by left-wing thinkers. The question is: how can individuals be 'free and equal', enjoy equal opportunities to participate in the determination of the framework which governs their lives, without surrendering the important issues of individual liberty and distributional questions to the uncertain outcomes of the democratic process? This question constitutes the leading theme of chapter 10. But before addressing it, the impact of the collapse of Soviet communism on democratic theory and practice needs to be appraised, as does the idea that democracies should be deliberative if they are to be legitimate (see chs 8 and 9 below, respectively).

---

[6] This is not to say that the problems are unrecognized (see, e.g., Macpherson, 1977, ch. 5).

8 Democracy after Soviet Communism

The revolutions which swept across Central and Eastern Europe at the end of 1989 and the beginning of 1990 stimulated an atmosphere of celebration. Liberal democracy was fêted as an agent of progress, and capitalism as the only viable economic system. Some political commentators even proclaimed (to borrow a phrase from Hegel) the 'end of history' – the triumph of the West over all political and economic alternatives. The two world wars, the division of Europe, a world wracked by ideological conflict during the Cold War and the political and economic pressures of the late 1960s and 1970s had previously shattered complacency about stability and progress in the liberal democratic world. Now, faith in democratic reason and market-orientated thinking could be fully restored.

The objective of this chapter is to explore the debate about the meaning of the transformations that swept through Central and Eastern Europe during 1989–90, and that were accelerated further by the developments in Russia in August 1991 – the popular counter-movement to the coup attempt on the 18th–21st of that month. Has Western democracy won? Has liberal democracy finally displaced the legitimacy of all other forms of government? Is ideological conflict at an end? In addressing these questions it will become apparent that the debate about 1989 is much more than one about the events of that year and subsequent occurrences, important as these are. For it is also a debate about the character and form of the constitutive processes and structures of the contemporary political world. In particular, the chapter presents in microcosm some of the key issues, problems and discussions about democracy, its past, present and possible futures. It does not present another model of democracy as such, but rather an account of the changing context of democracy – an account which will help frame the final part of this volume, which addresses the question: what should democracy mean today?

The chapter is divided into three sections. The first section offers a brief examination of the historical backdrop to 1989 and the events of that year. The second section focuses on the writings of Francis Fukuyama, which became a, if not the, *locus classicus* in subsequent discussion of the political transformations sweeping Eastern Europe, particularly in the Anglo-American world. Fukuyama's main thesis amounted to the claim that socialism is dead and liberalism is the sole remaining credible political philosophy. The third section addresses writings by Alex Callinicos, who wrote a timely challenge to Fukuyama's view. Callinicos interprets the East European revolutions as a victory for capitalism – a victory that makes Marxism and direct democracy more relevant today, not less. The chapter is concluded with a brief summary of how those different positions conceive the political good and the role and nature of democracy – an issue so forcefully put on the agenda by 1989 and the events since then.

The historical backdrop

The changes of political regime that swept through Central and Eastern Europe in 1989–90 – Poland, Hungary, East Germany, Bulgaria, Czechoslovakia, Romania – were world-shaking events by any standard. An extraordinary sense of exhilaration was created within and beyond Europe. As Callinicos aptly put it:

> Far beyond the countries directly affected, people shared a sense of suddenly widened possibilities. Parts of the furniture of the postwar world that had seemed irremovable suddenly disappeared – literally in the case of the Berlin wall. Previously unalterable assumptions – for example, that Europe would be permanently divided between the superpowers – abruptly collapsed. (1991, p. 8)

The sharp division between the democratic capitalist and state socialist worlds, created in the aftermath of World War II, began to disappear. The pattern of intense rivalry between the superpowers, perhaps the dominant fact of world politics in the second half of the twentieth century, was almost at a stroke transformed (see Lewis, 1990a). If this were not considered a revolution (or series of revolutions) within the affairs of the erstwhile communist bloc, and within the international order more generally, it is hard to see what would qualify as a revolutionary change.

But things are rarely as straightforward as they seem. While the term 'revolution' seems to describe accurately the sweeping, dramatic and unexpected transformations of the state socialist system, and the extraordinary movements of people who ushered in these changes on the streets of Warsaw, Budapest, Prague, Berlin, Bucharest and other cities, it detracts attention from the momentum of changes and processes already under way by 1989. Although the term 'revolutions' will continue to be used to refer to the events of 1989–90, it is as well to bear in mind that these had roots stretching back in time. To begin with, significant political changes had begun in Poland in the early 1980s and in Hungary a little later. The Communists had been defeated in elections in Poland and the principle of one-party rule had been renounced in Hungary before the 'dramatic' events of 1989–90 took place. Moreover, the massive student uprising in Tiananmen Square in China, so brutally put down on 3–4 June 1989, was a reminder, if one was necessary at all, that change in state socialist regimes might, at the very best, be tolerated only at a slow and managed pace.

Underpinning the slow but significant changes in Central and Eastern Europe in the late 1980s was the reform process initiated in the USSR by Mikhail Gorbachev – *perestroika*. It was shifts in strategic thinking in the Kremlin that were probably the proximate cause of the revolutions,[1] alongside the gradual

---

[1] These shifts reflected in part an accession to power of a new political generation with a distinctive social and cultural background and different perceptions of Soviet aims and possible solutions (see Lewin, 1988).

erosion of communist power in the civil societies and economies of the Soviet bloc (see Lewis, 1990a, 1990b). In particular, the Soviet decision to replace the Brezhnev Doctrine (the policy of protecting the 'achievements of socialism' in Eastern Europe by force if necessary) with the 'Sinatra Doctrine' (the policy of tolerating nationally chosen paths to progress and prosperity: 'do it your way') had decisive consequences – intended and otherwise – for the capacity of state socialist regimes to survive. By removing the threat of Red Army or Warsaw Pact intervention, and by refusing to sanction the use of force to crush mass demonstrations, the 'Sinatra Doctrine' effectively pulled the carpet from under East European communism. The developments in East Germany were a notable case in point. When Hungary opened its border with Austria, and triggered the massive emigration of East Germans to the West, pressures within East Germany rapidly intensified and demonstrations, held in Leipzig and nearby cities, escalated. Without the routine recourse to force, the East German authorities sought to placate their rebellious citizenry by sanctioning access to the West via new openings in the Berlin Wall. The result is well known: the authorities lost control of an already demanding situation, and within a short time both their legitimacy and their effectiveness were wholly undermined.

The roots of the 1989–90 'legitimation crisis' of state socialist societies can be traced back further. Three particular sets of pressures can usefully be mentioned, for they help shed some light not only on why a shift in strategic thinking occurred in the Kremlin, but also on why the changes took the direction they did. First, the Soviet economy's lack of integration into the world economic system protected it in the *short term* from the pressures and instabilities attendant on achieving competitive productivity levels necessary for a sustained role in the international division of labour; in the *long run*, however, it left it weak and uncompetitive, particularly in relation to technology and innovation. Ever more dependent on imported technology and foreign sources of funding and investment, the centrally administered economy, rigid and relatively inflexible at the best of times, found few avenues through which to deliver better economic performance. Second, this situation was compounded by renewed geo-political pressures that followed from the intensification of the Cold War in the late 1970s and 1980s, given particular momentum by Ronald Reagan and Margaret Thatcher. A new arms race, in which ever more sophisticated weapon-systems played an increasing role, put a greater and greater burden on the financial, technical and managerial resources of the Soviet Union. The costs of the Cold War became profoundly difficult to contain on both sides, but were especially draining to the crumbling organizations and infrastructure of the Soviet economy.

Third, significant conflicts and schisms had emerged in the Soviet bloc during the previous few decades, leading to massive acts of repression to contain dissent in Hungary (1956), in Czechoslovakia (1968) and in Poland (1981). While these acts may have effectively contained protest in the short term, they were not a permanent obstacle to the spawning of dissent, social movements and autonomous organizations in civil society. The developments in Poland in the 1980s, particularly the formation of Solidarity (the mass movement for freedom and self-determination), were by no means typical of what was happening in

Eastern Europe as a whole, shaped as they were by a remarkable ethnic and national unity, the power of the Catholic Church and a strong sense of a foreign enemy on Poland's soil corrupting its growth and identity. But they were indicative of a certain growing democratic pressure to 'roll back the state' and to create an independent civil society in which citizens could pursue their self-chosen activities free of immediate political direction (cf. ch. 7 above). Solidarity sought to foster such a society throughout the 1980s by creating independent networks of information, cultural interchange and social relations. In so doing, it recast and expanded the meaning of what it was to be a democratic social movement while drastically weakening the appeal of state-dominated political change.

The above account is by no means intended as a thorough analysis of the remarkable events and developments of 1989 onwards. Rather, it is intended as a historical sketch to provide a context for the main focus of this chapter: a consideration of what the revolutions meant, and what light they shed on democracy and its future.

The triumph of economic and political liberalism?

Following the defeat of the United States in the Vietnam war and the rise of the Japanese economic challenge – and before any major glimpse of the changes in the Soviet Union to come – a detectable gloom settled over Washington policy-makers in the late 1970s. This was reinforced by a spate of major academic publications in the 1980s, including Robert Keohane's *After Hegemony* (1984a) and Paul Kennedy's *The Rise and Fall of the Great Powers* (1988), which charted the (relative) decline of US power and considered its implications for world politics and political economy. Highlighting a growing mismatch between military strength and productive and revenue-raising capacities eroded by economic rivals, alarms were raised about the US's future and about the consequences of decline for the defence and stability of the West. Few foresaw how these considerations would have to be balanced by an assessment of the dramatic decline of Soviet communism at the end of the 1980s.

The publication of Francis Fukuyama's essays 'The end of history?' (1989) and 'A reply to my critics' (1989/90), the focus of the discussion below – and the appearance later of his *The End of History and the Last Man* (1992) – not only provided a reassuring counterpoint to early preoccupation with the US's fall from hegemony, but, in their confident and assertive tone, went some way to restore faith in the supremacy of Western values. Fukuyama, formerly deputy director of the US State Department Policy Planning Staff, celebrated not only the 'triumph of the West' but also, as he put it, 'the end of history as such; that is, the end point of mankind's ideological evolution and the universalization of Western liberal democracy as the final form of human government' (1989, p. 3). Fukuyama's message became widely reported in the press and the electronic media more generally. While it was subject to considerable criticism, most of Fukuyama's critics seemed to concede that his 'main point – the current lack of competitors against political and economic liberalism in the world ideological market place – is surely hard to refute' (Mortimer, 1989, p. 29).

Fukuyama's message recalls the earlier debate on 'the end of ideology' in the 1950s and 1960s (see ch. 7 above, esp. pp. 187–8). But whereas the latter debate focused on the significance in the West of a decline in support for Marxism, and on a reduction in the differences among political parties to a little more or a little less government intervention and expenditure, Fukuyama's thesis goes much further, philosophically and politically. It has four main components. First, there is a broad emphasis on conflicts among *ideologies* as the motor of history. Taking a certain inspiration from Hegel, Fukuyama argues that history can be understood as a sequence of stages of consciousness or ideology; that is, as a sequence of systems of political belief that embody distinctive views about the basic principles underlying social order (Fukuyama, 1989/90, pp. 22–3). The sequence represents a progressive and purposive path in human development from partial and particularistic ideologies, such as those which buttressed monarchies and aristocracies, to those with more universal appeal. In the modern period we have reached, in Fukuyama's judgement, the final stage of this development.

Second, the end of history has been reached because ideological conflict is virtually at an end. Liberalism is the last victorious ideology. At the heart of this argument, Fukuyama notes, 'lies the observation that a remarkable consensus has developed in the world concerning the legitimacy and viability of liberal democracy' (1989/90, p. 22). The chief rivals to liberalism in the twentieth century, fascism and communism, either have failed or are failing. And contemporary challengers – religious movements such as Islam or nationalist movements such as those found in East Europe today – articulate only partial or incomplete ideologies; that is to say, they champion beliefs that cannot be sustained without the support of other ideologies. Neither religious nor nationalist belief systems provide coherent alternatives to liberalism in the long term and, therefore, have no 'universal significance'. Only liberal democracy, along with market principles of economic organization, constitutes a development of 'truly world historical significance' (Fukuyama, 1989/90, p. 23).

Third, the end of history should not be taken to mean the end of all conflict. Conflict can arise, indeed is likely to arise, from diverse sources, including advocates of various (dated) ideologies; nationalist and religious groups; and peoples or collectivities locked into history or prehistory, i.e. those who remain 'outside' the liberal world (certain 'Third World' countries) or who remain 'outsiders inside' (individuals and groups within the liberal world who have not yet fully absorbed its inescapability). Moreover, there is a danger of a progressive *bifurcation* of the world, particularly between those in the 'post-historical' liberal societies and the rest – the traditional, unmodernized world. Bifurcation could certainly generate intense and violent struggles, but none of these will lead, Fukuyama maintains, to new systematic ideas of political and social justice that could displace or supersede liberalism.

Fourth, Fukuyama is not wholly unambivalent about the 'end of history'. It will, he suggests, be 'a very sad time' (1989, p. 18; cf. 1992, p. 311). There will no longer be daring leaps of human imagination and valiant struggles of great principle; politics will become an extension of the regulative processes of markets. Idealism will be replaced by economic management and the solving of technical problems in the pursuit of consumer satisfaction. In short, recalling some of the central themes of postmodernism (notably its account of the demise of universalistic belief systems and its critique of all claims to universality), Fukuyama asserts the exhaustion of the bold, even heroic, 'grand narratives' of human emancipation that once struggled with one another for dominance in the world. (Cf. Weber's account of this process, pp. 127–8 above.) But while there is a detectable note of regret in his tone, it barely qualifies his generally optimistic affirmation of liberalism. Ideological consensus today may be neither 'fully universal nor automatic', but it exists to a 'higher degree than at any time in the past century' (1989/90, p. 22). The 'liberal democratic revolution' and the 'capitalist revolution' are the end stage of a clear-cut pattern of historical evolution.[2]

Fukuyama's writings have been widely acclaimed as among the 'key texts for our age' (*Guardian*, 7 September 1990). In a sense, they provided a sophisticated justification for many of the commonplaces found among the leading governments of the West in the 1980s, especially those of Thatcher and Reagan (Hirst, 1989a, p. 14). They reinforced the message of the neo-liberal New Right, which proclaimed the death of socialism, and the market and minimal state as the only legitimate and viable future (see, for example, Friedman, 1989). But it would be wrong to suggest that Fukuyama's argument only resonated with the New Right. A broad spectrum of political opinion found its general political message hard to brush aside, even if there was intensive disagreement about most of its details.

None the less, there are serious questions to be raised about Fukuyama's argument. In the first instance, liberalism cannot be treated simply as a unity. There are, as we have seen, distinctive liberal traditions set down by such figures as John Locke, Jeremy Bentham and John Stuart Mill, which embody quite different conceptions from each other of the individual agent, of autonomy, of the rights and duties of subjects, and of the proper nature and form of political community. Fukuyama does not systematically analyse the different forms of liberalism, nor does he provide any arguments about how one might choose among them. This is a striking lacuna, since liberalism itself is an ideologically contested terrain.[3]

In addition, Fukuyama does not explore whether there are any tensions, or even perhaps contradictions, between the 'liberal' and 'democratic' components of liberal democracy; that is, between the liberal preoccupation with individual rights or 'frontiers of freedom' that 'nobody should be permitted

---

[2] The end of history would, Fukuyama proclaims, be a 'dog's life'. In a noteworthy passage he writes: 'A dog is content to sleep in the sun all day provided he is fed, because he is not dissatisfied with what he is. He does not worry that other dogs are doing better than him, or that his career as a dog has stagnated, or that dogs are being oppressed in a distant part of the world.' If human progress continues, 'life will come to resemble that of the dog' (1992, p. 311). For a discussion of this analogy, see Held (1993b).

[3] Fukuyama addresses some of these problems more fully in *The End of History and the Last Man*, especially part III, where he elaborates at greater length his metaphysical conception of history, philosophical anthropology and understanding of modernity. However, I find these elaborations ultimately unconvincing (see Held, 1993b).

to cross', and the democratic concern with the regulation of individual and collective action, with public accountability (Berlin, 1969, pp. 164ff). Those who have written at length on this question have frequently resolved it in quite different directions (see chs 3, 5, 6 and 7 above). Where Fukuyama stands on the balance between 'liberalism' and 'democracy' is unclear. Furthermore, there is, of course, not simply one undisputed form of democracy. Even liberal democracies have crystallized into a number of different institutional types – the Westminster and federal models, for example – which make any appeal to a liberal conception of public life vague at best (see Lijphart, 1984; Dahl, 1989; Beetham, 1994; Potter et al., 1997). Fukuyama essentially leaves unanalysed the whole meaning of democracy and its possible variants.

Fukuyama's affirmation of the principles of economic liberalism, and the mechanisms of the market, also raises major questions. Following a central assumption of *laissez-faire* liberalism – that markets are basically self-equilibrating and 'clear' if various 'imperfections' are eliminated (wage and price 'stickiness', for instance) – he interprets markets as essentially 'powerless' mechanisms of coordination. He thus neglects to inquire into the extent to which market relations are themselves power relations that can constrain and limit the democratic process (cf. the discussion of neo-pluralism and neo-Marxism in ch. 6 above and the discussion of the New Right in ch. 7). He fails to ask whether systematic asymmetries in income, wealth and opportunity may be the outcome of the existing form of market relations: minimally regulated capitalist market relations. And he fails to examine whether one particular liberty – the liberty to accumulate unlimited economic resources – poses a challenge to the extent to which political liberty can be enjoyed by all citizens, i.e. the extent to which citizens can act as equals in the political process. Not to examine this challenge is to risk ignoring one of the main threats to liberty in the contemporary world; a threat deriving not, as thinkers like de Tocqueville and J. S. Mill expected, from demands for equality, but from inequality, inequality so great as to create violations of political liberty and democratic politics (Dahl, 1985, p. 60; and see pp. 169–72 above).

Moreover, the degree to which inequalities of ownership and control, and serious asymmetries of life chances, create differences of interest that can spark clashes of value, principle, belief (i.e. ideology) within the West, and between the West and the 'developing world', is also barely considered, despite Fukuyama's remarks on the dangers of a bifurcated global order. The potential for struggles between different 'ideological' accounts of the nature of the economic system and of desirable alternative forms of economic organization at national and international levels is underestimated. It is by no means self-evident, for example, that the existing economic system can generate the minimum life conditions for millions of people who currently face death by starvation in Africa and elsewhere, or, for that matter, the minimum life conditions for all the planet's population faced with global warming and the continued destruction of life-sustaining natural resources (see Held, 2004). It is far from self-evident that the existing economic system is compatible with the liberal concern itself to treat all persons as 'free and equal' (see D. Miller, 1989). In the absence of such compatibility, one can surmise, liberalism is likely to face continued criticism, as the search for a 'fairer' and 'safer' economic order goes on. Indeed, the anti-globalization or social justice movement has put those issues firmly on the agenda in the current period (see Held and McGrew, 2002).

Fukuyama's own account of the potential sources of ideological conflict is, in addition, weak. Leaving aside his characterization of ideology that is itself problematic (see J. B. Thompson, 1990), his attempt to explain away the persistence of nationalism and religious movements, especially religious fundamentalism, is unconvincing. For example, he dismisses Islam as a political ideology on the grounds that it cannot generate a universal appeal; its appeal is restricted to the Muslim world. But put like this it is a poor argument; for the same reasoning must surely lead one to conclude that liberalism itself should be dismissed as a political ideology because it too cannot generate a universal appeal; it has, after all, had limited impact on the Muslim world, on China and so on. Furthermore, some of the most protracted sources of political debate that have emanated in the West recently from social movements like feminism, environmentalism and the anti-globalists are not examined.

Finally, Fukuyama's claims about 'the end of history' are implausible. For what these claims ignore is not only the continued contestability of liberalism and of the liberal conception of the political good within and beyond the borders of the Western nation-state (see chs 10 and 11 below), but also that we cannot fully know what all the major sources of conflict and ideological struggle will be in a world shaped by the contingent, the unanticipated, and the imponderable as much as by determinate causal trajectories and bounded patterns of institutional change (see Himmelfarb, 1989). What we know is largely based on what has happened – on what was, and not on what will be. In this particular sense Hegel can be turned against Fukuyama; for it was Hegel who reminded philosophers that 'the Owl of Minerva spreads its wings only with the falling of dusk' (Hegel, *Philosophy of Right*, p. 13). We cannot rule out the possibility of new doctrinal orthodoxies with mass-mobilizing potential, capable of legitimating new kinds of regime, benevolent or authoritarian (see Beetham, 1991). One of the abiding lessons of the twentieth century must surely be that history is not closed and human progress remains an extraordinarily fragile achievement, however one defines and approaches it. In all likelihood, the very form and shape of democracy will remain contested for generations to come.

The events of 9/11 are adequate testimony to all of this: the world after 9/11 is extraordinarily different from that predicted by Fukuyama. Fundamentalism is on the rise and not just in Islam. Islamic, Christian, Jewish groupings, among others, are altering the terms of political debate. Established systems of religious belief and of political ideas are evolving, in some cases radically. In addition, patterns of Western globalization are being challenged not just by the anti-globalization movement but by the counter-global project articulated by some radical Islamic groups as well. The incidents of political violence and terrorist acts have increased across the world, from Kabul and Baghdad to New York, Madrid and London. Liberalism and democracy are under renewed challenge. Far from being at the 'end of history', we could be at the start of another beginning. I shall return to these themes in chapter 11.

The renewed necessity of Marxism and democracy from 'below'?

Liberal theory – in its classical and contemporary guises – generally takes for granted, as indicated in the previous chapter, what has to be carefully examined: namely, whether existing relationships among men and women, working, middle and upper classes, blacks and whites, and various ethnic groups allow formally recognized liberties actually to be realized. If liberals like Fukuyama were to examine these issues seriously, they might have to come to terms more directly with the massive number of people who are restricted systematically, for want of a complex mix of resources and life opportunities, from participating actively in political and civil affairs.

Pursuing related themes, Alex Callinicos, one of the most vigorous defenders of classic Marxism today, argues that liberal democracy has broken its promises. Following the Italian political theorist Norberto Bobbio, he conceives these promises as: (1) political participation, (2) accountable government, and (3) freedom to protest and reform (Callinicos, 1991, pp. 108–9; cf. Bobbio, 1987, pp. 42–4). 'Really existing liberal democracy' fails, he contends, on all three counts; it is distinguished by the existence of a largely passive citizenry (significant numbers of eligible citizens do not vote in elections, for example); the erosion and displacement of parliamentary institutions by unelected centres of power (typified by the expansion of the role of bureaucratic authority, of functional representatives and of the security services); and substantial structural constraints on state action and, in particular, on the possibility of the piecemeal reform of capitalism (the flight of capital overseas, for example, is a constant threat to elected governments with strong programmes of social reform) (Callinicos, 1991, p. 109).

Against this background Callinicos seeks to defend and reaffirm the classic Marxist tradition and, in particular, the model of direct democracy (model IV, p. 120 above) by arguing that democracy can only come from 'below', from the self-activity of the working class. A democratic alternative to liberal democracy can be found, Callinicos avers, in Marx's texts and in the 'rich twentieth-century tradition of soviet democracy, of workers' councils' (1991, p. 110). From this point of view, Stalinism, which dominated the Soviet Union's history, can be seen as the negation of socialism. Callinicos interprets Stalinism as a counter-revolutionary force which created at the close of the 1920s an anti-democratic, state capitalist regime; that is, a regime in which the state bureaucracy extracted surplus value and regulated capital accumulation, fulfilling the role once performed by the propertied classes. Stalinism destroyed the possibility of a radical workers' democracy, installed briefly in the Soviet Union in October 1917 under Lenin's leadership (see Lenin, *State and Revolution*). The collapse of Stalinism in 1989, therefore, cannot be understood, following Fukuyama, as the defeat of classic Marxism; for what was defeated, Callinicos insists, was an authoritarian distortion of Marxism. And what won in 1989 was not 'democracy' but capitalism. The achievement of the East European revolutions was to effect a political reorganization of the ruling classes, allowing the technical, bureaucratic elites of Eastern Europe to integrate their economies fully into the world market and to aid the transition from state to globally integrated capitalism (Callinicos, 1991, p. 58).

Callinicos attacks the equation Marxism = Leninism = Stalinism. A 'qualitative break', he argues, separates Stalinism from Marx and Lenin (1991, p. 16). Neither Marx's theory nor Lenin's practice sanctioned a system characterized not simply by one person's rule, but by 'the hierarchically organized control of all aspects of social life, political, economic, and cultural, by a narrow oligarchy seated at the apex of the party and state apparatuses' (1991, p. 15). In addition, there are resources in the classic Marxist tradition that provide a basis for making sense of the demise of the Stalinist regimes. Three themes, according to Callinicos, are of special relevance (1991, pp. 16–20). First, Marx's work, subsequently enriched and refined by later Marxist scholars, provides an account of epochal transformations, cast in terms of the underlying conflict that develops between the relations and forces of production and between classes which both mediate and intensify such conflict (cf. ch. 4 above). This account offers an indispensable framework for understanding the progressive collapse of the Stalinist order.

Second, in the work of the Trotskyist tradition a basis exists for understanding the specific nature and evolution of Stalinism (see Cliff, 1974). The concept of 'state capitalism', in particular, identifies the contradictions that exist in Stalinist regimes – between an exploiting dominant class that runs the bureaucracy and state factories, and the working classes, excluded from any effective control of the productive forces. It was this contradiction that brought the Stalinist regimes to an 'immense crisis'. While the crisis has been resolved temporarily by the integration of the Central and East European economies into the world capitalist order, the contradictions of this latter order are likely to result in still greater economic and political instability in the future.

Finally, in defining a project of human emancipation, classic Marxists provide an alternative to existing class-ridden regimes, in the West and the East. In championing a conception of socialism as 'the self-emancipation of the working class', classic Marxism upholds a vision of a 'self-conscious independent movement of the immense majority, in the interests of the immense majority', as Marx once wrote. This is a vision of 'socialism from below', wholly at odds both with the form of governance that used to prevail in the USSR and the Eastern bloc and with the emasculated democracies of the liberal West (Callinicos, 1991, p. 18). Neither state socialism nor liberal democracy can provide a political programme to liberate the powers of the *demos*. The same can be said about the programme of participatory democracy, which ultimately failed to address the economic power of capital and, thus, the primary obstacle to the transformation of democratic politics. Despite the concessions of thinkers like Macpherson and Pateman to liberalism, Callinicos upholds the contemporary relevance of the classic Marxist framework in all fundamental respects (cf. pp. 209–14 above).

The present era is constituted by a single unified economic system, marked by exploitation and inequality (Callinicos, 1991, p. 134). 'Really existing capitalism', unlike the myth of self-equilibrating markets, is characterized by: the concentration and centralization of economic power; the growth of corporations beyond the control of individual nation-states; cyclical crises involving overproduction, anarchy and waste; poverty in the heartlands of the West and massive disparities in life chances between the West and the rest; and the creation of life-threatening side-effects of uncontrolled capitalist accumulation in the form of, for example, global warming (Callinicos, 1991, pp. 98–106). In Callinicos's judgement, 'capitalism stands condemned'; it is time to resume the classic Marxist project of direct democracy (pp. 106, 134–6).

In the liberal tradition of the nineteenth and twentieth centuries, the political has often been equated, as shown in chapter 3, with the world of government and the citizen's relation to it. Where this equation is made and where politics is regarded as a sphere apart from economy or culture, a vast domain of what is central to politics tends to be excluded from view. Marxism has been at the forefront of the criticism of this position, maintaining that the key source of contemporary power – private ownership of the means of production – is unacceptably depoliticized by liberalism. This critique, as Callinicos rightly stresses, raises important questions; above all, about whether productive relations and market economies can be characterized as non-political and, thus, about whether the interconnections between economic power and the state are a constitutive element of politics. But it also raises difficulties by postulating (even in its subtler versions) a direct connection between the political and the economic. By seeking to understand the political by reference to economic and class power, and by rejecting the notion of politics as a form of activity *sui generis*, Marxism itself tends to marginalize or exclude from politics certain types of issue: essentially, all those that cannot be reduced to class-related matters – a point lucidly made by participatory and deliberative democrats (see chs 7 and 9).

One of the chief problems with a position such as Callinicos's, therefore, concerns the questions that arise when the capitalist order is presented as an all-embracing totality within which all aspects of social, political and cultural life are, in principle, located. Some mechanisms of institutional ordering (the modern states-system, the representative principle, for instance) and some types of social relationship (gender inequality and ethnic discrimination, for example) existed before the advent of modern capitalism, and have retained distinctive roles in the formation and structuring of politics (see Held, 1995, part II). One implication of this is that the concepts of mode of production and class analysis are too limiting. The thesis of the primacy of production and class relations has to be discarded, though this should not be taken to mean that the analysis of class and class conflict becomes insignificant (see S. Hall et al., 1992).

There are additional questions to raise. If not all differences of interest can be reduced to class and if differences of opinion, for example about the allocation of resources, can stem from a variety of interpretations and social locations, it is important to create the institutional space for the generation of, and debate about, alternative political strategies and programmes, as many of the social movements in Central and Eastern Europe sought to do from 1989 onwards. Indeed, without such a space it is hard to see how citizens can be active participants in the determination of the conditions of their own association. Politics involves discussion, negotiation and deliberation about public policy – which cannot take place according to wholly impartial or objective criteria, for there are no criteria which are themselves uncontested (see p. 119 above). Accordingly, the form and nature of democratic and representative institutions need to be specified and elaborated. For without this, the spheres for public deliberation and decision-making cannot be properly demarcated. Marxism has consistently underestimated the significance of the liberal preoccupation with how to secure freedom of criticism and action, i.e. choice and diversity, in the face of political power, although this is by no means to say that the traditional liberal formulation of the problem is fully satisfactory (see below).

It does not follow from this that Marx's conception of communism is one that entails the suppression of all individual difference (cf. Callinicos, 1993). There are admirable aspects of Marx's conception, particularly his concern that the 'free development of each' be compatible with the 'free development of all'. However, Marx's political theory does not provide a remotely adequate basis for defending this ideal. Once again, the problems stem from a failure to treat politics as an autonomous sphere. It is not an accident, as previously noted, that Marxism does not have a systematic account of the nature of 'public power', of legitimate claims to authority, of the dangers of centralized political power and of the problem of accountability. These problems – at the heart of modern liberal thought – were displaced by Marxism in its search for the driving force of society in class relations. The question of how 'individual differences' are to be understood, articulated and nurtured is severely neglected. Callinicos believes that while social conflicts will persist under communism, they will diminish in intensity for, 'in the absence of poverty and inequality', they will be readily amenable to negotiation and resolution. Even allowing Callinicos's qualification to stand about the absence of severe material difference in a post-capitalist order, this position does not seem very plausible. Like Fukuyama's version of the 'end of history', this account projects an end of politics – an end of intense differences of interest and interpretation, differences that could stem from nationalism, religion, social movements such as environmentalism, and a vast array of other sources, from uneven development and contingent outcomes to the unintended consequences of action. However, it is not enough to paper over all these challenges and issues with an appeal to their resolution in and through the expansion of revolutionary mechanisms of 'democratic self-organization'. What, where, and how exactly?

The upshot of this argument is that Stalinism should not simply be interpreted as an aberration of the Marxist project, a wholly separate and distinct political phenomenon. Rather, it is an outcome – though by no means the only possible one – of the 'deep structure' of Marxist categories with their emphasis on the centrality of class, the universal standpoint of the proletariat, and a conception of politics that roots it squarely in production. The contributions to politics of other forms of social structure, collectivity, agency, identity, interest and knowledge are severely underestimated. This argument does not imply that Stalinism was the inevitable result of the revolution of 1917; there were many complex conditions that determined the fate of the revolution. But it does imply that Marxism has misunderstood the liberal and liberal democratic preoccupation with the form and limits of state power, and that this misunderstanding is an inextricable part of classical Marxist political theory (cf.

Hont, 1994). Moreover, it is a misunderstanding with implications, rich in consequences, for how one conceives politics, democracy and the nature of political agency.

The argument that what failed in the Soviet Union was simply Stalinism, or the state-capitalist regime, is deeply problematic. This reflection is reinforced by considering that it was not a form of capitalism that failed but, rather, a form of what I call 'state-administered socialism'. There are several different variants of state-administered socialism, from the state socialist societies of the former Eastern bloc to those social democratic regimes in the West which orientated themselves to programmes of nationalization and state ownership. Although there are major differences among these types, which I by no means wish to underestimate, they also have certain elements in common: all can be associated with centrally controlled bureaucratic institutions. The programme of state-administered socialism lost its radical appeal precisely because it failed, among other things, to recognize the desirable form and limits of state action, as liberals and neo-liberals have indicated (see pp. 79–84, 214–16).

In summary, the 'crisis of socialism', in theory and in practice, goes much further than the 'crisis of Stalinism'. The relation between socialism and democracy has to be rethought. There are notable theoretical and practical reasons, I have suggested, for scepticism about some of the dominant elements of the traditional socialist project.

In sum: the question of the political good

The East European revolutions were a historical watershed, without doubt. The collapse of the Soviet empire and the retreat of communism across Europe were major events not only of the twentieth century, but probably of modern history as well. Ripples of change spread through political institutions and conventional beliefs across the globe.

The diverse interpretations of the revolutions, and of their impact upon the contemporary world, reflect at least one thing: history is not at an end and ideology is not dead. Liberalism and Marxism, with their distinctive roots stretching back into the formative moments of modernity, remain active traditions. Although liberalism is clearly dominant today, Marxism – in its diverse variants – is not yet exhausted, a point reaffirmed by the recent debate on the US as an empire (see Hardt and Negri, 2000; cf. Held and Koenig-Archibugi, 2004). None the less, both traditions, I have argued, are wanting in fundamental respects.

Among these respects is a concern about how to conceive the meaning of the political good, or how one should define the 'good life' in contemporary politics. This is a matter about which Fukuyama and Callinicos have something to say (whether directly or indirectly) and it provides, accordingly, a useful basis around which to draw together some of the strands of the previous sections of this chapter.

For Fukuyama, the good life follows from the progressive recasting of the modern world on liberal principles. Political life, like economic life, is – or ought to be – a matter of individual freedom and initiative, and the more closely it approximates this state of affairs, the more it can justifiably be claimed that the political good has been achieved. The individual is, in essence, sacrosanct, and is free and equal only to the extent that he or she can pursue and attempt to realize self-chosen ends and personal interests. Equal justice can be sustained among individuals if, above all, individuals' entitlement to certain rights or liberties is respected and all citizens are treated equally before the law. The preoccupation is with the creation and defence of a world where 'free and equal' individuals can flourish with minimum political interference, in West and East, North and South.

By contrast, Callinicos and classic Marxists more generally defend the desirability of certain social or collective goals and means. For them, to take equality and liberty seriously is to challenge the view that these values can be realized by individuals left, in practice, to their own devices in a 'free market' economy and a restricted or minimal state. Equality, liberty and justice cannot be achieved in a world dominated by private ownership of property and the capitalist economy; these ideals can be realized only through struggles to ensure that the means of production are socialized, i.e. subject to collective appropriation and to procedures ensuring social control. Only the latter can ultimately guarantee that 'the free development of each' is compatible with the 'free development of all'.

Although the revolutions of Central and Eastern Europe put democracy at the forefront of politics across the regions of the globe, the appeal and nature of democracy itself remains inadequately considered by both Fukuyama and Callinicos. In Fukuyama's political writings, democracy is ultimately eclipsed by the affirmation of individualist political, economic and ethical doctrines (cf. Fukuyama, 1995). The question and problem of democratic accountability take second place to the imperative of individual liberty in the face of political regulation. In Callinicos's work, the categories of class, class conflict and production displace the necessity of a thorough analysis of democracy. Despite the recent consolidation of liberal democracy, the common use of democracy in political discourse, and its practically universal invocation by political regimes at the end of the twentieth century (see Potter et al., 1997), it has not been at the centre of these thinkers' political reflections and theoretical analyses. Neither the celebration of liberal democracy nor its dismissal as a purely formal mechanism or 'empty shell' provides adequate means of assessing its strengths and limitations. Democracy bestows an 'aura of legitimacy' on modern political life. Yet, under what conditions political regimes may reasonably be considered legitimate and when one can justifiably claim the mantle of democracy remain unclear. The next chapter reassesses this issue. It raises questions about the 'quality' of democracy; that is, about the extent to which democracy reflects and articulates informed and publicly tested judgements, and about the institutional conditions of such judgements.

9 Deliberative Democracy and the Defence of the Public Realm

A spectre haunts contemporary democratic politics, namely, that while entrenching the accountability of rulers to the ruled, and extending the scope of the *demos* across all facets of public life, politics could be reduced to the lowest possible denominator – to governance by the masses who are neither well informed nor wise. Such a fear was at the heart of Plato's despair about the prospects of democracy, elaborated in his parables about the ship's captain and what it takes to control a large, powerful animal (pp. 24–6 above). A preoccupation that rule by the many means the pursuit by them of unbridled desires and interests, on the one hand, and ignorant and short-sighted views, on the other, has led some to believe that democracy is either a dangerously mistaken ambition or something to be hedged and checked as much as possible by constitutional structures and mechanisms, and the careful delimitation of the scope of democratic action. If Plato is typical of thinkers in the first camp, Madison and Schumpeter are typical of the second. The story of democracy contains both a celebration of the end of arbitrary rule and paternalistic politics, and anxiety that democracy could mean rule by the rabble.

Of course, the history of democracy reveals a difficult struggle to define its proper meaning, and the models of democracy examined so far disclose the way this matter has been resolved and weighed at different times and periods. Within democratic thinking, a clear divide exists between those who value political participation for its own sake and understand it as a fundamental mode of self-realization, and those who take a more instrumental view and understand democratic politics as a means of protecting citizens from arbitrary rule and expressing (via mechanisms of aggregation) their preferences. From classical democrats and developmental republicans to developmental liberals and participatory democrats, political engagement is prized because it fosters a sense of political efficacy, generates a concern with collective problems and nurtures the formation of a knowledgeable citizenry capable of pursuing the common good. Democracy here is the unfolding of civic virtue and the democratic polity is the means to self-fulfilment. Against this understanding, there are those, no doubt the majority of democratic thinkers, who interpret democracy as a means to protect citizens from their governors and from each other, and to ensure that a sound political structure is in place which can generate a skilled and accountable elite capable of making essential public decisions. According to this position, democracy is a means not an end; it serves to protect the liberty of citizens and to maintain the minimum public goods (the rule of law, electoral politics, a social safety net, security) necessary for citizens to go about their self-chosen ends and objectives.

The eight models of democracy presented so far leave seemingly little room for new and innovative thinking about democracy. They appear to cover the spectrum of possible political spaces along two dimensions: the extension of political equality and citizenship to all adults, and the deepening of the scope of democracy to cover economic, social and cultural affairs. Yet there is a candidate for the status of a new (ninth) model which has emerged in the last twenty years or so: 'deliberative democracy', a term used for the first time by Joseph Bessette (1980, 1994). While the term now spans a wide range of positions, its main advocates use it to distinguish a political approach focused on improving the quality of democracy. At issue is enhancing the nature and form of political participation, not just increasing it for its own sake. Deliberative democrats often portray contemporary democracy, representative or direct, as a descent into personality clashes, celebrity politics, sound-bite 'debates' and the naked pursuit of personal gain and ambition. They champion, instead, informed debate, the public use of reason and the impartial pursuit of truth.

Reason and participation

The problem addressed by deliberative democrats is whether democratic processes and institutions should be built around the actual or empirical will of those engaged in politics, or whether it should be built around what might be called 'reasonable' political judgement. Deliberative democrats put a premium on refined and reflective preferences. Of course, as soon as one has stressed this point the issue of definition emerges. Claus Offe and Ulrich Preuss have addressed the matter head-on. According to them, a 'rational' or 'enlightened' political will or judgement is one that meets three criteria: 'ideally it would have to be at one and the same time "*fact-regarding*" (as opposed to ignorant or doctrinaire), "*future-regarding*" (as opposed to myopic) and "*other-regarding*" (as opposed to selfish)' (1991, pp. 156–7). Whenever deficiencies in political judgement are found it is usually because such judgements fail on one or more of these criteria, that is, they fail because they are uninformed and/or short-sighted and/or self-interested. The issue raised is whether democratic theory should regard preferences that are actually found in everyday life as already fully formed and reasonable, or whether it should steer political thinking into raising questions about the nature of 'political will' and, if so, whether the latter should only be regarded as justified or legitimate if it meets certain tests of impartiality.

As soon as these points are made, a connection emerges to the position adopted by critics of democracy from Plato onwards, who fear that democracy connotes the descent to the lowest common denominator and the necessary eclipse of refined, reflective political judgement. The issue for deliberative democrats is whether a concern with reflective preferences is necessarily elitist, in a sense that would have pleased Plato, or whether it can lead to new, innovative ideas about how democracy might function and work. The theoretical dilemma can be put in the following way: is the democratic conception of the common good little more than the aggregation of given individual preferences, or can it be articulated in relation to serious public debate and deliberation? For Offe and Preuss, the key point can be put bluntly:

'there is no positive linear relationship between participation and reasonableness' (1991, p. 167). The challenge for democratic theory is neither simply to think through the increasing categories of people who might be entitled to participate in politics, nor is it simply to reconsider the many substantive areas where democracy might be legitimately extended. Rather, the challenge today is to be concerned with 'the introduction of procedures that put a premium upon the formulation of carefully considered, consistent, situationally abstract, socially validated and justifiable preferences' (1991, p. 167).

The key focus for deliberative democrats was well put by Bernard Manin when he wrote 'it is . . . necessary to alter radically the perspective common to liberal theories and democratic thought: the source of legitimacy is not the pre-determined will of individuals, but rather the process of its formation, that is, deliberation itself'(1987, pp. 351ff). The major contention of deliberative democrats is to bid farewell to any notion of fixed preferences and to replace them with a learning process in and through which people come to terms with the range of issues they need to understand in order to hold a sound and reasonable political judgement. At issue is not the simple imposition of an abstract, preconceived standard of rationality but, rather, a commitment to politics as an open-ended and continuous learning process in which the roles of 'teacher' and 'curriculum' are raised, and where the matter of what is to be learnt has to be settled in the process of learning itself (Offe and Preuss, 1991, p. 168). In other words, a deliberative democratic process would not be one which treats people's judgements and processes as given, but one which effectively asks: do these judgements and processes meet an adequate standard of learning? And if not, how can they be improved?

As Offe and Preuss put it, 'it appears to be a largely novel task to think about institutional arrangements and procedures which could generate a selective pressure in favour of this type of reflective and open preference-learning, as opposed to fixed preferences that are entirely derivative from situational determinants, rigid beliefs or self-deception' (1991, p. 168). Thus, deliberative democrats make a very distinctive case; that is, they contend that no set of values or particular perspectives can lay claim to being correct and valid by themselves, but they are valid only in so far as they are justified. Moreover, individual points of view need to be tested in and through social encounters which take account of the point of view of others – the moral point of view.

The conclusion of this line of reasoning is that the institutional designs of modern democracy must be based on the 'principle of reciprocity'. This principle requires that democratic theorists, as well as people in everyday settings, place greater emphasis upon those settings and the procedures of preference formation and learning within politics and civil society. It demands that we adopt 'a multi-perspectival mode of forming, defending and thereby refining our preferences' (Offe and Preuss, 1991, p. 169). Why we come to adopt the views we do, and whether we could defend them in a complex social setting with people with opposed preferences, becomes the focus of attention. Democratic theory must direct itself to constitutional designs which help build in to the process of politics itself the opportunity to learn and to test publicly citizens' views. Democratic theory needs to upgrade the quality of citizenship by

> putting a premium on refined and reflective preferences, rather than 'spontaneous' and context-contingent ones. By reflective preferences [is meant] ... preferences that are the outcome of a conscious confrontation of one's own point of view with an opposing point of view, or of the multiplicity of viewpoints that the citizen, upon reflection, is likely to discover within his or her own self. Such reflectiveness may be facilitated by arrangements that overcome the monological seclusion of the act of voting in the voting booth by complementing this necessary mode of participation with more dialogical forms of making one's voice heard. (Offe and Preuss, 1991, p. 170)

The upshot of the argument, then, is that democratic theory needs to think not just about the contexts in which people form views and test their opinions, but also about the kinds of mechanisms that are in operation in democracies that either reinforce existing viewpoints, or help create new ones. There must be a shift in democratic theory from an exclusive focus on macro-political institutions to an examination of the various diverse contexts of civil society, some of which hinder and some of which nurture deliberation and debate.

The limits of democratic theory

A preoccupation with the deficiencies of contemporary political life motivates a great deal of the thinking of deliberative democrats. James Fishkin, one of the pioneers of deliberative democracy, is scathing about the apathy and lack of interest in public life today found among large swathes of the electorate, and the elitism of political parties and governing groups. Contemporary democracy presents 'a forced choice between politically equal but relatively incompetent masses and politically unequal but relatively more competent elites' (Fishkin, 1991, p. 1). The historical trend towards greater formal equality, represented by the extensions of the franchise won by excluded groups, has all too often been 'accompanied by massive non-participation and disinterest' (1991, p. 54). Voter turnout has declined despite the extension of the vote to formerly disfranchised groups. Debate in contemporary democracies is generally superficial, ill informed and thoughtless; voters exhibit a clear sense of disconnection from the political process, suffering alienation, disengagement or complacency. The emphasis on politicians' personalities, rather than a focus on policy, pervades the media-saturated world of electoral politics. Sound-bites replace arguments, celebrity glitz displaces principled political argument, and candidates are selected 'more or less the way we choose detergents' (1991, p. 3).

The elites that dominate US and European politics are also, Fishkin argues, increasingly disconnected from the wider processes and problems of political debate. The policy process has been invaded by opinion polling, focus groups and other marketing tools designed to adjust policy to extant views and interests rather than to explore the principles underpinning policy and to deliberate over policy direction. Elites drive politics by trying to second-guess their electorates. The ideal of a public sphere which upholds reason, argument and impartiality found in strands of both classical and liberal democratic theory is undermined by the reliance of elites and parties on opinion poll data, which they are free to interpret and manipulate in their own interests. As Fishkin puts it: 'instead of public opinions worthy of the name controlling leaders, preferences shaped by leaders and by the mass media too often are bounced back, reflected in polls, without sufficient critical scrutiny and without sufficient information and examination to represent any meaningful popular control' (1991, p. 19). Politics is increasingly shallow, media driven, mean and empty of both ideas and high quality leadership.

While Fishkin's characterization of liberal democracy echoes Schumpeter's account of democracy – with its affirmation of the democratic political process as a struggle of elites in the face of a vulnerable and susceptible electorate (pp. 146–52 above) – and Weber's portrayal of representative democracy as 'plebiscitary leadership democracy' with Caesarist tendencies (pp. 134–8 above), he does not affirm or celebrate it. On the contrary, he takes this to be the basis for a clarion call for an imaginative rethinking of democracy offering a new kind of participation, one that not only gives citizens more power, but also allows them more opportunities to exercise this power thoughtfully. He is joined in this by many contemporary political thinkers. Among them is Jon Elster.

Elster focuses attention on the way electoral politics creates winners and losers through the aggregation of private preferences. This process, he suggests, embraces a concept of rationality more appropriate to consumer choice, i.e. market relations, than to politics, which should be governed by a form of discursive rationality appropriate to a public meeting place or site of discussion. Reducing collective decision-making to the aggregation of private preferences

> embodies a confusion between the kind of behaviour that is appropriate in the market place and that which is appropriate in the forum. The notion of consumer sovereignty is acceptable because, and to the extent that, the consumer chooses between courses of action that differ only in the way they affect him. In political choice situations, however, the citizen is asked to express his preference over states that also differ in the way in which they affect other people. (Elster, 1997, pp. 33–4)

Consumer choice is self-regarding, the pursuit of objects and resources for the satisfaction of individual needs or wants. By contrast, political choice is other regarding and can, in John Stuart Mill's terms, 'concern others' because it can 'harm' them (p. 80 above). The difference between consumption and politics is, in short, the difference between choices affecting oneself and choices which shape and affect the preferences and life opportunities of others. If collective decisions in the latter case are to be effective, legitimate and just, then they need to be shaped by sound public reasons – that can stand up to public debate and inquiry.

John Dryzek shares this view. Drawing on work from the Frankfurt School (see pp. 188–9 above; Held, 1980, part I), Dryzek sets out a wide-ranging critique of the increasing dominance of instrumental rationality – that is, purely formal, means–end rationality – in public and private life. He contends that the spread of instrumental rationality leads to the bureaucratization and concentration of power in the hands of technically skilled elites who treat politics as the preserve of experts, not citizens. Experts seek to disaggregate complex problems into manageable constituent elements and to deal with each in isolation from the other and from the wider body politic. This prevents a complex, holistic approach to government, which must be based on a non-instrumental, socially orientated approach to politics. In addition, instrumental reason encourages people to treat each other as means to an end, and undermines a conception of persons as free and equal and capable of active citizenship. While liberal democracy recognizes only private views and interests, and seeks to legitimate the freedom of action of experts via the aggregation of individual choices through occasional elections, public problems require, Dryzek holds, moving the quality of decision-making into the centre of debate, and the creation of public fora in which private preferences are treated not as fixed but, rather, as amenable to transformation in the light of 'the discovery of generalizable interests' through argument and justification (Dryzek, 1990, p. 54).

At the heart of this position are the arguments of the leading contemporary critical theorist, Jürgen Habermas (1973, 1990, 1993, 1996; and see below). As Habermas conceives it, rationality need not only be thought of as a device employed by individuals to manipulate the world of discrete elements and objects, but can be considered also as the means to ensure the social coordination of action. The latter can be articulated as the body of norms which guide our activity and which are capable of becoming the subject of debate and cross-examination. Rationality on this model is inseparable from the idea of justification to others. For Dryzek, the deficiencies of existing models of liberal democracy can be overcome only by strengthening discursive or communicative rationality which allows us to seek collective solutions to the collective problems we face in modern societies, from the crisis of pensions to environmental degradation.

Going forward to rethink democracy does not mean going back to existing models of direct or participatory democracy. Many of what deliberative democrats regard as the limits of liberal democracy are reproduced in these conceptions as well. The ideal of face-to-face political decision-making and attempts to adapt this idea to various forms of direct or participative democracy are treated with scepticism for three reasons. The first and most obvious is that the ideal cannot be realized in highly complex and differentiated modern societies. The critiques of direct democracy by John Stuart Mill and Weber find an echo here (see pp. 84–6, 129–30 above). Second, the idealization of face-to-face decision-making in small communities is itself misplaced because the potential defects of small, relatively homogeneous communities – a tendency to conformity, intolerance, and the personalization of politics – risk being reproduced in all forms of direct political life. As Fishkin put it, small-scale democracy is 'more vulnerable to tyranny' because it is 'more vulnerable to demagoguery' (1991, p. 50). Third, increased participation alone does not address the problem of the quality of participation. Participatory democrats fail to focus on specifically deliberative deficits. Participation *per se* does not remedy this and can in fact make it worse in mass societies: 'the deliberative competence of mass publics is suspect. It is a dubious accomplishment to give power to the people under conditions when they are not really in a position to exercise that power … aroused publics might, on occasion, be vulnerable to demagoguery' (Fishkin, 1991, p. 21).

The critique of direct popular participation is also found in contemporary republican thinkers who wish to draw upon deliberative insights. Philip Pettit, for example, is concerned with constructing institutions which would avoid the risk of the exposure of individuals to domination, i.e. arbitrary interference in their lives. He is concerned that increasing participation for its own sake can enhance precisely the kinds of arbitrariness republicans seek to avoid. In his judgement, if the electorate is given direct control of policy issues, without improving the quality of political reflection and argument, it is liable to become the most arbitrary of all powers (Pettit, 2003, p. 154). This argument is reinforced by the work of Joshua Cohen, who is careful to separate an analysis of the ideal of deliberative democracy from the ideals both of voter aggregation and direct democracy. In an important early statement of deliberative democracy he argued that he sees 'no merit' in the claim that direct democracy best institutionalizes the ideals of deliberative democracy (1989). Direct democracy *per se* need not be deliberative. Deliberative democracy cannot accurately be portrayed as another version of direct participatory models of democracy.

The aims of deliberative democracy

Deliberative democracy, broadly defined, is 'any one of a family of views according to which the public deliberation of free and equal citizens is the core of legitimate political decision-making and self-governance' (Bohman, 1998, p. 401). Political legitimacy does not turn on the ballot box or on majority rule *per se* but, rather, on the giving of defensible reasons, explanations and accounts for public decisions (see Saward, 2003, pp. 120–4). The key objective is the transformation of private preferences via a process of deliberation into positions that can withstand public scrutiny and test.

Deliberation can overcome the limitations of private views and enhance the quality of public decision-making for a number of reasons. First, through sharing information and pooling knowledge, public deliberation can transform individuals' understanding and enhance their grasp of complex problems. People may come to understand elements of their situation which they had not appreciated before: for example, aspects of the interrelation of public issues, or some of the consequences of taking particular courses of action, intended or otherwise. Second, public deliberation can reveal how certain preference formations may be linked to sectional interests, thereby securing an ideological purpose. In this case, deliberation can expose the one-sidedness and partiality of certain viewpoints which may fail to represent the interests of the many. It may also reveal the limits of 'accommodationist preferences', that is, preferences shaped by reducing one's expectations to accommodate oneself to circumstances which seem fixed or unchangeable. Cohen has referred to these as 'psychological adjustments to conditions of subordination' (1989, p. 25). Examples might be forms of acceptance of a dominant political order based on 'tradition' or on 'pragmatic acquiescence', both analysed earlier (p. 155 above).

What deliberation can reveal under these conditions is the importance of an open, fluid and dynamic process of 'opinion formation' in public life; for it can help disclose socially distorted positions and lay the basis for a more thorough understanding.

Third, public deliberation can replace 'the language of interest with the language of reason' (Elster, 1989, p. 111). Deliberation may enhance collective judgement because it is concerned not just with pooling information and exchanging views, but also with reasoning about these and testing arguments. Fishkin emphasizes that in public deliberation 'participants must be willing to consider the arguments offered on their merits' (1991, p. 37). In short, deliberative democrats hope to strengthen the legitimacy of democratic procedures and institutions by embracing deliberative elements, elements designed to expand the quality of democratic life and enhance democratic outcomes. For some deliberative thinkers, this quality warrants the claim that deliberative democracy is the best conception of democratic procedure because it can generate the 'best' decisions; that is, produce outcomes that are the most thoroughly examined, justified and, hence, legitimate. The exchange of public reasons in deliberation creates a new principle of legitimate governance.

Deliberative democracy constitutes an independent political ideal. Cohen offers a succinct account of this when he argues that a democratic association should be conceived as one in which 'the justification of the terms and conditions of association proceeds through public argument and reasoning' and that citizens in such an order 'regard their basic institutions as legitimate in so far as they establish the framework for free public deliberation' (1989, p. 21). According to this position, deliberation is free if it is 'not constrained' by the authority of prior norms or requirements. Under conditions of ideal deliberation, as Habermas has stated, 'no force except that of the better argument is exercised' (1976, p. 108). Parties are required 'to state their reasons for advancing proposals, supporting them or criticising them' (Cohen, 1989, p. 22). Citizens cannot simply state their preferences without being prepared to justify them in public. For the ideal to be effective, citizens need to enjoy freedom from the distorting influences of unequal power, wealth, education and other resources. What matters is a rationally motivated agreement, not an outcome produced by coercion, manipulation or bargaining. The model requires that citizens enjoy formal and substantial equality. Deliberative democracy rests on a view of political justification, that is, that it proceeds through free deliberation among equal citizens. Institutions must be geared to making this possible (Cohen, 1989, p. 26).

What is sound public reasoning? Impartialism and its critics

According to deliberative democrats, there are better and worse ways to make public decisions. While there are a number of different ways of conceiving what this amounts to in the literature, two positions will be set out here: those of the impartialists and their critics. An examination of their positions helps map the debate over what constitutes sound public reasoning. The focus is on specifying the grounds on which it can be said something is right or just. If these grounds can be successfully disclosed, a critical basis is established for laying out guiding or regulative principles of public life.

Impartialism

Deliberative democrats do not take citizens' preferences as simply given or preset and, instead, seek to create the means for the examination of opinion about common problems. The aim is to establish a deliberative process whose structure grounds 'an expectation of rationally acceptable results' (see Habermas, 1996). Such a process can be conceived in terms of a broad set of public spheres in which views are considered, and collective judgements are arrived at, through deliberation guided by impartiality. Being impartial means being open to, reasoning from, and assessing all points of view before deciding what is right or just; it does not mean simply following the precepts of self-interest, whether based on class, gender, ethnicity or nationality. Political decisions that meet the standards of impartiality are those that would be defensible in relation to all significantly affected groups and parties if they had participated as equal partners in public debate. Impartialists do not assume that all relevant groups will always be able to engage in a public debate about a pressing matter (desirable though that might be in principle). Rather, they assume that a satisfactory deliberative process must be one that tests arguments against all possible relevant views and interests and thus meets the standards of inclusiveness and non-partisanship.[1]

To test the validity of preferences and interests involves 'reasoning from the point of view of others' (Benhabib, 1992, pp. 9–10, 121–47). Attempts to focus on this 'social point of view' find their clearest contemporary elaboration in John Rawls's original position, Jürgen Habermas's ideal speech situation and Brian Barry's formulation of impartialist reasoning (see Rawls, 1971; Habermas, 1973, 1996; Barry, 1989, 1995). These formulations have in common a concern to conceptualize an impartial moral standpoint from which to assess particular forms of practical or moral reasoning. This concern could be thought of as quite unrealistic or overdemanding. But as one commentator aptly put it: 'all the impartiality thesis says is that, if and when one raises questions regarding fundamental ... standards, the court of appeal that one addresses is a court in which no particular individual, group, or country has *special* standing' (Hill, 1987, p. 132, quoted in Barry, 1995, pp. 226–7). Before the court, suggesting 'I believe this is the case', 'I want it because I like it', 'it suits me', 'I think it's fair', 'it belongs to male prerogatives', 'it is in the best interest of my country', does not settle the issue at hand, for claims and principles must be defensible from a larger, social standpoint. The latter is an open-ended, critical argumentative device for focusing our thoughts on views, norms and rules that might reasonably command agreement.

Impartialist reasoning is a frame of reference for specifying standpoints that can be universally shared; and, concomitantly, it rejects as unjust all those

---

[1] The material in the following four paragraphs is adapted from my 'Principles of cosmopolitan order', in Brock and Brighouse (2005).

positions and practices anchored in principles not all could adopt (O'Neill, 1991). At issue is the establishment of principles and rules that nobody, motivated to establish an uncoerced and informed agreement, could reasonably discard (see Barry, 1989; cf. Scanlon, 1998). In order to meet this standard a number of particular tests can be pursued, including an assessment of whether all points of view have been taken into consideration; whether all parties would be equally prepared to accept the outcome as fair and reasonable irrespective of the social positions they might occupy now or in the future; and whether there are individuals in a position to impose on others in such a manner as would be unacceptable to the latter, or to the originator of the action (or inaction), if the roles were reversed (see Barry, 1989, pp. 372 and 362–3).

Impartialist reasoning cannot produce a simple deductive proof of the best or only moral principles that should guide institutional development; nor can it produce a deductive proof of the ideal set of principles and conditions which could overcome the deficiencies of political life. Rather, it should be thought of as a heuristic device to test viewpoints and principles, and their forms of justification (Kelly, 1998, pp. 1–8; Barry, 1998b). These tests are concerned with a process of reasonable rejectability, which can always be pursued in a theoretical dialogue open to fresh challenge and new questions (Gadamer, 1975). But to acknowledge this is not to say that the theoretical conversation is 'toothless'.

In the first instance, impartialism has a crucial critical role. This position is emphasized most clearly by Onora O'Neill (1991). Impartialist reasoning, in this account, is a basis for criticizing partial and one-sided views, non-generalizable principles, rules and interests, and of showing how justice is a matter of not basing actions, lives or institutions on principles that cannot be universally shared. But can it state a more positive position? Impartialists think so.

For example, they argue that within an impartialist framework it is possible to show that individual or collective social arrangements generating serious harm (urgent unmet need) cannot be simply upheld by reference to a special social standing, cultural identity, ethnic background, or nationality – in fact by reference to any particular social grouping – if the latter sanctions exclusion or closure in relation to the core conditions of human autonomy, development and welfare (see Caney, 2001). To the extent that a domain of activity operates to structure and delimit significantly the life expectancy and life chances of some to the disadvantage of others, deficits are disclosed in the structure of action of a political association. These can, furthermore, be regarded as illegitimate to the extent to which they would be rejected under conditions of impartialist reasoning. If people did not know their future social location and political identity, they would be unlikely to find the particular defence of specific exclusionary processes and mechanisms convincing. These justificatory structures cannot easily be generalized and are thus weak in the face of the test of impartiality. Unless exceptional arguments were available to the contrary, social mechanisms and processes generating serious harm for certain groups and categories of people would fall to the requirement of impartiality (see Barry, 1995, 1998a).

Impartialist reasoning is a basis for thinking about the problems posed by asymmetries of power, unevenness of resource distribution and stark prejudices. It provides the means for asking about the rules, laws and policies people might think right, justified or worthy of respect. It allows a broad distinction to be made between legitimacy as acquiescence to existing socioeconomic arrangements, and legitimacy as 'rightness' or 'correctness' – the worthiness of a political order to be recognized because it is the order people would accept as a result of impartialist reasoning. The latter can be conceived not as an optional element of a political and social understanding but, rather, as a requirement of any attempt to grasp the nature of the support and legitimacy enjoyed by particular social relations and institutions; for without this form of reasoning the distinction between legitimacy as 'acceptance' and legitimacy as 'rightness' could not be drawn. Hence, it is the basis of distinguishing compliance based on tradition, pragmatic acquiescence or instrumental agreement from compliance based on what people would consider as right and worthy of respect after deliberation (pp. 155–6, 197–8 above).

It should be emphasized that the pursuit of impartial reasoning is a social activity even when it is pursued as a solitary theoretical exercise. For as Hannah Arendt has written:

> The power of judgement rests on a potential agreement with others, and the thinking process which is active in judging something is not ... a dialogue between me and myself, but finds itself always and primarily, even if I am quite alone in making up my mind, in an anticipated communication with others with whom I know I must finally come to some agreement ... And this enlarged way of thinking ... cannot function in strict isolation or solitude; it needs the presence of others 'in whose place' it must think, whose perspective it must take into consideration, and without whom it never has the opportunity to operate at all. (*On Revolution*, as cited by Benhabib, 1992, pp. 9–10)

The aim of a debate about impartiality is an anticipated agreement with all those whose diverse circumstances are affected by a pressing issue or set of issues. Of course, as an 'anticipated agreement' it is a hypothetical ascription of a collective or intersubjective understanding. As such, the ultimate test of its validity must depend in contemporary life on the extension of the conversation to all those whom it seeks to encompass. Only under the latter circumstances can an analytically proposed interpretation become an actual understanding or agreement among others (Habermas, 1988). Critical reflection must link up with public debate and deliberative politics (see below).

The critics

Impartialist reasoning is argument designed to abstract from power relations and to test the force of the better argument. But it is a form of reasoning that has been criticized as too abstract and too narrow in its conception of what constitutes a good argument. Amy Gutmann and Dennis Thompson are leading voices in this regard. They reject the notion that deliberation under the right conditions – free of coercion and power relations – is necessary to legitimate laws and public policies (1996, p. 200). What is needed, they argue, is not an account of deliberation in unattainable conditions following very abstract argumentative rules but, rather, a better grasp of the nature and meaning of deliberation under 'non-ideal' conditions. They do not think that the likes of Habermas or Rawls have much to offer here.

Just as Weber spoke of the irreducible clash between 'warring gods' (p. 128 above), Gutmann and Thompson believe conflict over public choices cannot be eliminated from human affairs, and that self-interested political actors cannot be turned through deliberation into altruistic persons. 'Incompatible values' and 'incomplete understanding' are endemic to human politics, as endemic, in fact, as scarcity and limited altruism (1996, pp. 25–6). Moreover, we cannot expect to resolve all or even most moral conflicts because 'moral disagreement is a condition with which we must learn to live, not merely an obstacle to be overcome on the way to a just society' (1996, p. 26). This was the error of Marxism (cf. pp. 116f above) and is the error of all forms of political and social theory that hold that such conflicts and differences are simply the product of socioeconomic interests. Conflict over law and policy cannot be explained reductively as a product of self-interest because citizens' 'moral understanding [and lack of understanding] are part of what constitutes their interests' (1996, p. 19).

Impartiality is incapable of indicating how to handle moral conflicts such as that posed by whether or not abortions should be legalized, the extent of the teaching of religion in schools or the level of welfare benefits appropriate for those who are unemployed. This is so because in each of these and numerous other examples, the matter cannot be resolved by appeal to the facts (for what facts are to be counted as relevant will be determined by prior conceptual choices) or an analysis of the relevant concepts involved (for those will also be contested). Impartiality requires the exchange of general reasons to settle a dispute, and the searching out of positions capable of intersubjectivity and collective agreement. But precisely which will count as a 'general reason' or a position thought capable of generating agreement will inevitably be disputed.

Gutmann and Thompson argue that impartiality entails a type of moral absolutism: impartial reasoners in search of the better or clinching argument cannot recognize that dissenters may have good reasons for the positions they hold. All parties to a dispute about a matter of pressing concern may have sound grounds for not wanting to shift their views in the face of impartialist tests. Accordingly, deliberative democrats like Gutmann and Thompson stress the importance of recognizing that interlocutors are not necessarily disagreeing because they are poor reasoners, blindly self-interested or stupid. Instead, parties to deliberation should seek mutually acceptable reasons before deciding on a course of action and if they fail to find these they should seek an accommodation consistent with mutual respect (1996, pp. 79ff). In this context, public justification requires that 'a citizen offers reasons that can be accepted by others who are similarly motivated to find reasons that can be accepted by others' (1996, p. 53). They call this principle, in an argument that recalls Offe's and Preuss's position (see pp. 232–4 above), the principle of reciprocity. Citizens should aspire to a form of reasoning that is mutually justifiable and mutually accommodating.

The core of Gutmann's and Thompson's account of deliberation has been succinctly put by one commentator:

[deliberation] cannot hope to resolve all moral conflicts, but in imposing an obligation on citizens, in the first instance, to seek justifications which are acceptable to all, it focuses our attention on these and deliberation about them can then come to clarify them. If some problems remain, following clarification of the issues, and cannot be treated as the product of misunderstandings, then we . . . are required to seek an accommodation with those in opposition. The pursuit of accommodation manifests the mutual respect which citizens have for one another and it should exhibit 'civic integrity', i.e. the avoidance of strategic or hypocritical speech, and 'civic magnanimity', i.e. parties should strive to be open-minded and acknowledge the seriousness of the issue for both parties to the dispute. (McBride, 2004, p. 39)

Gutmann and Thompson refer to this position as seeking 'an economy of moral disagreement' (1996, p. 84). Citizens should pursue the argument that minimizes rejection of the position they oppose and avoid unnecessary conflict in characterizing the standpoint of their opponents. The aim is to search out 'significant points of convergence between one's own understandings and those of citizens whose positions, taken in their most comprehensive forms, one must reject' (p. 85). A majority vote on controversial issues should only be taken after all discursive avenues have been exhausted.

James Tully also warns of the dangers of a single model of deliberative reasoning. Dominant groups, who have their own customary ways of reasoning, often present these 'as canonical, as universal or as the uniquely reasonable' (2002, p. 223). In the West, this outcome has been achieved typically by presenting particular forms of cultural and historical reasoning as the modern or democratic way to present oneself and be heard – the 'free and equal' way of deliberating. The result has been a conflictual model of argument, oriented to winning an exchange with opponents rather than one that seeks mutual understanding and accommodation. The impartialist model promotes a single form of reasoning above all others and, hence, fails to see how it itself is shaped by particular cultural, social and linguistic practices and identities. If impartialism is oriented to a consensus produced by 'the force of the better argument', then some voices will be dismissed as weak, uninformed or irrational, and silenced along the way (see Tully, 2002; and Young, 2000, pp. 52–80).

Tully's critical point is conjoined with a positive emphasis on how different practices of reasoning are grounded in distinctive social practices and rules, local repertoires and genres of argumentation, and customary ways of relating to one another. These cultural and historical forms of knowledge and getting on with things – local 'know-hows' – are, he argues, the intersubjective bases of culturally diverse practices of deliberation, that is,

of raising questions and listening to others, of presenting a reason, a story, an example, a comparison, a gesture or a parable for consideration, showing rather than saying, expressing disagreement, deferring or challenging, taking a point, informing another, advising and taking advice, speaking for another and being spoken for, stonewalling, feet-dragging and feigning, dissenting through silence, breaking off talks, working towards a compromise, agreeing conditionally or unconditionally . . . and countless other discursive and non-discursive activities which make up deliberative language games. (Tully, 2002, p. 223)

There are many ways to be heard and make a point, yet impartialist reasoning risks excluding all these in a perverse search for *the* reasonable. Tully presents a strong case for deliberative democracy, but one based on an appreciation of diverse forms of reasoning and justification, not one fixed on a single form of deliberation. For him a legitimate political order is a continuously 'conciliated' or 'negotiated' order, always open to questioning in dialogues – the critical practice of thought and action that prevents political sclerosis and unwanted institutional sedimentation. In his judgement, 'the first and perhaps only universalizable principle of democratic deliberation is *audi alteram partem*, "always listen to the other side", for there is always something to be learned from the other side' (2002, p. 218).

The critique of the ideal of impartiality in deliberative democracy is taken a step further by Iris Young. She criticizes the ideal for a number of reasons. In the first instance, the ideal of impartiality expresses a fiction because it rests on the assumption that people can transcend their particularities when engaging in deliberation. In fact, we are all situated beings and nobody can completely set this aside and present an impersonal and dispassionate standpoint (1990, p. 103). Second, the ideal of impartiality 'represses difference' in that, as Tully also notes, it seeks to reduce diverse and complex forms of reasoning to a simple model of reasoning together. Third, it falsely reduces a multiplicity of possible standpoints in the world to one viewpoint – the viewpoint that, allegedly, 'all rational subjects can adopt' (p. 100). In contrast, Young proposes 'to promote a politics of inclusion' that nurtures 'the ideal of a heterogeneous public' (p. 119). This ideal does not presuppose that participants would surrender their social and cultural identity as the price of inclusion. Instead, it seeks the recognition and effective representation of diverse social groups in public life.

In Young's view, this can be achieved by:

- making available public funds to promote the self-organization of social groups, especially the marginal;
- group analysis and group generation of policy proposals to ensure all agendas are articulated;
- ensuring that decision-makers are accountable to all groups by obliging them to show that they have taken group perspectives into consideration in their deliberations;
- granting veto rights in public policy-making to those groups who are significantly affected by certain sets of issues (e.g. reproductive rights policy for women, or land use policy for indigenous peoples);
- altering public culture so that argumentative modes of reasoning are supplemented by other modes of communication, including greeting, rhetoric and narrative; this would help disclose experiences and needs which might otherwise go unnoticed, and the diverse ways these can be articulated. (1990, pp. 184–5; 2000, pp. 56ff)

Young has sought to emphasize recently that not all groups (e.g. youth subcultures) are to have special representation in her democratic model, but only 'structural groups', that is, those whose common social location tends to exclude them from political participation, the ability to express their group freedom and concepts of social justice (2000, p. 97). Public life needs to include 'differently situated voices' able to articulate their concerns and interests. Young argues that the representation of interests by the usual mechanisms of party politics must be supplemented in public deliberation by the representation of group perspectives. This can be achieved by a number of different means, e.g., quotas for representation on key political committees inside and outside formal political institutions, the reservation of seats in legislatures as a temporary means to promote the inclusion of marginal groups, among other possibilities (2000, p. 150; cf. Phillips, 1995).

The critics of impartialism are adamant that sound public reasoning in deliberative democracy can take a number of different forms. Yet impartialists are not thrown by this charge. In the first instance, they accept that there are diverse forms of reasoning; this hardly constitutes a discovery. The point is not to stress diversity *per se* but, rather, that not all forms of public reasoning are equally valid if political life is to be steered by refined and reflective preferences which are fact-, future- and other-regarding. If political judgements are to be legitimated in and through the processes out of which they emerge, then we need to be able to distinguish coerced from non-coerced agreements, and agreements which reflect the distortions of power from those which are formed in open and free communication. Only the latter can provide a true compass through the mire of social conflicts.

Moreover, impartialism does not entail the view that politics is or can be free of self-interest. Instead, in order to distinguish standpoints which directly reflect self-interest from those capable of intersubjective agreement, it requires one to weigh all the relevant interests affected by a particular course of action – without dogmatically assuming one's own position is valid and that it automatically trumps those of others. Impartiality imposes a formal constraint on the types of reasoning one can adopt if one is to distinguish successfully between the assertion of self-interest and the pursuit of a course of argument or action which other reasonable people would endorse under shared circumstances. Impartiality does not block the pursuit of one's own interests in all situations, but it insists that reasons for action, if they are to command legitimacy, must be those which all parties would accept as sound irrespective of where they are located in the relevant chain of action. Political philosophy must not blur the boundary between a legitimate and illegitimate public decision procedure. Public legitimacy requires that courses of action are chosen because they are based on reasons which all could accept. Of course, whether citizens will proceed in this way in actual deliberations is far from clear; they have and rely upon many different sources of power and action. However, political philosophers should not confuse, impartialists hold, the rightful basis of action with the mere assertion of identity and self-interested strategic action.

Any model of public reasoning can be manipulated in public life, and impartialism is no exception. When dominant groups or political elites try to legitimate their power by defining the idea of a good citizen in terms of their own particular cultural and historical qualities, and the proper form of political justification as that which adheres to the rules of discourse they have established, there is a clear risk that others will be marginalized and silenced. This could be an intended or unintended outcome. Thus, when dissenters from a dominant point of view are dismissed as partisan, irrational or merely self-interested, this might be because dominant forms of public justification are serving an ideological function. Claims to be impartial can be manipulated in public discourse, buttressing existing rule systems. That this can happen is not an argument against the notion of impartialism itself, but an argument against its one-sided application. In fact, any such critique presupposes that ideology can be unmasked from a non-ideological standpoint, and that a distorted public domain can be distinguished from the notion of a genuinely impartial public sphere (McBride, 2004, p. 87).

Institutions of deliberative democracy

The dispute between impartialists and their critics is likely to continue to divide how deliberative democrats understand their project. Yet, despite these controversies, they have in common a scepticism about many aspects of existing forms of liberal democracy – criticizing its excessive recognition of private interests, its aggregative conception of the public good (as the sum of private preferences), its reliance on instrumental forms of rationality, and its failure to place the quality of public decision-making at the centre of debate. While liberal democracy tends to treat private preferences as fixed and given, deliberative democrats are all committed to problematizing these, and to focusing on political mechanisms and social practices which facilitate the discovery of good arguments, sound justifications of action and, where possible, generalizable interests (Dryzek, 1990). Deliberative democrats offer some important new insights into the possible institutional structures of democracy. Typically, these involve proposals to supplement and enrich existing democratic procedures, and to enhance the quality of democratic life without assuming the high levels of political participation demanded by classical, Marxian and participatory democrats (which can be hard to sustain beyond the politics of protest or a revolutionary moment). (In the latter regard, it is sobering to reflect on the dissipation of political energy after the 'velvet revolutions' of 1989–90: see chapter 8.)

For deliberative theorists, the process of deliberation is regarded as essential to democracy. It is the means to turn democratic politics from the passive registration of interests, the know-all certainty of armchair critics and the inclination of the moment to a more refined and reflective process. As Fishkin boldly put it, 'political equality without deliberation is not much use for it amounts to nothing more than power without opportunity to think about how that power ought to be exercised' (1991, p. 36). But deliberation is not an all or nothing affair; and the task is to find ways of increasing the deliberative element in modern democracies. Among the suggested ways of doing this are the introduction of deliberative polls, deliberative days, citizens' juries, expanding voter feedback mechanisms and citizen communication, the reform of civic education to enhance the possibility of reflective choices, and the public funding of civic groups and associations seeking engagement with deliberative politics.

Deliberative polls and deliberative days

Like all polls, a deliberative opinion poll involves the random selection of a representative sample of the population, a 'microcosm' of the electorate as a whole. But while an ordinary opinion poll assesses 'what the electorate thinks given how little it knows', a deliberative poll is designed to reveal what 'the electorate would think if, hypothetically, it could be immersed in intensive deliberative processes' (Fishkin, 1991, p. 81). How is this organized? The idea is to bring a representative sample of the population together in one place for a few days in order to deliberate on a pressing matter of public concern. The sample is initially polled on its members' pre-deliberative views. Deliberation then takes place usually involving two elements: exposure to, and questioning of, a range of experts on the issue at stake; and a debate among the participants in the hope of arriving at more publicly defensible positions. After this everyone is polled again and the results of the pre- and post-deliberative polls are compared. Typically, the process of deliberation is expected to shift opinions because views have become informed by a careful consideration of the evidence, and those involved have taken account of the opinions and arguments of others.

Apart from the immediate impact of a deliberative poll on its participants, it is hoped that, if the results are well publicized (perhaps on radio and television), the general public would be stimulated to consider their own views more carefully. James Fishkin, one of the pioneers of deliberative polls, believes that their results carry greater authority than an ordinary opinion poll because they represent the 'reflective judgement' of the electorate. The outcome has particular 'recommending force', telling us that this is what the public would think if given an opportunity for extensive reflection and access to information (Fishkin, 1991, p. 81). Unlike official political representatives, who tend to be drawn from elites and who are the subject of enormous pressures from special interests (see chapter 6), the deliberative poll is a sample of the informed opinion of people drawn by lot, a key selection device recommended in classical democracy, to ensure everyone has an equal chance to be selected, no matter where they come in the social hierarchy (see chapter 1). Each person is equally likely to be chosen to participate and each person is equally interchangeable with another. Hence, the advocates of deliberative polls see them as combining two powerful ideals: deliberation and political equality. Elements of classical Athenian democracy (rotation of participants and open debate) are combined with elements of representative democracy (political equality, publicity and public debate) to create a new institutional mechanism (see Beetham, 2005, pp. 137–40).

Deliberative polls were not designed to replace the political institutions of liberal democracy, but to support and complement them. They have been utilized across a range of public issues, both in the US and in Europe. Evidence from their use generally supports the claim that deliberation does result in a significant transformation of the preferences of those involved. For example, participants in one poll in the US who were initially hostile to the notion of raising electricity prices shifted their views when prices were tied to higher levels of investment in renewable energy sources; another poll found that people hostile to foreign aid changed their minds once they discovered how relatively little money is committed to aid in national budgets; and yet another poll showed how people change their positions on appropriate tax levels if they have a better grasp of social expenditure budgets and the reasons some people receive social benefits and others do not (see Ackerman and Fishkin, 2003). However, there is less evidence that publicizing the results of deliberative polls has a positive effect on the mass of voters, although deliberative advocates argue that institutionalizing deliberative polling, making it a regular feature of public life, would modify the behaviour of other actors in the long run.

A subsequent proposal, developed by Fishkin and Bruce Ackerman, seeks to overcome the limited public effectiveness of deliberative polls by devoting whole days to public discussion of a critical issue. The initial version of this proposal focused on a 'deliberative day' to be built into presidential elections in the US. Samples of 500 citizens would be assembled in local schools and halls in order to spend the day deliberating over the choice of candidates. Local and national radio and television debates would be linked to these and scheduled into the day. The results of the day's deliberation, reporting pre- and post-deliberative preferences (and key reasons for shifts in position), could then be publicized, locally and nationally. In order to ensure that nobody is discouraged from participation on financial grounds, Ackerman and Fishkin suggest a 'substantial citizen stipend' of, say, $150 for the day. A 'deliberative day' would seek to engage as many people as possible in a reflective process of political judgement.

Ackerman and Fishkin consider that the regular use of deliberative days on matters of great public concern would enhance the quality of public debate and the grounds underpinning voting; shift politicians from a 'soundbite' culture to longer, more discursive practices focused on the reasons for policy preferences (in the expectation that these would better stand the test of public scrutiny); and expand the 'informational base' of party and non-party activists so that they are better able to operate effectively. Thus, it is hoped, an increasingly informed citizenry, and an increasingly responsive political class anticipating public accountability, would help bring about a 'genuine renaissance of civic culture' (Ackerman and Fishkin, 2003, p. 25).

Citizens' juries

Citizens' juries operate on a very similar basis to deliberative polls, and like them assume that citizens are capable of reflective decisions on complex public questions, given a suitable deliberative environment. The assumption is particularly significant in the context of democratic theory since it is in marked contrast to the pessimistic estimations of human capacity found among competitive elitists and legal democrats. Citizens' juries have been used to advise national governments on a wide range of controversial issues, including aspects of city design and planning; welfare reform and levels of social expenditure; competing budget claims; priorities for medical treatment; the choice of technology for energy production and appropriate pricing policy; and agricultural priorities, including the use of GM crops (see Beetham, 2005, p. 140).

Citizens' juries are assembled by public bodies to offer assessments of and policy priorities for pressing issues, once they have weighed the relevant evidence and considered relevant arguments. As in deliberative polls, deliberation is guided by expert witnesses and the testing of argument. The aim of citizens' juries is for lay people to reach a consensus on the matter at hand, and for these findings to be fed into formal decision-making procedures. Up to now, citizens' juries have had only an advisory role; they have not been regarded as a substitute for formal decision-making. Yet they have often produced striking conclusions at odds with the views of elected representatives. For instance, a citizens' jury on health reform in the US found unanimously in favour of comprehensive health coverage, and of members of government, Congress and the judiciary 'living under whatever healthcare plan they introduced for the rest of the country' (Beetham, 2005, p. 141). Despite this, there is considerable evidence that governments (in addition to citizen lobby groups) in many countries are interested in making use of them to help create an informed environment for public debate and political decision-making.

Expanding voter feedback mechanisms and citizen communication

A further domain of experimentation in enhancing the quality of public deliberation involves developing 'voter feedback' mechanisms on central public issues (Adonis and Mulgan, 1994). These are designed to improve communication and understanding between decision-makers and citizens. New voter feedback mechanisms can combine television, cable and computer networks, built by the public or private sector, with local governments and national institutions. The aim is, again, to improve the process by which citizens form political judgements and to enhance the mechanisms whereby career politicians are informed about citizens' views and priorities. Examples include email access to public fora, using email to place items on the public agenda if they meet a certain threshold of support, special internet 'noticeboards' to generate debate or survey preferences on troubling matters, and more elaborate and focused access to television and radio networks to generate new spheres of public discussion and information provision.

Other possibilities for the future include using the internet to create public solutions to key social or health care issues. The internet is already used to provide a space for the collective design and development of some software systems and computer games. Why could it not also be deployed by non-governmental organizations, governments or international bodies to tap into the 'know-how' of people significantly affected by a pressing public matter (traffic congestion, health threats or security concerns) and to help generate innovative bottom-up and bottom-tested solutions? Information technologies could be deployed to create sites for debate about the most appropriate characterization of a public issue; new ways of engaging in thinking about and designing solutions to it; and new forms of policy implementation. Citizens could be drawn in to these processes across national borders in so far as public problems and solutions transcend national frontiers, as they do with a huge range of contemporary challenges from HIV/Aids to environmental degradation and new modes of delivering aid to developing countries.

New technology can be used to enhance relations between citizens and governments and between citizens themselves. A distinction is sometimes made between e-government and e-democracy initiatives. The former is typically depicted as 'top-down' (concerned with dissemination of information, improving access to representatives and so on) and the latter 'bottom-up' (concerned with the creation of new citizens' fora for discussion and deliberation, and sites for mobilization and action) (Beetham, 2005, pp. 150–5). While the distinction has some analytical value, many democratic government initiatives to put key documents on line (e.g. the Special Prosecutor's report to the US Congress on the Clinton–Monica Lewinsky affair), to improve understanding of social policy entitlements through the use of web-based information and to seek voter opinion on a wide range of public questions can enhance responsiveness and accountability on both sides of government. None the less, probably the most significant democratic potential of digital technology for the development of citizen communication lies in its application to enhance lateral communication between citizens through the generation of online public fora. Examples of deliberative fora include Minnesota E-Democracy and DNet in California, both of which promote debate and evaluation of candidates for public office (see Hacker and Dijk, 2001; Beetham, 2005, pp. 153f); OpenDemocracy.net in the UK, which focuses on a wide range of global issues and aims to stimulate public discussion of them; and a host of activist sites focused on everything from environmental degradation to mobilization against the war in Iraq in early 2003.

Typically, experiments to enhance voter feedback and citizen communication provide avenues for deepening political participation within *existing* patterns of liberal representative politics. They create new opportunities for public engagement for those who have access to the new communication facilities. And they enrich, in principle, the scope and nature of public debate. Virtual communication adds a range of discursive dimensions unenvisaged, of course, from Plato to Schumpeter. The costs of deliberative participation are reduced, and the range of possible engagement enhanced. The extent of actual political change that results remains, of course, another question.

The final mechanism to be mentioned in this context involves extension of the use of referenda to include all citizens significantly affected by a policy question at local or national levels. This would link new communication avenues to the possibility of actually determining policy choices. Citizens could, in principle, have the opportunity to initiate referenda given a minimum level of support (measured, say, by 3 per cent of the electorate signing a petition). The nature of this 'minimum level' would need to be revised in the light of the impact of referenda on the process and efficacy of governance (see Butler and Ranney, 1994). But a range of referenda could be considered, from those which are purely consultative to those which offer either veto power or the possibility of positively framing public policy. Moreover, if such referenda were linked in to the use of deliberative polls or deliberative days, a powerful instrument could be deployed to record newly informed democratic opinion.

Civic education and public funding of deliberative bodies

Deliberative democrats hope that new forms of deliberative engagement will stimulate reflection not only on the part of those immediately involved, but also on the part of those who come into contact with 'deliberative activists' – family members, friends and workmates. They hope that re-engaging some citizens in politics will stimulate widespread networking which could eventually trigger a culture of far-reaching civic participation (Ackerman and Fishkin, 2003, p. 25). Integral to this possibility, according to Gutmann, is a strong civic education agenda to help cultivate the capacity for public reasoning and political choice (1987; see also Gutmann and Thompson, 1996).

Civic education needs to be part of every child's learning process, from early school through to higher education and beyond. If 'reasoning from the point of view of others' does not come naturally, it can be striven for both in play and in formal citizenship studies. Learning to place one's own desires and interests in the context of those of others should be an essential part of every child's education. Thinking in a way that is sensitive to others, and to the facts and future possibilities, is not an easy task and requires considerable mental discipline – above all, the capacity to put one's own immediate perspective on life in critical relation to those of others (see pp. 233–4 above). A multi-perspectival mode of forming, defending and refining one's preferences and judgements is a tough cognitive challenge (at all times) and needs to be acquired through schooling, a commitment to lifelong learning and a willingness to put oneself in discursive situations which unsettle one's point of view. The creation of an education system, which opens up people's understanding and horizons as a result of knowing about others, is a crucial element of the development of a democratic public culture.

Public funding of civil society associations which actively promote deliberative practices is strongly endorsed by some deliberative theorists. Organizations that directly or indirectly support lifetime learning, the mediation of traditions and cultures, and the broadening of individuals' capacities to give and exchange reasons for action are central to the conditions of a successful deliberative culture. Deliberative politics requires both the nurturing of a civic education programme and discursive public fora to help 'upgrade the quality of citizenship' (Offe and Preuss); that is, to generate a public culture supportive of refined and reflective preferences. The capacity of citizens to be able to sustain 'the public use of reason' – the pursuit of publicly justifiable reasons for action – is to be placed, in the deliberative account, at the centre of institutional design and development (see Cohen and Rogers, 1992).

An important question remains: where does or should deliberation occur in a public culture geared to transforming people's preferences? Surveying the options canvassed in the literature, Michael Saward emphasizes multiple possibilities:

- in specially constructed micro-forums . . . where a small representative sample of people debate and in some cases vote on issues [deliberative polls, citizens' juries, etc.];

- within political parties;
- in national and other parliaments;
- in supra-national committee networks such as those in the governing structures of the European Union;
- within private or voluntary associations;
- within courts; or
- within a diverse 'public' sphere of 'protected enclaves' or 'subaltern counterpublics', in other words, oppressed groups in society. (2003, pp. 123–4)

The extent to which deliberative democrats perceive deliberation as a supplement or enrichment of liberal democracy or as an alternative model of democracy varies across deliberative thinkers. The questions 'Who deliberates?' and 'Where do people deliberate?' evince quite different answers. For a figure like Fishkin deliberation is a way of renewing modern representative democracy via deliberative polls and days. By contrast, for theorists like Young and Dryzek, deliberation is a way of transforming democracy and creating a new language of radical politics – a deliberative, participatory political order. Where deliberation should be sited, and the extent of popular participation, are not questions about which there is a consensus among deliberative thinkers. To the extent that deliberation is seen as a supplement to liberal institutions, theorists tend to recommend it as a way of improving the quality of existing political institutions. To the extent that deliberation is regarded as a transformative mode of reasoning which can be drawn upon in diverse settings, from micro-fora and neighbourhood associations to national parliaments and transnational settings, it tends to be interpreted as a new radical model of democracy.

Value pluralism and democracy

Most of the chapters in this volume present accounts of established orthodoxies, although all traditions are open to hermeneutic contestation and revision. Deliberative democracy stands out from this somewhat because it represents a body of thought that is only about twenty years old and hence is better represented as a programme of research and discussion. In order to conform to the structure and presentational form of the book, its principles and key features are set out in model IX. But this particular characterization ought to be treated tentatively, for the reason given.

A number of questions have been addressed in this chapter, the answers to which affect the coherence of the notion of deliberative democracy: Why deliberate? When can it be concluded that deliberation is successful? Who deliberates and where should deliberation take place? As noted previously, responses to these questions are by no means settled in the deliberative literature, and a number of very distinctive positions and arguments are on offer. If views tend to converge on any point, it is on the first question, 'Why deliberate?', with an emphasis on elements of the following: refined and reflective views should be considered integral to democratic politics; the quality of decision-making should be at the centre of public debate; political rationality is inseparable from the idea of justification to others; the strengthening of

In sum: model IX

Deliberative Democracy

Principle(s) of justification

The terms and conditions of political association proceed through the free and reasoned assent of its citizens. The 'mutual justifiability' of political decisions is the legitimate basis for seeking solutions to collective problems

Key features

Deliberative polls, deliberative days, citizen juries

E-government initiatives from full on-line reporting to direct access to representatives

E-democracy programmes including on-line public fora

Group analysis and generation of policy proposals

Deliberation across public life, from micro-fora to transnational settings

New uses of referenda tied to deliberative polls, etc.

renewing representative democracy

Deepening of deliberation

radical, deliberative participatory democracy

General conditions

Value pluralism

Strong civic education programme

Public culture and institutions supporting the development of 'refined' and 'reflective' preferences

Public funding of deliberative bodies and practices, and of the secondary associations which support them

---

discursive rationality is vital to the search for the best substantive solutions to collective problems. Answers to the rest of the questions diverge, with significant implications. Impartialists and their critics dispute the very nature of public reasoning, and how it can be claimed that it is achieved (or not). There is no general agreement on the criterion which could determine when deliberation is successful. In my judgement, the position of the impartialists is by no means defeated by their critics (see pp. 239–45 above). Yet it has to be acknowledged that the ideal of impartiality and of the transformation of popular judgements in line with the requirements of mutual justification cannot accommodate all claims made on behalf of social differences; for impartialism takes a clear position on the equal moral and political worth of each and every individual and hence is incompatible with group claims as such, which can threaten the freedom and equality of individuals (McBride, 2004, p. 104). How far this matters depends on whether ontological priority is given to people as individuals or groups. Positions differ here with considerable consequences. (Arguments I develop later take moral or egalitarian individualism to be central to democracy in its contemporary form and to trump group demands. The claims of groups are interpreted as secondary to the rights and liberties of individuals. See chapters 10 and 11; see also Held 2002; 2004, appendix.)

Divergencies of assessment are also evident in reflections on who should be involved in deliberation, and where they should engage. At one end of the spectrum deliberative theorists are seeking a better understanding of what it is that actually happens in parliaments and constitutional courts, and are pursuing an extension of the use of public reason and mutual justification to new domains within representative democracy. At the other end of the spectrum discursive democracy is presented as a way of overcoming the deficiencies of liberal democracy by promoting a public sphere in which no individual may possess authority except on the basis of a compelling argument or idea; no institutional barriers should exist to the participation of all interested parties; and there should be no rules or regulations beyond challenge over time (Dryzek, 1990, pp. 41–2). The public domain, in short, should not be constrained by any formal or constitutional rules that are themselves beyond democratic accountability.

Whether deliberative democracy constitutes a 'paradigm shift' in democratic theory and practice remains, at this stage, an open question. None the less, I think it can reasonably be claimed that it has moved democratic thinking along new paths. Although a concern with deliberation and public reasoning can be found in classical democracy, developmental republicanism and developmental democracy, it is moved centre-stage by deliberative theorists. Preoccupied by the quality of democratic reasoning and the justification for action, it places an innovative concept of legitimacy at the heart of political reflection. Whether in the end it enriches and adds elements to modern representative democracy, or transforms it in fundamental ways, remains to be seen.

While deliberative theorists weigh value pluralism and ethical disagreement differently, they acknowledge these as more or less permanent features of everyday politics. For impartialists, differences of value are not *sui generis* and can be sifted and critically assessed through open, non-partisan argument; their critics take value pluralism as given and seek to find modes of mutual accommodation among the protagonists through the deployment of various discursive practices. A critic of both these positions, Jeremy Waldron, has expressed the concern that value disagreement might be so profound – even within settled democracies – that citizens could disagree not only about how to decide on daily ethical issues but also on more profound questions of justice (1999a, 1999b). The contention is that ongoing ethical disagreements show that deliberation cannot take the place of majority voting as a decision procedure. On the contrary, deliberation about deep ethical and moral disagreements needs to be regarded as a stepping stone to an authoritative (i.e. voted) collective decision. Waldron holds that it is a particular strength of liberal democratic proceduralism that it provides good grounds for citizens who disagree with a substantive decision to accept and comply with it; that is, that the decision has been arrived at by a fair procedure. Under these conditions losing minorities only have to surrender to a majority (vote winning) outcome, not to the judgement of the victor (Waldron, 1999a).

The criticism is telling but not necessarily decisive. A convergence of judgements is not required for a collective decision in accounts like that of Gutmann and Thompson (1996). In addition, deliberative democracy has recently been rearticulated to conceive of it as an ongoing process of public deliberation punctuated by elections. In this account, it is reasonable to interpret majoritarian views as indicators of where the balance of argument lies at a particular electoral moment, recognizing that the argument must continue (see Lafont, 2006). Thus, the safest conclusion at this juncture in the development of deliberative theory is that deliberation about deliberative democracy will continue! How far and to what extent deliberative democracy is understood as a new innovative model of democracy, or a change to the way representative democracy is understood and can function, is a question for further debate.

PART THREE

WHAT SHOULD DEMOCRACY MEAN TODAY?

10 Democratic Autonomy

The dispute over the contemporary meaning of democracy has generated an extraordinary diversity of democratic models: from technocratic visions of government to conceptions of social life marked by extensive political participation and deliberation. In pursuing the questions posed by the differences and contradictions between these models, Part Three will tentatively map out the contours of yet another conception of democracy. Is such an exercise justified?

There are several reasons why the critical assessment of existing models of democracy and the pursuit of alternative positions is important. First, we cannot escape an involvement in politics, although many people seek to do so. Whether one explicitly acknowledges adherence to a political perspective or not, our activities presuppose a particular framework of state and society which does direct us. The actions of the apathetic do not escape politics; they merely leave things as they are. Second, if we are to engage with problems of democracy, we need to reflect on why for so many people the fact that something is a recognizably 'political' statement is almost enough to bring it instantly into disrepute. Politics is frequently associated today with self-seeking behaviour, hypocrisy and 'public relations' activity geared to selling particular policy packages. The problem with this view is that, while it is quite understandable, the difficulties of the modern world will not be solved by surrendering politics, but only by the development and transformation of 'politics' in ways that will enable us more effectively to shape and organize human life. We do not have the option of 'no politics'.

Third, scepticism and cynicism about politics are not necessarily inevitable facts of political life. By establishing the credibility and viability of alternative models of 'governing institutions', and showing how these can be connected to systematic difficulties that occur and recur in the social and political world, a chance is created that mistrust of politics can be overcome. A political imagination for alternative arrangements is essential if the tarnished image of politics is to be eradicated. Fourth, we cannot be satisfied with existing models of democratic politics. Throughout this volume, we have seen that there are good grounds for not simply accepting any one model, whether classic or contemporary, as it stands. There is something to be learnt from a variety of traditions of political thought, and a propensity simply to juxtapose one position with another, or to play off one against another, is not fruitful.

In what follows, one strategy for advancing beyond the current debate between perspectives is elaborated. It is important to stress that the position set out below does not claim to represent a tightly knit, definitive series of ideas; rather, it amounts to a number of suggestions for further examination. It is an attempt to offer a plausible response to the question: what should democracy mean today? The response is pursued in two parts. In the first, arguments are explored with reference to the dominant political association of our times: the nation-state. This association has, of course, been at the heart of modern democratic discourse since the inception of liberal democracy. But whether it can remain exclusively at the centre of political life in the future is a question increasingly put on the agenda by intensifying regional and global relations and forces – from environmental change and security challenges to the progressive extension of economic life to regional and global networks. Chapter 10 will pursue the question of what democracy should mean today in the context of the nation-state and develop a model I call 'democratic autonomy' (model Xa). Chapter 11 will raise doubts about the adequacy of this framework and tentatively explore how democracy within nation-states must be complemented by democratic associations at the regional and global levels. I refer to this latter conception as 'cosmopolitan democracy' (model Xb). Models Xa and Xb may be thought of as two sides of a single position. Both sides, however, will need a considerably more detailed defence than can be offered here, if they are to be found ultimately compelling (for a more elaborate account of the issues see Held, 1995, esp. parts III and IV; and 2004).

Chapter 10 begins by examining the continuing appeal of democracy and why this idea remains so contested. Against this background, the claims and counter-claims of different traditions of democratic political theory are explored in relation to a set of problems which they share – problems which centre on the nature of liberty or autonomy and how one reconciles this value with other important political concerns. The chapter suggests that there is a common principle – which I call the 'principle of autonomy' – at the centre of the modern democratic project, a principle which can provide an anchor point for both conceiving and building a new and more robust account of democracy. This principle, however, has to be linked to a diversity of conditions of enactment, that is, institutional and organizational requirements, if it is to be fully entrenched in political life. An argument is made that none of the leading traditions of modern democratic thought can fully grasp these conditions. In exploring what these conditions might be, chapter 10 sets out a novel conception of the democratic polity which chapter 11 pursues further with reference to international and transnational relations and processes.

The appeal of democracy

Part of the attraction of democracy lies in the refusal to accept *in principle* any conception of the political good other than that generated by 'the people' themselves. From the pursuit of elements of popular sovereignty in early self-governing republics to the diverse struggles to achieve a genuinely universal franchise in the nineteenth and twentieth centuries, advocates of greater accountability in public life have sought to establish satisfactory means for authorizing and controlling political decisions. At issue has been the rejection of the power of monarchs, princes, leaders or 'experts' to determine political outcomes and the defence of 'tests' of consent in the determination of public concerns and interests. Democracy has been championed as a mechanism that bestows legitimacy on political decisions when they adhere to proper principles, rules and mechanisms of participation, representation and accountability. In the East European revolutions of 1989–91, the principles of self-determination and consent to government action once again challenged the principle of 'single person' or, in these particular cases, 'single party' rule. Democracy has been recelebrated as a way of containing the powers of the state, of mediating among competing individual and collective projects, and of rendering key political decisions accountable. In political circumstances constituted by a plurality of identities, cultural forms and interests, each perhaps articulating different prescriptive regimes, democracy is seen, moreover, to offer a basis for tolerating, discussing and negotiating difference.

In the ensuing two chapters I argue that democracy should be conceived as the privileged conception of the political good because it offers – in theory at least – a form of politics and life in which there are fair and just ways of deliberating over and negotiating values and value disputes. Democracy is the only 'grand' or 'meta-' narrative that can legitimately frame and delimit the competing 'narratives' of the contemporary age. But why exactly should this be so? What is significant about democracy in an age in which some think it represents the end-point of history, and others that it represents a sham in its existing form?

The *idea* of democracy is important because it does not just represent one value among many, such as liberty, equality or justice, but is the value that can link and mediate among competing prescriptive concerns. It is a guiding orientation that can help generate a basis for specifying relations between different normative concerns. Democracy does not presuppose agreement on diverse values; rather, it suggests a way of relating values to each other and of leaving the resolution of value conflicts open to participants in a public process, subject only to certain provisions protecting the shape and form of the process itself. In this lie further elements of its appeal.

The attempt to develop a democratic conception of the political good – the 'good life' defined under 'free and equal' conditions of political engagement and deliberation – does not offer, it should be stressed, a panacea for all injustices, evils and dangers (cf. Giddens, 1993). But it does lay down good grounds for the defence of a public dialogue and decision-making process about matters of general concern, and suggests institutional paths for its development. My argument is not that 'democracy' is the answer to all questions – far from it – but that, when adequately clarified and explicated, democracy can be seen to lay down a programme of change in and through which pressing, substantive issues will receive a better opportunity for deliberation, debate and resolution than they would under alternative regimes. How should this position be understood? To begin with, I shall address this question by reconsidering some of the leading claims of contemporary liberals, particularly New Right thinkers, and their critics, which have been the focus of chapters 7 and 8. The discussion will then be broadened to include other traditions discussed in this volume, including that of deliberative democracy. Throughout, the approach I adopt will involve an attempt to reconceptualize a concern which is common to a number of strands of political thought – the concern with how individual and collective self-determination can be reconciled – and to show how aspects of these strands can, indeed must, be integrated into an alternative position in order to grapple better with this fundamental matter.

The principle of autonomy

Contemporary liberal thinkers have in general tied the goals of liberty and equality to individualist political, economic and ethical doctrines. In their view, the modern democratic state should provide the necessary conditions to enable citizens to pursue their own interests; it should uphold the rule of law in order to protect and nurture individuals' liberty, so that each person can advance his or her own objectives while no one can impose a vision of the 'good life' upon others. This position has, of course, been a central tenet of liberalism since Locke: the state exists to safeguard the rights and liberties of citizens, who are ultimately the best judge of their own interests; the state is the burden individuals have to bear to secure their own ends; and the state must be restricted in scope and restrained in practice to ensure the maximum possible freedom of every citizen. Liberalism has been and is preoccupied with the creation and defence of a world in which 'free and equal' individuals can flourish with minimum political impediment.[1]

By contrast, socialist thinkers, from Marxists to the New Left, have defended the importance of certain social or collective means and goals. For them, to pursue liberty and equality earnestly involves rejecting the view that these values can be realized by people left, in practice, to their own devices in a 'free market' economy and a minimal state. These values can be entrenched only through struggles to ensure that society, as well as the polity, is democratized, i.e. subject to procedures that ensure maximum accountability. Only the latter can ultimately guarantee the reduction of all forms of coercive power so that human beings can develop as 'free and equal'. While New Left thinkers differ in many respects from traditional Marxist writers, they share a concern to uncover the conditions whereby the 'free development of each' is compatible with the 'free development of all'. This is a fundamental common goal.

The views of the New Right and their critics on the left are, of course, radically different. The key elements of their theories are fundamentally at odds. It is therefore somewhat paradoxical to note that they share a vision of reducing arbitrary power and regulatory capacity to its lowest possible extent. Both fear the extension of networks of intrusive power into society, 'choking', to borrow a phrase from Marx, 'all its pores'. They both have ways of criticizing the bureaucratic, inequitable and often repressive character of much state action. Moreover, they are both concerned with the political, social and economic conditions for the development of people's capacities, desires and interests. Put in this general and very abstract manner, there appears to be a convergence of emphasis on ascertaining the circumstances under which people can develop as 'free and equal'.

---

[1] Unless indicated to the contrary, 'liberalism' is used here in the broad sense to connote both liberalism since Locke and liberal democracy.

To put the point another way, the aspiration of these traditions for a world characterized by free and equal relations among mature adults reflects a concern to ensure:

1 the creation of the best circumstances for all humans to develop their nature and express their diverse qualities (involving an assumption of respect for individuals' diverse capacities and their ability to learn and enhance their potentialities);
2 protection from the arbitrary use of political authority and coercive power (involving an assumption of respect for privacy in all matters which are not the basis of potential and demonstrable 'harm' to others);
3 involvement of citizens in the determination of the conditions of their association (involving an assumption of respect for the capacity of individuals to come to reasoned standpoints);
4 expansion of economic opportunity to maximize the availability of resources (involving an assumption that when individuals are free from the burdens of unmet physical need they are best able to realize their ends).

There is, in other words, a set of general aspirations that 'legal' and 'participatory' theorists have in common. Moreover, these aspirations have been shared by thinkers as diverse as J. S. Mill and Marx, and by most of those eighteenth- and nineteenth-century theorists (considered in this volume) who have sought to clarify the proper relation between the 'sovereign state' and 'sovereign people'.

The concept of 'autonomy' or 'independence' links together these aspirations and helps explain why they have been shared so widely. 'Autonomy' connotes the capacity of human beings to reason self-consciously, to be self-reflective and to be self-determining. It involves the ability to deliberate, judge, choose and act upon different possible courses of action in private as well as public life. Clearly, the idea of an 'autonomous' person could not develop while political rights, obligations and duties were closely tied, as they were in the medieval worldview, to property rights and religious tradition (see ch. 3). Nor could it develop while people's political identitites were determined by their social category (male/female, black/white, native/foreigner) or status (lord/serf, property owner/worker). But with the changes that wrought a fundamental transformation of medieval notions, there emerged a widespread concern across Europe with the nature and limits of political authority, law, rights and duty.

Liberalism advanced the challenging view that individuals were 'free and equal', capable of determining and justifying their own actions, capable of entering into self-chosen obligations (Pateman, 1985, p. 176; cf. Gilligan, 1982; Chodorow, 1989; Giddens, 1992). The development of autonomous spheres of action, in social, political and economic affairs, became a (if not *the*) central mark of what it was to enjoy freedom and equality. While liberals failed frequently to explore the actual circumstances in which individuals lived – how people were integrally connected to one another through complex networks of relations and institutions – they none the less generated the strong belief that a defensible political order must be one in which people are able to develop their nature and interests free from the arbitrary use of political authority and coercive power. And although many liberals stopped far short of proclaiming that for individuals to be 'free and equal' they must themselves be sovereign, their work was preoccupied with, and affirmed the overwhelming importance of, uncovering the conditions under which individuals can determine and regulate the structure of their own association – a preoccupation they shared with figures such as Marx and Engels, although both dissented, of course, from liberal interpretations of this central issue (see J. Cohen and Rogers, 1983, pp. 148–9).

The broad aspirations that make up a concern with autonomy in modern political thought can be recast in the form of a general principle – the 'principle of autonomy'.[2] This can be stated as follows:

persons should enjoy equal rights and, accordingly, equal obligations in the specification of the political framework which generates and limits the opportunities available to them; that is, they should be free and equal in the processes of deliberation about the conditions of their own lives and in the determination of these conditions, so long as they do not deploy this framework to negate the rights of others.[3]

The principle of autonomy is a principle for the demarcation of legitimate power; it expresses a concern with the specification of the foundations of democratic consent. But a number of its elements require further clarification if its meaning is to be fully grasped. These can be elaborated in a preliminary way as follows:

1 The notion that persons should enjoy equal rights and obligations in the political framework which shapes their lives and opportunities means, in principle, that they should enjoy equal autonomy – that is, a common structure of political action – in order that they may be able to pursue their projects, both individual and collective, as free and equal agents (cf. Rawls, 1985, pp. 245ff).

2 The concept of 'rights' connotes entitlements, entitlements to pursue action and activity without the risk of arbitrary or unjust interference. Rights define legitimate spheres of independent action (or inaction). They enable – that is, create spaces for action – and constrain – that is, specify limits on independent action so that the latter does not curtail and infringe the liberty of others. Hence, rights have a structural dimension, bestowing both opportunities and duties.

3 The idea that people should be free and equal in the determination of the conditions of their own lives means that they should be able to participate in a process of debate and deliberation, open to all on a free and equal basis, about matters of pressing public concern. A legitimate decision, within this

---

[2] See Beetham (1981) and J. Cohen and Rogers (1983), whose writings helped stimulate the argument set out below.

[3] I have modified my earlier conception for this principle, to be found in the first edition of *Models of Democracy* (1987) and in Held (1991a).

framework, is not one that necessarily follows from the 'will of all', but rather one that results from the deliberation of all in the political process (Manin, 1987, p. 352). As such, the democratic process is compatible with the procedures and mechanisms of majority rule.

4 The qualification stated in the principle – that individual rights require protection – represents a familiar call for constitutional government. The principle of autonomy specifies both that individuals must be 'free and equal' and that 'majorities' should not be able to impose themselves on others. There must always be institutional arrangements to protect the individual's or the minority's position, i.e. constitutional rules and safeguards.

5 Group demands or group claims (those, for instance, of men or women, of settlers or indigenous peoples, of heterosexuals or homosexuals) will always be of secondary standing to individual rights or freedoms; for the unitary or homogeneous nature of these can always be overstated, and individual differences neglected (see ch. 9 above; Barry, 2001; Kelly, 2002). None the less, participation in public debate on a free and equal basis means necessarily that the nature of these claims should be heard and examined, and their generalizability tested.

The concern that individual rights require explicit protection reflects the traditional liberal position from Locke to Hayek. Hayek's distinction between 'sources of power' and 'limitations on power' restates the liberal view, as does Nozick's claim that liberty means that people should not be able to impose themselves on others. Liberals have always argued that 'the liberty of the strong' must be restrained, although they have not, of course, always agreed about who constitutes 'the strong'. For some 'the strong' has included those with special access to certain kinds of resource (political, material and cultural), but for others 'the strong' has been elements of the *demos* itself. But whatever the precise conception of the proper nature and scope of individual liberty, liberals have been committed to a conception of the individual as 'free and equal' and to the necessity of creating institutional arrangements to protect their position, i.e. they have been committed to a version of the principle of autonomy.

Could Marxists (orthodox or otherwise) and the New Left theorists subscribe to the principle of autonomy? There is a fundamental sense, explored in chapters 4, 7 and 8, in which the answer to this question is 'no'. They have not thought it necessary to establish a theory of the 'frontiers of freedom' (rights, cultural ends, objective interests or whatever we choose to call them) which 'nobody should be permitted to cross' in a post-capitalist political order (cf. Berlin, 1969, pp. 164ff). This is precisely the sense in which the left's account of democratic politics does not have an adequate assessment of the state and, in particular, of democratic government as it exists and as it might be. Its dominant view of the future has always been that its 'music' could not and should not be composed in advance. To the extent that theories have been developed about existing or possible 'governing processes', they are wanting in many respects (cf. Lukes, 1985; Pierson, 1986, 1995). However, matters ought not to be left here; for there is a sense in which this position is misleading.

Marx's attempt to unpack the broad conditions of a non-exploitative society – an order arranged 'according to need' which maximizes 'freedom for all' – presupposes that such a society will be able to protect itself rigorously against all those who would seek to subject productive property and the power to make decisions once again to private appropriation. In the account offered by New Left thinkers, a similar assumption is also clearly crucial; in fact, in many passages of their work it is quite explicit (see Macpherson, 1977, ch. 5). But the ideas in these vital passages remain undeveloped. Participatory democracy requires a detailed theory of the 'frontiers of freedom', and a detailed account of the institutional arrangements necessary to protect them, if it is to be defended adequately. A conception of the principle of autonomy is an unavoidable presupposition of radical democratic models, but it is not addressed and developed by them. It is also a presupposition, whether formally stated or not, of those versions of deliberative theory which focus on the equal moral standing and equal political worth of each and every human being (see ch. 9, pp. 238–41 and 252–5 above).

What is the status of the principle of autonomy? This principle ought to be regarded as an essential premiss of all traditions of modern democratic thought. For it is a principle at the heart of the political project preoccupied with the capability of persons to choose freely, to determine and justify their own actions, to enter into self-chosen obligations, and to enjoy the underlying conditions for political freedom and equality. The principle of autonomy is a basic and inescapable element of all those forms of politics which have given, and continue to give, priority to the nurturing of 'autonomy' or 'independence'. (For an elaboration and development of this position, see Held, 1995, ch. 7.) However, to state this – and to try to articulate its meaning in a fundamental but highly abstract principle – is not yet, it must be stressed, to say very much. For the full meaning of a principle cannot be specified independently of the conditions of its enactment. Different political traditions may give priority to 'autonomy', but they differ radically over how to secure it and, hence, in the end over how to interpret it.

The specification of a principle's 'conditions of enactment' is a vital matter; for if a theory of the most desirable form of democracy is to be at all plausible, it must be concerned with both theoretical and practical issues, with philosophical as well as organizational and institutional questions. Without this double focus, an arbitrary choice of principles and seemingly endless abstract debates about them are encouraged. A consideration of principles, without an examination of the conditions for their realization, may preserve a sense of virtue, but it will leave the actual meaning of such principles barely spelt out at all. A consideration of social institutions and political arrangements, without reflecting upon the proper principles of their ordering, might, by contrast, lead to an understanding of their functioning, but it will barely help us come to a judgement as to their appropriateness and desirability.[4]

---

[4] Hence, it is useful to recall, each model of democracy presented in this volume has been elaborated in relation to its general, sometimes explicit but often implicit, conditions of enactment.

Bearing this double focus in mind, I shall contend that a number of variants of democratic theory can contribute to the development of a proper understanding of the conditions of enactment of the principle of autonomy. Further justification of the principle alone will not be attempted here: first, because the reasons for its significance have already been set out: it ought to be thought of as a fundamental axiom of key strands of modern democratic thought. And, second, because its further justification depends on a satisfactory elucidation of its meaning in relation to the conditions for its realization. For the sake of simplicity, the discussion below will focus to begin with on broad issues raised by classic republicanism, liberalism and Marxism. In drawing on republicanism as well as on liberalism and Marxism in this context, I do not mean to imply that republicanism is a 'modern' political tradition which can be linked to the principle of autonomy as such. It is more appropriately thought of as late medieval (or very early modern), and as having developed before the pre-occupation set in with autonomy, rights and the limits of public power (see chs 2 and 3). None the less, many of its insights can fruitfully be referred to in what follows, especially in the consideration of the links between freedom, participation, deliberation and the proper form of governance. The focus below will be on the developmental republican tradition, from Marsilius of Padua to Rousseau, which forged an intimate connection between the notions of political community, self-governance and democracy. The complexities introduced into democratic theory by other strands of thought do not alter the basic structure of the argument given here, although they do contribute important insights, which will be returned to below. In short, I shall argue in what follows that the conditions of enactment of the principle of autonomy can be specified adequately only if one (1) draws upon aspects of republicanism, liberalism and Marxism, (2) appreciates some of the limitations of these overall positions, and (3) builds connections between these and the insights of other democratic traditions.

Enacting the principle

A starting point for reflection is provided by table 10.1, which sums up (albeit in rather stark form) some of the central positions of developmental republicanism, liberalism and Marxism, the significance of which has been shown in chapters 2–8. There are good grounds for taking seriously some of the central arguments and, thus, some of the central prescriptions of all three of these traditions. The principle of autonomy can only be conceived adequately if we adopt this somewhat eclectic approach. It is important to appreciate, above all, the complementarity of republicanism's scepticism about the power of monarchs and princes, liberalism's scepticism about concentrated political power in all its forms, and Marxism's scepticism about economic power. To focus exclusively on any one of these is to negate the possibility of realizing the principle of autonomy. However, to appreciate the complementarity of these sceptical positions is, of course, only a general starting point in the reappraisal of the legacy of democratic thinking; each of the traditions has important limitations which need to be kept in mind as well.

Table 10.1 Central tenets of developmental republicanism, liberalism and Marxism

Developmental republicanism	Liberalism	Marxism
1 Hostility to and scepticism about the power of monarchs and princes	1 Hostility to and scepticism about state power, and emphasis on the importance of a diversity of power centres	1 Hostility to and scepticism about concentration of economic power in private ownership of the means of production
2 Civic liberty requires a self-governing polity in which participation is essential	2 Separation of state from civil society as an essential prerequisite of a democratic order	2 Restructuring of civil society, i.e. transformation of relations of production, as a prerequisite of a flourishing democracy
3 Freedom and participation are inextricably linked; the business of government is the business of citizens	3 The desirable form of the state is an impersonal (legally circumscribed) structure of power	3 The 'impersonality' or 'neutrality' of the state can only be achieved when its autonomy is no longer compromised by capitalism
4 The wisest and most effective laws are those made by citizens bearing the 'common good' in mind. Sovereign authority rests with the people and the executive should be conceived as a 'commission' for the enactment of their will	4 Centrality of constitutionalism to guarantee formal equality (before the law) and formal freedom (from arbitrary treatment) in the form of civil and political liberties or rights essential to representative democracy: above all, those of free speech, expression, association, belief and (for liberal democrats) one-person-one-vote and party pluralism	4 The transformation of the rigid social and technical division of labour is essential if people are to develop their capacities and involve themselves fully in the democratic regulation of political as well as economic and social life
5 Civic greatness depends on citizens' involvement in a 'free way of life'	5 Protected space enshrined in law for individual autonomy and initiative	5 The equally legitimate claims of all citizens to autonomy are the foundation of any freedom that is worth the name
6 A 'complete community' depends on all economic functionaries (farmers, traders, artisans, etc.) fulfilling their ends while these are politically moderated and regulated	6 Importance of markets as mechanisms for coordinating diverse activities of producers and consumers	6 Unless there is public direction of investment, production will remain exclusively geared to profit, not to need

The republican preoccupation, articulated by Marsilius and Rousseau above all others, with the creation of a self-governing order – a participatory polity – in which the community is sovereign presupposed a fundamental connection between freedom and participation. In arguing that the citizen's liberties depend directly on participation in the business of politics, republicans set out an innovative conception of the ideal of the active citizen (see ch. 2). In addition, their argument that the political good can only be fully known in and through political interaction and deliberation – and, thus, that autonomy must be understood as a social achievement rather than an attribute of the individual – set down a powerful legacy affirming the centrality of political involvement in the maintenance of liberty (see Farrar, 1992). The difficulty with these views, however, is that they did not specify fully enough how such a participatory politics might be secured in the face of concentrations of state power, the frailty of citizens (i.e. the absence of civic virtue or restraint) and weak political institutions. How these matters might be addressed, in particular, in a world of nation-states with large populations, whose members are typically quite remote from each other in time and space, became a pressing matter, especially with the demise of the independent cities. It was here that republican arguments were vulnerable to liberal objections. And it was in exploring these vulnerabilities that liberalism displayed some of its most profound strengths (see ch. 3).

Yet liberalism's thrust to create a democratic state, a diversity of power centres and a world marked by openness, controversy and plurality is compromised by the reality of the 'free market', the structure and imperatives of the system of private capital accumulation. One of liberalism's central weaknesses is to see markets as 'powerless' mechanisms of coordination, and thus to neglect – as neo-pluralists, among others, point out – the distorting nature of economic power in relation to democracy. Insights into this question are at the heart of the strengths of Marxism. But its overall position, in turn, is weakened by the reduction of political power to economic power and, thus, the neglect – as participatory democrats, among others, point out – of the dangers of centralized political power and the problems of political accountability. Marxism's embodiment in East European societies was marked by the growth of the centralized bureaucratic state; its claim to represent the forces of progressive politics was tarnished by socialism's relation in practice, in the East and also in the West, with bureaucracy, surveillance, hierarchy and state control (see chs 4 and 8). Accordingly, the republican case for the possibility of a participatory order must be questioned, liberalism's account of the nature of markets and economic power must be doubted and Marxism's account of the nature of democracy must be critically appraised.

It is important to take note, furthermore, of some of the limitations shared by republicanism, liberalism and Marxism. Generally, these three political traditions have failed to explore the impediments to participation in democratic life other than those imposed, however important these may be, by unaccountable state and economic power. The roots of the difficulty here lie in narrow conceptions of 'the political'. In the republican and liberal traditions the political is equated with the business of rulership or the world of government. Where this equation is made, a vast domain of politics is excluded from view:

above all, the spheres of productive and reproductive relations. This is particularly apparent in liberal doctrines.[5] The Marxist conception of politics raises related matters. Although the Marxist critique of liberalism is of considerable significance, its value is ultimately limited because of the direct connection it postulates between the political and the economic. Whole clusters of issues, from the nature of sovereignty to the development of power in organizations, are inadequately conceived (see chs 4, 8 and 9).

The narrow conception of 'the political' in these traditions has meant that key conditions for the realization of the principle of autonomy have been eclipsed from view: conditions concerning, for example, the necessary limits on private control of productive and financial resources if democratic outcomes are not to be skewed systematically to the advantage of the economically powerful (insufficiently examined by liberalism); and the necessary changes in the organization of the household and childrearing, among other things, if women are to enjoy a common structure of political action (insufficiently examined by republicanism, liberalism and Marxism). (This is not to say, of course, that no thinker within these three traditions has been concerned with these problems; rather, it is to argue that their frameworks of analysis cannot adequately encompass them.) In order to grasp the diverse conditions necessary for the adequate institutionalization of the principle of autonomy, a broader conception of 'the political' is required than is found in any one of these modes of thought.

In my view, politics is about power; that is, it is about the *capacity* of social agents, agencies and institutions to maintain or transform their environment, social or physical. It is about the resources that underpin this capacity and about the forces that shape and influence its exercise (Held and Leftwich, 1984, p. 144; cf. Giddens, 1979). Accordingly, politics is a phenomenon found in and between all groups, institutions and societies, cutting across public and private life. It is expressed in all the activities of cooperation, negotiation and struggle over the use and distribution of resources. It is involved in all the relations, institutions and structures which are implicated in the activities of production and reproduction in the life of societies. Politics creates and conditions all aspects of our lives and it is at the core of the development of problems in society and the collective modes of their resolution. While politics, thus understood, raises a number of complicated issues – above all, about whether a concept of the private is compatible with it (a matter returned to later) – it usefully highlights the nature of politics as a universal dimension of human life, unrelated to any specific 'site' or set of institutions.

If politics is conceived in this way, then the specification of the conditions of enactment of the principle of autonomy amounts, in the first instance, to the specification of the conditions for the participation of citizens in decisions

[5] Republicanism largely developed, of course, against the backdrop of small cities, artisan and trading enclaves, and rural economies. As such it emerged before the industrial revolution and the spread of mass commodity production; it did not foresee many of the dilemmas of politics which followed in the wake of these transformations. However, as chapter 2 above shows, republicans affirmed a gendered conception of politics, predominantly by omission, although sometimes by an explicit hostility to women in the public sphere.

concerning issues which impinge upon and are important to them (i.e. us). I say 'in the first instance' because it is here that deliberative theory comes into its own. In stressing that the terms and conditions of political association require the free and reasoned assent of its members, that mutual justifiability of outcomes is central to political legitimacy and that the conditions of *informed* participation need to be problematized, it adds a new dimension to democratic thinking. And what it adds is the insight that if democracy is to be constituted by refined and reflective preferences, and steered by arguments and positions that would be defensible in relation to all significantly affected groups, then the quality of the public realm needs to be transformed from a set of mechanisms to aggregate preferences to one for examining them and pursuing those which are fact-, other- and future-regarding (see pp. 232–3).

Thus, it is necessary to strive towards a state of affairs in which political life – democratically and deliberatively organized – is, in principle, a central part of all people's lives. Can this state of affairs be specified more precisely?

The heritage of classic and twentieth-century democratic theory ▪

If the force of the above argument is accepted, it follows that the realization of the principle of autonomy would require the creation of a system of collective, reflective decision-making which allowed the engagement of citizens in the diverse forms of political affairs that significantly affect them. A powerful case can be made, as it has been by Dahl (1979, 1985, 1989), that for such a system to be fully democratic it would have to meet the following criteria:

1 effective participation – citizens must have adequate and equal opportunities to form their preferences, to place questions on the public agenda, and to express reasons for affirming one outcome rather than another;
2 enlightened understanding – citizens must enjoy ample and equal opportunities for discovering and affirming what choice in a matter before them would best serve their interests;
3 voting equality at the decisive stage – each citizen must be assured that his or her judgement will be counted as equal in weight to the judgements of other citizens at the decisive stage of collective decision-making;
4 control of the agenda – the *demos* must have the opportunity to make decisions as to what matters are and are not to be decided by processes that meet the first three criteria;
5 inclusiveness – the provision of the powers of citizenship to all mature persons with a legitimate stake in the polity (i.e. transients and visitors can be exempted) (see Dahl, 1989, chs 6–9).

These criteria can be examined further in order to help specify the general conditions of democratic decision-making.

If citizens are unable to enjoy the conditions for 'effective participation' and 'enlightened understanding', then it is unlikely that the marginalization of large categories of citizens in the democratic process will ever be overcome, or that the vicious circles of limited or non-participation will be broken. For in the absence of these conditions, citizens will not have the discursive means or the participatory channels to pursue collective decision-making effectively. If the right to 'equal votes' is not established, then there will be no mechanism that can take equally into account, and provide a decision procedure to resolve differences among, the views and preferences of citizens (even though the latter may decide not to deploy a decision-making system based on voting in all circumstances). If the 'final control' of the 'political agenda' is out of the hands of citizens, then 'rule by the people' will exist largely in name only, and Schumpeter's technocratic vision is more likely to be the order of the day. If the *demos* does not include all adults (with the exception of those temporarily visiting political 'units', whether these be nation-states or smaller-scale associations, and those who 'beyond a shadow of doubt' are legitimately disqualified from participation due to mental incapacity and/or records of serious crime), then it will clearly fail to create the conditions for 'equal involvement'. In short, for persons to be 'free and equal' the above criteria would have to be met. It is hard to see how persons could be politically equal if any of the criteria were violated and how, as Dahl put it, 'any process that failed to satisfy one or more of the criteria could be regarded as fully democratic' (Dahl, 1985, p. 60; 1989, p. 130; cf. Held, 1991c, for a discussion).

Many questions remain, however, including: under what conditions might it be possible for citizens to be in a position to enjoy equal political status and effective opportunities for participation and deliberation, i.e. a common structure of political action? If the principle of autonomy is to be realized, how is it to be institutionalized in a way that might guarantee collective decision-making? Answers to these questions are, unfortunately, by no means straightforward. In the first instance, to recognize the centrality of democracy and to argue for its wide relevance to many social spheres does not entail the simple affirmation of any of those models of democracy, considered in this volume, which proclaim democracy to be the only legitimate mode of organizing the general structures of life. For reasons already set out, neither the arguments nor the features of these models can be simply accepted.

The classical Athenian model, which developed in a tightly knit community, cannot be adapted to 'stretch' across space and time. Its emergence in the context of city-states and under conditions of 'social exclusivity' was an integral part of its successful development. In circumstances that are socially, economically and politically highly differentiated, it is very hard to envisage how a democracy of this type could succeed without drastic modification (see Budge, 1993). Furthermore, in coming to terms with the classical model one is forcefully reminded that a form of impersonal (legally circumscribed) public power, with a diversity of centres of authority, is an essential feature of a democratic order. The pertinent question is: what is the most appropriate form of this 'impersonal power'? What kind of a structure should it be and how should it be developed?

The significance of these questions is reinforced by reflecting upon the models of democracy advocated by Marsilius and Rousseau, on the one hand, and by Marx, Engels and their followers, on the other. It could be argued that Marsilius's and Rousseau's radical conceptions of republican democracy might function successfully in small-scale communities with limited access to citizenship in which politics was conducted in face-to-face fora. Their exclusion of women from participation in politics would no doubt have helped to reduce the scale of the political problems posed by social differentiation, at the cost, of course, of perpetuating 'the divine right of men' (see Wollstonecraft's argument, pp. 49–54 above). But even if, for instance, the circumstances in which model IIb could operate were tightly delimited, the model could still not be straightforwardly adopted. For the problem would remain of how the reach of 'the democracy' might be limited in the interests of preserving the liberty of individuals and minorities; and of how an adequate space might be created, and procedures established, for debate and decision-making around issues to which citizens brought divergent views and interests. (The same may be said about model IIa, protective republicanism, with its emphasis on self-rule as the key obstacle to domination by others: see ch. 2.) Weber's assessment – that a system of exclusively direct participation can only work in associations with limited numbers of members, where those involved share similar sets of views, skill levels and social positions, and where they are faced by relatively simple and stable administrative functions – is highly persuasive (see ch. 5, pp. **129–30** above).

Much of the above also applies to Marx's and Engels's conception of direct democracy. Its suitability as an institutional arrangement which allows for mediation, negotiation and compromise among struggling factions, groups or movements does not stand up well to criticism. Unless we can be sure that the need for such political processes will soon be overcome, that is, unless we believe in the plausibility of a world in which not only are Wittgenstein, Freud, Eminem and members of our local community agreed on a common vision of life, but the social basis of all group and class conflicts is eliminated as well, direct democracy is in itself not a good gamble. A system to promote discussion, debate and competition among often divergent views – a system encompassing the formation of movements, pressure groups and/or political parties with leaderships to help press their cases – seems unavoidable.

What of participatory democracy? While participatory democracy recognizes many of the difficulties associated with the above three models and, hence, unquestionably represents an advance upon them, the model leaves several fundamental questions unresolved, including how the conditions of its own existence are to be secured adequately. In addition, while the evidence certainly indicates that we learn to participate by participating, and that participation does help foster – as Rousseau, Wollstonecraft and J. S. Mill all contended – an active citizenry, the evidence is by no means conclusive that increased participation *per se* will trigger a renaissance in deliberation and human development. Moreover, it is questionable whether participation *per se* leads to consistent and desirable political outcomes; an array of possible tensions can exist between individual liberty, distributional questions (social justice) and democratic decisions (see ch. 7 above; McLean, 1986, 1991). As deliberative theorists have suggested, these matters are only likely to be dealt with if the quality of participation is itself examined. Yet participatory democracy has not in general addressed deliberative deficits.

The possibility of political participation needs to be secured within a legal framework that protects and nurtures the enactment of the principle of autonomy. The principle of autonomy must have priority over any objective of creating unlimited or uncircumscribed participation. Further, if the form of political participation involved is one that simply registers fixed or given preferences, and fails to address the problem of deliberation, it will leave itself open to many of the objections levelled by deliberative theorists at existing democratic arrangements (see ch. 9). Thus, a complex programme of democratic institution-building is required.

Remoulding democratic institutions

One cannot escape the necessity, therefore, of recognizing from the outset the importance of a number of fundamental liberal tenets: concerning the centrality, in principle, of an 'impersonal structure' of public power, of a constitution to help guarantee and protect rights, of a diversity of power centres within and outside the state, of mechanisms to promote competition and debate between alternative political platforms. What this amounts to, among other things, is confirmation of the fundamental liberal notion that the 'separation' of the state from civil society must be a central feature of any democratic political order. Models of democracy that depend on the assumption that 'state' could ever replace 'civil society' or vice versa must be treated with the utmost caution.

Within the history of liberalism alone the concept of 'civil society' has, of course, been interpreted in a variety of different ways (cf. Pelczynski, 1985; Keane, 1988a; Bobbio, 1989). There is a profound sense, moreover, in which civil society can never be 'separate' from the state; the latter, by providing the overall legal framework of society, to a significant degree constitutes the former. None the less, it is not unreasonable to claim that civil society retains a distinctive character to the extent that it is made up of areas of social life – the domestic world, the economic sphere, cultural activities and political interaction – which are organized by private or voluntary arrangements between individuals and groups outside the *direct* control of the state. It is in this sense that the notion is used here.[6] Thus understood, the terms of the argument can be restated as follows: centralized, representative state institutions – *pace* the advocates of highly radical models of democracy (models I, IIa, IIb, IV and VIII) – must be viewed as necessary devices for, among other things, enacting legislation, enforcing rights and obligations, promulgating new policies and containing inevitable conflicts between particular interests. Representative electoral institutions, including a parliament and the competitive party system, are an inescapable element for authorizing and coordinating these activities.

However, to make these points is not to affirm any one liberal democratic model as it stands. It is one thing to accept the arguments concerning the

---

[6] The concepts of public and private are frequently associated directly with the state/civil society distinction. Although similar in meaning, the two pairs of concepts do not have identical referents (see Okin, 1991). I shall return to the 'public' and 'private' below.

necessary protective, conflict-mediating and redistributive functions of the democratic state, quite another to accept these as prescribed in the models of liberal democracy from Bentham to Schumpeter. Similarly, it is one thing to agree on the significant role of democracy in the development of a knowledgeable and informed citizenry, quite another to accept that it must lead to J. S. Mill's conception of the proper role of representative government. There are profound difficulties, previously discussed, with each of the major models of liberal democracy (see esp. chs 3, 5, 6 and 9). Accordingly, in order for state institutions to become effective, deliberative and accountable centres of public life, they have to be rethought and indeed transformed in a number of distinctive respects.

Advocates of liberal democracy have tended to be concerned, above all else, with the proper principles and procedures of democratic government. By focusing on 'government', they have attracted attention away from a thorough examination of the relation between: formal rights and obligations and actual rights and obligations; commitments to treat citizens as free and equal and practices which do neither sufficiently; citizens' expressed opinions and the conditions for the development of reflective views; conceptions of the state as, in principle, an independent authority and involvements of the state in the reproduction of the inequalities of everyday life; notions of political parties as appropriate structures for bridging the gap between state and society and the array of power centres which such parties (and their leaders) cannot reach; conceptions of politics as governmental affairs and systems of power which negate this concept. None of the models of liberal democracy is able to specify adequately the conditions for the possibility of a common structure of political action, on the one hand, and the set of governing institutions capable of regulating the forces which actually shape everyday life, on the other. The conditions of democratic participation and deliberation, the form of democratic control, the scope of democratic decision-making – all these matters are insufficiently questioned in the liberal democratic tradition. The problems are, in sum, twofold: the structures of civil society (including the prevailing forms of productive and financial property, sexual and racial inequalities) – misunderstood or endorsed by liberal democratic models – do not create conditions for equal votes, effective participation and deliberation, proper political understanding and equal control of the political agenda; while the structures of the liberal democratic state (including large, frequently unaccountable bureaucratic apparatuses, institutional dependence on the imperatives of private capital accumulation, political representatives preoccupied with their own re-election) do not create an organizational force which can adequately regulate 'civil' power centres.

Democracy: a double-sided process

The implications of these points are profound: for democracy to flourish today it has to be reconceived as a double-sided phenomenon: concerned, on the one hand, with the *re*form of state power and, on the other hand, with the restructuring of civil society (Held and Keane, 1984).[7] The principle of autonomy can only be enacted by recognizing the indispensability of a process of *double democratization*: the interdependent transformation of both state and civil society. Such a process must be premissed by the acceptance of the axiom that the division between state and civil society must be a central feature of democratic life, and of the axiom that the power to make decisions must be free of illegitimate constraints imposed by the private flows of capital and other resources. But, of course, to recognize the importance of both these positions is to recognize the necessity of recasting substantially their traditional connotations.

The enactment of the principle of autonomy requires us to rethink the forms and limits of state action and the forms and limits of civil society. The questions arise: How, and in what ways, might state policy be made more accountable? How, and in what ways, might 'non-state' activities be democratically reordered? To address these problems with any thoroughness is beyond the scope of this volume (though it is a task begun in Held and Pollitt, 1986, and a central concern of Held, 1995, 2004; cf. Hirst, 1994; J. Cohen and Rogers, 1995). However, it is clearly important to add some institutional detail to the argument presented so far if the conditions of enactment of the principle of autonomy are to be envisaged at all. What follows is nothing other than the briefest of sketches: an agenda for further thought.

In the North and West the need to democratize political institutions has mostly been confined to questions of reforming the process whereby party leaders are selected and changing electoral rules. Other issues which are raised include the public funding of elections for all parties meeting a minimum level of support; genuine access to, and more equitable distribution of, media time; freedom of information (for example in Britain, abolition of many of the regulations concerning state secrecy); decentralization of the civil service to the regions; the defence and enhancement of local government powers against rigid, centralized state decisions; and experiments to make government institutions more accountable and amenable to their 'consumers'. All these are important issues, which must be developed further if adequate strategies are to be found for democratizing state institutions (see Barnett et al., 1993; Beetham, 2005). But none of them will make a decisive contribution to making the polity more democratic unless a further fundamental problem (set out in chs 2, 3, 4, 7 and 9) is confronted: how can the requirements of democratic public life (open debate, reasoned deliberation, access to power centres, general political participation, etc.) be reconciled with those institutions of state (from the executive to branches of the administration) whose task it is to uphold the rule of law, mediate disputes and negotiate among conflicting interests? How can the

---

[7] I would like to acknowledge my debt to John Keane in formulating elements of this argument. Some of the ideas in this section of the chapter were discussed in our joint essay (1984), although he may well not agree with aspects of their elaboration here. In addition, it should be noted that the attempt to reassess the relation between 'state' and 'civil society' has been influenced not only by a variety of writings from thinkers in the East and the West, but also by social movements, again in both East and West, that made this attempt a central element of their agenda (see, e.g., J. L. Cohen, 1982; Offe, 1984; Keane, 1988a; J. L. Cohen and Arato, 1992; and cf. ch. 8 above).

requirements of both a 'sovereign state' and a 'sovereign people' be met? At issue, in other words, is establishing the sovereignty of citizens over the state while resisting the surrender of lawmaking and enforcement – and the powers of the state in general – to the unlimited power of the people with its possible threat to the entrenchment of the principle of autonomy, to the liberty of individuals and minorities, and to the quality of public reasoning (the reduction of public argument to the lowest possible denominator) (see ch. 9 above). The state requires democratization, but also the protection and development of some of its independent or impartial powers if democracy is to maintain a shape and form that respects and enforces, in principle, the rights and obligations of all citizens. How can this be done?

In many countries, the limits of 'government' are explicitly defined in constitutions and bills of rights which are subject to public scrutiny, parliamentary review and judicial process. This idea is fundamental, and especially so to the principle of autonomy. However, the principle of autonomy requires these limits on 'public power' to be reassessed in relation to a far broader range of issues than has hitherto been commonly presupposed. If people are to be free and equal in the determination of the conditions of their own lives, and enjoy equal rights as well as equal obligations in the specification of the framework which generates and limits the opportunities available to them, they must be in a position to enjoy a range of rights not only in principle, but also in practice. This entails a 'system of rights' which would both constrain and enable collective activities across a broad domain.

A democracy would be fully worth its name if citizens had the actual power to be active as citizens; that is to say, if citizens were able to enjoy a bundle of rights which allowed them to demand democratic participation and to treat it as an entitlement (cf. Sen, 1981, ch. 1). Such a bundle of rights, it is important to stress, should not be thought of as merely an extension of the sphere of accumulated private demands for rights and privileges over and against the state, as many liberal thinkers have conceived rights (see ch. 3 above). Nor should it be thought of as simply redistributive welfare measures to alleviate inequalities of opportunity, as many of the theorists of the welfare state have interpreted rights (see Marshall, 1973). Rather, it should be seen as entailed by, and integral to, the very notion of democratic rule itself. It is a way of specifying certain conditions necessary for the equal autonomy of all citizens, that is, for a common structure of political action. *If one chooses democracy, one must choose to operationalize a radical system of rights and obligations* – obligations which follow from the necessity to respect the equal rights of others and to ensure that they enjoy a common structure of political activity.

What would be included in such a system? In the first instance, a constitution and bill of rights which enshrined the principle of autonomy would specify equal rights with respect to the processes that determine state outcomes. This would involve not only equal rights to cast a vote, but also equal rights to enjoy the conditions for effective participation, enlightened understanding and the specification of the political agenda. Such broad 'political' rights would, in turn, entail a broad bundle of social rights linked to reproduction, childcare, health and education, as well as economic rights to ensure adequate economic and financial resources for democratic autonomy. Without tough social and economic rights, rights with respect to the state could not be fully enjoyed; and without state rights, new forms of inequality of power, wealth and status could systematically disrupt the implementation of social and economic liberties.

A system of rights of this type would, in addition, specify certain obligations of citizens towards one another as well as responsibilities of the state to groups of citizens, which particular governments could not (unless permitted by an explicit process of constitutional amendment) override. The authority of the state would thus, in principle, be clearly circumscribed; its capacity for freedom of action bounded. For example, a right to reproductive freedom for women would entail making the political community responsible not only for the medical and social facilities necessary to prevent or assist pregnancy, but also for providing the material conditions which would help make the choice to have a child a genuinely free one, and thereby ensure a crucial condition for women if they are to be 'free and equal'. A right to childcare would entail making the polity accountable for the provision of adequate childcare facilities and would, therefore, also limit public expenditure options. The recognition of this priority is a vital component of the possibility of equal opportunities for women in work and in the broader framework of civic and political life. A right to economic resources for women and men, in order that they may be in a position to choose among possible courses of action, would oblige the state to be preoccupied with the ways in which wealth and income can be more equitably arranged. Such resources might be made available through, among other things, a guaranteed income for all adults irrespective of whether they are engaged in wage-labour or household labour (see Jordan, 1985). Strategies of the latter type should be treated with some caution; their implications for collective or societal wealth creation and distribution are complex, and by no means fully clear. However, without a minimum resource base of some kind, many people will remain vulnerable and highly dependent on others, unable fully to exercise an independent choice or to pursue different opportunities that are formally before them.[8] The 'rule of law', then, must involve a central concern with distributional questions and matters of social justice: anything less would hinder the realization of the principle of autonomy and the rule of democracy (see Held, 1989, ch. 7; 1995, chs 7–9; 2004).

Accordingly, in this scheme of things, a right to equal membership of a democratic, political community, that is, citizenship, would entail not only the responsibility of the state to ensure formal equality before the law, but also that citizens would have the actual capacity (the health, education, skills and resources) to take advantage of opportunities before them. Such a constitution and bill of rights would radically enhance the ability of citizens to take action against the state to redress unreasonable encroachment on liberties. It would help tip the balance from state to parliament and from parliament to citizens, while also specifying independent points of orientation for the polity. It would,

---

[8] Or, as Galbraith boldly put it, 'there is, first, the absolute, inescapable requirement that everyone in the good . . . society has a basic source of income. And if this is not available from the market system . . . it must come from the state. Nothing, let us not forget, sets a stronger limit on the liberty of the citizen than a total absence of money' (1994, p. 2).

thus, be an *empowering legal system*, for citizens and political agencies alike. Of course, 'empowerment' would not thereby be guaranteed; no legal system alone is able to offer such guarantees. But it would specify rights which could be fought for by individuals, groups and movements (wherever pressure could most effectively be mounted), and which could be tested in, among other places, open court.[9]

Such a legal framework, important as it is to the delimitation of a democratic community, would be insufficient to create greater fluidity and accountability of political power. If political power is not merely to pass from one set of politicians to another, albeit operating through new modes and spheres of activity, then citizens' actual involvement in politics needs to be deepened. Moreover, if citizens are, in principle, to enjoy both the capacities for autonomy and the ability to exercise these effectively, then how the latter is to occur needs further explication. But can political participation be deepened given that models of direct citizen involvement, from classic republicanism to participatory democracy, cannot simply be adapted to embrace all citizens in the contemporary world? How can an empowering legal system be complemented by enhanced channels of communication, deliberation and decision-making among citizens and their relevant representatives, local and national? In addition, if enhanced political participation is to be informed participation – participation that bears directly on the quality of the decision-making process – then how political power should be exercised becomes a pressing matter; both enlightened understanding and effective participation are essential for creating the possibility of an informed share in government (see Fishkin, 1991; cf. J. Cohen, 1989).

To analyse the nature of democracy in this way is more than simply an attempt to clarify the theoretical framework that might help empower citizens in the business of politics. The limits and possible forms of democracy are becoming crucial themes in North American and European discussions of alternative deliberative public fora and procedures, as documented in chapter 9. Deliberative polls, deliberative days, citizens' juries, certain e-government and e-democracy mechanisms, new civic education initiatives, the public funding of deliberative public spheres and the associations that support them, are all among new ways of thinking about how to 'upgrade citizenship' (Offe and Preuss) and to nurture the development of informed and reflective political preferences (see model IX). The development of deliberative democratic public spaces is important not because they can be straightforwardly adopted or 'imported' into all countries, but because they recognize the need to break vicious circles of limited or non-participation while also acknowledging that the

---

[9] The existing judicial system in most countries is unlikely to provide sufficiently representative personnel to oversee such a judicial process. An alternative would have to be found, comprising perhaps judicial bodies composed of people who were chosen from a 'statistically representative' sample of the population; that is, who were statistically representative of key social categories (gender, race, age) (see Burnheim, 1985). There is no reason to suppose that such bodies would be less capable of independent judgement than the existing judiciary and many reasons for believing that their judgements over the specific matter of how to interpret human rights would be more representative of collective opinion.

question of informed participation is a central matter to the future of democracy. Without new deliberative initiatives it is hard to see how the democratization of the state, in principle and in practice, could advance in the long term.

The implications of all this for the organization of civil society are in part clear. To the extent that the anatomy of civil society comprises elements that undermine the possibility of effective collective decision-making, they would have to be addressed. A democratic state and civil society are incompatible with powerful sets of social relations and organizations which can, by virtue of the very basis of their operations, systematically distort democratic arguments and outcomes. At issue here is, among other things, the curtailment of the power of corporations to constrain and influence the political agenda, the restriction of the activities of powerful interest groups (whether they be representatives of particular industries or some trade unions with workers in key industrial sectors) to pursue their own interests unchecked, and the erosion of the systematic privileges enjoyed by some social groups (for instance, certain religious groups) at the expense of others. The state and civil society must, then, become the condition for each other's democratic development.

Under such conditions, strategies would have to be adopted to break up old patterns of power in civil society and, in addition, to create new circumstances which allowed citizens to enjoy greater control of their own projects (see Keane, 1988b). If individuals are to be free and equal in the determination of the conditions of their own existence, there must be a multiplicity of social spheres – for example, sectors of socially regulated enterprises, independent communications media and health centres – which allow their members control of the resources at their disposal without direct interference from the state, political agencies or other third parties. The models for the organization of these spheres would have much to learn from the conceptions of direct participation discussed earlier. A system of open (face-to-face) meetings or of delegated representatives finds its most appropriate domain of application precisely in these contexts. Many of the 'units' of civil society might approximate to, or come to share, the conditions under which direct democracy could flourish while meeting deliberative standards. But an experimental view of such organizational structures would have to be taken. The condition of democratic theory and the knowledge we have of radical democratic experiments do not allow wholly confident predictions about the most suitable strategies for organizational change. In this particular sense, the 'music of the future' can only be composed in practice. The nature and form of different types of democracy and their pertinence to different social and political conditions need careful further examination.

The enactment of the principle of autonomy, around a process of 'double democratization', produces a model of state and society which I call 'democratic autonomy' (or 'liberal socialism'). Its principles and features are sketched in model Xa. The model amounts to a number of proposals which together might create the conditions for the defence and development of democracy in contemporary circumstances. In the following section, a further step will be taken to clarify the model.

Democratic autonomy: compatibilities and incompatibilities

If democratic life involves no more than a periodic vote, the locus of people's activities will be the 'private' realm of civil society and the scope of their actions will depend largely on the resources they can command. Few opportunities will exist for citizens to act as citizens, as participants in public life. Democratic autonomy seeks to redress this state of affairs by creating opportunities for people to establish themselves 'in their capacity of being citizens' (Arendt, 1963, p. 256). But if the aim and overall structure of the model of democratic autonomy are clear, there remains, it must be said, an array of unanswered questions. Each of these questions in itself raises an extensive series of considerations. The attempt to survey these issues here should be taken as further acknowledgement that the argument presented calls for detailed additional thought. I believe each of the issues can be satisfactorily dealt with within the framework of the model of democratic autonomy, but it cannot be claimed that they are fully addressed here.

Participation: an obligation?

The principle of autonomy lays down the right of all citizens to participate in and deliberate on public affairs. What is at issue is the provision of a *rightful share* in the process of 'government'. The idea of such a share was, of course, central to Athenian democrats, for whom political virtue was in part synonymous with the right to participate in the final decisions of city-state politics (cf. Finley, 1983, p. 140). The principle of autonomy preserves 'the ideal of the active citizen'; it requires that people be recognized as having the right and opportunity to act in public life. However, it is one thing to recognize a right, quite another to say it follows that everyone must, irrespective of choice, actually participate in public debate and activity. Participation is not a necessity. Deliberative democracy presupposes, according to some of its leading advocates, that publicly upheld positions can meet the test that all significantly affected would assent to them, but it does not presuppose that all will or could necessarily engage in debate (see Habermas, 1996, for example). It has been argued that one of the most important negative liberties established since the end of the ancient world is 'freedom from politics', and that such a liberty is an essential part of the contemporary democratic heritage (Arendt, 1963, p. 284). Democratic autonomy is certainly compatible with this element of our heritage. Citizens may decide that extensive participation is unnecessary in certain circumstances, and they may decide this for very rational reasons, including a conviction that their interests are already well protected (see Mansbridge, 1983). Clearly, all systems of law – and the legal system of democratic autonomy would be no exception – specify a variety of obligations. Within the model of democratic autonomy obligations would clearly exist. Citizens would be obliged to accept democratic decisions in a variety of circumstances unless it could be proved that their rights were violated by such decisions. But the obligation to get involved in all aspects of public life would not be a legal one. The right to a life of one's own, within a framework of democratic autonomy, is important.

In sum: model Xa

Democratic Autonomy

Principle(s) of justification

Persons should enjoy equal rights and, accordingly, equal obligations in the specification of the political framework which generates and limits the opportunities available to them; that is, they should be free and equal in the processes of deliberation about the conditions of their own lives and in the determination of these conditions, so long as they do not deploy this framework to negate the rights of others

Key features

State

Principle of autonomy enshrined in constitution and bill of rights

Parliamentary or congressional structure (organized around two chambers based on PR)

Judicial system to include specialized fora to test interpretations of rights (SR)

Competitive party system (recast by public funding and DP)

Central and local administrative services, internally organized to include elements of DP with a requirement to coordinate 'local user' demands

Civil society

Diversity of types of household and of sources of information, cultural institutions, consumer groups, etc.

Community services such as childcare, health centres and education internally organized to include elements of DP but with priorities set by adult users

Development and experimentation with different types of self-managed enterprises

Diverse forms of private enterprise to promote innovation and economic flexibility

General conditions

Open and free information to help ensure informed decisions in public affairs

Full use of deliberative democratic mechanisms and procedures from deliberative polls to 'voter feedback' to enhance the processes of enlightened participation

Overall regulatory objectives of the economy set by government in discussion with public and private agencies

Entrenchment of rules governing labour, welfare, health and the environment in the operational dynamics of corporations

Minimization of unaccountable power centres in public and private life

Maintenance of institutional framework receptive to experiments with organizational forms

---

Note: The institutional features of democratic autonomy are set out here, it must be stressed, in a highly tentative mode. They include a variety of forms of democratic decision-making and of methods of election. The key abbreviations refer to:

DP Direct participation of particular sets of citizens (involving open meetings, local referenda and delegated representatives) in the regulation of an organization

PR Election of representatives on the basis of a form of proportional representation

SR Representatives chosen on the basis of 'statistical representation' (that is, a sample of those who are statistically representative of key social categories, including gender and race)

(For further discussion of methods of election, see Held and Pollitt, 1986.)

This position, of course, raises further issues. What exact bundle of rights and obligations does the model of democratic autonomy require? What exact obligations would citizens have to accept? Under what circumstances could they legitimately refuse such obligations? If citizens would be entitled to refuse a decision on the grounds that it violated their rights, what means of resistance would they be justified in deploying in these circumstances? These are just a few of the problems which a fully explicated model of democratic autonomy would have to address.

Politics and the private: what is the private?

If democratic autonomy is compatible with a concept of the private, what exactly should this concept be? In contrast to narrower views of political life, the argument here entails a broad notion of politics embracing all systems of power, where power is understood as 'transformative capacity' (pp. 270–1 above). While this concept of politics is essential in order to elucidate adequately the range of issues that impinges on, and affects the possibility of, democratic life, it raises a number of difficulties. Schumpeter rightly warned that an 'unbounded' concept of politics provides no clear-cut barrier between the polity, on the one hand, and the everyday life of citizens, on the other. By making politics potentially coextensive with all realms of social, cultural and economic life, it opens these domains to public regulation and control. Schumpeter thought politics so conceived would offer an enormous temptation to those with power, whether they were majorities or minorities, to control all aspects of life. Broad concepts of politics, he suggested, might become connected for many, in practice, to a diminution of freedom. This is, again, a fundamental matter.

While a broad concept of politics is defensible and necessary to the adequate consideration of the problems and questions of democracy, it must be thought through carefully in relation to a conception of the limits of the justifiable reach of democracy. The argument here has been that the principles of political engagement and participation are applicable to a large array of domains. However, they are not necessarily applicable to what I wish to call the 'sphere of the intimate'; that is, to all those circumstances where people live out their personal lives without systematically harmful consequences for those around them. Just like Mill's principle of harm, a concept of the intimate when used in this way would need very careful elaboration and defence. And just like Mill's principle of harm, it would be hard to find satisfactory grounds for its elucidation and justification. None the less, the examination of such grounds is an indispensable task. Clear criteria will have to be found for demarcating the public and the political from the sphere of the intimate, and for defining the limits to legitimate legislation in the latter realm. Considerable theoretical inquiry remains to be undertaken in this field (see Pateman, 1985, pp. 174–5).

Public decision-making: Who deliberates? Who governs?

It is possible to conceive of different types of democracy as forming a continuum from the local to the national, with the local marked by direct and participatory processes while larger areas with significant populations are progressively mediated by representative mechanisms. The possibilities for direct participatory democracy in communities and workplaces are clearly extensive compared to those which exist in highly differentiated social, economic and political circumstances (see Beetham, 1993; Phillips, 1993). However, the simple juxtaposition of participatory with liberal representative democracy is now in flux given developments in deliberative theory and in information technology, which has put simultaneous two-way communication within reach of larger populations. The merits of participatory democracy have to be re-examined now aspects of its technical feasibility are closer at hand. As one commentator has recently argued, it is unacceptable to dismiss all types of direct democracy as if they could be realized only through 'unmediated popular voting on a take it or leave it basis'; for direct democracy can take several different institutional forms, just as liberal representative democracy does (Budge, 1993, pp. 136–49). While some of these forms are open to serious reservations, it is possible to conceive, for instance, a type of party-based deliberative direct democracy in which the electorate would be able, in the first instance, to consider and choose among competing parties for office and, in the second, to act like a parliamentary assembly – deliberating over and voting directly on proposed legislation set out and advocated by the party in office. The stability of such a political system would require a complex set of rules and procedures to be in place, but these are not in principle difficult to specify (see Budge, 1993, pp. 136–55; 1996). In practice, of course, a great many issues remain unresolved and, at the time of writing, they are clearly open to extensive debate. (For a range of views on this matter, see Held, 1993c, part II; Fishkin, 1991; Saward, 2003.)

Among the outstanding issues are these: How should the role of political representatives and citizens be reconceived if citizens gain new direct powers of deliberation and decision-making on controversial public issues? What should be the balance between the extension of consultative procedures and decision-making mechanisms? If representative and direct democracy are combined progressively through the extension of citizens' juries, referenda and the like, what mechanisms and institutions can ensure independent deliberative or electoral procedures? How can these procedures be satisfactorily scrutinized and regulated? Who should frame the issues and questions put to citizens' bodies? What should be the balance between citizens' rights to initiate and veto legislation? How should these considerations be weighed in relation to other important political values such as fairness, efficacy and efficiency? Within the framework of democratic autonomy, an experimental view would have to be taken of the new rules, technologies and procedures; dogmatism about any of these issues might risk weakening those aspects of our political traditions which need protection and nurturing – such as the notion of an impartial and circumscribed political authority, and the maintenance of many key liberal democratic rights and obligations (see ch. 3) – without necessarily gaining new and effective political resources.

The entrenchment of democracy in economic life: reframing the market?

Democracy is challenged by powerful sets of economic relations and organizations which can – by virtue of the bases of their operations – deflect or distort democratic processes and outcomes. Accordingly, if democracy is to prevail, the key groups and associations of the economy will have to be rearticulated with political institutions so that they become part of the democratic process – adopting, within their very *modus operandi*, a structure of rules, principles and practices compatible with democracy. The possibility of such a structure depends upon groups and economic associations functioning within agreed and delimited frameworks (cf. Hirst, 1990, pp. 75–8). What is at issue is the inscription of the principles, rules and procedures of democracy and democratic autonomy into the organizational rules and procedures of companies, and of all other forms of economic association.

If democratic processes and relations are to be sustained, corporations will have to uphold, *de jure* and *de facto*, a commitment to the requirements of democratic autonomy. What this entails is that companies, while pursuing strategic objectives, must operate within a framework which does not violate the requirement to treat their employees and customers as free and equal persons. But how exactly should this be conceived? What would constitute such a framework? How can a common structure of political action be built into corporate and market relations?

In the first instance, it is useful to distinguish between different types of property and, in particular, between productive and financial property, on the one hand, and consumption property (items possessed for private consumption), on the other. The principle of autonomy requires the rigorous pursuit of questions concerning the structure of productive and financial property, but it certainly does not presuppose the rigorous pursuit of such issues with respect to items we choose to consume in daily life, whether these are shirts, washing machines or personal computers. Entitlements to consumption property need to be separated from the right to unlimited accumulation of economic resources. Rousseau was one of the first to make this argument powerfully (see pp. 46–7 above; cf. Connolly, 1981, ch. 7). Recently, the point has been argued incisively by Dahl, who affirms that we cannot leap from an 'entitlement to secure possession of the shirt on my back or the cash in my pocket to a fundamental moral right to acquire shares in IBM and therewith the standard rights of ownership that shareholdings legally convey' (Dahl, 1985, pp. 74–5). A choice in favour of 'the standard rights of ownership' is a choice against political equality and a common structure of political action. If political equality is a moral right, so too is greater equality in the conditions governing productive and financial resources. Recognition of the necessity to transform aspects of the ownership and control of the productive and financial systems is fundamental to the possibility of an open, unbiased political agenda. Without clear restrictions on the private governance and use of economic resources, a necessary condition of democracy cannot be met.

However, there are further complex questions to be raised about the proper form of ownership and control of economic goods. There are sound reasons for criticizing and worrying about high concentrations of both private and state forms of ownership (see chs 3, 4 and 7). Other options, for instance, cooperative forms of ownership, involving the collective possession of enterprises by work groups, might be more compatible with democratic autonomy than either state or private ownership alone. But a thoroughly convincing case for social or cooperative ownership has yet to be made. Among the central questions which require further examination are the following: What exactly are the nature and boundaries of an enterprise? Would all existing companies have to be broken up into small units (a wholly unrealistic prospect) for cooperative ownership to be viable? How can consumer preferences – other than through the market – be taken into account and what weight should they be given? How can the requirements of cooperative ownership be fully reconciled with the requirements of democratic control and/or efficient management?[10] Forms of ownership, and experiments with different types, need more rigorous attention, as do their respective implications for the distribution of political power (see Ruggie, 2003; Held, 2004).

Democratic autonomy: the tyranny of sameness?

Does the pursuit of the principle of autonomy and a common structure of political action entail that people should always be treated in a similar way by the state? State outcomes may well be unequal for individuals, and justifiably so. From the perspective of democratic autonomy, to secure the conditions which enable individuals to play an active role as citizens requires different sets of strategies and policies for different sets of people. In the first instance, it will be necessary to treat those who currently control vast amounts of productive or financial property, with minimum public accountability, unequally. But the matter goes much further than this. For instance, if women are to enjoy 'free and equal' conditions, not only will the typical circumstances under which they bear and raise children have to be transformed, but the traditional privileges of men with respect to jobs, income and access to cultural activities, among other things, will have to be eroded as well. This double-sided policy process – of alleviating the conditions of the least powerful while restricting the scope and circumstances of the most powerful – would apply to a variety of areas marked by systematic inequality (from wealth and gender to race and ethnicity), where it could be shown that such inequality *undermines* or *artificially limits* the pursuit of democratic deliberation and decision-making by others.

But does the creation of greater equality of political and economic circumstances mean, as is often claimed, that people must or should eventually do all the same things, pursue all the same activities and live under identical conditions – in short, be the same? Is the pursuit of a common structure of political action the pursuit of a tyrannically conceived order in which all people

---

[10] It could be objected that the above account fails to examine whether or not private property, and private property in productive resources, is essential for the achievement of a number of important ends, e.g. efficiency and innovation. There is not the space here to investigate all the issues involved in such an objection, but they are examined by Dahl, who develops a compelling argument about many of the problems (1985).

are reduced to similar status and similar activities? It is unquestionably the case that a commitment to democratic autonomy entails a commitment to reducing the privileges of the privileged if these restrict the participative possibilities of others and deny their capacity for democratic engagement. But it would not involve, and would be quite incompatible with, an attack on personal, social, cultural and (in certain respects) economic 'differences'. The *raison d'être* of the model of democratic autonomy is to enhance the choices and benefits which flow from living in a society that does not leave large categories of citizens in a permanently subordinate position, at the mercy of forces entirely outside their control. Furthermore, if broadly common political conditions were established, it would not follow that the correct and only principle of justice would be the constant and further pursuit of such conditions. It is going to be a matter for citizens themselves to consider and decide, within the framework set down by the principle of autonomy, how exactly goods and services are to be distributed (cf. Pateman, 1985, p. 188).

However, it must again be stressed that additional theoretical work is required on these problems. If political equality and democratic life require greater equality of economic and social conditions, the exact nature of the principles of social justice will have to be spelt out more carefully and their scope thoroughly examined. While the model of democratic autonomy clearly circumscribes the direction of distributive forms of state action, it remains to be specified in what precise ways and with what order of priorities. In addition, the many *practical* issues of *policy* involved require careful thought. New types of social and economic policies and new ways of implementing them will have to be developed. The point is not just to interpret or change the world, but to explore the justifiable *and* feasible ways in which it can be altered.

Democratic autonomy: limited autonomy?

In any given political system there are clearly limits to the extent of liberty which citizens can enjoy. What distinguishes the model of democratic autonomy from many of the other models discussed in this book is a fundamental commitment to the principle that the liberty of some individuals must not be allowed at the expense of others, where others can be a majority or significant minority of citizens. In this sense, the concept of liberty presupposed by the model of democratic autonomy allows in some respects a smaller range of actions for certain groups of individuals. If the principle of autonomy is to be realized, then some people will no longer have the scope to, for instance, pollute the environment of others, accumulate vast unregulated resources, or pursue their own life opportunities at the expense of those of their lovers or wives. The liberty of persons within the framework of democratic autonomy will have to be one of progressive accommodation to the liberty of others. While, therefore, the scope of action may be more limited for some in certain respects, it will be substantially enhanced for others.

It does not follow from this, as is sometimes remarked about related theoretical positions, that such a fundamental transformation of life opportunities entails the end of the division of labour or the end of a role for specialized competencies. As one critic rightly commented: 'a political future which promised to dispense with expertise will be necessarily an idiot's promise or a promise made in the deepest bad faith' (Dunn, 1979, p. 19). The model of democratic autonomy is and must be fully compatible with people choosing to develop particular talents and skills. The conditions of such choices will be different, but this does not mean that there will be no choices. Moreover, the model of democratic autonomy presupposes explicitly the existence of centralized decision-making in government. Democratic autonomy does not promote the levelling of all authority and of those clusters of institutions which can provide skilled, predictable administration. Weber's argument about the importance of the latter in preventing public affairs becoming a quagmire of infighting among factions, wholly inefficient in settling pressing collective issues, is particularly significant (see ch. 5 above). But the *form* and *structure* of such institutions would have to be altered. It would, again, be fallacious to claim we know exactly how and in what precise ways this would happen. We need to reflect and deliberate much more on types and forms of possible political organization and their connecting relations with markets, when the latter function within a framework of broad accountability.

Legitimacy: would democratic autonomy create political legitimacy?

Political order today, as argued in chapters 5–7, is not achieved through common value systems, or general respect for the authority of the state, or legitimacy, or, by contrast, simple brute force; rather, it is the outcome of a complex web of interdependencies between political, economic and social institutions and activities which divide power centres and which create multiple pressures to comply. State power is a central aspect of these structures but it is not the only key variable.

The precariousness of 'government' in contemporary circumstances is linked both to the limits of state power in the context of national and international conditions and to the remoteness, distrust and scepticism that are expressed about existing institutional arrangements, including the effectiveness of liberal representative democracy. The institutions of liberal representative democracy remain crucial to the formal control of the state, but the disjuncture between the agencies which possess formal control and those with actual control, between the power that is claimed for the people and their limited actual power, between the promises of representatives and their actual performance, is striking. The perception of this disjuncture contributed to the formation of a number of powerful social movements – including the women's movement, the environmental movement and the anti-globalization or social justice movement – which have pressed and continue to press for greater spheres of autonomy and accountability in politics. These movements, in addition, have been an important impetus to those – from segments of the labour movement and civil society to the innovative wings of political parties – who have had related objectives. But in the context of the many factors which fragment opposition forces, it is, of course, hard to predict how successful these will be: the 'balance' of political life always depends on debate, negotiation and conflict, and its results cannot, therefore, be easily read off from a consideration of current circumstances.

The notion of an 'ideal normative agreement' was introduced in chapter 5; it is an agreement to follow rules and laws on the grounds that they are the regulations we would have agreed to in ideal conditions, with, for instance, all the knowledge we would like and all the opportunity we would want to discuss the requirements of others (pp. 155–6, 197–8 above). This idea is useful because it provides a basis for a 'thought experiment' into how people would interpret their needs, and which rules and laws they would consider justified, under conditions of unconstrained knowledge and discussion. It enables us to ask what the circumstances would have to be like for people to follow rules and laws they think right, justified and worthy of respect. It conjoins with the arguments of those deliberative theorists who seek to test candidate principles of social and political order against the requirements of impartiality (see pp. 239–41 above). Surveying the issues and evidence explored in Parts One and Two of this volume, it can be said that a political system implicated deeply in the creation and reproduction of systematic inequalities of power and opportunities will rarely (the exceptions perhaps being occasions like war) enjoy sustained support by groups other than those whom it directly privileges. Or, more contentiously, only a political order that places the transformation of those inequalities at its centre will enjoy legitimacy in the long run. The principle of autonomy, enacted through a double-sided process of democratization, might be the basis for such an order. The pursuit of political legitimacy, of a political order marked by respect for authority and law, suggests the importance of pursuing the model of democratic autonomy. Critical reflection must, at this point, link up with public debate and deliberative politics if this analytically proposed account is to become part of the democratic conversation and encompass all those whom it seeks to address. Only under the latter circumstances can a theoretical model become an actuality in the understanding and practices of citizens.

11 Democracy, the Nation-State and the Global System

There has been an assumption at the heart of modern democratic theory, manifest in the last chapter as well, concerning a 'symmetrical' and 'congruent' relationship between political decision-makers and the recipients of political decisions. In fact, symmetry and congruence have been assumed at two crucial points: first, between citizen-voters and the decision-makers whom they are, in principle, able to hold to account; and second, between the 'output' (decisions, policies, etc.) of decision-makers and their constituents – ultimately, 'the people' in a delimited territory (Held, 1991a, pp. 198–204).

Throughout the twentieth century, especially, democratic theory has focused on the organizational and socioeconomic context of democratic procedures and the effects this context has on the operation of 'majority rule'. From the development of the theory of competitive elitism to the elaboration of classic pluralism, or to the critique of these ideas in the writings of radical thinkers, the focus of modern democratic theory has been on the conditions which foster or hinder the democratic life of a nation. It has been assumed, furthermore, by theorists and critics of modern democracy alike, that 'the fate of a national community' is largely in its own hands and that a satisfactory theory of democracy can be developed by examining the interplay between 'actors' and 'structures' in the nation-state.

At the centre of the debate about democracy has been a taken-for-granted conception of 'sovereignty'. The sovereignty of the nation-state has generally not been questioned (cf. Laski, 1932; Figgis, 1913; Hirst, 1989b). It has been assumed that the state has control over its own fate, subject only to compromises it must make and limits imposed upon it by actors, agencies and forces operating within its territorial boundaries, and by the agents and representatives of other governments and states. It is evident that nineteenth- and twentieth-century democratic theory, along with much of the rest of social and political theory, has generally regarded the world beyond the nation-state as a given – subject to an 'all else being equal' clause. Leading perspectives on social and political change have assumed that the origins of societal transformation are to be found largely in processes internal to society (cf. Dunn, 1990, ch. 8; Giddens, 1985). Change is presumed to occur via mechanisms 'built in', as it were, to the very structure of a given society and governing its development. The world putatively 'outside' the nation-state – the dynamics of the world economy, the rapid growth of transnational links and major changes to the nature of international law, for example – has barely been examined, and its implications for democracy have not been thought out at all by democratic political theorists. Up to this point, the argument in favour of democratic autonomy has barely touched on these questions either.

In what follows these matters are explored as a complement to the issues raised in chapter 10. The focus is on the 'other side' of democracy: the interrelation between democracy and the global system. The chapter begins with an account of some of the particular ways in which national politics intersects with regional[1] and global forces. Against this background an assessment is made of the changing forms and limits of democracy. While the main purpose of this chapter is to set out a number of additional unresolved problems facing democratic thought, in the final section some remarks are offered on the changing meaning of democracy in the global system, and on how the theory of democratic autonomy must be recast further to embrace the global networks of states and civil societies.

Democratic legitimacy and borders

The limits of a theory of politics that derives its terms of reference exclusively from the nation-state become apparent from a consideration of the scope and efficacy of the principle of majority rule; that is, the principle that decisions that attract the largest number of votes should prevail. The application of this principle is at the centre of all contemporary conceptions of democracy, and it is at the root of the claim of democratic political decisions to be regarded as worthy or legitimate. Problems arise, however, from a number of sources. In the first instance, they arise because many of the decisions of 'a majority' or, more accurately, its representatives, affect (or potentially affect) not only their communities but citizens in other communities as well.

To take some topical examples: a decision to build a nuclear plant near the borders of a neighbouring country is likely to be a decision taken without consulting those in the nearby country (or countries), despite the many risks and ramifications for them. A decision to increase interest rates in an attempt to stem inflation or exchange rate instability is most often taken as a 'national' decision, although it may well stimulate economic changes internationally. A decision to permit the 'harvesting' of the rainforests may contribute to ecological damage far beyond the borders that formally limit the responsibility of a given set of political decision-makers. These decisions, along with policies on issues as diverse as security, arms procurement and AIDS, are typically regarded as falling within the legitimate domain of authority of a sovereign nation-state. But in a world of regional and global interconnectedness, there are major questions about the coherence, viability and accountability of national decision-making entities themselves.

Further difficulties emerge for the nature of democratic legitimacy from decisions made by quasi-regional or quasi-supranational organizations such as the European Union (EU), the World Trade Organization (WTO), or the International Monetary Fund (IMF). For these decisions can also diminish the range of decisions open to given national 'majorities'. (Illustrations of such decisions will be discussed later.) The idea of a community that rightly governs

---

[1] By a region I mean a cluster of nation-states in a geographical area which share a number of common concerns and which may cooperate with each other through limited membership organizations (such as the European Union).

itself and determines its own future – an idea at the very heart of the democratic polity – is today, accordingly, problematic. Any simple assumption in democratic theory that political relations are now or could be 'symmetrical' or 'congruent' is open to question.

The examples offered above of the regional and global interconnectedness of political decisions and outcomes raise issues which go to the heart of the categories of classic and contemporary democratic thought. The idea that consent legitimates government and the state system more generally has been central to nineteenth- and twentieth-century liberal democrats. These democrats have focused on the ballot box as the mechanism whereby the individual citizen expresses political preferences and whereby the citizen body as a whole periodically confers authority on government to enact the law and regulate economic and social life. But the very idea of consent through elections, and the particular notion that the relevant constituencies of voluntary agreement and debate are the communities of a bounded territory or a state, become open to question as soon as the matter of national, regional and global interconnectedness is considered and the nature of a so-called 'relevant community' is contested.

Whose agreement is necessary and whose participation is justified in decisions concerning, for example, the use of non-renewable resources, or the disposal of nuclear waste, or the management of financial flows, or the rules of trade, or AIDS? What is the relevant constituency: national, regional or international? To whom do decision-makers have to justify their decisions? To whom should they be accountable? Further, what are the implications for the idea of legitimate rule of decisions taken in polities, with potentially life-and-death consequences for large numbers of people, many of whom might have no democratic stake in the decision-making process?

Territorial boundaries specify the basis on which individuals are included and excluded from participation in decisions affecting their lives (however limited the participation might be), but the outcomes of these decisions, and of the decisions of those in other political communities and agencies, often stretch beyond national frontiers. The implications of this are troubling, not only for the categories of consent and legitimacy but for all the key ideas of democracy: the nature of a constituency, the meaning of representation, the proper form and scope of political participation, the extent of deliberation, and the relevance of the democratic nation-state as the guarantor of the rights, duties and welfare of subjects. The very process of governance seems to be 'escaping the categories' of the nation-state. Regional and global interconnectedness contests the traditional national resolutions of the central questions of democratic theory and practice.

Regional and global flows: old and new

There is a striking paradox to note about the contemporary era: from Africa to Eastern Europe, Asia to Latin America, more and more people are championing the idea of 'rule by the people'; but they are doing so at just that moment when the very efficacy of democracy as a national form of political organization appears open to question. As substantial areas of human activity are progressively organized on a regional or global level, the fate of democracy, and of the independent democratic nation-state in particular, is fraught with difficulty.

It could be objected that there is nothing particularly new about regional or global interconnections, and that the significance of such interconnections for politics has, in principle, been plain for people to see for a long time. Such an objection could be elaborated by emphasizing that a dense pattern of global interconnections began to emerge with the initial expansion of the world economy and the rise of the modern state from the late sixteenth century (see ch. 3). Further, it could be suggested that domestic and international politics have been interwoven throughout the modern era: domestic politics has always to be understood against the background of international politics, and the former is often the source of the latter (see Gourevitch, 1978). However, it is one thing to claim that there are elements of continuity in the formation and structure of modern states, economies and societies, and quite another to claim that there is nothing new about aspects of their form and dynamics. For there is a fundamental difference between, on the one hand, select military and naval operations which have an impact on certain towns, rural centres and territories, or the development of particular trade routes connecting a number of geographically dispersed cities, and, on the other hand, an international order involving the emergence of a global economic system which stretches beyond the control of any single state (even of leading states); the expansion of networks of transnational relations and communications over which particular states have limited influence; the enormous growth in international organizations and regimes which can limit the scope for action of the most powerful states; and the development of a global military order, with the build-up of global security challenges (terrorism and 'war on terrorism' in the current period), which can alter the range of policies available to governments and their citizens. While trade routes and military expeditions can link distant populations together in long loops of cause and effect, contemporary developments in the global order link peoples through multiple networks of transaction and coordination, reordering the very notion of distance itself. Politics unfolds today, with all its customary uncertainty and indeterminateness, against the background of a world shaped and permeated by the movement of goods and capital, the flow of communication, the interchange of cultures and the passage of people (Kegley and Wittkopf, 1989, p. 511) – in short, against the backdrop of processes of 'globalization'.

What is globalization? Globalization denotes a shift in the spatial form of human organization and activity to transcontinental or interregional patterns of activity, interaction and the exercise of power. It involves a stretching and deepening of social relations and institutions across space and time such that, on the one hand, day-to-day activities are increasingly influenced by events happening on the other side of the globe and, on the other, the practices and decisions of local groups or communities can have significant global reverberations (cf. Giddens, 1990, p. 64).

Globalization today implies at least two distinct phenomena. First, it suggests that many chains of political, economic and social activity are becoming worldwide in scope and, second, it suggests that there has been an intensification of levels of interaction and interconnectedness within and between states and societies. What is new about the modern global system is the stretching of social relations in and through new dimensions of activity – technological, organizational, administrative and legal, among others – and the chronic intensification of patterns of interconnectedness mediated by such phenomena as modern communication networks and new information technology. It is possible to distinguish different historical forms of globalization in terms of the extensivity of networks of relationships and connections; the intensity of flows and levels of enmeshment; and the impact of these phenomena on particular communities (see Held et al., 1999).

Globalization is neither a singular condition nor a linear process. Rather, it is best thought of as a multi-dimensional phenomenon involving diverse domains of activity and interaction including the economic, political, technological, military, legal, cultural and environmental. Each of these spheres involves different patterns of relationships and activity – each with its distinctive forms of logic and implications for other domains. A general account of globalization cannot simply predict from one domain what will occur in another. In addition, nation-states, democratic or otherwise, are themselves variably enmeshed in regional and global flows. The significance of globalization differs for individuals, groups and countries depending on, for instance, a nation-state's location in the international division of labour, its place in particular power blocs, its position with respect to the international legal system and its relation to major international organizations. Not all states, for example, are equally integrated into the world economy; thus, while national political outcomes will be heavily influenced by global processes in some countries, in others regional or national forces might well remain supreme.

It needs to be emphasized, furthermore, that processes of globalization do not necessarily lead to growing global integration; that is, to a world order marked by the progressive development of a homogeneous or unified society and politics. For globalization can generate forces of both fragmentation and unification. Fragmentation or disintegrative trends are possible for several reasons. The growth of dense patterns of interconnectedness among states and societies can increase the range of developments affecting people in particular locations. By creating new patterns of transformation and change, globalization can weaken old political and economic structures without necessarily leading to the establishment of new systems of regulation. In order to put flesh on an account of the impact of globalization on democracy and of the democratic nation-state on globalization, it is necessary to turn from a general concern with its conceptualization to an examination of the distinctive domains and processes of activity and interaction.

Sovereignty, autonomy and disjunctures

While the nation-state manifests continuing vitality, this does not mean that the sovereign structure of individual democratic nation-states remains unaffected by the intersection of national, international and transnational forces and relations: rather, it signals, in all probability, shifting patterns of powers and constraints. The precise scope and nature of the sovereign authority of democratic nation-states can be mapped by looking at a number of 'disjunctures' between, on the one hand, the formal domain of political authority they claim for themselves and, on the other, the actual practices and structures of the state and economic system at the regional and global levels (see Held, 1995, part I). At the latter levels, there are disjunctures between the idea of the democratic state as in principle capable of determining its own future, and the world economy, international organizations, regional and global institutions, international law and military alliances which operate to shape and constrain the options of individual nation-states. In the discussion that follows the focus will be on these 'external' disjunctures. But their enumeration, it should be stressed, is simply illustrative – it is neither complete nor systematic. It is intended simply to indicate questions about the extent to which globalization in a number of key domains can be said to constitute constraints or limits on political agency, and about the extent to which the possibility of a democratic polity has been transformed. Once these matters are addressed, their implications can be pursued for the nature and prospects of democracy, within and beyond borders.

When assessing the impact of disjunctures, it is important to consider that sovereignty is eroded only when it is displaced by forms of 'higher' and/or independent authority which curtail the rightful basis of decision-making within a national framework. For sovereignty demarcates the political authority within a community which has the right to determine the framework of rules, regulations and policies within a given territory and to govern accordingly (see ch. 3 above; and Held, 1995, for a fuller account). However, in thinking about the impact of globalization upon the nation-state, one needs to distinguish sovereignty – the entitlement to rule over a bounded territory – from state autonomy – the actual power the nation-state possesses to articulate and achieve policy goals independently.[2] In effect, state autonomy refers to the ability of nation-states to act free of international and transnational constraints, and to achieve goals once they have been set. Bearing these distinctions in mind, it can be shown that external disjunctures map a series of processes which alter the range and nature of the decisions open to democratic decision-makers within a delimited terrain. The central question to pose is: has sovereignty remained intact while the autonomy of the state has altered, or has the modern state actually faced a loss of sovereignty? In addressing this question, I shall draw most of my examples from the processes and relations which impinge most directly on the states of Europe.[3] It is the fate of these states which will be uppermost, although the discussion will be broadened out to include other regions.

[2] The concept of 'state autonomy' should not be confused with the principle of autonomy defined earlier. Broadly, the former refers to the capacity of the state to fulfil policy objectives, while the latter is focused on the extent to which the proper form and direction of these policies are shaped by citizen deliberation and involvement, i.e. it is a principle of political legitimacy. Sovereignty is the intervening or mediating link between these two notions; for sovereignty specifies the rightful basis for acting on behalf of the political community and for representing it in a manner which is authoritative and accountable.

[3] For a detailed and carefully measured account of regional and global trends affecting these states, see Held et al. (1999). I am indebted to this volume, and to the guidance of McGrew, Goldblatt and Perraton, for many of the examples below, especially the trend data on trade, finance and multinational corporations, and on cultural developments and the environment.

Disjuncture 1: the world economy

There is a disjuncture between the formal authority of the state and the actual system of production, distribution and exchange which in many ways serves to limit the power or scope of national political authorities (R. O. Keohane and Nye, 1989; Frieden, 1991; Held et al., 1999, chs 3–5).

1   Two elements of global economic processes are central: the globalization of production and the globalization of financial transactions, organized in part by fast growing multinational companies. Multinational corporations (MNCs) plan and execute their production, marketing and distribution with the world economy firmly in mind. Even when MNCs have a clear national base, their interest is above all in global profitability. Financial organizations such as banks are also progressively more global in scale and orientation; they are able to monitor and respond to developments, be they in London, Tokyo or New York, almost instantaneously. New information technology has radically increased the mobility of economic units – currencies, stocks, shares, 'futures' and so on – for financial and commercial organizations of all kinds.

2   Trade has grown substantially in the postwar period, reaching unprecedented levels. Not only has there been an increase in intraregional trade around the world, but there has also been sustained growth among regions as well. More countries are involved in rapidly expanding trading arrangements, for instance, India and China, and more people and nations are affected by such arrangements. If there is a further lowering of tariff barriers across the world, these trends are likely to continue. The expansion of global financial flows has, moreover, been staggering in the last twenty-five years. Foreign exchange turnover is now over a trillion dollars a day.[4] Much of this financial activity is speculative and generates fluctuations in values (in stocks, shares, etc.) in excess of those which can be accounted for by changes in the fundamentals underlying asset values. Furthermore, MNCs now account for more than a quarter of world production, 80 per cent of world industrial output and a third of world trade (McGrew, 2005). They are essential to the diffusion of technology, and are key players in international money markets.[5] In addition, MNCs have profound effects on macroeconomic policy; they can respond to variations in interest rates by raising finance in whichever capital market is most favourable. They can shift their demand for employment to countries with much lower employment costs (outsourcing). And in the area of industrial policy, especially technological policy, they can move their activities to where the maximum benefits accrue.

3   There is considerable evidence to support the claim that technological advances in communication and transportation are eroding the boundaries between hitherto separate markets – boundaries which were a necessary

[4] The proportion of foreign exchange turnover to trade has mushroomed from eleven dollars to one to nearly sixty dollars to one in the last twenty to twenty-five years; that is, for every sixty dollars turned over in the foreign exchange markets, one dollar is turned over in real trade (Held and McGrew, 2002, p. 48).

[5] Although evidence suggests that many of the largest MNCs still generate most of their sales and profits domestically, this is largely due to the influence of US companies, which have a large domestic market. The proportion of sales and profits generated domestically are much lower for non-US companies and, significantly, for higher-tech companies.

condition for independent national economic policies (R. O. Keohane and Nye, 1972, pp. 392–5). Markets, and societies, are becoming more sensitive to one another even when their distinctive identities are preserved: the East Asian crash of the late 1990s is one obvious example of this. The very possibility of a national economic policy is, accordingly, problematic. The costs and benefits of deploying whole ranges of economic policies have altered. For instance, although there are many reasons why national Keynesianism may no longer work today, one fundamental reason is that it is much harder for individual governments to intervene and manage their economies when faced with a global division of labour and monetary system (cf. Gilpin, 1987; Cox, 1987; Kolko, 1988). Keynesianism functioned well in the context of the system of 'embedded liberalism' which existed in the years following World War II; it was the operating framework of both international and national economic agreements across the Western world (see R. O. Keohane, 1984b). But with the breakdown of the postwar 'liberal consensus' in the wake of the 1973 oil crisis, among other events, the possibility of managing an economy and 'bucking' international economic trends became more difficult. Moreover, it has become increasingly costly for individual countries to pursue independent monetary policies and independent exchange rate strategies, given current levels of international turnover in currencies and bonds.

    4   The loss of control of national economic programmes is, of course, not uniform across economic sectors or societies more generally: some markets and some countries can isolate themselves from transnational economic networks by such measures as attempts to restore the boundaries or 'separateness' of markets and/or to extend national laws to cover internationally mobile factors and/or to adopt cooperative policies with other countries for the coordination of policy (Cooper, 1986, pp. 1–22; Gilpin, 1987, pp. 397ff). In addition, the regionalization of sections of the world economy, with economic activity clustering around a number of poles (among them the European market, the United States and the Asia–Pacific region), provides scope for some regulation of market trends. The particular tensions between political and economic structures are likely to be different in different spheres, and between them: West–West, North–South, East–West. It cannot, therefore, simply be said that the very idea of a national economy is superseded. However, the globalization of production, finance and other economic resources is unquestionably challenging the capacity of an individual state (whether democratic or not) to control its own economic future. At the very least, there appears to be a shift in the costs and benefits of the policy choices before governments, thereby affecting their autonomy; and a disjuncture between the idea of a sovereign state determining its own future and the circumstances of modern economies, marked as they are by the intersection of national, regional and global economic forces.

Disjuncture 2: international political decision-making

A second significant area of disjuncture between the theory of the sovereign state and the contemporary global system lies at the intersection of a vast array of international regimes and organizations that have been established to manage whole areas of transnational activity (trade, transportation, the use of the oceans and so on) and collective policy problems. The growth in the number of these new forms of political organization reflects the rapid expansion of transnational links, the growing interpenetration of foreign and domestic policy, and the corresponding desire by most states for some form of international governance and regulation to deal with collective policy problems (see Luard, 1977; Krasner, 1983; Held and McGrew, 2002, chs 2–7).

1   The formation of international and transnational organizations has led to important changes in the decision-making structure of world politics. New forms of multilateral and multinational politics have been established and with them distinctive styles of collective decision-making involving governments, international governmental organizations (IGOs) and a wide variety of transnational pressure groups and international non-governmental organizations (INGOs). In 1909 there were 37 IGOs and 176 INGOs, while in 1996 there were 4,667 active IGOs and 25,260 INGOs (UIA, 2002). In the middle of the nineteenth century there were two or three conferences or congresses per annum sponsored by IGOs; today the number is over 9,000 annually (see UIA, 2002). Against this background, the range and diversity of the participants at the Earth Summit in Rio de Janeiro in June 1992, or at the Women's Conference in Beijing in August 1995, or the people who participated in the 2005 Make Poverty History campaign, may not seem quite as remarkable as the events initially suggested.

2   Among the extensive range of international agencies and organizations are those whose primary concerns have been technical: the Universal Postal Union, the International Telecommunications Union, the World Meteorological Organization and a host of other bodies. These agencies have tended to work effectively and uncontroversially – providing, in most cases, extensions to the services offered by individual nation-states (Burnheim, 1986, p. 222). To the extent that their tasks have been sharply delimited, they have been politically unexceptionable. At the opposite pole lie organizations like the World Bank, the IMF, the WTO, the United Nations Educational, Scientific and Cultural Organization (UNESCO) and the United Nations (UN). Preoccupied with more central questions of the management and allocation of rules and resources, these bodies have been highly controversial and politicized. Unlike the smaller, technically based agencies, these organizations are at the centre of continual conflict over the control of policy (Burnheim, 1986, pp. 220ff). While the mode of operation of these agencies tends to vary, they have all benefited over the years from a certain 'entrenchment of authority' which has bestowed on some decisive powers of intervention. The operations of the IMF provide an interesting case. In pursuing a particular line of economic policy, the IMF has often insisted as a condition of its loan to a government that the latter cut public expenditure, devalue its currency and cut back on subsidized welfare programmes. It has to be borne in mind that IMF intervention takes place routinely at the request of governmental authorities or particular political factions within a state, and is often the result of the recognition that there is minimal scope for independent national policies; it cannot straightforwardly be

interpreted, therefore, as a threat to sovereignty. None the less, a striking tension has emerged between the idea of the sovereign state – centred on national politics and political institutions – and the nature of decision-making at the international level. The latter raises serious questions about the conditions under which a community is able to determine its own policies and directions, given the constraints of the international economic order and the operating rules of agencies like the IMF, the World Bank and the WTO.

3   The European Union provides an important additional illustration of the issues posed by international organizations. Although elements of its structure are in question at the time of writing, the impact and efficacy of the EU reaches further than that of any other kind of international organization by virtue of its right to make laws which can be imposed on member states; more than any other international agency, it justifies the label 'quasi-supranational'. Within EU institutions, the Council of Ministers has a unique position, for it has at its disposal powerful legal instruments (above all, 'regulations', 'directions' and 'decisions') which allow it to make and enact policy. Of all these instruments 'regulations' are the most notable, because they have the status of law independently of any further negotiation or action on the part of member states. Accordingly, the member states of the EU are no longer the sole centres of power within their own borders (see Hoffman, 1982; Wallace, 1994). On the other hand, it is important to bear in mind that the EU's powers were gained by the 'willing surrender' of aspects of sovereignty by member states – a 'surrender' that, arguably, has actually helped the survival of the European nation-state given the dominance of the US in the first three decades after World War II and the generation of intense economic competition with many countries in Pacific Asia. In short, like many other international organizations, the EU provides both opportunities and constraints. Its states retain the final and most general power in many areas of their domestic and foreign affairs; and the EU itself seems to have strengthened their options in some of these domains. However, within the EU sovereignty is now also clearly divided: any conception of sovereignty which assumes that it is an indivisible, illimitable, exclusive and perpetual form of public power – embodied within an individual state – is defunct.[6]

4   All these developments have engendered a shift away from a purely state-centred international system of 'high politics' to new and novel forms of geo-governance. Perhaps one of the most interesting examples of this can be drawn from the very heart of the idea of a sovereign state – national security and defence policy. There has been a noticeable increase in emphasis among many states upon collective defence and cooperative security. The enormous costs, technological requirements and domestic burdens of defence are contributing to the strengthening of multilateral and collective defence arrangements as well as international military cooperation and coordination. The rising density of technological connections between states now challenges the very idea of national security and national arms procurement. Some of the most advanced

[6] It is important to bear in mind that this structure remains intact after the 'no' votes in France and Holland in 2005 concerning whether to adopt a new European constitution, which was proposed in the hope of streamlining EU decision-making.

weapon systems in the world, e.g. fighter aircraft, depend on components which come from many countries.[7] There has been a globalization of military technology linked to a transnationalization of defence production. And the proliferation of weapons of mass destruction makes all states insecure and problematizes the very notion of 'friends' and 'enemies'.

None of this is to deny, of course, the resurgence of American power since 9/11, its attempt to put together a 'coalition of the willing' (more successful in Afghanistan than Iraq), and the pursuit under George W. Bush of unilateral strategies. The US (along with China) can resist the collective security trends discussed above, and is clearly able to mount massive military interventions. It can fight wars across the world, alone if necessary. Yet it cannot easily win the peace; and unilateralism proves a weak basis for winning the hearts and minds of people. Without widespread cooperation with other states and without the widespread cooperation of the peoples of Afghanistan and Iraq, conventional military power is vulnerable to defeat (see Held and Koenig-Archibugi, 2004, for a debate about this point). Today, much of Afghanistan is once again in the hands of warlords and drug barons, and Iraq is embroiled in a violent insurgency. Great powers can be humbled under these conditions, forcing them back to seeking cooperative and collaborative solutions. It appears that in a democratic and global age, acting alone may, when dealing with international and transnational questions, be the grounds for generating neither legitimacy nor success.

Disjuncture 3: international law

The development of international law has subjected individuals, governments and non-governmental organizations to new systems of legal regulation. International law has recognized powers and constraints, and rights and duties, which transcend the claims of nation-states and which, while they may not be backed by institutions with coercive powers of enforcement, none the less have far-reaching consequences.

1 There are two legal rules which, since the very beginnings of the international community, have been taken to uphold national sovereignty: 'immunity from jurisdiction' and 'immunity of state agencies'. The former prescribes that 'no state can be sued in courts of another state for acts performed in its sovereign capacity'; and the latter stipulates that 'should an individual break the law of another state while acting as an agent for his country of origin and be brought before that state's courts, he is not held "guilty" because he did not act as a private individual but as the representative of the state' (Cassese, 1988, pp. 150–1). The underlying purpose of these rules is to protect a government's autonomy in all matters of foreign policy and to prevent domestic courts from ruling on the behaviour of foreign states (on the understanding that all domestic courts everywhere will be so prevented). And the upshot has traditionally been that governments have been left free to pursue their interests subject only to the constraints of the 'art of politics'. It is

---

[7] I am indebted to Anthony McGrew for many interesting discussions on this point.

notable, however, that these internationally recognized legal mainstays of sovereignty have been progressively questioned by Western courts. And while it is the case that national sovereignty has most often been the victor when put to the test, the tension between national sovereignty and international law is now marked, and it is by no means clear how it will be resolved in the long term.

2 Of all the international declarations of rights which were made in the post-war years, the European Convention for the Protection of Human Rights and Fundamental Freedoms (1950) is especially noteworthy. In marked contrast to the UN's Universal Declaration of Human Rights (1948) and subsequent UN conventions of rights, the European initiative was concerned, as its preamble indicates, 'to take the first steps for the *collective enforcement* of certain of the Rights of the UN Declaration' (emphasis added). The European initiative was committed to a most remarkable and radical legal innovation: an innovation which in principle would allow individual citizens to initiate proceedings against their own governments. European countries have now accepted an (optional) clause of the Convention which permits citizens to petition directly the European Commission on Human Rights, which can take cases to the Committee of Ministers of the Council of Europe and then (given a two-thirds majority on the Council) to the European Court of Human Rights. While the system is far from straightforward and is problematic in many respects, it has been claimed that, alongside legal changes introduced by the EU, it no longer leaves the state 'free to treat its own citizens as it thinks fit' (Caportorti, 1983, p. 977).

3 The gap between the idea of membership of a national community, i.e. citizenship, which traditionally bestows upon individuals both rights and duties, and the creation in international law of new forms of liberties and obligations is exemplified further by the results of the International Tribunal at Nuremberg. The Tribunal laid down, for the first time in history, that when *international rules* that protect basic humanitarian values are in conflict with *state laws*, every individual must transgress the state laws (except where there is no room for 'moral choice') (Cassese, 1988, p. 132). The legal framework of the Nuremberg Tribunal marked a highly significant change in the legal direction of the modern state, for the new rules challenged the principle of military discipline and subverted national sovereignty at one of its most sensitive points: the hierarchical relations within the military.

4 International law is a 'vast and changing corpus of rules and quasi-rules' which sets out the basis of coexistence and cooperation in the international order. Traditionally, international law has identified and upheld the idea of a society of sovereign states as 'the supreme normative principle' of the political organization of humankind (Bull, 1977, pp. 140ff). In recent decades, the subject, scope and source of international law have all been contested; and opinion has shifted against the doctrine that international law is and should be a 'law between states only and exclusively' (see Oppenheim, 1905, ch. 1). At the heart of this shift lies a conflict between claims made on behalf of the states system and those made on behalf of an alternative organizing principle of world order: ultimately, a transnational or cosmopolitan community (see Held, 2004, part

III). This conflict is, however, far from settled, and the renewed intensity of many fundamentalist and nationalist conflicts, the resurgence of the US's pursuit of its geopolitical interests under the administrations of George W. Bush, and the weakening of the EU project in the face of the derailment of its proposed constitution in 2005 indicate that claims mobilized on behalf of a new principle of world order can, at the very least, seem hastily made.

Disjuncture 4: culture and the environment

There is a further disjuncture involving the idea of the state as an autonomous centre of culture, able to foster and sustain a national identity, with a secure environment for its people, and interlinked changes in the spheres of media and environmental forces.

1   Evidence of globalization in the realms of media and culture is complex and uncertain. A great deal of research remains to be carried out (see J. B. Thompson, 1995, ch. 5). None the less, a number of remarkable developments in recent times can be pointed to. English has spread as the dominant language of elite cultures throughout the world: it is now the dominant language in business, computing, law, science and politics. The internationalization and globalization of telecommunications have been extraordinarily rapid: international telephone traffic has increased over fivefold since the early 1980s; there has been a massive increase in transnational cable links; there has been an explosion in satellite links; and the internet has provided a remarkable increase in the infrastructure of horizontal and lateral communication capacity within and across borders. Moreover, substantial multinational media conglomerates have developed, such as the Murdoch empire, Sony and Bertelsmann. In addition, there has been a huge increase in tourism. For example, in 1960 there were 70 million international tourists, while by the mid-1990s there were over 500 million. And in television and film there are similar trends: 60–90 per cent of box office receipts in Europe come from foreign films (although, it has to be said, this is largely the story of American dominance).

2   None of the above examples, or the accumulated impact of parallel cases, should be taken to imply the development of a single global, media-led culture – far from it. But certainly, taken together, these developments do imply that many new forms of communication and media range in and across borders, linking nations and peoples in new ways. Accordingly, the capacity of national political leaders to sustain a national culture has become more difficult. For example, China sought to restrict access to and use of the internet, but it has found this virtually impossible to do.

3   Environmental problems and challenges are, however, the clearest and starkest examples of the global shift in human organization and activity, creating some of the most fundamental pressures on the efficacy of the nation-state and state-centric democratic politics. There are three types of problem at issue:

(a)   The first is shared problems involving the global commons, i.e. fundamental elements of the ecosystem. The clearest examples of the environmental commons are the atmosphere, the climate system and the oceans and seas;

and among the most fundamental challenges here are global warming, ozone depletion and the general pollution of the global commons.

(b) A second category of global environmental problems involves the interlinked challenges of demographic expansion and resource consumption. Examples of great importance under this category include questions of bio-diversity and challenges to the very existence of certain species.

(c) A third category of problems is transboundary pollution such as acid rain or river pollutants. More dramatic examples arise from the siting and operation of nuclear power plants, for instance that at Chernobyl.

4 In response to the progressive development of, and publicity surrounding, environmental problems, there has been an interlinked process of cultural and political globalization as illustrated by the emergence of new cultural, scientific and intellectual networks; new environmental movements with transnational organizations and transnational concerns; and new institutions and conventions like those agreed in 1992 at the Earth Summit in Brazil. Not all environmental problems are, of course, global. Such an implication would be quite false. But there has been a striking physical and environmental shift in the circumstances – that is, in the extent and intensity of environmental problems – affecting human affairs in general.

In sum: democracy and the global system

The global order, and with it the role of the nation-state, is changing. While a complex pattern of global interconnections has been evident for a long time, there is little doubt that there has recently been a further 'internationalization' of domestic activities and an intensification of decision-making in international frameworks (Kaiser, 1972, p. 370). The evidence that international and transnational relations have altered the powers of the modern sovereign state is certainly strong. Global processes have moved politics a long way from activity which simply crystallizes first and foremost around state and interstate concerns.

The 'disjunctures' identified above reveal a set of forces which combine to restrict the freedom of action of governments and states by blurring the boundaries of domestic politics, transforming the conditions of political decision-making, changing the institutional and organizational context of national polities, altering the legal framework and administrative practices of governments and obscuring the lines of responsibility and accountability of national states themselves. These processes alone warrant the statement that the operation of states in an ever more complex global system both alters their autonomy (by changing the balance between the costs and benefits of policies) and impinges increasingly upon their sovereignty. Any conception of sovereignty which interprets it as an illimitable and indivisible form of public power is undermined. Sovereignty itself has to be conceived today as already divided among a number of agencies – national, regional and international – and limited by the very nature of this plurality.

The modern theory of the sovereign democratic state, liberal and radical, presupposes the idea of a community which rightly governs itself and determines its own future. This idea is challenged fundamentally by the nature of the pattern of global interconnections and the issues that have to be confronted by a modern state. National communities by no means exclusively 'programme' the actions, decisions and policies of their governments and the latter by no means simply determine what is right or appropriate for their own citizens alone (Offe, 1985, pp. 283–4). The meaning of democracy, and of the model of democratic autonomy in particular, has to be rethought in relation to a series of overlapping local, regional and global structures and processes. While it is a mistake to conclude from the seeming flux of contemporary interaction networks that political communities today are without distinctive degrees of division or cleavage at their 'borders', they have been shaped by multiple interaction networks and power systems over time. Accordingly, questions are raised both about the fate of the idea of the political community and about the appropriate locus for the articulation of the democratic political good. If the agent at the heart of modern political discourse, be it a person, a group or a collectivity, is locked into a variety of overlapping forces, developments and communities – domestic, international and transnational – then the proper 'home' of politics, and of the model of democratic autonomy especially, becomes a puzzling matter.

Rethinking democracy for a more global age: the cosmopolitan model

We live today at a fundamental point of transition. On the one hand, there are clear tendencies which are combining to weaken democracy and accountability within and beyond the nation-state. A clear scenario exists suggesting the progressive concentration of power in the hands of multinational capital (productive and financial), and the weakening role of states faced with global market processes and forces. In this context, the risk is that democratic politics will increasingly be reduced to adapting to global markets – second-guessing their tendencies and accommodating to them. At the same time, the susceptibility of the UN to the agendas of the most powerful states, the weaknesses of many of its enforcement operations (or lack of them altogether), the underfunding of its organizations, the continued dependency of its programmes on the financial support of a few countries, the inadequacies of the policing of many environmental regimes (regional and global) – all these are indicative of the very limited efficacy and reach of democracy at the global level. The multilateral system is shaped disproportionately by the agendas of leading states, a tendency which could accelerate further in the years to come (see Held 2004; Held and Koenig-Archibugi, 2004). This scenario suggests that global politics will be shaped increasingly by global economic priorities and 'club-driven' or executive-led (G1, G7, G8)[8] multilateralism.

---

[8] The G1 refers to the United States; the G7 (Group of Seven) to the US, Canada, Britain, France, Germany, Italy and Japan; and the G8 to the G7 plus Russia.

On the other hand, political alternatives to this state of affairs might be developed by deepening and extending democracy across nations, regions and global networks. Such a process can be referred to as the entrenchment of democratic autonomy on a cosmopolitan basis – or 'cosmopolitan democracy' for short. This would involve the development of administrative capacity and independent political resources at regional and global levels as a necessary complement to those in local and national polities. At issue would be strengthening the administrative capacity and accountability of regional institutions like the EU, along with developing the administrative capacity and forms of accountability of the UN system itself. A cosmopolitan democracy would not call for a diminution *per se* of state capacity across the globe. Rather, it would seek to entrench and develop democratic institutions at regional and global levels as a necessary complement to those at the level of the nation-state. This conception of democracy is based upon the recognition of the continuing significance of nation-states, while arguing for a layer of governance to constitute a limitation on national sovereignty.

The case for cosmopolitan democracy is the case for the creation of new political institutions which would coexist with the system of states but which would override states in clearly defined spheres of activity where those activities have demonstrable transnational and international consequences (see Held, 1995, ch. 10, for an elaboration of this argument). At issue, in addition, is not merely the formal construction of new democratic institutions, but also the construction, in principle, of broad avenues of civic participation in and deliberation over decision-making at regional and global levels. How should this conception of democracy be understood? Addressing this question requires recalling earlier arguments about the need to conceive democracy as a double-sided process, while reappraising the proper domain for the application of this process (see pp. 275–82 above). For if the arguments in this chapter are correct, democracy has to become not just a national but a transnational affair if it is to be possible both within a restricted geographic territory and within the wider international community. The possibility of democracy today must, in short, be linked to an expanding framework of democratic institutions and agencies.

Two distinct requirements arise: first, that the territorial boundaries of systems of accountability be restructured so that those issues which escape the control of a nation-state – aspects of monetary management, the rules of the global trading system, environmental questions, elements of security, new forms of communication – can be brought under better democratic control; and, second, that the role and place of regional and global regulatory and functional agencies be rethought so that they may provide a more coherent and effective focal point in public affairs. The basis for meeting these requirements can be elaborated by focusing on some of the institutional components of the cosmopolitan model.

A cosmopolitan polity would need to establish an overarching network of democratic public fora, covering cities, nation-states, regions and the wider transnational order. It would need to create an effective and accountable political, administrative and regulative capacity at global and regional levels to complement those at national and local levels. This would require:

- The formation of an authoritative assembly of all states and agencies – a reformed General Assembly of the United Nations, or a complement to it. The focus of a global assembly would be the examination of those pressing problems which are at the heart of concerns about life expectancy and life chances – concerns, for instance, about health and disease, food supply and distribution, the debt burden of the developing world, global warming and the reduction of the risks of nuclear, chemical and biological warfare. Its task would be to lay down, in framework-setting law, the standards and institutions required to embed the rule of law, democratic principles, and the minimum conditions for human agency to flourish.[9]

- The creation where feasible of regional parliaments and governance structures (for example, in Latin America and Africa) and the enhancement of the role of such bodies where they already exist (the European Union) in order that their decisions become recognized and accepted as legitimate independent sources of regional and international regulation.

- The opening up of functional international governmental organizations (such as the WTO, IMF and World Bank) to public examination and agenda setting. Not only should such bodies be transparent in their activities, but they should be open to public scrutiny (on the basis perhaps of elected supervisory bodies, or functional deliberative fora, representative of the diverse interests in their constituencies), and accountable to regional and global assemblies.

- The establishment, where IGOs are currently weak and/or lacking in enforcement capability, of new mechanisms and organizations, e.g. in the areas of the environment and social affairs. The creation of new global governance structures with responsibility for addressing poverty, welfare and related issues is vital to offset the power and influence of market-oriented agencies such as the WTO and IMF.

---

[9] Agreement on the terms of reference of a global assembly would be difficult to say the least, although there is no shortage of plausible schemes and models. Ultimately, its terms of reference and operating rules would need to command widespread agreement and, hence, ought to be generated in a stakeholder process of consensus-building – a global constitutional convention – involving states, IGOs, INGOs, citizen groups and social movements. A global process of consultation and deliberation, organized at diverse levels, represents the best hope of creating a legitimate framework for accountable and sustainable global governance. Three core issues would need to be addressed: Who is to be represented, governments or citizens? What is to be the principle of representation, one state, one vote, proportional representation, or a mixture of both? What are the proper scope and limits of action of a global assembly? These are demanding questions which admit of a number of sound theoretical answers. The case for each would have to be considered and weighed in the context of the diversity of interests which would be brought to a global constitutional convention; for example, the inevitable differences that would emerge between the developed and developing countries on whether population size or economic strength or a mixture of both should count in the determination of the basis of representation. While the legitimacy and credibility of a new global assembly would depend on it being firmly grounded on the principle of consent and electoral inclusiveness, it is likely that any assembly in the foreseeable future would be constituted by compromises between theoretical ideas and practical constraints. Accordingly, rather than set out blueprints for the nature and form of a global assembly, it seems better to stress the importance of a legitimate process of consensus-building in and through which these issues might be deliberated upon and settled (see Held, 2004).

- The enhancement of the transparency and accountability of the organizations of national and transnational civil society, addressing the potentially disturbing effects of those who are able to 'shout the loudest' and of the lack of clarity about the terms of engagement of non-state actors with IGOs and other leading political bodies (Edwards and Zadek, 2003). Experiments are necessary to find ways of improving the internal codes of conduct and modes of operation of non-state actors, on the one hand, and of advancing their capacity to be represented in IGOs and other leading political bodies preoccupied with global policy processes, on the other. Moreover, to avoid citizens of developed countries being unfairly represented twice in global politics (once through their governments and once through their NGOs) special attention and support needs to be given to enhance the role of NGOs from developing countries.
- The use of general referenda cutting across nations and nation-states at regional or global levels in the case of contested priorities concerning the implementation of core cosmopolitan concerns. These could involve many different kinds of referenda, including of a cross-section of the public, and/or of targeted and significantly affected groups in a particular policy area, and/or of the policy-makers and legislators of national parliaments.
- The development of law enforcement and coercive capability, including peace keeping and peace-making, to help deal with serious regional and global security threats. It is necessary to meet the concern that, in the face of pressing and violent challenges to fundamental human rights and democratic priorities, 'covenants, without the sword, are but words' (Hobbes).

Hand in hand with these changes, the cosmopolitan model of democracy assumes the entrenchment of a cluster of rights and obligations, including civil, political, economic and social rights and obligations, in order to provide shape and limits to democratic decision-making (see ch. 10). This requires that they be enshrined within the constitutions of parliaments and assemblies (at the national, regional and global levels); and that the influence of international courts be extended so that groups and individuals have an effective means of suing political authorities for the enactment and enforcement of key rights, both within and beyond political associations.

If the history and practice of democracy have until now been centred on the idea of locality and place (the city-republic, the community, the nation), is it likely that in the future democracy will be centred exclusively on the international or global domain, if it is to be centred anywhere at all? To draw this conclusion is, I think, to misunderstand the nature of contemporary globalization and the argument being developed here. Globalization is, to borrow a phrase, 'a dialectical process': 'local transformation is as much a part of globalization as the lateral extension of social connections across time and space' (Giddens, 1990, p. 64). New demands are made for regional and local autonomy as groups find themselves buffeted by global forces and by inappropriate or ineffective political regimes. Although these circumstances are clearly fraught with danger, and the risk of an intensification of sectarian politics, they also portend a new possibility: the recovery of an intensive,

In sum: model Xb

Cosmopolitan Democracy

Principle(s) of justification
In a world of intensifying regional and global relations, with marked overlapping 'communities of fate', the principle of autonomy requires entrenchment in regional and global networks as well as in national and local polities

Key features

Short-term	*Long-term*
Polity/governance	
Reform of leading UN governing institutions such as the Security Council (to give developing countries a significant voice and effective decision-making capacity)	New charter of rights and obligations locked into different domains of political, social and economic power
Creation of a UN second chamber (following an international constitutional convention)	Global parliament (with limited revenue-raising capacity) connected to regions, nations and localities
Enhanced political regionalization (EU and beyond) and the use of transnational referenda	Separation of political and economic interests; public funding of deliberative assemblies and electoral processes
Creation of a new, international Human Rights Court; compulsory jurisdiction before the International Criminal Court	Interconnected global legal system, embracing elements of criminal and civil law
Establishment of an effective, accountable, international, military force	Permanent shift of a growing proportion of a nation-state's coercive capability to regional and global institutions
Economy/civil society	
Enhancement of non-state, non-market solutions in the organization of civil society	Creation of a diversity of self-regulating associations and groups in civil society
Experimentation with different democratic organizational forms in the economy	Multi-sectoral economy and pluralization of patterns of ownership and possession
Provision of resources to those in the most vulnerable social positions to defend and articulate their interests	Public framework investment priorities set through general deliberation and government decision, but extensive market regulation of goods and labour

General conditions

   Continuing development of regional, international and global flows of resources and networks of interaction

   Recognition by growing numbers of peoples of increasing interconnectedness of political communities in diverse domains, including the social, cultural, economic and environmental

   Development of an understanding of overlapping 'collective fortunes' which require democratic deliberation – locally, nationally, regionally and globally

   Enhanced entrenchment of democratic rights and obligations in the making and enforcement of national, regional and international law

   Transfer of increasing proportion of a nation's military coercive capability to transnational agencies and institutions with the ultimate aim of demilitarization and the transcendence of the states' war system

Note: The institutional requirements of cosmopolitan democracy, and the complexity of the major issues of reform, are only laid out here in a rudimentary manner. For further discussion see Archibugi and Held (1995), Held (1995), Held (2004).

participatory and deliberative democracy at local levels as a complement to the deliberative assemblies of the wider global order. That is, they portend a political order of democratic associations, cities and nations as well as of regions and global networks. In such an order, the principle of autonomy would be entrenched in diverse sites of power and across diverse spatial domains.

The key features of this conception of democracy are set out in model Xb. The model presents a programme of possible transformations with short- and long-term political implications. It does not present an all-or-nothing choice, but rather lays down a direction of possible change with clear points of orientation.

A utopian project?

In the last hundred years political power has been reshaped and reconfigured. It has been diffused below, above and alongside the nation-state. Political power is multilevel and multilayered. Globalization has brought large swathes of the world population 'closer together' in overlapping communities of fate. Life chances are affected by national, international and transnational processes. Democratic and human rights values are entrenched in important sectors of international law and new regional and global courts have been set up to examine some of the more heinous crimes humans can commit. Transnational movements, agencies and corporations have established the first stages of a global civil society. These, and related developments, create anchors for the development of cosmopolitan democracy. The latter does not have to start from scratch, but can develop from legal and institutional stepping stones laid down in the twentieth century.

There arc, obviously enough, many reasons for pessimism. Globalization has not just integrated peoples and nations, but created new forms of antagonism. The globalization of communications does not just make it easier to establish mutual understanding, but often highlights what it is that people do not have in common and how and why differences matter. The dominant political game in the 'transnational town' remains geopolitics. Ethnic self-centredness, religious fundamentalism, right-wing nationalism and unilateralist politics are once again on the rise, and not just in the West. Yet the circumstances and nature of politics have changed. Like national culture and traditions, cosmopolitan democracy is a cultural and political project, but with one difference: it is better adapted and suited to our regional and global age. However, the arguments in support of this have yet to be articulated in the public sphere in many parts of the world; and we fail here at our peril.

It is important to add a reflection on 9/11 and to say what it means in this context. One cannot accept the burden of putting accountability and justice right in one realm of life – physical security and political cooperation among defence establishments – without at the same time seeking to put it right elsewhere. If the political and the security, the social and the economic dimensions of accountability and justice are separated in the long term – as is the tendency in the global order today – the prospects of a peaceful and civil society will be bleak indeed. Popular support against terrorism, as well as against political violence and exclusionary politics of all kinds, depends upon convincing people that there is a legal, responsive and specific way of addressing their grievances. Without this sense of confidence in public institutions the defeat of terrorism and intolerance becomes a hugely difficult task, if it can be achieved at all.

Against the background of 9/11, the current unilateralist stance of the US and the desperate cycle of violence in the Middle East and elsewhere, the advocacy of cosmopolitan democracy may appear like an attempt to defy gravity or walk on water! And, indeed, if it was a case of having to adopt cosmopolitan principles and institutions all at once or not at all, this would be true. But it is no more the case than was the pursuit of the modern state at the time of Hobbes. Over the last several decades the growth of multilateralism and the development of international law have created cosmopolitan anchors to the world. These are the bases for the further consolidation of the hold of cosmopolitan principles and institutions. Moreover, a coalition of political groupings could emerge to push these achievements further, comprising European countries with strong commitments to the multilateral order and the human rights regime; liberal groups in the US polity which support multilateralism and the rule of law in international affairs; developing countries struggling for freer and fairer trade rules in the world economic order; non-governmental organizations from Amnesty International to Oxfam, campaigning for a more just, democratic and equitable world order; transnational social movements contesting the nature and form of contemporary globalization; and those economic forces that desire a more stable and managed global economic order (see Held and McGrew, 2002, chs 8 and 9).

Although the interests of these groupings would inevitably diverge on a wide range of issues, there is potentially an important overlapping sphere of concern among them for the strengthening of multilateralism, building new institutions for providing global public goods, regulating global markets, deepening accountability, protecting the environment and ameliorating urgently the social injustices that kill thousands of men, women and children daily. Of course, how far such forces can unite around these objectives – and can overcome fierce opposition from well-entrenched geopolitical and geoeconomic interests – remains to be seen. The stakes are high, but so too are the potential gains for human security and development if the aspirations for cosmopolitan governance can be slowly realized.

The explosion of interest in democracy in recent times has all too often conceived of democracy in terms of liberal democracy, assumed that democracy can only be applied to 'governmental affairs' (and has no place in economic and social spheres) and presupposed that the nation-state is the most appropriate locus for democracy. By questioning these terms of reference, Part Three of this volume has sought to help establish a new agenda for political thought and deliberation. Clearly, to set out a new agenda is not to resolve all the deep and protracted difficulties faced by democratic theory and practice. But it is hoped, at the least, that a case has been made for the deepening and extending of democracy within and between countries – a development which is essential if democracy is to retain its relevance, efficaciousness and legitimacy in the centuries ahead.

Acknowledgements

The author and publishers are grateful to the following publishers for permission to reproduce previously published material:

Penguin Books Ltd for an extract from Aristotle, *The Politics*, translated by T. A. Sinclair, revised and re-presented by Trevor J. Saunders (Penguin Classics, 1962, revised edition 1981), copyright © the Estate of T. A. Sinclair, 1962; copyright © Trevor J. Saunders, 1981.

J. M. Dent & Sons Ltd, an imprint of the Orion Group, for an extract from Xenophon, 'History of Greece', in Cosmo Rodewald (ed.), *Democracy: Ideas and Realities*, 1974.

Some sections of this book have been adapted from previously published essays. While the substance of each of these essays has been extensively modified and developed for the purposes of this volume, the details of the original publications are as follows:

'Central perspectives on the modern state'. In D. Held et al. (eds), *States and Societies*, Oxford: Martin Robertson, 1983, pp. 1–55. Parts of this essay helped inform chapter 3.

'Theories of the state: some competing claims' (with Joel Krieger). In S. Bornstein, D. Held and J. Krieger (eds), *The State in Capitalist Europe*, London: Allen and Unwin, 1984, pp. 1–20. An adapted version of this essay forms part of chapter 6.

'Power and legitimacy in contemporary Britain'. In G. McLennan, D. Held and S. Hall (eds), *State and Society in Contemporary Britain*, Cambridge: Polity, 1984, pp. 299–369. Sections of this essay helped structure chapter 7.

'Liberalism, Marxism and democracy', *Theory and Society*, 22, 1993, pp. 249–81. A section of this essay informed chapter 8.

'Principles of cosmopolitan order'. In G. Brock and H. Brighouse (eds), *The Political Philosophy of Cosmopolitanism*. Cambridge: Cambridge University Press, 2005. The discussion of impartialism in chapter 9 draws upon a section of this essay.

'Socialism and the limits of state action' (with John Keane). In J. Curran (ed.), *The Future of the Left*, Cambridge: Polity, 1984, pp. 170–81. Some material from this essay was adapted for a section of chapter 10.

'Democracy, the nation-state and the global system', *Economy and Society*, 20(2), 1991, pp. 138–72; and in D. Held (ed.), *Political Theory Today*, Cambridge: Polity, 1991, pp. 197–235. Parts of this essay were drawn upon in chapter 11.

Bibliography

Abercrombie, N., Hill, S. and Turner, B. 1980: *The Dominant Ideology Thesis*. London: Allen and Unwin.

Ackerman, B. 1989: Why dialogue? *Journal of Philosophy*, 86.

Ackerman, B. and Fishkin, J. 2003: Deliberation day. In J. Fishkin and P. Laslett (eds), *Debating Deliberative Democracy*. Oxford: Blackwell.

Adonis, A. and Mulgan, G. 1994: Back to Greece: the scope for direct democracy. *Demos*, 3.

Albrow, M. 1970: *Bureaucracy*. London: Pall Mall.

Almond, A. and Verba, S. 1963: *The Civic Culture: Political Attitudes and Democracy in Five Nations*. Princeton: Princeton University Press.

Almond, A. and Verba, S. (eds) 1980: *The Civic Culture Revisited*. Boston: Little, Brown.

Anderson, B. 1983: *Imagined Communities*. London: Verso.

Anderson, P. 1974a: *Passages from Antiquity to Feudalism*. London: New Left Books.

Anderson, P. 1974b: *Lineages of the Absolutist State*. London: New Left Books.

Andrewes, A. 1967: *The Greeks*. London: Hutchinson.

Annas, J. 1981: *An Introduction to Plato's Republic*. Oxford: Clarendon Press.

Anweiler, O. 1974: *The Soviets*. New York: Random House.

Aquinas, St Thomas: *De regimine principum*. In *Aquinas: Selected Political Writings*, ed. A. P. D'Entrèves. Oxford: Blackwell, 1948.

Archibugi, D. and Held, D. 1995: *Cosmopolitan Democracy: An Agenda for a New World Order*. Cambridge: Polity.

Arendt, H. 1963: *On Revolution*. New York: Viking Press.

Aristotle: *The Politics*. Harmondsworth: Penguin, 1981.

Astell, M.: *Some Reflections upon Marriage*. Dublin, 1730.

Augustine: *The City of God against the Pagans*, 7 vols. London: Heinemann, 1957–72.

Avineri, S. 1972: *Hegel's Theory of the Modern State*. Cambridge: Cambridge University Press.

Bachrach, P. and Baratz, M. S. 1962: The two faces of power. *American Political Science Review*, 56(4).

Baldwin, T. 1992: The territorial state. In H. Gross and T. R. Harrison (eds), *Cambridge Essays in Jurisprudence*. Oxford: Clarendon Press.

Ball, T. 1988: *Transforming Political Discourse: Political Theory and Critical Conceptual History*. Oxford: Blackwell.

Barber, B. 1984: *Strong Democracy: Participatory Politics for a New Age*. Berkeley: University of California Press.

Barnett, A., Ellis, C. and Hirst, P. 1993: *Debating the Constitution: New Perspectives on Constitutional Reform*. Cambridge: Polity.

Barry, B. 1989: *Theories of Justice*. London: Harvester Wheatsheaf.

Barry, B. 1995: *Justice as Impartiality*. Oxford: Oxford University Press.

Barry, B. 1998a: International society from a cosmopolitan perspective. In D. Mapel and T. Nardin (eds), *International Society: Diverse Ethical Perspectives*. Princeton: Princeton University Press.

Barry, B. 1998b: Something in the disputation not unpleasant. In P. Kelly (ed.), *Impartiality, Neutrality and Justice*. Edinburgh: Edinburgh University Press.

Barry, B. 2001: *Culture and Equality*. Cambridge: Polity.

Bauman, Z. 1991: *Modernity and Ambivalence*. Cambridge: Polity.

Beer, S. 1969: *Modern British Politics*. London: Faber.

Beer, S. 1982: *Britain against Itself*. London: Faber.

Beetham, D. 1981: Beyond liberal democracy. *Socialist Register*, 1981. London: Merlin Press.

Beetham, D. 1985: *Max Weber and the Theory of Modern Politics*. Cambridge: Polity.

Beetham, D. 1991: *The Legitimation of Power*. London: Macmillan.

Beetham, D. 1993: Liberal democracy and the limits of democratization. In D. Held (ed.), *Prospects for Democracy: North, South, East, West*. Cambridge: Polity.

Beetham, D. 1994: Conditions for democratic consolidation. *Review of African Political Economy*, 60.

Beetham, D. 2005: *Democracy*. Oxford: Oneworld.

Beitz, C. 1979: *Political Theory and International Relations*. Princeton: Princeton University Press.

Bellamy, R. 1996: The political form of the constitution: the separation of powers, rights and representative democracy. *Political Studies*, 44(3), special issue.

Benhabib, S. 1992: *Situating the Self*. Cambridge: Polity.

Benn, S. I. 1955: The uses of sovereignty. *Political Studies*, 3.

Bentham, J.: *Constitutional Code*, book I. In *The Works of Jeremy Bentham*, vol. IX, ed. Jeremy Bowring. Edinburgh: W. Tait, 1843.

Bentham, J.: *Fragment on Government*, ed. W. Harrison. Oxford: Blackwell, 1960.

Bentham, J.: *Principles of the Civil Code*. In *The Works of Jeremy Bentham*, vol. I, ed. Jeremy Bowring. Edinburgh: W. Tait, 1838.

Bentham, J.: *The Works of Jeremy Bentham*, 11 vols, ed. Jeremy Bowring. Edinburgh: W. Tait, 1838–43.

Berelson, B. 1952: Democratic theory and public opinion. *Public Opinion Quarterly*, 16 (autumn).

Berelson, B., Lazarfeld, P. F. and McPhee, W. 1954: *Voting*. Chicago: University of Chicago Press.

Berlin, I. 1969: *Four Essays on Liberty*. Oxford: Oxford University Press.

Bernal, M. 1987: *Black Athena*, vol. 1. London: Free Association Books.

Bessette, J. 1980: Deliberative democracy: the majority principle in republican government. In R. A. Goldwin and W. A. Schambra (eds), *How Democratic is the Constitution?* Washington: American Enterprise Institute.

Bessette, J. 1994: *The Mild Voice of Reason: Deliberative Democracy and American National Government*. Chicago: University of Chicago Press.

Bobbio, N. 1987: *Which Socialism?* Cambridge: Polity.

Bobbio, N. 1989: *Democracy and Dictatorship*. Cambridge: Polity.

Bohman, J. 1996: *Public Deliberation: Pluralism, Complexity, and Democracy, Studies in Contemporary German Social Thought*. Cambridge, MA: MIT Press.

Bohman, J. 1998: The coming of age of deliberative democracy. *Journal of Political Philosophy*, 6.

Bornstein, S., Held, D. and Krieger, J. (eds) 1984: *The State in Capitalist Europe*. London: Allen and Unwin.

Bottomore, T. 1985: *Theories of Modern Capitalism*. London: Allen and Unwin.

Bradley, H. 1995: *Fractured Identities*. Cambridge: Polity.

Brittan, S. 1975: The economic contradictions of democracy. *British Journal of Political Science*, 5(1).

Brittan, S. 1977: Can democracy manage an economy? In R. Skidelsky (ed.), *The End of the Keynesian Era*. Oxford: Martin Robertson.

Brock, G. and Brighouse, H. (eds) 2005: *The Political Philosophy of Cosmopolitanism*. Cambridge: Cambridge University Press.

Brown, R. and Scase, R. (eds) 1991: *Poor Work*. Buckingham: Open University Press.

Budge, I. 1993: Direct democracy: setting appropriate terms of debate. In D. Held (ed.), *Prospects for Democracy: North, South, East, West*. Cambridge: Polity.

Budge, I. 1996: *The New Challenge of Direct Democracy*. Cambridge: Polity.

Bull, H. 1977: *The Anarchical Society*. London: Macmillan.

Burnheim, J. 1985: *Is Democracy Possible?* Cambridge: Polity.

Burnheim, J. 1986: Democracy, the nation state and the world system. In D. Held and C. Pollitt (eds), *New Forms of Democracy*. London: Sage.

Butler, D. and Ranney, A. 1994: *Referendums around the World*. Basingstoke: Macmillan.

Butler, D. and Stokes, D. 1974: *Political Change in Britain*. London: Macmillan.

Callinicos, A. 1991: *The Revenge of History: Marxism and the East European Revolutions*. Cambridge: Polity.

Callinicos, A. 1993: Liberalism, Marxism, and democracy: a response to David Held. *Theory and Society*, 22.

Campbell, A., Converse, P., Miller, W. and Stokes, D. 1960: *The American Voter*. New York: John Wiley.

Caney, S. 2001: Cosmopolitan justice and equalizing opportunities. In T. Pogge (ed.), *Global Justice*. Oxford: Blackwell.

Canovan, M. 1987: Republicanism. In D. Miller, J. Coleman, W. Connolly and A. Ryan (eds), *The Blackwell Encyclopaedia of Political Thought*. Oxford: Blackwell.

Caportorti, F. 1983: Human rights: the hard road towards universality. In R. St J. Macdonald and D. M. Johnson (eds), *The Structure and Process of International Law*. The Hague: Martinus Nijhoff.

Cassese, A. 1986: *International Law in a Divided World*. Oxford: Clarendon Press.

Cassese, A. 1988: *Violence and Law in the Modern Age*. Cambridge: Polity.

Cassese, A. 1991: Violence, war and the rule of law. In D. Held (ed.), *Political Theory Today*. Cambridge: Polity.

Chodorow, N. J. 1989: *Feminism and Psychoanalytic Theory*. Cambridge: Polity.

Cicero: *De re publica*, trans. G. H. Sabine and S. B. Smith as *On the Commonwealth*. Indianapolis: Bobbs-Merrill, 1929.

Cliff, T. 1974: *State Capitalism in Russia*. London: Pluto.

Cohen, J. 1989: Deliberation and democratic legitimacy. In A. Hamlin and P. Pettit (eds), *The Good Polity: Normative Analysis of the State*. Oxford: Blackwell.

Cohen, J. and Rogers, J. 1983: *On Democracy*. New York: Penguin.

Cohen, J. and Rogers, J. 1992: Secondary associations and democratic governance. *Politics and Society*, 20(4).

Cohen, J. and Rogers, J. 1995: *Associations and Democracy*. London: Verso.

Cohen, J. L. 1982: *Class and Civil Society: The Limits of Marxian Critical Theory*. Oxford: Martin Robertson.

Cohen, J. L. and Arato, A. 1992: *Civil Society and Political Theory*. Cambridge, MA: MIT Press.

Coleman, J. 2000: *A History of Political Thought from the Middle Ages to the Renaissance*. Cambridge: Cambridge University Press.

Colletti, L. 1972: *From Rousseau to Lenin*. London: New Left Books.

Connolly, W. 1981: *Appearance and Reality*. Cambridge: Cambridge University Press.

Cooper, R. J. 1986: *Economic Policy in an Interdependent World*. Cambridge, MA: MIT Press.

Corcoran, P. E. 1983: The limits of democratic theory. In G. Duncan (ed.), *Democratic Theory and Practice*. Cambridge: Cambridge University Press.

Coward, R. 1983: *Patriarchal Precedents: Sexuality and Social Relations*. London: Routledge and Kegan Paul.

Cox, R. W. 1987: *Production, Power and World Order: Social Forces in the Making of History*. New York: Columbia University Press.

Cranston, M. 1968: Introduction. In J.-J. Rousseau, *The Social Contract*. Harmondsworth: Penguin.

Crompton, R. 1993: *Class and Stratification*. Cambridge: Polity.

Crozier, M. 1964: *The Bureaucratic Phenomenon*. London: Tavistock.

Dahl, R. A. 1956: *A Preface to Democratic Theory*. Chicago: University of Chicago Press.

Dahl, R. A. 1957: The concept of power. *Behavioural Science*, 2(3).

Dahl, R. A. 1961: *Who Governs? Democracy and Power in an American City*. New Haven: Yale University Press.

Dahl, R. A. 1971: *Polyarchy: Participation and Opposition*. New Haven: Yale University Press.

Dahl, R. A. 1978: Pluralism revisited. *Comparative Politics*, 10(2).

Dahl, R. A. 1979: Procedural democracy. In P. Laslett and J. Fishkin (eds), *Philosophy, Politics and Society*. Fifth series. New Haven: Yale University Press.

Dahl, R. A. 1985: *A Preface to Economic Democracy*. Cambridge: Polity.

Dahl, R. A. 1989: *Democracy and its Critics*. New Haven: Yale University Press.

de Tocqueville, A.: *Democracy in America*, 2 vols. London: Fontana, 1968.

Devine, F. 1993: *Affluent Workers Revisited*. Edinburgh: Edinburgh University Press.

Devine, P. 1988: *Democracy and Economic Planning*. Cambridge: Polity.

Dickenson, D. 1997: *Property, Women and Politics: Subjects or Objects?* Cambridge: Polity.

Dominelli, L. 1991: *Women across Continents*. Hemel Hempstead: Harvester Wheatsheaf.

Draper, H. 1977: *Karl Marx's Theory of Revolution*, vol. I. New York: Monthly Review Press.

Dryzek, J. 1990: *Discursive Democracy: Politics, Policy, and Science*. Cambridge: Cambridge University Press.

Dryzek, J. 2000: *Deliberative Democracy and Beyond: Liberals, Critics, Contestations*. Oxford: Oxford University Press.

Duncan, G. 1971: *Marx and Mill*. Cambridge: Cambridge University Press.

Duncan, G. and Lukes, S. 1963: The new democracy. In S. Lukes (ed.), *Essays in Social Theory*. London: Macmillan.

Dunn, J. 1969: *The Political Thought of John Locke*. Cambridge: Cambridge University Press.

Dunn, J. 1979: *Western Political Theory in the Face of the Future*. Cambridge: Cambridge University Press.

Dunn, J. 1980: *Political Obligation in its Historical Context: Essays in Political Theory*. Cambridge: Cambridge University Press.

Dunn, J. 1990: *Interpreting Political Responsibility*. Cambridge: Polity.

Dunn, J. (ed.) 1992: *Democracy: The Unfinished Journey, 508 BC to AD 1993*. Oxford: Oxford University Press.

Duverger, M. 1974: *Modern Democracies: Economic Power versus Political Power*. Hindsale, IL: Dryden Press.

Edwards, M. and Zadek, S. 2003: Governing the provision of global public goods: the role and legitimacy of nonstate actors. In I. Kaul et al. (eds), *Providing Global Public Goods*. Oxford: Oxford University Press.

Eisenstein, Z. R. 1980: *The Radical Future of Liberal Feminism*. New York: Longman.

Elster, J. 1976: Some conceptual problems in political theory. In B. Barry (ed.), *Power and Political Theory*. London: John Wiley.

Elster, J. 1989: Deliberation and constitution making. In J. Elster (ed.), *Deliberative Democracy*. Cambridge: Cambridge University Press.

Elster, J. 1997: The market and the forum: three varieties of political theory. In J. Bohman and W. Rehg (eds), *Deliberative Democracy*. Cambridge, MA: MIT Press.

Engels, F.: Letter to A. Bebel, March 1875. In K. Marx and F. Engels, *Selected Works*. New York: International Publishers, 1968.

Engels, F.: *The Origins of the Family, Private Property, and the State*. New York: International Publishers, 1972.

Falk, R. 1969: The interplay of Westphalian and Charter conceptions of the international legal order. In R. Falk and C. Black (eds), *The Future of the International Legal Order*, vol. 1. Princeton: Princeton University Press.

Falk, R. 1975: *A Study of Future Worlds*. New York: Free Press.

Farrar, C. 1992: Ancient Greek political theory as a response to democracy. In J. Dunn (ed.), *Democracy: The Unfinished Journey, 508 BC to AD 1993*. Oxford: Oxford University Press.

Featherstone, M. 1991: *The Body, Social Processes and Cultural Theory*. London: Sage.

Figgis, J. N. 1913: *Churches in the Modern State.* London: Longman, Green.

Fine, B. and Harris, L. 1979: *Rereading Capital.* London: Macmillan.

Finley, M. I. 1963: *The Ancient Greeks.* Harmondsworth: Penguin.

Finley, M. I. 1972: Introduction. In Thucydides, *The Peloponnesian War.* Harmondsworth: Penguin.

Finley, M. I. 1973a: *The Ancient Economy.* London: Chatto and Windus.

Finley, M. I. 1973b: *Democracy Ancient and Modern.* London: Chatto and Windus.

Finley, M. I. 1975: *The Use and Abuse of History.* London: Chatto and Windus.

Finley, M. I. 1983: *Politics in the Ancient World.* Cambridge: Cambridge University Press.

Fishkin, J. 1991: *Democracy and Deliberation: New Directions for Democratic Reform.* New Haven: Yale University Press.

Foucault, M. 1977: *Discipline and Punish.* London: Allen Lane.

Frankel, B. 1979: On the state of the state: Marxist theories of the state after Leninism. *Theory and Society*, 7(1–2).

Franklin, J. H. 1978: *John Locke and the Theory of Sovereignty.* Cambridge: Cambridge University Press.

Fraser, N. 1997: Rethinking the public sphere: a contribution to the critique of actually existing democracy. In *Justice Interruptus.* London: Routledge.

Frieden, J. 1991: Invested interests: the politics of national economic policies in a world of global finance. *International Organization*, 45(4).

Friedman, J. 1989: The new consensus. Part 1: The Fukuyama thesis. *Critical Review* (3–4).

Fukuyama, F. 1989: The end of history? *National Interest*, 16.

Fukuyama, F. 1989/90: A reply to my critics. *National Interest*, 18.

Fukuyama, F. 1992: *The End of History and the Last Man.* London: Hamish Hamilton.

Fukuyama, F. 1995: *Trust.* London: Hamish Hamilton.

Gadamer, H.-G. 1975: *Truth and Method.* London: Sheed and Ward.

Galbraith, J. K. 1994: The good society. *Guardian*, 26 January.

Gamble, A. 1996: *Hayek.* Cambridge: Polity.

Gewirth, A. 1951: *Marsilius of Padua and Medieval Political Philosophy.* New York: Columbia University Press.

Gewirth, A. 1980: Introduction. In Marsilius of Padua, *Defensor pacis.* Toronto: Toronto University Press.

Giddens, A. 1972: *Politics and Sociology in the Thought of Max Weber.* London: Macmillan.

Giddens, A. 1979: *Central Problems in Social Theory: Action, Structure and Contradiction in Social Analysis.* London: Macmillan.

Giddens, A. 1981: *A Contemporary Critique of Historical Materialism*, vol. I. London: Macmillan.

Giddens, A. 1984: *The Constitution of Society.* Cambridge: Polity.

Giddens, A. 1985: *The Nation-State and Violence*, vol. II of *A Contemporary Critique of Historical Materialism.* Cambridge: Polity.

Giddens, A. 1990: *The Consequences of Modernity.* Cambridge: Polity.

Giddens, A. 1992: *The Transformation of Intimacy.* Cambridge: Polity.

Giddens, A. 1993: Modernity, history and democracy. *Theory and Society*, 22.

Giddens, A. 1994: *Beyond Left and Right: The Future of Radical Politics.* Cambridge: Polity.

Giddens, A. 1998: *The Third Way.* Cambridge: Polity.

Giddens, A. and Held, D. (eds) 1982: *Classes, Power and Conflict.* London: Macmillan.

Gilbert, F. 1965: *Machiavelli and Guicciardini.* Princeton: Princeton University Press.

Gilligan, C. 1982: *In a Different Voice: Women's Conceptions of the Self and Morality.* Cambridge: Harvard University Press.

Gilpin, R. 1987: *The Political Economy of International Relations.* Princeton: Princeton University Press.

Gourevitch, P. 1978: The second image reversed: the international sources of domestic politics. *International Organization*, 32(4).

Gray, J. 1993: *Beyond the New Right.* London: Routledge.

Green, P. 1981: *The Pursuit of Inequality*. New York: Pantheon Books.

Gutmann, A. 1987: *Democratic Education*. Princeton: Princeton University Press.

Gutmann, A. 1999: Deliberative democracy and majority rule: reply to Waldron. In H. H. Koh and R. C. Slye (eds), *Deliberative Democracy and Human Rights*. New Haven: Yale University Press.

Gutmann, A. and Thompson, D. 1996: *Democracy and Disagreement*. Cambridge: Belknap Press.

Habermas, J. 1962: *Strukturwandel der Öffentlichkeit*. Neuwied: Luchterhand.

Habermas, J. 1971: *Towards a Rational Society*. London: Heinemann.

Habermas, J. 1973: Wahrheitstheorien. In H. Fahrenbach (ed.), *Wirklichkeit und Reflexion*. Pfüllingen: Neske.

Habermas, J. 1976: *Legitimation Crisis*. London: Heinemann.

Habermas, J. 1987: *The Philosophical Discourse of Modernity: Twelve Lectures*. Cambridge, MA: Polity.

Habermas, J. 1988: *Theory and Practice*. Cambridge: Polity.

Habermas, J. 1990: Discourse ethics: notes on a program of philosophical justification. In *Moral Consciousness and Communicative Action*. Cambridge: MIT Press.

Habermas, J. 1993: Remarks on discourse ethics. In *Justification and Application*. Cambridge, MA: MIT Press.

Habermas, J. 1996: *Between Facts and Norms: Contributions to a Discourse Theory of Law and Democracy*. Cambridge: Polity.

Hacker, A. 1967: Power to do what? In W. Connolly (ed.), *The Bias of Pluralism*. Chicago: Atherton.

Hacker, K. and Dijk, J. 2001: *Digital Democracy*. London: Sage.

Hall, P. 1986: *Governing the Economy*. Cambridge: Polity.

Hall, S. 1983: Themes and questions. In *The State and Society*, 3(7). Milton Keynes: Open University.

Hall, S. 1992: The question of cultural identity. In S. Hall, D. Held and A. McGrew (eds), *Modernity and its Futures*. Cambridge: Polity.

Hall, S. and Gieben, B. (eds) 1992: *Formations of Modernity*. Cambridge: Polity.

Hall, S., Critcher, C., Jefferson, T., Clarke, J. and Roberts, B., 1978: *Policing the Crisis*. London: Macmillan.

Hall, S., Held, D. and McGrew, A. (eds) 1992: *Modernity and its Futures*. Cambridge: Polity.

Halsey, A. H. 1981: *Change in British Society*. Oxford: Oxford University Press.

Hansen, M. H. 1991: *The Athenian Democracy in the Age of Demosthenes*. Oxford: Blackwell.

Hardt, M. and Negri, A. 2000: *Empire*. Cambridge: Harvard University Press.

Harrison, R. 1993: *Democracy*. London: Routledge.

Hartmann, H. 1976: Capitalism, patriarchy and job segregation by sex. *Signs*, 1(3). Also in A. Giddens and D. Held (eds), *Classes, Power and Conflict*. London: Macmillan, 1982.

Hayek, F. A. 1960: *The Constitution of Liberty*. London: Routledge and Kegan Paul.

Hayek, F. A. 1976: *The Road to Serfdom*. London: Routledge and Kegan Paul.

Hayek, F. A. 1978: *New Studies in Philosophy, Politics, Economics and the History of Ideas*. London: Routledge and Kegan Paul.

Hayek, F. A. 1982: *Law, Legislation and Liberty*, vol. 3. London: Routledge and Kegan Paul.

Hegel, G. W. F.: *Lectures on the Philosophy of World History*. Cambridge: Cambridge University Press, 1975.

Hegel, G. W. F.: *Philosophy of Right*, trans. T. M. Knox. Oxford: Oxford University Press, 1967.

Held, D. 1980: *Introduction to Critical Theory: Horkheimer to Habermas*. Cambridge: Polity.

Held, D. 1983: Central perspectives on the modern state. In D. Held et al. (eds), *States and Societies*. Oxford: Martin Robertson. Revised and reprinted in D. Held, *Political Theory and the Modern State*. Cambridge: Polity, 1989.

Held, D. 1984: Power and legitimacy in contemporary Britain. In G. McLennan, D. Held and S. Hall (eds), *State and Society in Contemporary Britain*. Cambridge: Polity. Revised and reprinted in D. Held, *Political Theory and the Modern State*. Cambridge: Polity, 1989.

Held, D. 1986: Liberalism, Marxism and the future direction of public policy. In P. Nolan and S. Paine (eds), *Re-thinking Socialist Economics*. Cambridge: Polity. Revised and reprinted in D. Held, *Political Theory and the Modern State*. Cambridge: Polity, 1989.

Held, D. 1989: *Political Theory and the Modern State*. Cambridge: Polity.

Held, D. 1991a: Democracy, the nation-state and the global system. In D. Held (ed.), *Political Theory Today*. Cambridge: Polity.

Held, D. 1991b: Introduction. In D. Held (ed.), *Political Theory Today*. Cambridge: Polity.

Held, D. 1991c: The possibilities of democracy: a discussion of Robert Dahl, *Democracy and its Critics*. *Theory and Society*, 20.

Held, D. 1992: The development of the modern state. In S. Hall and B. Gieben (eds), *Formations of Modernity*. Cambridge: Polity.

Held, D. 1993a: Democracy: from city-states to a cosmopolitan order? In D. Held (ed.), *Prospects for Democracy: North, South, East, West*. Cambridge: Polity.

Held, D. 1993b: Liberalism, Marxism and democracy. *Theory and Society*, 22.

Held, D. 1993c: Anything but a dog's life? Further comments on Fukuyama, Callinicos and Giddens. *Theory and Society*, 22.

Held, D. (ed.) 1993d: *Prospects for Democracy: North, South, East, West*. Cambridge: Polity.

Held, D. 1995: *Democracy and the Global Order: From the Modern State to Cosmopolitan Governance*. Cambridge: Polity.

Held, D. 2002: Law of states, law of peoples. *Legal Theory*, 8(1), pp. 1–44.

Held, D. 2004: *Global Covenant: The Social Democratic Alternative to the Washington Consensus*. Cambridge: Polity.

Held, D. and Keane, J. 1984: Socialism and the limits of state action. In J. Curran (ed.), *The Future of the Left*. Cambridge: Polity.

Held, D. and Koenig-Archibugi, M. (eds) 2004: *American Power in the Twenty-First Century*. Cambridge: Polity.

Held, D. and Krieger, J. 1983: Accumulation, legitimation and the state. In D. Held et al. (eds), *States and Societies*. Oxford: Martin Robertson.

Held, D. and Krieger, J. 1984: Theories of the state: some competing claims. In S. Bornstein, D. Held and J. Krieger (eds), *The State in Capitalist Europe*. London: Allen and Unwin. Revised and reprinted in D. Held, *Political Theory and the Modern State*. Cambridge: Polity, 1989.

Held, D. and Leftwich, A. 1984: A discipline of politics? In A. Leftwich (ed.), *What is Politics?* Oxford: Blackwell. Revised and reprinted in D. Held, *Political Theory and the Modern State*. Cambridge: Polity, 1989.

Held, D. and McGrew, A. 2002: *Globalization/Anti-Globalization*. Cambridge: Polity.

Held, D. and Pollitt, C. (eds) 1986: *New Forms of Democracy*. London: Sage.

Held, D. and Thompson, J. B. 1989: *Social Theory of Modern Societies: Anthony Giddens and his Critics*. Cambridge: Cambridge University Press.

Held, D., McGrew, A., Goldblatt, D. and Perraton, J. 1999: *Global Transformations: Politics, Economics and Culture*. Cambridge: Polity.

Hill, T. 1987: The importance of autonomy. In E. Kittay and D. Meyers (eds), *Women and Moral Theory*. Towata: Roman and Allanheld.

Himmelfarb, G. 1989: Response to Fukuyama. *National Interest*, 16.

Hinsley, F. H. 1986: *Sovereignty*, 2nd edn. Cambridge: Cambridge University Press.

Hirst, P. Q. 1989a: Endism. *London Review of Books*, 23 November.

Hirst, P. Q. 1989b: *The Pluralist Theory of the State*. London: Routledge.

Hirst, P. Q. 1990: *Representative Democracy and its Limits*. Cambridge: Polity.

Hirst, P. Q. 1994: *Associative Democracy*. Cambridge: Polity.

Hobbes, T.: *Leviathan*, ed. C. B. Macpherson. Harmondsworth: Penguin, 1968.

Hoffman, S. 1982: Reflections on the nation-state in Western Europe today. *Journal of Common Market Studies*, 21(1, 2).

Hont, I. 1994: The permanent crisis of a divided mankind. *Political Studies*, 42, special issue.

Hornblower, S. 1992: Creation and development of democratic institutions in ancient Greece. In J. Dunn (ed.), *Democracy: The Unfinished Journey, 508 BC to AD 1993*. Oxford: Oxford University Press.

Huntington, S. 1975: Post-industrial politics: how benign will it be? *Comparative Politics*, 6.

Hutton, W. 1995: *The State We're In*. London: Jonathan Cape.

Hyde, M. 1985: The British welfare state: legitimation crisis and future directions. Research paper.

Ignatieff, M. 1978: *A Just Measure of Pain*. London: Macmillan.

Jessop, B. 1977: Recent theories of the capitalist state. *Cambridge Journal of Economics*, 1(4).

Jessop, B. 1990: *State Theory*. Cambridge: Polity.

Jones, A. H. M. 1957: *Athenian Democracy*. Oxford: Blackwell.

Jordan, B. 1985: *The State: Authority and Autonomy*. Oxford: Blackwell.

Jowell, R. and Airey, C. (eds) 1984: *British Social Attitudes*. London: Gower.

Kaiser, K. 1972: Transnational relations as a threat to the democratic process. In R. O. Keohane and J. S. Nye (eds), *Transnational Relations and World Politics*. Cambridge: Harvard University Press.

Kavanagh, D. 1980: Political culture in Great Britain. In A. Almond and S. Verba (eds), *The Civic Culture Revisited*. Boston: Little, Brown.

Keane, J. 1984a: *Public Life and Late Capitalism*. Cambridge: Cambridge University Press.

Keane, J. 1984b: Introduction. In C. Offe, *Contradictions of the Welfare State*. London: Hutchinson.

Keane, J. (ed.) 1988a: *Re-discovering Civil Society*. London: Verso.

Keane, J. 1988b: *Socialism and Civil Society*. London: Verso.

Kegley, C. W. and Wittkopf, E. R. 1989: *World Politics*. London: Macmillan.

Kelly, P. (ed.) 1998: *Impartiality, Neutrality and Justice*. Edinburgh: Edinburgh University Press.

Kelly, P. (ed.) 2002: *Multiculturalism Reconsidered*. Cambridge: Polity.

Kennedy, P. 1988: *The Rise and Fall of the Great Powers*. London: Unwin.

Keohane, N. O. 1972: Virtuous republics and glorious monarchies: two models in Montesquieu's political thought. *Political Studies*, 20(4).

Keohane, R. O. 1984a: *After Hegemony: Cooperation and Discord in the World Political Economy*. Princeton: Princeton University Press.

Keohane, R. O. 1984b: The world political economy and the crisis of embedded liberalism. In J. H. Goldthorpe (ed.), *Order and Conflict in Contemporary Capitalism*. Oxford: Oxford University Press.

Keohane, R. O. and Nye, J. S. (eds) 1972: *Transnational Relations and World Politics*. Cambridge: Harvard University Press.

Keohane, R. O. and Nye, J. S. 1989: *Power and Interdependence*, 2nd edn. Boston: Little, Brown.

King, A. 1976: *Why Is Britain Becoming Harder to Govern?* London: BBC Publications.

Kolko, J. 1988: *Restructuring the World Economy*. New York: Pantheon.

Korpi, W. 1978: *The Working Class in Welfare Capitalism*. London: Routledge and Kegan Paul.

Kramnick, M. 1982: Introduction. In M. Wollstonecraft, *Vindication of the Rights of Woman*. Harmondsworth: Penguin.

Krasner, S. 1983: *International Regimes*. Ithaca: Cornell University Press.

Krieger, J. 1983: *Undermining Capitalism*. Princeton: Princeton University Press.

Krieger, J. 1986: *Reagan, Thatcher and the Politics of Decline*. Cambridge: Polity.

Krouse, R. W. 1983: Classical images of democracy in America: Madison and Tocqueville. In G. Duncan (ed.), *Democratic Theory and Practice*. Cambridge: Cambridge University Press.

Lafont, C. 2006: Is the ideal of deliberative democracy coherent? In S. Besson and J. L. Marti (eds), *Deliberative Democracy and its Discontents*. Aldershot: Ashgate.

Larsen, J. A. O. 1948: Cleisthenes and the development of the theory of democracy at Athens. In M. R. Konvitz and A. E. Murphy (eds), *Essays in Political Theory Presented to George Sabine*. Port Washington, NY: Kennikat Press.

Laski, H. 1932: *Studies in Law and Politics*. London: Allen and Unwin.

Laslett, P. 1963: Introduction. In Locke, *Two Treatises of Government*. Cambridge and New York: Cambridge University Press.

Lee, D. 1974: Introduction. In Plato, *The Republic*. Harmondsworth: Penguin.

Lehmbruch, G. 1979: Consociational democracy, class conflict, and the new corporatism. In P. C. Schmitter and G. Lehmbruch (eds), *Trend toward Corporatist Intermediation*. New York: Sage.

Lenin, V. I.: *State and Revolution*. New York: International Publishers, 1971.

Lewin, M. 1988: *The Gorbachev Phenomenon*. London: Verso.

Lewis, P. 1990a: The long goodbye: party rule and political change in Poland since martial law. *Journal of Communist Studies*, 6(1).

Lewis, P. 1990b: Democratization in Eastern Europe. *Coexistence*, 27.

Lijphart, A. 1984: *Democracies*. New Haven: Yale University Press.

Lindblom, C. E. 1977: *Politics and Markets*. New York: Basic Books.

Lipset, S. M. 1963: *Political Man*. New York: Doubleday.

Lively, J. 1975: *Democracy*. Oxford: Blackwell.

Livy: *History of Rome*, vol. XIII, bks XLIII–XLV, trans. A. F. Schlesinger. Cambridge, MA: Harvard University Press, 1951.

Locke, J.: *Two Treatises of Government*. Cambridge and New York: Cambridge University Press, 1963.

Luard, E. 1977: *International Agencies: The Framework of Interdependence*. London: Macmillan.

Lukes, S. 1973: *Individualism*. New York: Harper and Row.

Lukes, S. 1974: *Power: A Radical View*. London: Macmillan.

Lukes, S. 1985: *Marxism and Morality*. Oxford: Oxford University Press.

McBride, C. 2003: Self-transparency and the possibility of deliberative democracy. *Journal of Political Ideologies*, 8.

McBride, C. 2004: Deliberative democracy: a review. Paper.

McDonald, F. 1986: *Novus Ordo Seclorum: The Intellectual Origins of the Constitution*. Lawrence: University Press of Kansas.

McGrew, A. G. 1992: Conceptualizing global politics. In A. G. McGrew, P. G. Lewis et al., *Global Politics*. Cambridge: Polity.

McGrew, A. 2005: The logics of globalization. In J. Ravenhill (ed.), *Global Political Economy*. Oxford: Oxford University Press.

Machiavelli, N.: *The Discourses*. Harmondsworth: Penguin, 1983.

Machiavelli, N.: *The Prince*. Harmondsworth: Penguin, 1975.

MacIntyre, A. 1966: *A Short History of Ethics*. New York: Macmillan.

McLean, I. 1986: Mechanisms of democracy. In D. Held and C. Pollitt (eds), *New Forms of Democracy*. London: Sage.

McLean, I. 1991: Forms of representation and systems of voting. In D. Held (ed.), *Political Theory Today*. Cambridge: Polity.

McLennan, G. 1984: Capitalist state or democratic polity? Recent developments in Marxist and pluralist theory. In G. McLennan, D. Held and S. Hall (eds), *The Idea of the Modern State*. Milton Keynes: Open University Press.

McLennan, G. 1995: *Pluralism*. Buckingham: Open University Press.

Macpherson, C. B. 1962: *The Political Theory of Possessive Individualism*. Oxford: Clarendon Press.

Macpherson, C. B. 1966: *The Real World of Democracy*. Oxford: Oxford University Press.

Macpherson, C. B. 1968: Introduction. In Hobbes, *Leviathan*. Harmondsworth: Penguin.

Macpherson, C. B. 1973: *Democratic Theory: Essays in Retrieval*. Oxford: Clarendon Press.

Macpherson, C. B. 1977: *The Life and Times of Liberal Democracy*. Oxford: Oxford University Press.

Madison, J.: *The Federalist Papers*. New York: Doubleday, 1966.

Madison, J.: Reflecting on representation. In Marvin Meyers (ed.), *The Mind of the Founder: Sources of the Political Thought of James Madison*. Indianapolis: Bobbs-Merrill, 1973.

Maguire, J. M. 1978: *Marx's Theory of Politics*. Cambridge: Cambridge University Press.

Main, J. T. 1973: *The Sovereign States: 1775–1783*. New York: Franklin Watts.

Mandel, E. 1972: *Marxist Economic Theory*, 2 vols. New York: Monthly Review Press.

Manin, B. 1987: On legitimacy and deliberation. *Political Theory*, 15(3).

Manin, B. 1994: Checks, balances and boundaries: the separation of powers in the constitutional debate of 1787. In B. Fontana (ed.), *The Invention of the Modern Republic*. Cambridge: Cambridge University Press.

Mann, M. 1970: The social cohesion of liberal democracy. *American Sociological Review*, 35. Also in A. Giddens and D. Held (eds), *Classes, Power and Conflict*. London: Macmillan, 1982.

Mann, M. 1973: *Consciousness and Action among the Western Working Class*. London: Macmillan.

Mann, M. 1986: *The Sources of Social Power*, vol. I. Cambridge: Cambridge University Press.

Mansbridge, J. J. 1983: *Beyond Adversary Democracy*. Chicago: Chicago University Press.

Mansfield, S. 1980: Introduction. In J. S. Mill, *The Subjection of Women*. Arlington Heights, IL: AHM Publishing.

Marcuse, H. 1964: *One-Dimensional Man*. Boston: Beacon.

Margolis, M. 1983: Democracy: American style. In G. Duncan (ed.), *Democratic Theory and Practice*. Cambridge: Cambridge University Press.

Marshall, T. H. 1973: *Class, Citizenship and Social Development*. Westport: Greenwood Press.

Marsilius of Padua: *Defensor pacis* (*The Defender of Peace*), trans. and ed. A. Gewirth. First published in English, New York: Columbia University Press, 1956; edition consulted, Toronto: Toronto University Press, 1980.

Marwick, A. 1982: *British Society since 1945*. Harmondsworth: Penguin.

Marx, K.: *Capital*, 3 vols. London: Lawrence and Wishart, 1970.

Marx, K.: *The Civil War in France*. Peking: Foreign Languages Press, 1970.

Marx, K.: *Critique of the Gotha Programme*. New York: International Publishers, 1970.

Marx, K.: *The Critique of Hegel's Philosophy of Right*. Cambridge: Cambridge University Press, 1970.

Marx, K.: *Economic and Philosophical Manuscripts*. In T. B. Bottomore (ed.), *Early Writings*. London: C. A. Watts, 1963.

Marx, K.: *The Eighteenth Brumaire of Louis Bonaparte*. New York: International Publishers, 1963.

Marx, K.: Letter two from the *Deutsch-Französische Jahrbücher*, 1843. In *Collected Works*, vol. 3. London: Lawrence and Wishart, 1975.

Marx, K.: *The Poverty of Philosophy*. New York: International Publishers, 1963.

Marx, K.: Preface to *A Contribution to the Critique of Political Economy*. London: Lawrence and Wishart, 1971.

Marx, K.: Value, price and profit. In K. Marx and F. Engels, *Selected Works*. New York: International Publishers, 1968.

Marx, K. and Engels, F.: *The Communist Manifesto*. In *Selected Works*, vol. I. Moscow: Progress Publishers, 1969.

Marx, K. and Engels, F.: *The German Ideology*. London: Lawrence and Wishart, 1970.

Masters, R. D. 1968: *The Political Philosophy of Rousseau*. Princeton: Princeton University Press.

Mattick, P. 1969: *Marx and Keynes*. Boston: Porter Sargent.

Meyers, M. (ed.) 1973: *The Mind of the Founder: Sources of the Political Thought of James Madison*. Indianapolis: Bobbs-Merrill.

Michels, R.: *Political Parties*. New York: Free Press, 1962.

Middlemas, K. 1979: *Politics in Industrial Society: The Experience of the British System since 1911*. London: André Deutsch.

Miliband, R. 1965: Marx and the state. *Socialist Register, 1965*. London: Merlin Press.

Miliband, R. 1969: *The State in Capitalist Society*. London: Weidenfeld and Nicolson.

Mill, J.: *An Essay on Government*. Cambridge: Cambridge University Press, 1937.

Mill, J.: Prisons and prison discipline. In *Essays on Government*. London: J. Innis, 1828.

Mill, J. S.: *Autobiography*, ed. John Jacob Coss. New York: Columbia University Press, 1873.

Mill, J. S.: Centralisation. *Edinburgh Review*, CXV, 1862.

Mill, J. S.: *Considerations on Representative Government*. In H. B. Acton (ed.), *Utilitarianism, Liberty, and Representative Government*. London: Dent, 1951.

Mill, J. S.: Essays on socialism. In Geraint L. Williams (ed.), *John Stuart Mill on Politics and Society*. London: Fontana, 1976.

Mill, J. S.: M. de Tocqueville on democracy in America. In Geraint L. Williams (ed.), *John Stuart Mill on Politics and Society*. London: Fontana, 1976.

Mill, J. S.: *On Liberty*. Harmondsworth: Penguin, 1982.

Mill, J. S.: *Principles of Political Economy*. In *Collected Works of J. S. Mill*, vols II and III. Toronto: University of Toronto Press, 1965.

Mill, J. S.: *The Subjection of Women*, ed. S. Mansfield. Arlington Heights, IL: AHM Publishing, 1980.

Mill, J. S.: Thoughts on parliamentary reform. In *Dissertations and Discussions Political, Philosophical, and Historical, Reprinted Chiefly from the Edinburgh and Westminster Reviews*. London: Longmans, Green, Reader and Dyer, 1868, vol. 3.

Miller, D. 1983: The competitive model of democracy. In G. Duncan (ed.), *Democratic Theory and Practice*. Cambridge: Cambridge University Press.

Miller, D. 1989: *Market, State and Community: Theoretical Foundations of Market Socialism*. Oxford: Clarendon Press.

Miller, D. 2000: *Citizenship and National Identity*. Cambridge: Polity.

Miller, J. 1984: *Rousseau: Dreamer of Democracy*. New Haven: Yale University Press.

Modelski, G. 1972: *Principles of World Politics*. New York: Free Press.

Mommsen, W. J. 1974: *The Age of Bureaucracy*. Oxford: Blackwell.

Montesquieu: *The Spirit of Laws*. Chicago: William Benton, 1952.

Moore, H. 1987: *Feminism and Anthropology*. Cambridge: Polity.

Moore, S. 1980: *Marx on the Choice between Socialism and Communism*. Cambridge: Harvard University Press.

Morgenthau, H. 1948: *Politics among Nations*. New York: Alfred A. Knopf.

Morse, E. 1976: *Modernization and the Transformation of International Relations*. New York: Free Press.

Mortimer, E. 1989: The end of history? *Marxism Today*, November.

Moss, L. 1982: People and government in 1978. Prepared for a Joint Meeting of Applied Statistics and Social Statistics Committees of the Royal Statistical Society (April).

Mouffe, C. 1992: *Dimensions of Radical Democracy*. London: Verso.

Mouffe, C. 2000: *The Democratic Paradox*. New York: Verso.

Nagel, J. H. 1975: *The Descriptive Analysis of Power*. New Haven: Yale University Press.

Nordhaus, W. D. 1975: The political business cycle. *Review of Economic Studies*, 42.

Nordlinger, E. A. 1981: *On the Autonomy of the Democratic State*. Cambridge, MA: Harvard University Press.

Nove, A. 1983: *The Economics of Feasible Socialism*. London: Macmillan.

Nozick, R. 1974: *Anarchy, State and Utopia*. Oxford: Blackwell.

O'Connor, J. 1973: *The Fiscal Crisis of the State*. New York: St Martin's Press.

Offe, C. 1975: The theory of the capitalist state and the problem of policy formation. In L. Lindberg, R. Alford, C. Crouch and C. Offe (eds), *Stress and Contradiction in Modern Capitalism*. Lexington: Lexington Books.

Offe, C. 1979: The state, ungovernability and the search for the 'non-political'. Paper presented to the Conference on the Individual and the State, Center for International Studies, University of Toronto (3 February). Reprinted in C. Offe, *Contradictions of the Welfare State*. London: Hutchinson, 1984.

Offe, C. 1980: The separation of form and content in liberal democratic politics. *Studies in Political Economy*, 3. Reprinted in C. Offe, *Contradictions of the Welfare State*. London: Hutchinson, 1984.

Offe, C. 1984: *Contradictions of the Welfare State*. London: Hutchinson.

Offe, C. 1985: *Disorganized Capitalism*. Cambridge: Polity.

Offe, C. 1996a: *Modernity and the State: East, West*. Cambridge: Polity.

Offe, C. 1996b: *Varieties of Transition: The East European and East German Experience*. Cambridge: Polity.

Offe, C. and Preuss, U. 1991: Democratic institutions and moral resources. In D. Held (ed.), *Political Theory Today*. Cambridge: Polity.

Offe, C. and Ronge, V. 1975: Theses on the theory of the state. *New German Critique*, 6. Reprinted in C. Offe, *Contradictions of the Welfare State*. London: Hutchinson, 1984.

Okin, S. M. 1979: *Women in Western Political Theory*. Princeton: Princeton University Press.

Okin, S. M. 1991: Philosopher queens and private wives: Plato on women and the family. In M. L. Shanley and C. Pateman (eds), *Feminist Interpretations and Political Theory*. Cambridge: Polity.

Ollman, B. 1971: *Marx's Theory of Alienation*. Cambridge: Cambridge University Press.

Ollman, B. 1977: Marx's vision of communism: a reconstruction. *Critique*, 8 (summer).

O'Neill, O. 1991: Transnational justice. In D. Held (ed.), *Political Theory Today*. Cambridge: Polity.

O'Neill, O. 1996: *Towards Justice and Virtue*. Cambridge: Cambridge University Press.

Oppenheim, L. 1905: *International Law*, vol. 1. London: Longman.

Paine, T.: *The Rights of Man*. Harmondsworth: Penguin, 1984.

Paine, T. 1987: *The Thomas Paine Reader*. Harmondsworth: Penguin.

Pangle, T. L. 1973: *Montesquieu's Philosophy of Liberalism: A Commentary on 'The Spirit of the Laws'*. Chicago: Chicago University Press.

Panitch, L. 1976: *Social Democracy and Industrial Militancy*. Cambridge: Cambridge University Press.

Panitch, L. 1980: Recent theorizations of corporatism. *British Journal of Sociology*, 31(2).

Parker, N. 1983: Democracy and revolution. In *The State and Society*, 2(3). Milton Keynes: Open University.

Parry, G. 1969: *Political Elites*. London: Allen and Unwin.

Parsons, T. 1960: Voting and the equilibrium of the American political system. In E. Burdick and A. J. Brodbeck (eds), *American Voting Behaviour*. Glencoe: Free Press.

Pateman, C. 1970: *Participation and Democratic Theory*. Cambridge: Cambridge University Press.

Pateman, C. 1971: Political culture, political structure and political change. *British Journal of Political Science*, 1.

Pateman, C. 1980: The civic culture: a philosophic critique. In G. Almond and S. Verba (eds), *The Civic Culture Revisited*. Boston: Little, Brown.

Pateman, C. 1983: Feminism and democracy. In G. Duncan (ed.), *Democratic Theory and Practice*. Cambridge: Cambridge University Press.

Pateman, C. 1985: *The Problem of Political Obligation: A Critique of Liberal Theory*. Cambridge: Polity.

Pateman, C. 1988: *The Sexual Contract*. Cambridge: Polity.

Pelczynski, Z. A. (ed.) 1985: *The State and Civil Society*. Cambridge: Cambridge University Press.

Perez-Diaz, M. 1978: *State, Bureaucracy and Civil Society*. London: Macmillan.

Peters, R. S. 1956: *Hobbes*. Harmondsworth: Penguin.

Pettit, P. 1999: Republican liberty, contestatory democracy. In I. Shapiro and C. Hacker-Cordon (eds), *Democracy's Value*. Cambridge: Cambridge University Press.

Pettit, P. 2003: Deliberative democracy, the discursive dilemma, and republican theory. In J. Fishkin and P. Laslett (eds), *Debating Deliberative Democracy*. Oxford: Blackwell.

Phillips, A. 1991: *Engendering Democracy*. Cambridge: Polity.

Phillips, A. 1993: Must feminists give up on liberal democracy? In D. Held (ed.), *Prospects for Democracy: North, South, East, West*. Cambridge: Polity.

Phillips, A. 1995: *The Politics of Presence*. Oxford: Oxford University Press.

Phillips, A. 1999: *Which Equalities Matter?* Cambridge: Polity.

Pierson, C. 1986: *Marxist Theory and Democratic Politics.* Cambridge: Polity.

Pierson, C. 1991: *Beyond the Welfare State?* Cambridge: Polity.

Pierson, C. 1995: *Socialism after Communism: The New Market Socialism.* Cambridge: Polity.

Pitkin, H. F. 1967: *The Concept of Representation.* Berkeley and Los Angeles: University of California Press.

Pitkin, H. F. 1984: *Fortune is a Woman: Gender and Politics in the Thought of Niccolò Machiavelli.* Berkeley: University of California Press.

Plamenatz, J. 1963: *Man and Society,* vol. 1. London: Longman.

Plant, R. 1985: Welfare and the value of liberty. *Government and Opposition,* 20(3).

Plant, R. 1992: Citizenship, rights and welfare. In A. Coote (ed.), *The Welfare of Citizens.* London: IPPR/Rivers Oram Press.

Plato: *The Laws.* Harmondsworth: Penguin, 1970.

Plato: *The Republic.* Harmondsworth: Penguin, 1974.

Plato: *The Statesman.* London: Routledge and Kegan Paul, 1952.

Pocock, J. G. A. 1975: *The Machiavellian Moment: Florentine Political Thought and the Atlantic Republican Tradition.* Princeton: Princeton University Press.

Poggi, G. 1978: *The Development of the Modern State.* London: Hutchinson.

Poggi, G. 1990: *The State: Its Nature, Development and Prospects.* Cambridge: Polity.

Polan, A. J. 1984: *Lenin and the End of Politics.* London: Methuen.

Pollitt, C. 1984: The state and health care. In G. McLennan, D. Held and S. Hall (eds), *State and Society in Contemporary Britain.* Cambridge: Polity.

Potter, D., Goldblatt, D., Kiloh, M. and Lewis, P. (eds) 1997: *Democratization.* Cambridge: Polity.

Poulantzas, N. 1972: The problem of the capitalist state. In R. M. Blackburn (ed.), *Ideology in Social Science: Readings in Critical Social Theory.* London: Fontana.

Poulantzas, N. 1973: *Political Power and Social Classes.* London: New Left Books.

Poulantzas, N. 1975: *Classes in Contemporary Capitalism.* London: New Left Books.

Poulantzas, N. 1980: *State, Power, Socialism.* London: Verso/New Left Books.

Rahe, P. A. 1994: *Republics Ancient and Modern,* vol. 2. Chapel Hill: University of North Carolina Press.

Rawls, J. 1971: *A Theory of Justice.* Cambridge, MA: Harvard University Press.

Rawls, J. 1985: Justice as fairness: political not metaphysical. *Philosophy and Public Affairs,* 14(3).

Rawls, J. 1993a: *Political Liberalism.* New York: Columbia University Press.

Rawls, J. 1993b: Reply to Habermas. In *Political Liberalism.* New York: Columbia University Press.

Rawls, J. 1999: The idea of public reason revisited. In S. Freeman (ed.), *Collected Papers.* Cambridge, MA: Harvard University Press.

Rodewald, C. (ed.) 1974: *Democracy: Ideas and Realities.* London: Dent.

Rose, R. and Peters, G. 1977: The political consequences of economic overload. Glasgow: University of Strathclyde Centre for the Study of Public Policy.

Roth, G. 1978: Introduction. In Max Weber, *Economy and Society,* 2 vols. Berkeley: University of California Press.

Roth, G. and Schluchter, W. 1979: *Max Weber's Vision of History.* Berkeley: University of California Press.

Rousseau, J.-J.: *Émile.* London: Dent, 1974.

Rousseau, J.-J.: *The Social Contract.* Harmondsworth: Penguin, 1968.

Rubinstein, N. 1982: Political theories in the Renaissance. In *The Renaissance: Essays in Interpretation.* London: Methuen.

Ruggie, J. G. 2003: Taking embedded liberalism global: the corporate connection. In D. Held and M. Koenig-Archibugi (eds), *Taming Globalization.* Cambridge: Polity.

Rutland, P. 1985: *The Myth of the Plan.* London: Hutchinson.

Ryan, A. 1974: *J. S. Mill.* London: Routledge and Kegan Paul.

Ryan, A. 1983. Mill and Rousseau: utility and rights. In G. Duncan (ed.), *Democratic Theory and Practice*. Cambridge: Cambridge University Press.

Ryle, G. 1967: Plato. In *The Encyclopedia of Philosophy*, vol. 6. New York: Macmillan.

Sabine, G. H. 1963: *A History of Political Theory*. London: Harrap.

Sallust: *The Jugurthine War/The Conspiracy of Catiline*. Harmondsworth: Penguin, 1963.

Sandel, M. (ed.) 1984: *Liberalism and its Critics*. Oxford: Blackwell.

Sartori, G. 1987: *The Theory of Democracy Revisited*. Chatham, NJ: Chatham House.

Saward, M. 2003: *Democracy*. Cambridge: Polity.

Saxonhouse, A. 1991: Aristotle: defective males, hierarchy, and the limits of politics. In M. L. Shanley and C. Pateman (eds), *Feminist Interpretations and Political Theory*. Cambridge: Polity.

Scanlon, T. 1982: Contractualism and utilitarianism. In A. Sen, T. Scanlon, and B. Williams (eds), *Utilitarianism and Beyond*. Cambridge: Cambridge University Press.

Scanlon, T. 1998: *What We Owe to Each Other*. Cambridge, MA: Belknap Press.

Schama, S. 1989: *Citizens*. New York: Alfred A. Knopf.

Schattschneider, E. F. 1960: *The Semi-Sovereign People: A Realist View of Democracy in America*. New York: Rinehart and Winston.

Schmitter, P. C. 1974: Still the century of corporatism? *Review of Political Studies*, 36(1).

Schmitter, P. C. 1979: Modes of interest intermediation and models of societal change in Western Europe. *Comparative Political Studies*, 10(1).

Schumpeter, J.: *Capitalism, Socialism and Democracy*. London: Allen and Unwin, 1976.

Sen, A. 1981: *Poverty and Famine*. Oxford: Clarendon Press.

Sen, A. 1999: *Development as Freedom*. Oxford: Oxford University Press.

Shapiro, I. 1999: Enough of deliberation: politics is about interests and power. In S. Macedo (ed.), *Deliberative Politics: Essays on Democracy and Disagreement*. New York: Oxford University Press.

Shklar, J. 1969: *Men and Citizens: A Study of Rousseau's Social Theory*. Cambridge: Cambridge University Press.

Sigler, J. 1983: *Minority Rights*. Westport: Greenwood Press.

Siltanen, J. and Stanworth, M. (eds) 1984: *Women and the Public Sphere*. London: Hutchinson.

Skinner, Q. 1978: *The Foundations of Modern Political Thought*, 2 vols. Cambridge: Cambridge University Press.

Skinner, Q. 1981: *Machiavelli*. Oxford: Oxford University Press.

Skinner, Q. 1986: The paradoxes of liberty. In S. McMurrin (ed.), *The Tanner Lectures on Human Values*, VII. Cambridge: Cambridge University Press.

Skinner, Q. 1989: The state. In T. Ball, J. Farr and R. L. Hanson (eds), *Political Innovation and Conceptual Change*. Cambridge: Cambridge University Press.

Skinner, Q. 1992: The Italian city-republics. In J. Dunn (ed.), *Democracy: The Unfinished Journey, 508 BC to AD 1993*. Oxford: Oxford University Press.

Soboul, A. 1962: *Histoire de la Révolution Française*, 2 vols. Paris: Éditions Sociales.

Spencer, M. E. 1979: Marx on the state. *Theory and Society*, 7(1–2).

Springborg, P. 1992: *Western Republicanism and the Oriental Prince*. Cambridge: Polity.

Sweezy, P. 1942: *The Theory of Capitalist Development*. New York: Monthly Review Press.

Taylor, B. 1983: *Eve and the New Jerusalem*. London: Virago.

Taylor-Gooby, P. 1983: Legitimation deficit, public opinion, and the welfare state. *Sociology*, 17(2).

Taylor-Gooby, P. 1985: Attitudes to welfare. *Journal of Social Policy*, 10(4).

Taylor-Gooby, P. 1988: The future of the British welfare state: public attitudes, citizenship and social policy under the Conservative government. *European Sociological Review*, 4(1).

Thompson, D. and Gutmann, A. 2003: Deliberative democracy beyond process. In J. Fishkin and P. Laslett (eds), *Debating Deliberative Democracy*. Oxford: Blackwell.

Thompson, J. B. 1984: *Studies in the Theory of Ideology*. Cambridge: Polity.

Thompson, J. B. 1990: *Ideology and Modern Culture*. Cambridge: Polity.

Thompson, J. B. 1995: *The Media and Modernity: A Social Theory of the Media.* Cambridge: Polity.

Thompson, W. 1970: *Appeal of One Half of the Human Race, Women, against the Pretensions of the Other Half, Men, to Retain them in Political, and Hence in Civil and Domestic Slavery.* New York: Source Book Press.

Thucydides: *The Peloponnesian War.* Harmondsworth: Penguin, 1972.

Tilly, C. (ed.) 1975: *The Formation of National States in Western Europe.* Princeton: Princeton University Press.

Tomalin, C. 1985: *Mary Wollstonecraft.* Harmondsworth: Penguin.

Truman, D. B. 1951: *The Governmental Process.* New York: Alfred A. Knopf.

Tully, J. 2002: The unfreedom of the moderns in comparison to their ideals of constitutional democracy. *Modern Law Review,* 65(2).

UIA (Union of International Associations). 2002: *Yearbook of International Organizations 2001/2002:* Vol. 1B (Int-Z). Munich: K. G. Saur.

Vajda, M. 1978: The state and socialism. *Social Research,* 4 (November).

Waldron, J. 1999a: Legislation, authority, and voting. *In Law and Disagreement.* Oxford: Oxford University Press.

Waldron, J. 1999b: Rawls's *Political Liberalism.* In *Law and Disagreement.* Oxford: Oxford University Press.

Wallace, W. 1994: Rescue or retreat? The nation state in Western Europe. *Political Studies,* 42, special issue.

Weber, M.: *Economy and Society,* 2 vols. Berkeley: University of California Press, 1978.

Weber, M.: *General Economic History.* London: Allen and Unwin, 1923.

Weber, M.: Politics as a vocation. In H. H. Gerth and C. W. Mills (eds), *From Max Weber.* New York: Oxford University Press, 1972.

Weber, M.: *The Protestant Ethic and the Spirit of Capitalism.* London: Allen and Unwin, 1971.

Weber, M.: Science as a vocation. In H. H. Gerth and C. W. Mills (eds), *From Max Weber.* New York: Oxford University Press, 1972.

West, P., Illsey, R. and Kelman, H. 1984: Public preferences for the care of dependency groups. *Social Science and Medicine,* 18(4).

Whiteley, P. 1981: Public opinion and the demand for social welfare in Britain. *Journal of Social Policy,* 10(4).

Williams, G. L. (ed.) 1976: *John Stuart Mill on Politics and Society.* London: Fontana.

Williams, R. 1976: *Keywords.* London: Fontana/Croom Helm.

Williamson, P. J. 1989: *Corporatism in Perspective.* London: Sage.

Winkler, J. T. 1976: Corporatism. *Archives européennes de sociologie,* 17(1).

Wollstonecraft, M.: *Vindication of the Rights of Woman.* Harmondsworth: Penguin, 1982.

Wood, G. S. 1969: *The Creation of the American Republic.* Chapel Hill: University of North Carolina Press.

Wootton, D. 1992: The Levellers. In J. Dunn (ed.), *Democracy: The Unfinished Journey, 508 BC to AD 1993.* Oxford: Oxford University Press.

Wright, E. O. 1978: *Class, Crisis and the State.* London: New Left Books.

Young, I. 1990: *Justice and Politics of Difference.* Princeton: Princeton University Press.

Young, I. 2000: *Inclusion and Democracy.* New York: Oxford University Press.

Young, I. 2001: Activist challenges to deliberative democracy. *Political Theory,* 29.

Index